THE ILLUSTRATED ENCYCLOPEDIA OF WEAPONRY & WARFARE

THE ILLUSTRATED ENCYCLOPEDIA OF WEAPONRY & WARFARE

ROBIN CROSS

METRO BOOKS
New York

METRO BOOKS
New York

387 Park Avenue South
New York, NY 10016-8810

This 2013 edition published by Metro Books by arrangement with Quantum Books.

Publisher: Sarah Bloxham
Managing Editor: Samantha Warrington
Project Editor: Marion Paull
Assistant Editor: Jo Morley
Editorial Intern: Isabelle Bourton
Production Manager: Rohana Yusof
Design: Natalie Clay, www.styloclay.com

Map and image reproduction:
Gumlohar Press and PICA Industries Ltd.

ISBN 978-1-4351-4428-6

For information about custom editions, special sales, and premium and corporate purchases, please contact Sterling Special Sales at 800-805-5489 or specialsales@sterlingpublishing.com.

Manufactured in Indonesia
2 4 6 8 10 9 7 5 3 1
www.sterlingpublishing.com

CONTENTS

INTRODUCTION

Looking Back at the story of warfare from the vantage point of the 21st century, it is all too easy for even the most conscientious military historian to draw obvious conclusions and slip into generalities. Today, for instance, the popular view is that both Napoleon and Hitler made the same fatal error of embarking on all-out campaigns to defeat Russia. Napoleon was defeated as much by a primitive and overextended communication and supply system as by the military muscle of the Tsarist armies. Hitler's failure was due to a mixture of military amateurishness, exemplified by his own confused orders, and a grotesque over-estimation of the power of the German armed forces to defeat their Soviet opponents.

Yet at the time, many well-informed observers did not share these views. Russia, after all, had made peace with Napoleon before, and the impressionable young Tsar Alexander I had dangled before him the prospect of a grand alliance in which French and Russian troops would march side by side to carve out an eastern empire at the expense of the British in India. As far as Hitler's invasion of the USSR was concerned, the informed view of the British War Office at the start of the campaign was that Soviet resistance would last for a matter of weeks, or at the most a few months. The power of hindsight is a potent one, but the duty of the modern chronicler is—or should be—to see "how it really was," as the German historian Ranke put it.

If historians can be misled, how much more difficult must it have been for the men on the battlefield to gain a distinct, comprehensive view of what they were fighting for and what they were actually achieving. Frequently it is only the civilian observers, tucked up safely at home or well behind the lines, who claim to have a clear vision. It is they who can visualize a grand strategy, and see war in terms of glorious victories or gallant defeats.

Thomas Hardy, in *The Dynasts*, wrote that war makes "rattling good history," but the Duke of Wellington, one of the greatest commanders of all time, grimly commented that "next to a battle lost, there is nothing so melancholy as a battle won." Most military men would agree with Napoleon's reply to a question about how he went about planning a battle: "Well, you engage your opponent and then you see!"

What is clear, as this book demonstrates, is that man is on the whole a pugnacious animal and certainly has never been a pacifist by nature. Throughout human history there has rarely been a moment of total peace. Somewhere, somehow, and at some time or other, some form of conflict is taking place, whether on a small or a large scale. Political philosophers, sociologists, and psychologists have long debated whether war is a weakness of human nature or an inevitable consequence of the emergence of organized societies and civilizations.

If the first premise is true—if, in common with Thomas Hobbes, we take the grim view that man's life is inevitably "nasty, brutish, and short"—then it follows that the art and practice of war, however sophisticated it has become, is merely camouflage for an innate barbarism. According to the military historian David Chandler, it is only by "an intensive and long process of education for peace" that this might be eradicated. He suggests that if the second theory is correct, war can be eventually eliminated, just like a disease.

What such arguments ignore is the clear link between war and historical change and evolution. Though some would claim that economic considerations are equally important, it is undeniable that the rise and the fall of the world's great empires have always been linked to military success and failure. Without falling into the trap of slavishly following the "Cleopatra's nose" theory of history (the French philosopher Blaise Pascal seriously argued that the entire history of the world would have been changed, if Cleopatra's nose had been half an inch shorter), the fact remains that it is possible to identify battles, sometimes fought in the space of a few brief hours, as true historical turning-points. What would the future of America have been, for instance, had the Confederacy triumphed at Gettysburg? What if the Japanese had won the battle of Midway? What would have been the consequences, not just for medieval Britain but for Europe as a whole, had Harold and his Saxons driven Duke William and his invading Normans into the sea at Hastings? It is this type of speculation that instantly appeals to the romantic in all of us, young and old.

Of course, it goes without saying that war is basically wrong. There is no such thing as a totally "just" war; whatever the justifications produced for embarking on war it is always as much motivated by national self-interest as by ideals. Britain did not go to war in 1914 solely to honor its treaty obligations to "gallant little Belgium;" an equal consideration was that of preserving the European balance of power and Britain's own world position. The same might be said of the USA in 1917. Though the *causus belli* was undoubtedly Germany's decision to resume unrestricted submarine warfare, the injudicious telegram sent by the German Foreign Minister Artur Zimmermann, with its offer of military support to Mexico, was obviously an additional factor, as were the billions tied up in the financing of the Allied war effort.

When Clausewitz wrote that "war is the continuation of politics by other means," he was emphasizing a truism that is as accurate today as it ever was. Bismarck put it even more brutally and succinctly, saying that most states at some stage or another will almost inevitably adopt a policy of "blood and iron" if they feel their national interests or ambitions are at stake.

What must be remembered also is that for much of human history—in fact up to the present century—wars have on the whole been fought by relatively small numbers, though obviously—particularly in the ancient world—defeat could bring about political consequences that affected whole nations or states.

The actual battles were fought by levies of peasants who had no voice or choice in the matter, officered by professionals largely drawn from the aristocracy. Even though in 1792 Revolutionary France raised a citizen-army of over 600,000 men when faced with a hostile Europe, the long years of war that followed left national ways of life relatively untouched, even with the later introduction of the levee-enmasse and conscription. Napoleon might have sought to impose his Continental System on his European allies and vassals, but it was still possible for, say, a Beethoven or a young Schubert to live in Hapsburg Vienna relatively unscathed.

The American Civil War saw the beginning of a wholesale change, and the siege of Paris in 1870-1 also pointed the way to the future. It was not until the advent of airpower, however, that civilians as well as soldiers found themselves well and truly in the firing line. In both world wars, modern technology was married to national ambitions to broaden the scope and cost of conflict to a point where whole populations were involved.

Even so, developments in warfare can be seen as having a positive side. The rate of technological advance witnessed in the last 100 years would have been much slower without the stimulus of the two world conflicts. For example, the Allied blockade of imperial Germany between 1914 and 1918 led German chemists to pioneer the development of a whole range of synthetics, which have gone on to alter our entire way of life and many key inventions ranging from radar to penicillin and other antibiotics were also the children of war. War has its uses, though such benefits as it has indirectly conferred can certainly never make up for its destructive cost.

1 THE FIRST MILITARY EMPIRES

Bellicosity is as old as mankind, but the origins of warfare are shrouded in the darkness of prehistory. Nevertheless, the colossal circular tower at the Neolithic settlement of Jericho demonstrates that warfare in the ancient Near East is virtually as old as urban life and the practice of agriculture. Indeed, it was the material wealth of such settlements—Jericho itself dominated an oasis—that helped promote human strife.

The first kingdoms of the ancient Near East flourished early in the third millennium BC in southern Mesopotamia or Sumer. Politically, Sumer was divided into several petty, warring temple-states, consisting of a capital city ringed by outlying towns and villages and surrounded by rich, irrigated, agricultural land and uncultivated pasturage. Endemic squabbles over watercourses and hinterland were the norm.

The turning point came with the rise of Sargon of Akkad, the foremost figure of his age. One-time cupbearer of Ur-Zababa and king of Kish, Sargon survived his master's overthrow by his rival, the king of Uruk and overlord of southern Sumer, Lugalzaggisi. Eventually (ca.2316 BC) Sargon liberated Kish and went on to bring the whole of Sumer under his sole rule.

In order to suppress the fiercely independent traditions of the conquered temple-states, Sargon replaced their rulers with his own governors, invariably Akkadians and members of his own clan. But his imperialistic designs did not terminate at Sumer's frontiers. Following Sumer's conquest, he campaigned in Iran against a confederation of four kings headed by the ruler of Awan, a powerful state centered on the southern Zagros mountains, and established his own governors in the subjugated territories. Campaigns to the northwest resulted in the crushing of the Syrian states of Mari, Iarmuti, Ibla, and Tutul, and, more importantly, the control of the cedar forests and silver mines of the Lebanon. Akkad became an empire that recognized no boundaries of language, religion, or geography, for Sargon's writ ran, according to one inscription, "from the Lower Sea [the Gulf] to the Upper Sea [the Mediterranean]."

Sargon's instrument for controlling this polyglot empire was a large standing army. In one inscription he boasts that no less than 5,400 soldiers ate daily in his palace, and these household retainers undoubtedly formed the professional core of his army. During times of war, the king would levy both royal and temporal feoffees for military service and this feudatory militia provided the main battle line of close order spearmen and shield bearers. Alongside these were ranged the four-wheeled "battle cars," vehicles bearing two soldiers whose primary function was to charge, frighten the enemy, and engage him at medium range with javelins, then close in with the spear.

But it is the nature of empires to rise and fall and Akkad was no exception. The far-flung empire of Sargon jolted through a multitude of internal revolts, and finally collapsed with the sacking of Kish (ca.2154 BC).

THE EGYPTIAN NEW KINGDOM

"I will take over the chariotry," trumpets the early sixteenth-century BC document recording the boast of the Theban pharaoh, Kamose, as he set out to reunite Egypt and break the rule of the Hyksos king Apophis, although it was left to his brother and founder of the Eighteenth Dynasty, Ahmose, to complete the expulsion of the Hyksos and thus launch the Egyptian New Kingdom. Nevertheless, Kamose was shrewd enough to see the potential advantages of incorporating the chariot into the Egyptian armory. Introduced into Egypt by the Hyksos, it had played an important part in their conquest of the country by the mid-seventeenth century BC. Now, as a result of the successful struggle against the Hyksos, Ahmose and his successors, particularly Thutmose III and Rameses II, were able to forge a "New Model Army," which was to spearhead an imperial expansion into Palestine, Syria, and Nubia.

THE "GOLDEN AGE" OF THE CHARIOT

Under the Rameside pharaohs, the Egyptian chariot was a formidable weapon, light, maneuverable, and stable, drawn by two horses, each around 12.5 hands. The crew comprised a charioteer-cum-shield bearer and an armored warrior wielding a composite bow, javelins, and sidearm. The Hittite chariot was more robust. The crew consisted of a shieldless charioteer and spearman and a shield-bearer, all armored. The sturdier, less-maneuverable Hittite chariots would try to interpenetrate the opposing lines, where their heavier weaponry and extra crewmen would tell against the lighter, more agile Egyptians.

Amenhotep III (1417–1379 BC) demonstrates his martial prowess.

AXES AND HAMMERS

To begin with, the hand-axe was a simple piece of flint or stone, shaped with a cutting edge at one end and the other rounded to provide something to grip. Such implements as these were developed independently in every region where suitable stone was available and are probably among the first artifacts to be made. Specimens from the Paleolithic era (12,000 BC and earlier) have been found in Africa and Europe. At some time, the additional power provided by a shaft was discovered. Initially, a hand-axe may have been lashed to a suitable stick, but certainly toward the end of the Neolithic period (8000–3000 BC) axe heads with holes for a handle were being made. At the same time, grinding and polishing to a relatively high degree of finish became common. With this skill came that of shaping the axe head to incorporate a more efficient blade, and by 2000 BC, curved and double-bladed heads were in use.

(Above) This painted limestone stele (nineteenth Dynasty of Egypt) depicts Merneptah holding a prisoner by his hair and apparently threatening him with a typical stone-headed axe of the period. (Left) Axe heads from the early Bronze Age (1800–1400 BC).

By this time, bronze had made its appearance, and the technique of shaping stone axes was soon applied to working in metal. Early bronze axes were more or less the same shape as those made of stone, but the adaptability of metal led to the development of other shapes as axe-makers attempted to produce axes adapted to either domestic or martial roles. Some began to add decoration, either in the form of patterns worked into the metal or by adding cast or worked decorative bosses.

The attachment of the head to the handle went through several stages. Early metal axe heads were wrought, rather than cast, and it was some time before the casting of a head with a socket for the handle was mastered. In the interim, the head was formed with a splayed back and tied to the handle; or with a spiked lower end, which could be driven into the handle; or formed with holes in the blind edge, alongside the handle, through which bindings could be tied; or formed with a central groove that could be inserted into the split end of the handle and then secured by lashing. Eventually, however, the socket became the universal method of attachment and has remained so ever since. An exception can be found in some Indian and Persian axes in which blade, head, and handle are forged as one piece.

This Bronze Age looped and socketed axe heads found in Essex, England. It has a lateral loop to assist in attaching the head to the shaft. The cutting edge is slightly convex and the socket squared with a raised rib at the mouth.

War hammer

A simpler, and perhaps more brutal, weapon was the war hammer. Although called a hammer (implying a blunt head), in fact, it usually had a pointed head that was more in the nature of a pick. Such weapons were developed by many primitive tribes and were comparable to stone or metal axes but with a pointed shape. They were adopted in Europe during the fourteenth century when chain mail and other forms of armor protection were in vogue. The pointed head of a war hammer proved to be an effective method of defeating mail, provided that the point and head were thin enough, and it could also be used to penetrate the joints of plate armor. With a pointed head on one side and a blunt head on the other, the war hammer became a twofold weapon. The blunt head could be used to stun the opponent or unhorse him, after which the pick could be used to defeat his armor and give the finishing blow. The war hammer was fairly common in Europe during the fifteenth and sixteenth centuries, but its use declined as the armored knight disappeared from the battlefield.

Weapons as symbols

Besides being a utilitarian weapon, commonly used in the field of battle, the axe took on a symbolic role, which was reflected in its style and appearance. Kings, princes, and nobility required battle axes that made their owner's status apparent. This was done by decoration, size, or being of a stylized shape, which showed that the bearer, while of the military caste and supremely capable, had no need to do his own fighting. As with axes, the formidable war hammer was also decorated and used as a symbol of rank.

CAMPAIGN OF THUTMOSE III

DATE ca.1481 BC
OBJECT To crush revolt in Syria and northern Palestine, led by Qadesh, a city commanding upper Orontes.
DESCRIPTION The king of Qadesh, leading a coalition of Canaanite and Syrian princes, moved south to bar Thutmose's advance at Megiddo, between Palestine's coastal plain and the Jezreel valley. Thutmose's response was dynamic: in nine days, averaging 16 miles a day, his army reached Gaza; three days later he held a council of war in Yehen. Three routes offered access to the coalition's position: a direct route via the Aruna defile, a northern alternative through Djefti, and a southern alternative to Ta'anach. Although Egyptian commanders cautiously urged avoidance of the first option because it meant moving in column-of-march against an enemy in line of battle, Thutmose decided to follow that course of action, establishing a camp along Qina Brook.

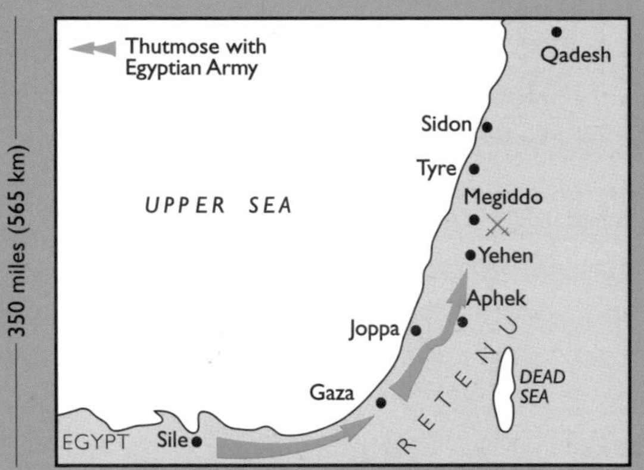

MEGIDDO

The king of Qadesh had been wrong-footed by Thutmose's boldness. The coalition's forces lay northwest of Megiddo and to the southeast near Ta'anach. At dawn Thutmose unleashed his attack. He had divided his army into three battles, "one to attack defenders in the north, another in the south, and the main battle," under himself, to strike at Canaanite and Syrian chariotry outside Megiddo. In the ensuing engagement, Egyptians swept away the coalition's forces, pursuing them to the city walls. Fugitives abandoned their chariots in order to be hauled up the walls—924 chariots were captured, but Thutmose failed to storm Megiddo since his troops had stopped to loot the enemy camp.

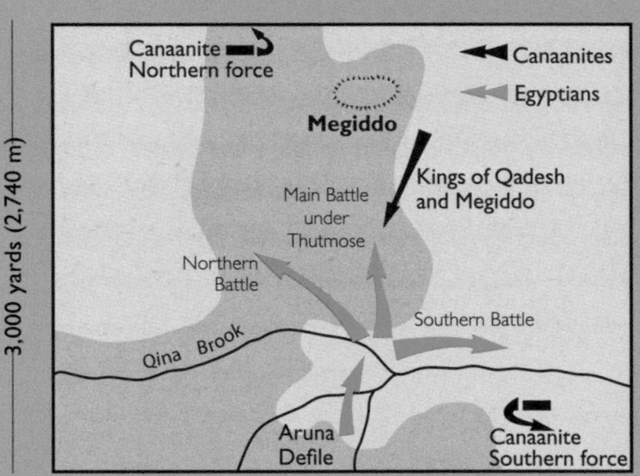

RESULT Megiddo eventually fell after seven months.

Thutmose III (ca.1504–1450 BC) was a compulsive imperialist who extended the Egyptian empire to its furthest limits. For 20 years he led campaigns into Asia, some involving bitter fighting, others mere parades of strength, against the Mitanni—Indo-European warriors who had subjugated northern Syria—and their Canaanite vassals who ruled the mercantile city-states of Syria-Palestine. His martial endeavors netted him the strongholds of Megiddo, Qadesh, and Carchemish, thus setting the Taurus Mountains and the Euphrates River as the northern boundary of his empire, while his generals extended the conquest of Nubia up to the 5th Cataract of the Nile. Eventually his empire stretched 1,500 miles (2,414 km) from north to south.

The northern domains did not long remain quiescent. The Hittites, a more formidable race of

Indo-Europeans, descended from their Anatolian fastness and rapidly devoured the decaying Mitannian empire. By the mid fourteenth century BC, Hittite and Egyptian were in head-on conflict, and it was left to the self-assertive Rameses II (ca.1304–1237 BC) to bring this to a climax. After a series of hard-fought campaigns across Syria, which seriously weakened both sides, a pact was signed (ca.1283 BC) defining the common border as the Orontes, south of Qadesh.

The pharaonic army at this time consisted of the royal guard, or "Pharoah's Braves," and four autonomous divisions. Each division marched under the divine protection of the patron deity of the town where the unit was quartered: Amon of Thebes, Re of Heliopolis, Ptah of Memphis, and Seth of Pi-Rameses. Egyptians were conscripted as either "shooters" or "strong-arm boys." Archers drew up in close order and supported the close-combat troops, who advanced at a rapid pace, shields slung over their backs, leaving both hands free to wield side arm and spear. If compromised by missiles, shields would be swung around to the front and the pace slackened. Chariotry was employed to support and protect the infantry as well as adding long-range mobility to operations.

In contrast, Hittite tactics were based on the offensive use of chariots with infantry in support. A feudal military aristocracy formed the chariotry, fiefs being held from the king with an obligation to serve. Infantry included native Hittites and imperial levies, predominantly armed with spear, dagger, and shield, although Syrians were best suited for skirmishing, being equipped with javelins, hurling sticks, and bows.

About 1200 BC, the ancient Near East was turned topsy-turvy. Egypt was suffering from repeated Libyan incursions and with these came the first wave of "Sea Peoples," a ragbag of predatory wanderers. Egyptian records are blunt: "all at once nations were moving and scattered by war. No land stood before their arms ... they were wasted." The Hittites attempted to stem the onslaught but were overrun, as were the Levantine city-states. Egypt itself survived, thanks to the efforts of Rameses III, but its empire was extinct.

QADESH CAMPAIGN

DATE ca.1296 BC
OBJECT Domination of Syria.
NUMBERS Muwatallis, king of the Hittites, moved south from Asia Minor with an army of 17,000. Rameses II commanded 20,000 in four divisions, each composed of subunits of archers, spearmen, and chariots.
DESCRIPTION The Hittite army lay outside Qadesh, but Rameses, arriving at Shabtuna from the south, was deceived into believing they were at Aleppo. He rushed ahead with his retinue to establish a camp northwest of Qadesh, hoping to invest the city before the Hittites arrived. While Rameses awaited his army, two prisoners revealed that the entire Hittite army was nearby; Rameses was trapped. As Re division marched northward, Muwatallis launched 2,500 chariots into its flank; that division broke in panic, followed by Amon. Hittites encircled Rameses' camp but, leading his retinue, Rameses counterattacked, checking the enemy and rallying his troops. Sensing victory, Hittite charioteers began to plunder, but Rameses reorganized the remnants of Re and Amon and took the offensive, aided by the fortuitous arrival of Canaanite mercenaries. Muwatallis now committed a further 1,000 chariots, but Rameses drove them back across the Orontes, pursued by the newly arrived Ptah division. At dusk Seth division was also deployed. Alone with his infantry, Muwatallis was powerless. He withdrew into Qadesh.
RESULT Both sides were badly mauled, and a non-aggression pact was signed, Rameses being too weak to besiege Qadesh, and Muwatallis happy to sit inside.

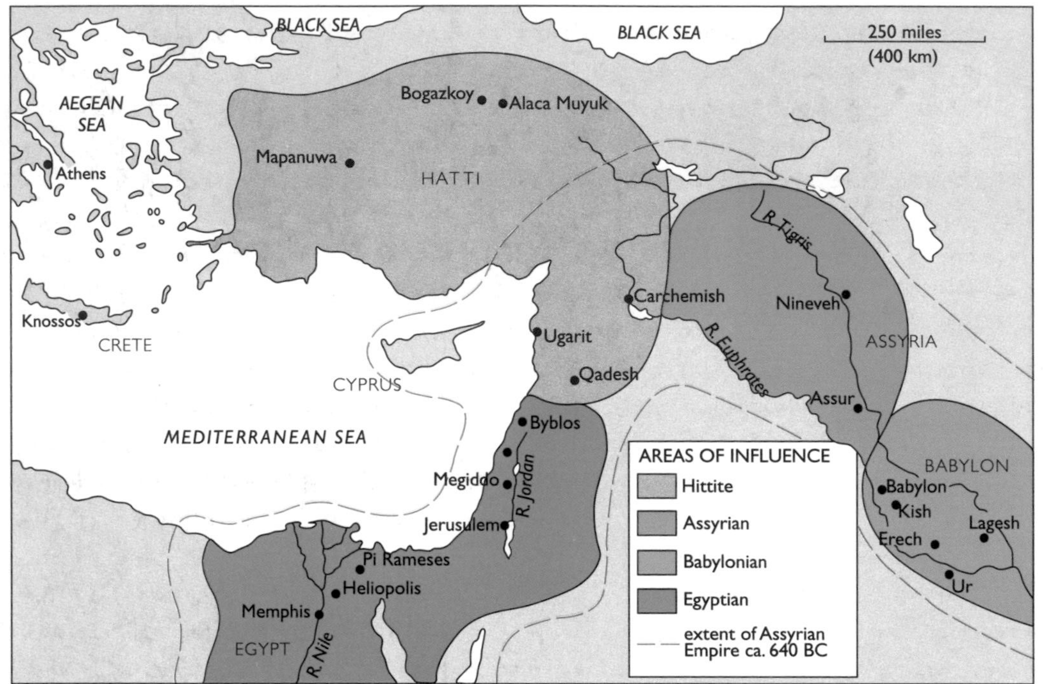

Areas of influence in the ancient Near East, ca. thirteenth century BC.

RISE AND FALL OF THE ASSYRIAN EMPIRE

When he died, Shalmaneser III of Assyria (859–824 BC) left behind a kingdom in decline. Despite their military prowess, the Assyrians had not been able to forge a viable empire out of their conquests, only a sphere of influence within which they ruled supreme, and their far-flung obligations had begun to stretch their empire's limited capabilities—in his 35-year reign, Shalmaneser had to levy his "feudal" army at least 31 times. Civil war and rebellion took hold as a succession of weak kings followed, each unable to maintain stability and thus preserve Assyria's suzerainty over the Fertile Crescent.

Out of chaos came order, and Assyria's fortunes rose like a phoenix from the ashes when, in 745 BC, a revolt in Nimrud elevated a certain general Pulu to the throne. Pulu took the name Tiglath-Pileser III (745–727 BC), and proceeded to remodel the government of Assyria in order to strengthen the central authority and weld its conquests into an empire. Assyria itself was reorganized into smaller provinces, while vassal states were annexed and transformed into further provinces. Each was under the authority of a state-appointed governor, and an efficient courier system was established, enabling the king to maintain an iron grip throughout his realm.

A full-time army was created, reinforced in times of war by a well-organized call up of men obliged to render military service. This imperial war machine was made up of four components: the "household troops," who protected the royal family and could include mercenaries; the "king's standing army," a large force composed of regular professional soldiers—chariot, cavalry, spearmen, shield bearers, archers, and slingers—maintained by the state and including the better soldiery from subjugated nations (elements of this force garrisoned the empire); the "king's men," holders of land grants from the king duty bound to serve in times of war; and the "general levy," imperial subjects called in times of national crisis.

The paramount section of the Assyrian army was the chariotry. The large, four horsed chariot was primarily employed in a "shock-charge" capacity to break the enemy line either through fear or collision. Initially, the crew had consisted of three, but by the seventh century

BC the standard crew comprised four heavily armored men—a driver, archer, and two spearmen-cum-shield bearers. Chariotry would be closely supported by cavalry—mounted warriors instead of scouts or messengers. Originally, riders operated in pairs. A shield bearer held the reins of an archer's horse, and screened him with the shield while the archer shot. However, by the seventh century BC, horsemen were equipped with both spear and bow, wore armor, and rode barded mounts (horses protected with textile armor), thus enabling them to charge into contact. This equestrian revolution hastened the redundancy of the war chariot, being more economical and tactically flexible.

Rise and fall

Assyrian campaigns were swift and ruthless. Tiglath-Pileser systematically reduced the Urartian kingdom, Babylonia, the Aramaean states, and Israel. Subject peoples were deported en masse and resettled in other parts of the empire. Imperial expansion reached its zenith in the first half of the seventh century BC. In 671, Sennacherib's son, Esarhaddon (681–668 BC), marched into Lower Egypt, toppled the pharaoh Taharqa, and installed his own governors. Two years later, he was forced to mount another Egyptian campaign, Taharqa having overthrown the Assyrian governors, but en route Esarhaddon fell ill and died. His son, Ashurbanipal (668–627 BC), mobilized the forces of 22 vassal kings along the Levantine coast, and crushed Egypt. The empire now extended over the entire Fertile Crescent.

Assyria's empire collapsed with surprising rapidity. Ashurbanipal's successors found themselves between two emerging rivals, Babylonia and the Medes, both of whom abetted the Assyrian imperial disintegration. Egypt had already freed itself from the Assyrian yoke. In 612 BC, Nineveh fell to a Babylonian–Median coalition.

BABYLONIAN EXPLOITS

Under Nebuchadnezzar II (604–562 BC) the Babylonians created an empire that encompassed virtually all the previous Assyrian domains. A resurgent Egypt under the Saite pharaohs attempted to prevent this but was pushed back from the Euphrates to its own borders. Babylonian efforts to conquer Egypt were unsuccessful but, in 598 BC, Nebuchadnezzar stormed Jerusalem after the Judaeans had risen in arms. Ten years later, following another revolt, Jerusalem was razed to the ground.

Nebuchadnezzar was succeeded by three kings who ruled amid internal disorder, until Nabonidus was placed on the throne by a coup d'état. In 550 BC, the Persian prince Cyrus conquered Achmetha (Ecbatana) and inherited the vast kingdom of the Medes, the rivals of Babylonia. Four years later he defeated Croesus, king of Lydia. In 539 BC, according to the Babylonian Chronicle, "the army of Cyrus entered Babylon without battle." Thus was inaugurated the Persian empire, the largest the Near East had ever seen. Under Cambyses (530–522 BC) and Darius (522–486 BC), it stretched from the Indus to Macedonia and from the Caucasus to Egypt. However, Xerxes' failure to conquer Greece halted the empire's expansion, and it was eventually destroyed by Alexander the Great.

SENNACHERIB'S CAMPAIGN IN PALESTINE

DATE 701 BC

OBJECT The Assyrian king Sennacherib marched west to crush a rebellion of Assyrian vassals in Palestine, headed by the Judaean king Hezekiah.

DESCRIPTION Advancing along the Levantine coast, Sennacherib dethroned the king of Tyre; Ashkelon and Ekron surrendered. In Judah, Hezekiah was prepared: he had strengthened Jerusalem's defenses, controlled access to water, and fortified and provisioned central towns. Sennacherib still took 46 walled towns and countless villages, besieging Lachish and Jerusalem in turn. Judah was wasted, but Jerusalem was not taken. An Egyptian army threatened Sennacherib's retreat northward; the forces clashed on the plain of Eltekeh.

RESULT Although Sennacherib claimed victory, the Assyrians mysteriously withdrew.

DAGGERS AND KNIVES

(Above) Dating from the sixth century BC, this bronze dagger was discovered in Italy. Its hilt has been carefully shaped to give an excellent grip, with a pommel and return to prevent the weapon from sliding out of the hand. The scabbard has been decorated with animals and fish, and a geometric pattern, embossed into the bronze.

A dagger is defined as a "short, edged, stabbing weapon," a knife as a "metal blade with a long sharpened edge, held in a handle, and used as a cutting instrument or weapon." The distinction between cut and thrust tends to become blurred.

The dagger is undoubtedly one of the oldest weapons. Flint daggers dating from about 20,000 BC are well known. In their earliest form these were no more than elliptical or wedge-shaped pieces of flint, carefully chipped to form a point and a cutting edge, and left blunt at the rear end to provide a grip. Over time the grip became more pronounced and was shaped to fit the hand. Some late flint knives have symmetrical and even ornate handles.

Besides flint, daggers were made from any other material that offered a sharp point—wood, bone, and horn were common. Knives and daggers made of semi precious materials, such as agate and jade, were invariably for ceremonial use and were not weapons of war—although those used by the Aztecs, among others, for human sacrifice were certainly capable of killing and maiming.

The advent of metal provided a material more suitable for cutting than had previously been available, and gave the maker more scope in the matter of shape. The first metal to be used was copper. Generally, this is too soft to be useful for weapons, but it was eventually discovered that hammering could "work-harden" the metal sufficiently for it to be given a reasonably sharp edge and point. It was usually necessary to make the blade broad, almost triangular, to obtain the desired stiffness.

By about 2000 BC, pure copper began to give way to bronze, an alloy of copper and tin that was developed by the Sumerian smiths of Mesopotamia. Bronze knives began with shapes similar to those of the copper knives they replaced, but as the superior hardness of bronze began to be appreciated, the knife became more slender and ornate. More significantly, bronze was capable of taking a reasonable cutting edge—a great advantage on the battlefield. Another feature of bronze was that it could be cast, and this, in turn, led to the development of cast handles riveted to forged blades, and more utilitarian knives cast in one piece.

Between 1000 and 5000 BC, bronze gradually yielded its place to iron, but this, although easier to work than bronze, was less rigid.

Japanese daggers (or tanto*) are virtually miniature versions of Japanese swords, having the same gentle curve and oblique-cut tip.*

It was not until the discovery of "steeling"—repeatedly hammering spongy iron—that a really satisfactory blade could be produced. This "blister steel" remained the common material for weapons until about the twelfth century, when the technique of hammering several strips of blister steel to form "shear steel" finally provided a metal with all the desirable attributes of rigidity and the ability to take and hold a good cutting edge.

Curved blades

The shape of the knife or dagger was, to some extent, dictated by the material and form of construction. The straight pointed blade was adequate for stabbing, whatever material it was made from, but for cutting or slashing purposes, copper and early bronze were less satisfactory. To compensate, the blade was shaped so as to aid the cutting motion and, as a result, the curved blade came to be the cutter, the straight blade the thruster.

The curvature of the blade took many different forms, depending upon the makers and users. Some forms have become identified with particular places; for example, the wavy edged *kris* of Malaysia, also characterized by an asymmetrical spur beneath the handle; or the broad-bladed *katar* of India, provided with a transverse grip that enabled the user to punch it into his opponent.

Curved blades became popular in the Middle East and India, an area where a pointed dagger with a T-section blade was also introduced. This blade was capable of piercing joints of various types of armor. Double bladed daggers, allowing for an upward and downward thrust, were known, as well as daggers with slotted blades with which an astute fighter could trap his opponent's blade and break or bend it.

Utility knives

Knives and daggers still find a place in warfare, even in the twenty-first century; commandos and other special forces carry them for close-quarter fighting, and utility knives capable of anything from combat to chopping down small trees are still popular with soldiers of all countries, even if mostly they are not officially issued with them.

The earliest Scottish dirks were generally made from broken sword blades. Thereafter, to reflect their origin, they frequently had a single edged blade with a short false edge for the first few inches from the tip. By the eighteenth century, they had become articles of dress instead of serious weapons, and ornamentation became all important.

2 HOPLITES TO HANNIBAL

At first sight it may seem surprising that when Greek warfare emerges into the light of history, it not only soon comes to be dominated by the close-packed, heavy infantry known as "hoplites," but continues to be so for some three centuries (ca.650–350 BC). Greece is a mountainous country, whereas, as a Persian general is supposed to have remarked, hoplites required flat land to be effective, and even there the necessity to maintain formation meant that a hoplite army was unwieldy and inflexible. Moreover, because hoplites were normally expected to provide their own equipment, the majority of the population in any given state was necessarily excluded.

WHY HOPLITES?

There were, however, good geographical, sociopolitical, and military reasons for this situation. First, areas of flat land, even relatively small ones, were vital to the very existence of the city states, because that was where most of their food was grown, and, sooner or later, an invading army could be compelled to confront the defending hoplites. Second, in many states the full rights of citizenship were accorded only to those who could afford to take their place in the hoplite line of battle, so that the hoplites effectively were the "nation in arms," and it would have been unthinkable to arm the poor majority. It was only in a state such as Athens, where the navy became important, that the poor, who rowed the ships, came to have a significant military role—hence Athenian democracy. Horses, on the other hand, were too expensive for all but the richest citizens, so that cavalry forces, south of Boeotia, were necessarily small. Finally, as events were to show, hoplites were formidable in the extreme. Anyone who doubts this should, above all, read Xenophon's account of the experiences of himself and his fellow mercenaries in their march, first, to confront the Persian king at Cunaxa, near Baghdad, where their employer, the rebel prince Cyrus, was killed, and then home again via Armenia and the Black Sea coast.

EQUIPMENT

Hoplites began to appear when the spread of Greek colonies around the shores of the Mediterranean and the Black Sea brought about a more general prosperity in the homeland, and increasing numbers of men could afford to arm themselves in the latest gear. At first, this included bronze helmets that covered the back and sides of the head, and had a nose piece, which left only the eyes and lower face exposed. Chest and back were protected by solid bronze plates, and the lower legs by bronze

The Eastern Mediterranean in early Classical times. The city-states of Classical Greece united in the face of invasion by the mighty Persian empire, first defeating Darius at Marathon and then routing the fleet of his successor, Xerxes, at Salamis. The victors fell out, however, and in the Peloponnesian Wars, Athens and Sparta battled for supremacy, Sparta eventually triumphing with its victory over the Athenian fleet at Aegospotami and the surrender of Athens the following spring. Spartan domination came to an end in its turn at Leuctra in 371 BC.

greaves. For offense, the throwing spear was soon abandoned in favor of the stabbing spear, and a sword for use if the spear was broken. Later on, metal armor probably gave way to jerkins of laminated linen strips of leather, and some hoplites may have discarded armor altogether. Helmets, too, were modified in various ways.

But, together with the stabbing spear, their shield remained characteristic of hoplites throughout their existence. Thus Spartan hoplites were allegedly exhorted to "come back with their shields or on them," and when in the 220s BC they finally abandoned the hoplite shield for a smaller, Macedonian-style buckler, they effectively ceased to be hoplites. However, the double grip with which the hoplite shield was fitted meant that, if carried comfortably, it covered only the left side, and hence a man depended on the shield of the man on his right for the protection of the other half of his body. Thus the phalanx was born—ranks of warriors standing shoulder to shoulder, with interlocked or overlapping shields—and to leave the line became the worst offense a soldier could commit, because it might cause the death of his comrades.

HOPLITE WARFARE

The first real test of the effectiveness of hoplites against different types of troops came with the two Persian invasions of Greece in 490 and 480–479 BC. In the first, the Athenians and their Plataean allies shattered a Persian army at Marathon; in the second, a tiny force of some 7,000 hoplites, with a hard core of 300 Spartans, successfully defended the pass of Thermopylae for two days before being taken in the rear. Then, in 479 BC, the Persian army was almost totally destroyed at Plataea in Boeotia. Herodotus, our main source for these wars, leaves no doubt that, at Plataea, the Persians, largely depending as they did on missile-armed troops, had no answer to the impact of hoplites fighting en masse, like a huge, armored rugby scrum, although the Greek army had split into three parts, and the crucial encounter involved just 11,500 of the 38,700 hoplites present.

Hoplites could, of course, be beaten by other troops in particular circumstances. Caught on terrain that did not suit them, they could, for example, be destroyed by javelins thrown from a distance. This happened to a small Athenian force in the Aetolian hills in 426 BC. Cavalry could occasionally ride them down if they were caught in the open and not properly formed, as happened to part of the Greek army at Plataea. But an earlier stage in the Plataea campaign demonstrated that cavalry could not defeat hoplites by frontal assault. Light troops armed with missiles had to be very skillfully handled and, above all, had to be backed up by hoplites of their own, if they were to stand any chance. The cutting to pieces of a *mora* (regiment) of the Spartan army by Athenian *peltasts* (light troops) under Iphicrates, in 390 BC, was a rare occurrence, and here Athenian hoplites were certainly present, although they played no part in the actual fighting until the very end.

Weight of numbers

Morale was supremely important, and many a hoplite battle ended almost as soon as it had begun, with one side breaking and running. If this did not happen, the two phalanxes would close to within a few feet, whereupon those in the front two or three of the eight or more ranks would try to stab their opposite numbers, aiming for the face, neck, or shoulders over the rim of the shield. But the pressure of those behind inevitably, sooner or later, brought the two formations crashing together, and then it is quite clear that it was literally a question of trying to "shove" the enemy back. Finally, one side or the other would have to give way and the rout would begin, men trampling each other underfoot as they tried to run. But the pursuit was not usually carried far, mainly because it would cause the pursuers to break formation and so expose themselves to the danger of a counterattack. Thus losses were comparatively slight in most hoplite battles, ranging from about 2 percent for the winners to about 15 percent for the losers.

HOPLITE SHIELDS

Possibly invented in Caria (in the southwest of modern Turkey) and introduced to the mainland via Argos between 700–650 BC, the shield (*aspis*) was 2½–3 feet (75–90 cm) in diameter, with a wooden core, offset rim and facing of bronze, and lining of leather. It was held by inserting the left arm through the central armband (*porpax*) and taking hold of the hand grip of bronze or cord (*antilabê*) straight ahead near the rim. Thus half the shield projected to the left. Shields usually carried blazons, either individualized— gorgon heads or roosters, for example—or referring to the hoplite's city (e.g. "A" for Athenians, or a club for the Thebans.) The shield was a hoplite's essential piece of equipment and to throw it away was a sign of cowardice.

A typical "Corinthian" helmet, which probably dates from the fifth century BC. Made of bronze, it is of the type worn by the hoplites.

Obviously there was a limit to the tactical skills that could be employed in this kind of fighting, and it is important to realize that nearly all hoplites, from the generals downward, were almost entirely untrained. This is made clear by the constant references in ancient literature to the uniqueness of the Spartan training system, and even in Sparta generals were picked for their social standing instead of their ability—indeed, the commander in chief of a Spartan army was usually a king or another member of one of the two royal families. All generals could do was to get their men into formation and then lead them into battle, and many a hoplite general fell as a result.

THE SPARTANS

The Spartans, however, demonstrated that highly trained hoplites, articulated into units as small as 30 to 40 men and with a proper chain of command—things that were unique in Greece until at least the fourth century BC—could be maneuvered on the battlefield. In particular, they could exploit the tendency of hoplite armies to edge to the right, described by Thucydides, as each man sought the protection of the shield of the man to his right. Often this led to stalemate, as each side won on its right and set off in pursuit of the enemy left. But by ignoring the fleeing enemy left, the Spartans learned to wheel in order to take the victorious enemy right in the flank, as it returned across the battlefield. At Mantinea in 418 BC, this seems to have been almost accidental, but at the Nemea in 394 BC there is not much doubt that the Spartans deliberately sacrificed their left in order to be in a position to outflank the enemy's left and roll up their line. Most strikingly of all, at the second battle of Coronea just after the Nemea, they even managed to countermarch their phalanx when the Thebans got in their rear by breaking through their left.

Theban genius

In the end, however, even the Spartans met their match in the genius of the one hoplite general who seems to have thought in anything but the simplest tactical terms—Epaminondas of Thebes. At Leuctra, he deliberately massed his left 50 deep, and refused his center and right, thus negating the usual Spartan tactics and overwhelming their 12-deep line; at the second battle of Mantinea, he added to these tactics the charge of a mixed formation of cavalry and light troops, trained perhaps to run into battle holding the horses' tails. But even this battle, which foreshadows in some ways the tactics of the Macedonians, Philip and Alexander, ended in typically hoplite fashion with Epaminondas falling mortally wounded as the phalanx he was leading crashed into the enemy.

THE SPARTAN ARMY

The Spartan army evolved from a primitive, tribal force, based on kinship groups, probably through an organization based on locality, to one in which men from different families and localities fought in the same unit. Eventually, it was articulated into units of 40 men or fewer (*enômotiai*), and had a command structure, unlike other Greek armies, enabling it to carry out maneuvers beyond their capacity. Probably four *enômotiai* made up a *pentekostyes*, four of these a *lochos* and two *lochoi* a *mora* (regiment.)

All Spartans from 20 to 60 were liable for military service, and were grouped in age classes, probably in such a way that there were five men from each group of five age classes in each full-strength *enômotia*. By varying the number of age classes called up, different numbers of men could be mobilized simply and swiftly. Thus, before the battle of Leuctra, the first 35 age classes in four *morai* (regiments) were called up, and after it the remaining five age-classes and two *morai*.

In battle, men were also ranged by age, with the youngest in front, so that the first 5, 10, or 15 age classes, as the case might be, could be ordered out, e.g. to drive off missile-armed troops. On at least one occasion, young Spartan hoplites managed to catch light troops armed with javelins who had not yet even come within range. They could also attack uphill and cooperate with cavalry, although Spartan cavalry was neither numerous nor efficient. It, too, was divided into *morai*, but it is not known how many men each of these contained.

Full citizens

In addition to the six infantry *morai*, there were 300 *hippies* ("horsemen" or "knights"), who, despite their name, fought on foot and acted as the king's guard. They were probably recruited from the 10 youngest age classes and drawn from noble families.

By the age of 14, Spartan boys had begun their training, although they did not join the army until they were 20. Originally, the entire army consisted of full citizens, *Spartiatai* or *homoioi* ("equals"), who were elected to a military mess (*phidition* or *sussition.*) They were expected to dine there each evening, and to sleep there until they were 30. This gave the army a magnificent *esprit de corps*.

From about 460 BC onward, however, the number of full citizens declined, and the deficit was made up either from the *perioikoi* ("neighbors," that is, men from the small, semi-independent communities in the southern Peloponnese, allied to Sparta,) or more probably from *hypomeiones* ("inferiors," for example, Spartans who had lost their full status.) At Leuctra, just 700 *Spartiatai* were present, of whom 400 were killed.

The formation of a solid body of "hoplites", armed with long spears, brought to perfection by Alexander of Macadon (ca. 330 BC).

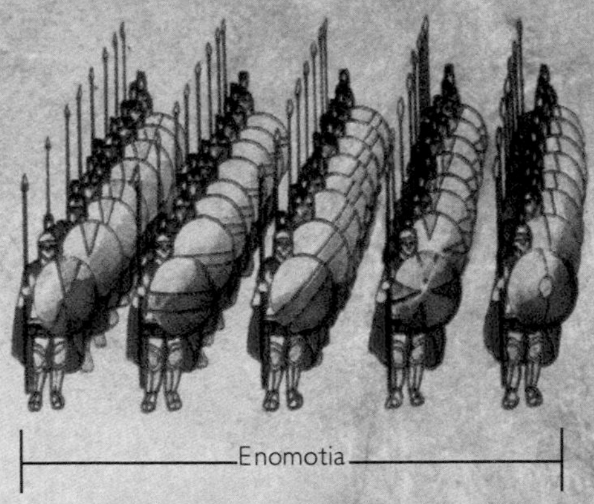

In battle, hoplites formed up shoulder to shoulder, shields touching or even overlapping, but for some maneuvers, such as the countermarch, a more open order would have been used, and a certain amount of space left between each file (right).

Spartan hoplites were organized into units called enomotiai. *Each had a maximum strength of 40 men, but usually contained 30–35 men on campaign, the oldest age-classes being left to defend Sparta. The number and depth of files could be varied, depending on maneuvers, giving generals a degree of control in battle.*

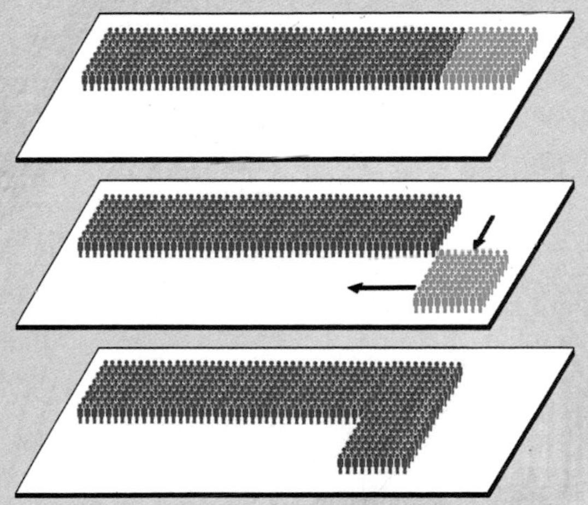

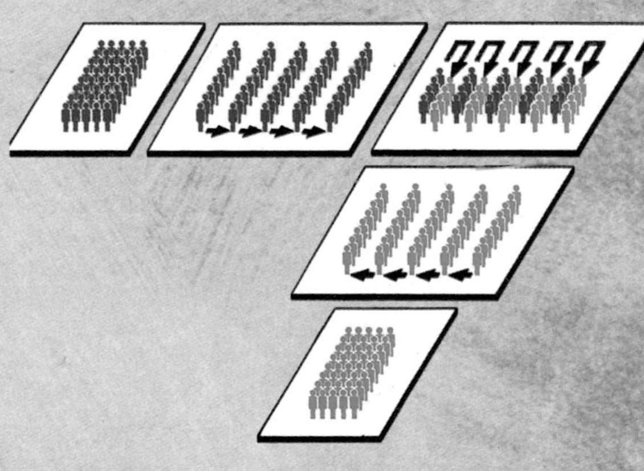

Anastrophe was the maneuver used by the Spartan army to double the depth of the phalanx. A number of files about turned, marched to the rear, and wheeled left or right to come up behind the files in front. This was a dangerous tactic if the enemy attacked during the maneuver, which is what may have happened at Leuctra in 371 BC.

Countermarch was the maneuver used to reverse the phalanx if the enemy appeared in the rear. The phalanx adopted open order, each file about turned, the rear man stood fast, and the front man led the rest of the file to take post in front of him. The ranks thus remained in the same order and it gave an impression of the phalanx advancing. This was used at Coronea in 394 BC.

Climax of the battle of Gaugamela (331 BC) as depicted on an anonymous tapestry dating from from the first half of the eighteenth century. Victory in this decisive battle between Alexander the Great of Macedonia and Darius III of Persia gave Alexander mastery of southwest Asia, signifying the end of the Persian empire.

MACEDONIA AND THE COMING OF ROME

Greek warfare was transformed by Philip II of Macedon (359–336 BC). His kingdom had long had fine cavalry— the king's "companions" (*hetairoi*), armed with lances instead of the missile weapons of Persian and other Greek cavalry—but, lacking a "middle class," had never developed hoplites. Philip was a hostage in Thebes in the 360s, and while there he may have become convinced of the need to complement his cavalry with solid infantry. It was almost certainly Philip who created the "foot companions" (*pezhetairoi*.) Their 18-foot (5.5-in) pike, the *sarisa*, required two hands, so they could not carry a hoplite shield, but the hedge of *sarisai* itself afforded protection, so they needed only a small buckler, probably hung from the neck to cover the left shoulder, and little or no body armor. Thus the equipment was cheap and large numbers of troops could be recruited.

Macedonian "phalangites," however, were not intended to be battle winners. Their job was to hold the enemy infantry long enough for the cavalry to exploit any opportunity. These were the tactics used by Philip in his first battle, against the Illyrians, and at Chaeronea. On both occasions, significantly, the king appears to have commanded the infantry, not the cavalry, perhaps to show his confidence in his new soldiers. It was this combination of different types of troops that was Philip's chief contribution to the art of war.

Alexander, Philip's son, inherited both his army and his plans for the invasion of the Persian empire, but he was to fight far more wide-ranging and complex campaigns. He was a different kind of general: Philip's great strength lay in his grasp of grand strategy, Alexander's in his tactical sense of timing. Nevertheless, it is interesting that the two greatest ancient generals—Alexander and Hannibal—should both have been sons of fine generals.

Integration of all types of troops reached fruition in Alexander's army. The heavy infantry—the foot companions and "shield bearers" (*hypaspistai*, derived from the old royal bodyguard)—were probably all armed with the *sarisa* for the set piece, but a shorter spear for other purposes, and were articulated into even smaller units than the Spartan army, with greater potential for maneuver. Light infantry armed with missile weapons screened the phalanx and performed specialized tasks, while allied and mercenary hoplites were used in minor roles. The shock troops were the Macedonian cavalry, but there was also other cavalry. The Thessalians, in particular, were of high caliber.

WAR ELEPHANTS

Elephants were first encountered by Alexander at Gaugamela and later at the Hydaspes in India. These would have been Indian elephants large enough to carry a number of armed men. Such elephants were used by Alexander's successors. Carthaginian elephants were the smaller, "forest" variety, found in west Africa. Ridden by a single mahout, the elephant itself was the weapon. Hannibal made effective use of them at the Trebbia, but all but one died during the winter of 218–217 BC. The last, possibly called "Surus" ("the Syrian"), may have been an Indian elephant. A few were landed at Locri, in 215 BC, and took part in Hannibal's attempt to relieve Capua in 211 BC. At Zama, they proved useless.

In siege warfare, Alexander followed his father. Philip had perhaps been the first mainlander to use the recently invented catapult, and Alexander used not only the conventional mounds, towers, and rams, but also both arrow-firing and stone-throwing catapults, above all in his siege of Tyre (332 BC). Philip had, finally, developed an efficient commissariat, enabling him to move fast from one end of Greece to the other, and to campaign all year round, to the consternation of his enemies, and modern studies have illuminated the sound logistical back up behind Alexander's campaigns.

After Alexander, there was a tendency for cavalry to become less important and infantry more unwieldy. This was to be of crucial significance. At both Cynoscephalae in 197 and Pydna in 168 BC, the phalanxes, despite carrying all before them in parts of the field, were eventually routed by the more flexible Roman legions.

PYRRHUS AND HANNIBAL

Pyrrhus came to Italy in 280 BC with 25,000 soldiers trained in Macedonian methods and 20 war elephants. At Heraclea, he used his phalanx to hold the Roman infantry while his cavalry and elephants—which untrained horses will not face—broke the Roman cavalry, and at Asculum in 279 BC, he broke the Roman infantry with his elephants. But on both occasions he lost heavily—hence the term "Pyrrhic victories"—and then, somewhat surprisingly, he left for Sicily on a new adventure. When he returned to Italy, he was fought to a standstill at Beneventum in 275 BC and went back to Greece.

BATTLE OF CHAERONEA

DATE ca. August 2, 338 BC
OBJECT Philip of Macedon, determined to assert authority in central Greece, confronted a coalition mainly of Athenians and Boeotians on the main route into Boeotia from the north.
NUMBERS Philip had ca. 30,000 infantry and 2,000 cavalry, the enemy a total of 30,000–35,000.
DESCRIPTION The course of the battle is uncertain. It is usually thought that Philip, commanding the right, deliberately withdrew, drawing Athenians on the allied left after him, thereupon stretching the allied line and creating a gap on the right into which his son, Alexander, charged at the head of the cavalry, while Philip launched a counterattack.
CASUALTIES Losses on the allied side were severe. Half the Athenians were killed or taken prisoner, and the Boeotians probably suffered even more. The Sacred Band of Thebes, an elite unit, was annihilated—the "Lion of Chaeronea" may mark their burial place; a mound by the River Cephisus, 2 miles (3 km) to the east, is where the Macedonian dead were cremated.
RESULT A decisive battle, Chaeronea effectively ended the hoplite era and the independence of the Greek city-states.

BATTLE OF GAUGAMELA

DATE ca. 1 October 331 BC
OBJECT Conquest of Persia by Alexander the Great of Macedon. NUMBERS Alexander had ca. 40,000 infantry and 7,000 cavalry, while Darius III of Persia had more numerous forces, including Greek mercernary hoplites, cavalry of good quality, scythed chariots, and elephants, precise numbers unknown.
DESCRIPTION The course of the battle is uncertain: Alexander formed his army in a rough oblong, with allied cavalry, foot companions, hypaspists, and companions in front, allied infantry behind, mixed cavalry and light infantry at the sides, and advanced obliquely to the right. As the Persian left moved left to forestall outflanking, a gap appeared between it and the center, into which Alexander led the companions, wheeling left. The enemy center crumpled before this attack and a frontal assault by foot companions and hypaspists, and Darius fled. Meanwhile the outflanked Macedonian left stood its ground, although hard pressed, until the rout elsewhere caused the enemy right to retreat.
CASUALTIES ca. 500 Macedonians killed, Persian losses unknown.
RESULT Victory for the Macedonians meant the end of the Persian empire and gave Alexander mastery of southwest Asia.

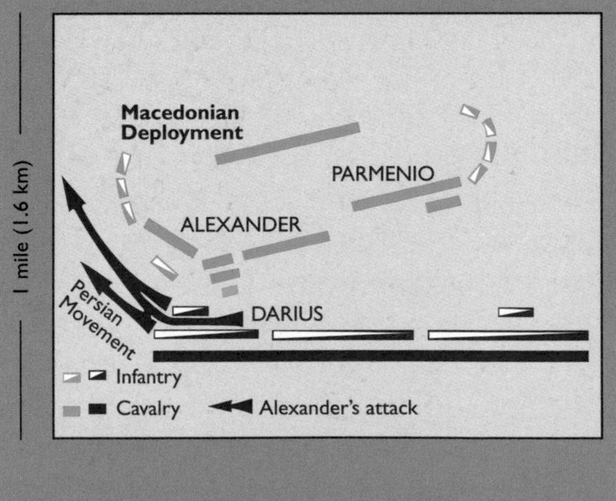

The true heir to Alexander, and the last great threat to Rome, was the Carthaginian Hannibal. The story goes that when asked by Scipio to list the world's greatest generals, he put Alexander first, Pyrrhus second, and himself third, adding that, had he won Zama, he would have put himself first. He was certainly too modest: he was not only a better tactician than Pyrrhus, but a far greater strategist, and it is even arguable that he surpassed Alexander. He never enjoyed the immense superiority in quality of troops that enabled the latter to fight his way out of difficulties, and at Zama, the only battle he lost, he had to depend on inferior mercenaries and raw levies for two-thirds of his infantry, while his cavalry was weaker both in number and in quality. Hannibal's holding back of his third line here was possibly the first example of a true reserve, and he might still have won the battle if the Roman cavalry, perhaps deliberately lured from the field, had not returned in the nick of time.

Hannibal's army

Unfortunately, we know little about Hannibal's army. The Spaniards and north Italian Celts who fought in the line were certainly swordsmen and the Africans possibly were, too, because Hannibal later armed them with captured Roman equipment. The light infantry probably included some troops armed with stabbing spears and slingers from the Balearic islands. The Numidians, from what is now Algeria, were mostly light cavalry, superb for scouting, raiding, and screening in battle or on the march, but certainly not capable of riding down unbroken infantry, and the Spanish and Celtic cavalry, although in some sense clearly regarded as "heavy," equally certainly did not consist of shock troops like Alexander's Macedonians.

Out of these heterogeneous elements, only the higher-ranking officers being Carthaginians, Hannibal succeeded in forging a precision instrument, and one of his great qualities was that he never asked his men to do something that was beyond them. He never won a "Pyrrhic" victory and one cannot imagine him being faced with mutinous troops refusing to go any farther, as Alexander finally was.

BATTLE OF CANNAE

DATE 2 August, 216 BC
CAMPAIGN Second Punic War
OBJECT Carthaginian attempt to destroy the Roman army and compel Rome to negotiate.
NUMBERS 40,000 infantry, 10,000 cavalry, under Hannibal, against 80,000 infantry, 6,000 cavalry under Varro and Paullus.
DESCRIPTION The Roman infantry was drawn up in three lines, behind a screen of skirmishers, the Carthaginian in a single, convex line, screened by skirmishers, with Celts and Spaniards in the center, Africans on the wings; Celtic and Spanish horse were on the left, Numidians on the right. The Celtic and Spanish cavalry routed the Roman cavalry, then rode round behind the advancing Roman infantry to fall on the rear of the Italian cavalry, opposite the Numidians. The Roman infantry pushed back the Celtic and Spanish foot, but avoided the Africans, who swung inward to attack the flanks. The Celtic and Spanish cavalry left the Numidians to pursue the Italian cavalry, and attacked the rear of the Roman infantry, drawing pressure off the Celtic and Spanish infantry and effectively surrounding the Roman infantry.
CASUALTIES 48,200 Romans killed, 4,500 captured on the field, 14,800 elsewhere; up to ca.8000 Carthaginians killed.
RESULT Battle of Cannae is regarded by military historians as a classic example of victorious double envelopment.

Because we know more about Alexander's army, his victories seem more sophisticated, but his tactics were, in essence, simple, and Hannibal's three great victories were subtler. The battle of Trebbia was a trap, which depended on the Roman belief that no trap was possible in such apparently open terrain; the terrain at Trasimene, by contrast, was "made by nature for an ambush," as a Roman historian said, but what general in command of 25,000 men could really have imagined that he could be ambushed? Cannae was the masterpiece. The terrain was open again, and no part of Hannibal's army concealed. But his dispositions themselves constituted a trap, inviting the Romans to attack the projecting center and hinting that the cavalry could have little part to play because most of it was on the left, apparently confined by the river, and only the Numidians were out on the open flank. Yet, by the end of the day, outnumbered two to one in infantry, and for the loss of at most 16 percent of his own men, Hannibal had inflicted on the Romans the greatest losses ever suffered by a European army in a single day, and more than 78 percent of their soldiers were either dead or in his hands.

Even more remarkable was Hannibal's strategic genius. Rome was a "superpower," able ultimately to call on three-quarters of a million men, and so to absorb defeats, such as Cannae, which would have crushed almost all other ancient states. Lesser generals might have realized that the way to defeat Rome was to invade Italy and break its hold on the allies who furnished over half its manpower. But few other generals would have believed it possible, particularly without command of the sea. Alexander, in contrast, merely had to contend with the vastness of the Persian empire, and although, for example, his strategy of nullifying Persia's naval superiority by capturing her naval bases, was brilliant, his invasion of Egypt allowed the king of Persia time to assemble another and more numerous army.

In the end, too, what was the point of it all? Alexander evidently saw himself as some kind of "hero" and conquest as an end in itself. Hannibal fought for a purpose, and when he finally lost at Zama, insisted that Carthage make peace. Alexander seems the more brilliant and charismatic, but there was something feverish about his genius. Hannibal's was perfectly tuned.

NAVAL WARFARE

Strategy and tactics in ancient naval warfare were dependent on the warships used, which were oar-powered galleys. Sails were used for moving from place to place, and a galley could probably move faster under sail than under oar, but they could really only sail before the wind and it was too dangerous to rely on the wind in combat. Masts and sails were invariably lowered before battle, sometimes left ashore, and to hoist sail was a sign of flight. Warships were designed to pack as many men as possible into a given length, to provide maximum motive power, and hence had little living or storage space. They were not designed to remain at sea for any length of time, and this limited their strategic capabilities.

Aside from the armed men on board, the only weapon was the ram. From the fourth century BC onward, there are references to the mounting of catapults on warships, but these were "man killers" rather than "ship killers," and there seems to be no reference to the sinking of a ship by catapult fire. The ram could smash a hole in an enemy galley and so cripple her, but probably could not literally sink her: ancient sources use words meaning "sink," but it is evident that ships so "sunk" could still be towed away. But whether boarding or ramming, ships had to collide, and this also limited their tactical capabilities.

Sea power was a factor in strategic thinking by the sixth century BC, and ca. 499 BC the Greeks of Asia Minor, about to rebel against Persian rule, are said to have been advised to win command of the sea. It was certainly their defeat off Lade in ca. 494 BC that ensured their revolt failed. The Persians sent the expeditionary force to Marathon by sea, and a large navy accompanied Xerxes' invasion in 480 BC. Its job was to protect communications and to bypass Greek positions, but not to convoy supplies, as is often said; it would have needed all the supplies it could carry or convoy itself. The Persian army continued the struggle after the navy's defeat at Salamis and clearly either had its own supplies or lived off the land.

BATTLE OF ARGINUSAE

DATE 406 BC
CAMPAIGN Peloponnesian War
OBJECT An attempt to relieve the Athenian fleet blockaded at Mytilene.
NUMBERS 143 Athenian and allied triremes in a hastily assembled scratch fleet, partly rowed by freed slaves, under eight admirals, against 120 Spartan and allied vessels under Callicratidas.
DESCRIPTION Callicratidas had fewer but faster ships in a single line abeam, ready for *diekplous* or *periplous*. Athenians, as counter, were in double line abeam, possibly on either side of the western island. The course of battle is uncertain: Callicratidas, on the right, was lost overboard when his ship rammed another, possibly after cutting the first Athenian line, and the Athenian right got the better of the Spartan left. After the battle, bad weather prevented the Athenians from picking up survivors who were clinging to wrecks.
CASUALTIES Spartans lost 9 of their 10 ships, and more than 60 of their allies'; the Athenians lost 25.
RESULT The last Athenian victory of the war.

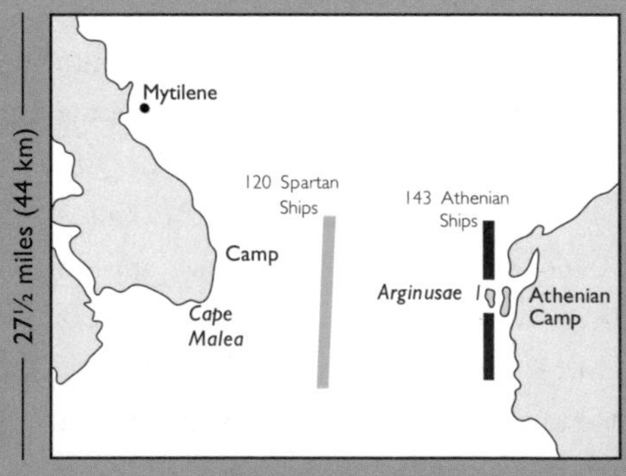

THE RISE AND FALL OF ATHENS: THE LIMITATIONS OF SEA POWER

After Xerxes' defeat, Athens used sea power to liberate the Greeks under Persian rule and to create the first great maritime empire, mainly around the Aegean and the Sea of Marmara, although her navy enabled her to strike as far as Cyprus and Egypt, the latter about 1,000 miles (1,600 km) away by sea. Inevitably, sea power formed the basis for her strategy in the Peloponnesian War with Sparta and her allies (431–404 BC). Basically, the strategy was to avoid confrontation with the Spartan army by withdrawing the population inside the fortified complex formed by Athens and the Piraeus, linked by the "long walls," and to supply it by sea.

This war perfectly illustrates the advantages and limitations of sea power. It is vital to the defense of an island or archipelago, or any state that depends on imports, but cannot be effective against a continental enemy because that enemy is self-sufficient. Athens could hit any of her enemies within reach of the sea, and even transport an expeditionary force to Sicily. But she could not prevent the enemy sending help to Sicily, let alone effectively blockade the Peloponnese, because her warships could not remain permanently at sea, and her raiding had a limited effect. Even when, from 425 BC, Athens established permanent bases on or off the enemy coasts, they were too easy to confine. In any case, the enemy did not depend upon imports and so was not vulnerable to sea power. The only time Athens could have won the war was in 418 BC when, backed by a temporary coalition of Peloponnesian states, she forced the Spartans to take a stand at Mantinea but lost.

But Athens herself was vulnerable to sea power. She depended upon it not only to protect her sea-borne supplies, but also to maintain her hold on her empire, from which she derived revenue and manpower, and in the end it was sea power that brought her down. Her Sicilian expeditionary force was destroyed in 413 BC, and this gave Sparta the chance to match her at sea, encouraged her allies to revolt, and induced the Persians to throw their financial weight behind her enemies. Once the Spartans had found a competent admiral in Lysander, and Persian gold had started to flow, it was only a question of time. When the Athenian fleet was annihilated at Aegospotami in the Hellespont, in 405 BC, Athens was forced to surrender.

THE PUNIC WARS

The wars between Rome and Carthage (264–241 and 218–201 BC) also illustrate these points. The First Punic War was essentially a struggle for control of an island, Sicily, and the decisive battle was fought at sea, off western Sicily.

BATTLE OF ECNOMUS

DATE 256 BC
CAMPAIGN First Punic War
OBJECT Roman attempt to invade Carthage in North Africa.
NUMBERS 330 Roman against 350 Carthaginian quinqueremes, Romans under Atilius Regulus and Manlius Vulso, Carthaginians under Hanno and Hamilcar.
DESCRIPTION The Roman fleet was in four squadrons—1st, 2nd, and 3rd formed a triangle, with 3rd at its base, towing transports, covered by the 4th at the rear. The Carthaginians had 263 ships in the center and on the right, in a single line abeam extending out to sea, and 87 more on the left at an angle along the shore. The Carthaginian center feinted retreat and was pursued by the first two Roman squadrons. Meanwhile, the right attacked the 4th and the left drove the 3rd, which had cast off the transports, toward shore. Having defeated the Carthaginian center, the 2nd Roman squadron returned to help the 4th, driving the Carthaginian right out to sea, and finally the 1st, 2nd, and 4th Roman squadrons joined the 3rd in defeating the Carthaginian left.
CASUALTIES Romans lost 24 "sunk," Carthaginians 30 "sunk" and 64 captured; *corvus* still much in evidence on Roman side.
RESULT The Romans were able to land their army, although it was defeated in the following year.

THE EVOLUTION OF THE FIGHTING GALLEY

The earliest Greek warships were pentekonters, that is, ships with 50 oars, probably rowed at one level, 25 each side. But as early as the eighth century BC, there is evidence of ships rowed at two levels, and around 650 BC comes the first reference in surviving literature to a trireme (in Greek *triêrês*, i.e. "three rower.") Such ships may have been invented at Corinth and used in battle against her recalcitrant colony Corcyra (Corfu) in about 610 BC. They were expensive because the large numbers of rowers had to be paid; slaves were used only in an emergency and were then freed. Thus it was probably not until the sixth century BC that triremes came into general use. A lucky strike in the Laureum silver mines enabled the Athenians to build the first really large fleet of triremes—up to 200 vessels—just in time to face Xerxes' invasion in 480 BC.

By this time, triremes were the standard warships used by the maritime powers of the eastern Mediterranean, although some old-fashion pentekonters were still to be seen. By then, too, the normal complement of a trireme seems to have been 200 men, and later evidence suggests that these would have been made up of 170 oarsmen, 85 each side (31 in the upper row, 27 each in the middle and bottom rows), 16 officers and deck-crew, and 14 marines. But the number of marines could be varied. At Lade (ca. 494 BC), the Chiot ships carried 40, and each ship in Xerxes' fleet had 30 extra, perhaps because of Persian experiences with the Chiots at Lade.

How a trireme may have looked with side screens in position. Sails were carried for cruising, and triremes could probably move faster under sail than under oar, with a favorable wind. But such a rig made tacking virtually impossible and thus fighting under sail too risky, it being essential to avoid presenting vulnerable sides or sterns to the enemy. Hence both masts and sails were lowered before battle, or even left ashore.

THE TRIREME RECONSTRUCTED

Trials for the trireme *Olympias* (*right*), built to the ancient design in the 1980s, have shown that such a ship is very maneuverable, can exceed seven knots, and cruise for more than seven hours at four or five knots. Conditions on board would have been very cramped but nevertheless light and airy. This was in marked contrast to the "ships of the line" in the late 18th and early 19th centuries.

Unfortunately, we do not know how many marines the Greek triremes carried in 480 BC, but it is doubtful whether it was less than the Persians, and the best evidence suggests that the Phoenician triremes in Xerxes' fleet, and particularly those of Sidon, were the fastest vessels on either side. Hence the significance of the narrow waters at Salamis, where the Persian advantages in speed and numbers were nullified. Earlier in the campaign, off Artemisium in Euboea, in waters nowhere narrower than five miles (8 km), the Greeks had barely managed to hold their own.

Later, warships carried more men—at Ecnomus, for example, the Roman quinqueremes had crews of 300 and 120 marines—but it is not certain how they were rowed. Probably no warship ever had more than three banks of oars, and the larger numbers were accommodated by doubling up on some of the oars. The largest warship ever built was the *tesserakontêrês* ("40 rower") under the auspices of Ptolemy IV of Egypt (221–204 BC), and it is inconceivable that it had 40 banks of oars—in any case, it apparently never sailed.

The evolution of oarage systems, from a single bank rowed across gunwales, via three banks of the trireme, to a doubling up on one or more banks to produce quinqueremes.

The corvus*, a device invented by the Romans in the early years of the First Punic War to counteract the speed and maneuverability of Carthaginian warships. First used at the battle of Mylae in 260 BC, it led to a number of Roman successes, down to the battle of Cape Hermaeum in 255 BC, but was apparently thereafter abandoned.*

The limitations of sea power were shown up again by Carthaginian failure to prevent Rome from transporting an army to Sicily in 264 BC. The Carthaginians themselves later demonstrated the impossibility of an effective blockade, when Hannibal "the Rhodian" repeatedly managed to run supplies into the besieged Carthaginian base at Lilybaeum (Marsala.)

In the First Punic War, while a Roman expeditionary force was on its way to Africa, there occurred the greatest naval battle of ancient history when 330 Roman quinqueremes, each carrying 420 men, defeated 350 Carthaginian quinqueremes off Ecnomus in southern Sicily.

In the Second Punic War, Roman sea power was one factor in her victory. It prevented Hannibal from transporting his army to Italy by sea, which would have been quicker and less costly, and effectively starved him of reinforcements. It checkmated his ally, Philip V of Macedonia, and enabled Rome to transport armies to Spain, Greece, Sardinia, Sicily, and Africa, and to supply and reinforce them. Indeed, Roman sea power is often forgotten in attempts to explain her rise in dominance in the Mediterranean world.

TACTICS AND COUNTERTACTICS

Ancient warships had no means of eliminating enemy vessels without colliding with them, so naval tactics were necessarily limited. Once the ram had been invented, the ship itself could be used as a weapon, but the problem was to avoid self-damage and entanglement with the enemy vessel. Speed and maneuverability made it possible to attack vulnerable sides and sterns, and during the fifth century BC, maneuvers known as *diekplous* and *periplous* were developed, particularly by the Athenians. The difference they could make was shown at the battle of Sybota, in 432 BC, when a mere 10 Athenian triremes prevented the Corinthians from defeating Athens' Corcyran allies, and by the exploits of Athenian admiral Phormio in the Gulf of Corinth in 429 BC, when, in command of just 20 ships, he first defeated 44 Peloponnesian ships, then 77.

Circles and crows

But such tactics were too easily countered to be decisive in normal circumstances. Slower and less maneuverable ships could contrive to fight in a confined space, as the Greeks did at Salamis, or the Syracusans in the Grand Harbor of Syracuse in 413 BC. They could adopt a defensive formation, such as the "circle" adopted by Phormio's opponents in the first of his victories, and allegedly by the

Greeks off Artemisium in 480 BC, although whether 271 triremes could literally have formed a circle is doubtful—it would have been about 3 miles (5 km) in circumference. A larger fleet could form up in two lines abeam, instead of the usual one, as the Athenians did at Arginusae, thus making the *diekplous*, if not impossible, at any rate very risky, since ships trying it would have to cut through two lines instead of through one.

Most famous of all the methods for nullifying faster and more maneuverable enemy vessels was the *corvus* (crow), invented by the Romans in the First Punic War. This was a boarding plank, with a spike at the far end, that could be rotated around a spar in the bows of the ship, and let down on to an approaching enemy, thus joining the two ships and providing a means of boarding. This device enabled the Romans to win most of the early battles of the war, including Ecnomus, but was apparently abandoned after ca. 255 BC. Perhaps it rendered Roman ships liable to capsize in heavy seas, and was responsible for their devastating losses in a storm off southern Sicily in that year.

It is clear from ancient accounts that sea battles rapidly degenerated into chaos, and it is doubtful whether any except minor skirmishes were won by tactics. An admiral really just arranged his ships, and it is worth noting that the same men commanded on both land and sea: Lysander, for example, perished in a land battle, and even Epaminondas once led a fleet to sea. Fleet tactics had to wait for a means whereby one fleet could damage the other, without its ships literally coming into contact with the enemy, and so risking equal damage.

TRIREME BATTLE TACTICS

The most famous maneuver was the *diekplous*, almost certainly involving single ships in line abeam—the normal battle formation—trying to cut through the enemy line. Each helmsman would try to steer for a gap between enemy ships, and either turn suddenly to port or starboard to ram one in the side, or row clean through the line, swing around, and attack from the stern. Sheering away enemy oars as a ship cut through the line might have been possible, but only if one's own oars could be shipped in time, which seems unlikely. The *periplous* was either a variation involving outflanking the enemy line, or the final stage of a *diekplous*, when the maneuvering vessel, having cut through the line, swung around to attack from the stern.

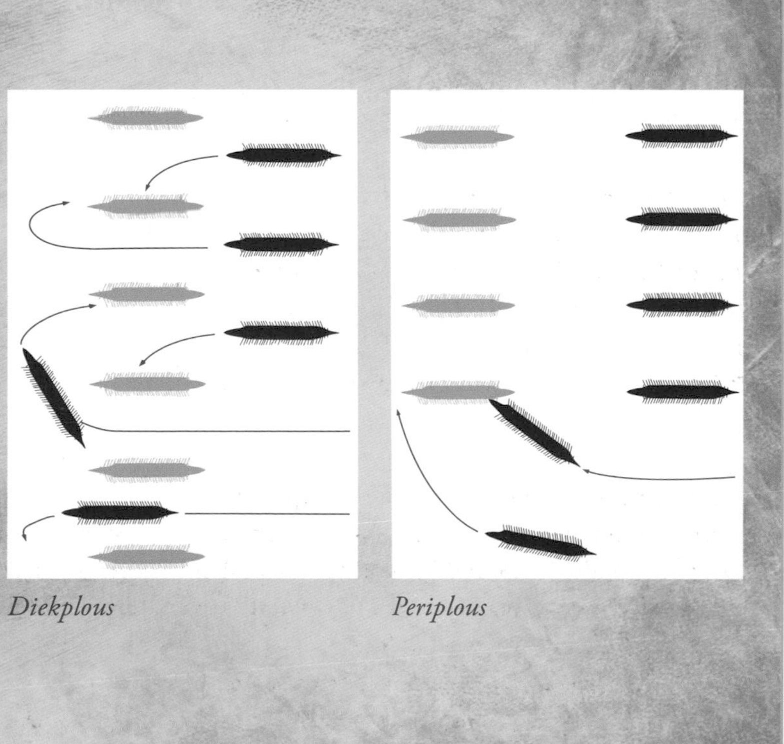

Diekplous *Periplous*

3 THE MIGHT OF ROME

Before the Second Punic War (218–201 BC), Rome's influence extended no farther than the Alps; within a century, the seeds of empire had been sown in Spain, Africa, and the Greek east.

THE MIDDLE REPUBLIC (ca. 200–100 BC)

In 211 BC, Rome had become embroiled in war against Philip V of Macedon, when he made common cause with Hannibal; an uneasy peace had ensued in 205, but no sooner had Rome humbled Carthage than her troops were again taking the field against Philip.

After a false start, the command passed to T. Quinctius Flamininus in 198 BC; his peace terms were rejected by Philip and, in the fighting that followed, he pushed the Macedonians back into Thessaly. In 197, the Romans met Philip's army near Pherae; the Macedonians numbered around 26,000, against a Roman force of 30,000. However, both sides disengaged, preferring to seek a more suitable battlefield. Two days later, after torrential rain and in the middle of a thick mist, they met again in a chance encounter at Cynoscephalae; the battle ended in victory for Flamininus, and delivered Greece into the hands of the Romans.

It was here that the legion first proved its superiority over the phalanx. The great hedge of pikes was effective only as long as it remained together, with its flanks guarded; lack of flexibility meant that rough ground was enough to break the line and disorganize

BATTLE OF CYNOSCEPHALAE

DATE 198 BC
CAMPAIGN Second Macedonian War
DESCRIPTION The armies of Philip V of Macedon and Flamininus were encamped on either side of a ridge, each ignorant of the other's whereabouts. It was misty, and the advance forces, which both commanders had sent to occupy the heights, met unexpectedly. Reinforcements arrived on both sides, and Flamininus led out his whole army—two legions at full strength with allied troops. A large part of the Macedonian army was absent foraging, so Philip deployed just half of his phalanx (ca. 8,000 men) on the ridge and charged down onto the Roman left, driving all before him. Flamininus took command of the Roman right, positioning his elephants in front, and charged uphill against Philip's left, where the rest of his forces were arriving in disorder; the Romans quickly routed them.
RESULT The initiative of one of Flamininus's officers won the day: he wheeled 20 maniples (ca. 2,000 men) around from the victorious Roman right, and fell upon the rear of the Macedonian right. Philip was completely defeated.

The Mediterranean ca. 100 BC.

its formation. Antiochus III of Syria tried to remedy the problem when he met the Romans in battle at Magnesia.

Antiochus had crossed to Europe late in 192 BC, attracted by the power vacuum that Philip's defeat had created. The Romans crushed his army at Thermopylae (191 BC) by emulating the tactics that the Persians had used in 480 BC. The Romans carried the conflict over to Asia Minor and met Antiochus on ground of his own choosing at Magnesia (winter 190–189 BC). Antiochus' grand army numbered more than 70,000 men and comprised several discrete elements with little cohesion. Central to the whole force was a 16,000-strong phalanx; unusually, it was articulated—that is to say, the ten blocks of pike-men were separated, one from another, by elephants. However, Antiochus and his cavalry abandoned the phalanx in their pursuit of the Roman left wing, and it was a simple matter for the Roman center to stampede the elephants and breach the line.

Rome became embroiled in conflict with Macedon again in the late 170s, this time against Perseus, eldest son of Philip V, who had acceded in 179 BC on his father's death. Roman incompetence prolonged the war to 168, when the veteran L. Aemilius Paullus took command and brought Perseus to battle at Pydna. Yet again, the flexibility of the legion proved superior to the massive weight of the phalanx. From now on, Macedon's days of independence were numbered: in 149 BC, Rome finally, and reluctantly, annexed the country. Three years later, Carthage was razed to the ground by Scipio Aemilianus, a son of Aemilius Paullus and a grandson (by adoption) of the great Scipio Africanus.

Meanwhile, the Romans faced a different situation in Spain. Roman troops had first set foot in the peninsula in 218 BC, during the war with Hannibal, but sporadic fighting in the interior kept two legions (and later, four) busy for another 85 years; indeed, Spain was not formally annexed until the time of Augustus.

The Lusitanians of the far west and the Celtiberians of the north gave constant trouble down to the late 140s BC, by which time only the hilltop town of Numantia still held out against Rome. A series of camps at Renieblas, 5 miles (8 km) to the east, housed the troops of successive Roman commanders in their attempts to reduce the town. Finally, in 134 BC, the task was entrusted to Scipio Aemilianus. He was something of a siege-craft expert, having reduced Carthage, and his blockade of Numantia, reportedly the first operation of its kind, eventually forced the capitulation of the inhabitants in 133 BC.

One man who had served as a Roman ally at Numantia was Jugurtha, a prince (and later, king) of Numidia. Many years later, affairs arising out of the murder of some Italian merchants in his country escalated into war with Rome. A succession of commanders sent to restore the situation culminated in the appointment of Gaius Marius (107 BC), another veteran of Numantia. Jugurtha was finally captured in 105, having been betrayed to one of Marius's officers, a certain L. Cornelius Sulla. Both Marius and Sulla were destined to play major parts in the unfolding drama of the next decade.

MARIUS' MULES

Marius' reforms meant that arms and armor had to be mass-produced, resulting in some standardization. Every legionary was uniformly equipped with a short, thrusting sword (the *gladius*), a long oval shield (the *scutum*), two javelins (*pila*), and a mail shirt. One *pilum* was heavy, the other light; the iron point of the heavy one was joined to the wooden shaft by a rivet and a wooden peg, which was intended to splinter on impact, so denying the enemy use of the weapon. Full armor, including helmet, must have weighed around 66 pounds (30 kg). Besides all this, the legionaries were obliged to carry much of their own luggage: entrenching equipment, cooking utensils, emergency rations, and personal baggage, all strapped onto a forked pole. It was as a result of this that the soldiers gained the nickname of "Marius's mules."

Professional army

Marius is usually credited with the institution of a professional Roman army; in fact, the two major changes ascribed to him were probably the result of a gradual process that had been gathering momentum for many years. First, Rome's amateur militia of conscripted men serving for six years was replaced by a professional long-service army of volunteers. The crucial factor was the lowering of the prescribed property qualification for service in order to draw upon the vast pool of *capite censi*, those citizens who owned no property and were thus normally excused military service. This, in turn, necessitated the equipping of soldiers at the state's expense.

The second major change was a tactical reform, discarding the maniple as the chief subunit in favor of the cohort. Each cohort resulted from the fusion of three maniples, one from each of the old divisions of *hastati*, *principes*, and *triarii* (or *pilani*.)The six centuries probably comprised 80 men, as the centuries of the Imperial army did, although pre-Marian centurions had commanded 60 men or fewer. The six centurions of the cohort preserved the old manipular terminology in their titles, such as *hastatus*.

In the later 90s BC, civil war erupted in Italy, with consequent repercussions on the army. Rome's Italian allies (the *socii*) were discontented with their military obligations and, in 91 BC, rose in rebellion. Marius (now almost 70) was active in putting down the revolt in northern Italy, Sulla in the south. The war was over by 88 BC, and Sulla was feted as consul and promised the command against Mithridates VI of Pontus, who was threatening war in the east by invading Greece. As a result of the Social War, the allied contingents, which used to accompany the legions on campaign, ceased to exist. All Italian recruits were now entitled to become legionaries. The number of legions consequently multiplied, particularly in preparation for major campaigns.

THE LATER REPUBLIC (c.100–44 BC)

Sulla's war with Mithridates was inconclusive, despite two victories in the field (one at Chaeronea), and he was forced to seek a diplomatic agreement. He had left Rome under a cloud—his army had marched on the city after the Senate tried to deprive him of his eastern command—and he returned to renewed civil unrest. By the end of 80 BC, as dictator, he was master of the Roman world. His death in 78 BC ushered in a new round of civil war in which the main players were the late dictator's legates. One, Gnaeus Pompey, was active against rebel forces in Spain. Another, M. Licinius Crassus, crushed Spartacus and his army of renegade slaves; he employed an elaborate system of earthworks to confine his quarry to the toe of Italy, a device perhaps inspired by Scipio Aemilianus's blockade of Numantia. A third, L. Licinius Lucullus, enjoyed initial success against a renascent Mithridates, until a mutiny paralyzed his army (67 BC); the command was given to Pompey, who finally consolidated Roman authority in the east.

Gnaeus Pompey (106–48 BC), who was given the name Magnus (the Great) by Sulla, was consul three times before meeting an untimely end.

BATTLE OF CHAERONEA

DATE 86 BC
CAMPAIGN First Mithridatic War
NUMBERS Sulla's forces amounted to some 15,000 infantry and 1,500 cavalry; Archelaus, Mithridates' general, commanded an army at least three times as large.
DESCRIPTION Sulla and Archelaus met on the Boeotian plain, north of the town of Chaeronea. As Sulla crossed the plain, he was obliged to turn his column left into the line of battle to meet Archelaus's approach. His left wing was seriously outflanked, but reserve cohorts were posted on the foothills to the rear. Archelaus' army comprised a phalanx of 15,000 liberated slaves, protected by scythed chariots, and strong contingents of cavalry and light troops on the wings. As he engaged with his right wing, the Roman reserve advanced to protect its outflanked comrades, but was driven back. Therefore, Sulla himself came across with his cavalry from the right and flung Archelaus back. The Roman left was again reinforced by the reserve and Sulla returned to the right wing, where Archelaus was now pressing the attack. Here, the Romans prevailed again, breaking through the enemy line.
RESULT Archelaus' army fled in confusion.

BATTLE OF ALESIA

DATE 52 BC
CAMPAIGN Gallic Wars
DESCRIPTION Caesar encamped his forces at key points around the hilltop town of Alesia, enclosing Vercingetorix and his 80,000 men within siegeworks. One line of fortifications confined them within Alesia; another faced outward against the inevitable Gallic relieving force. Each line had several elements—first, the rampart with a palisade and fortified with towers every 27 yards (24 m); forked branches (*cervi*) projected horizontally from the top. Next, there was a pair of ditches, each 5½ yards (5 m) wide, the inner one filled with water. Beyond these lay various booby traps: sharpened branches (*cippi*) set in trenches and interwoven to form a hedge of spikes; eight rows of pointed stakes (*lilia*) embedded vertically in pits and concealed with brushwood; and a scattering of barbed spikes (*stimuli*) anchored in blocks of wood. The inner line ran for some 10 miles (16 km); the outer was over 17 miles (27 km) long.

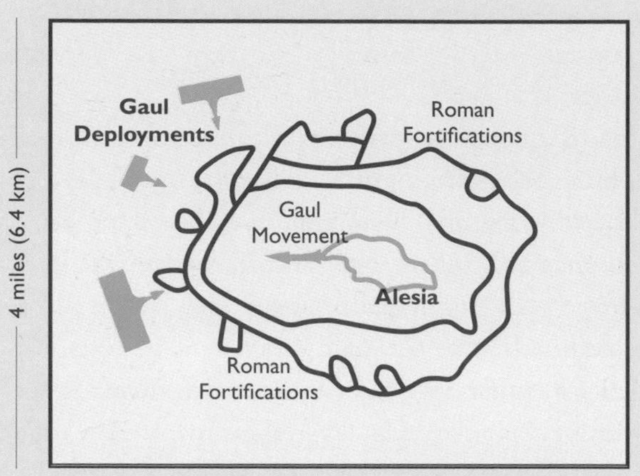

RESULT Gallic attempts to coordinate attacks on the Roman lines from within and without were unsuccessful, and Vercingetorix surrendered.

At around this time, a young nobleman named C. Julius Caesar rose to prominence. Born ca. 100 BC, by 60 BC, he had joined Pompey and Crassus in an informal alliance known to us as the First Triumvirate; until the death of Crassus in 53 BC, this trio successfully imposed their collective will on the State. In 58 BC, Caesar embarked upon a 5-year command in Gaul (later extended to 10 years.) He was immediately called upon to deal with the Helvetii, who were in the process of migrating west from the area of modern Switzerland. In order to deny them access to Roman territory, Caesar required the only legion available to him to construct a barrier along the Rhône for a distance of some 17½ miles (28 km). The whole thing, comprising rampart, ditch, and guard posts, was completed in around two weeks, testifying to the engineering skills of the legionaries. Caesar later brought up three more legions and raised two for the final confrontation, the battle of Bibracte, in which the Helvetii were utterly defeated.

From now on, Caesar intervened directly in Gallic affairs, raising a further two legions in 57 BC and campaigning as far afield as Brittany. Disaffection smoldered as the Gauls gradually realized that Caesar planned to occupy their territories. A legion was destroyed in the winter of 54–53 BC, but Caesar increased his complement to 10 in the following year (borrowing a legion from Pompey in the process.) In the summer of 52 BC, the great Gallic revolt flared up under the leadership of Vercingetorix. By this time, Caesar's army probably consisted of 12 legions. His first move was to attack the town of Avaricum, which the inhabitants had chosen to defend, rather than retreat with Vercingetorix; such was the Roman engineering expertise that the town was reduced by siege in less than a month. His attempt to storm Gergovia, however, ended in failure, but he was able to trap Vercingetorix in the hilltop town of Alesia, where the Gauls were starved into submission. One or two actions in the following year, 51 BC, effectively finished off the Gallic War.

When Caesar's command in Gaul was renewed (55 BC), his fellow Triumvirs, Pompey and Crassus, were granted respectively as their provinces Spain and Syria. Crassus unwisely provoked the sleeping giant of Parthia, a loosely organized confederation of states under the authority of a central monarchy. In 53 BC, he crossed the Euphrates with an army of seven legions accompanied by light troops, and ran into a force of Parthian cavalry and horse archers in the vicinity of Carrhae. The legionaries presented a sitting target for enemy missiles and were unable to retaliate. The Romans reportedly lost 20,000 killed (Crassus among them) and 10,000 prisoners.

Meanwhile, a breach had opened between Caesar and Pompey. The Senate put their trust in Pompey, whereupon Caesar swept down into Italy (49 BC.) Pompey rapidly retreated before Caesar's advance and embarked for the east; Caesar pursued him across the Adriatic, after quickly neutralizing his forces in Spain. Pinning Pompey on the coast south of his base at Dyrrhachium, Caesar hemmed him in with a circumvallation, but Pompey built a line of counterworks in reply. After fierce skirmishing, Caesar withdrew. Pompey followed and the two forces met at Pharsalus, where the Pompeians were soundly beaten. Pompey fled to meet his death in Egypt, and his troops were reorganized into four more legions for Caesar's huge army. Caesar released his veteran legions from service and, as dictator, made plans for a Parthian campaign; these were foiled by his assassination in 44 BC.

Julius Caesar's success in Gaul brought him to the English Channel and the Rhine.

THE LATER REPUBLIC LEGIONS

Roman legions each bore a numeral reflecting the sequence of their creation; the numbers I to IV were traditionally reserved for the consuls each year. At the time of Marius, the legions appear to have been reconstructed every year, but during the later Republic they began to retain their identity for more than a year. Service was, in the first instance, for 6 years, although the total period of liability to service was 16 years.

During the 70s BC, there were around 14 legions in the field in any one year. Throughout the 50s, Caesar steadily increased his Gallic army, and by 49 BC, he controlled some 30 legions. During the civil war, there were almost 50 legions under arms. The rank and file had to be rewarded: Caesar doubled his soldiers' pay to 225 *denarii* a year to secure their loyalty, and time-served veterans were entitled to a plot of land.

THE FOUNDATION OF THE EMPIRE

By late 43 BC, the major players in the next phase of fighting had resolved themselves into two camps: Caesar's murderers, the self-styled "Liberators" (principally Brutus and Cassius) in exile east of the Adriatic; and the coalition known to us as the Second Triumvirate, comprising the Caesarian partisans Mark Antony and Aemilius Lepidus, and Caesar's great-nephew and heir, Octavian. There were still some 37 legions under arms; several of Caesar's veteran legions had been reformed into the bargain. Leaving Lepidus in charge of Rome, Antony and Octavian transported 20 or so legions across the Adriatic to meet the 19 legions of the Liberators. The two armies met at Philippi in Macedonia, where the Triumvirs eventually prevailed. After the battle, the time-served veterans were released and sent to Italy with Octavian; the remainder were regrouped into 11 legions, three of which accompanied Octavian. The eight remaining to Antony included his favorite legion, V *Alaudae*, raised by Caesar in 52 BC.

The Triumvirate was due to expire in 33 BC. Relations between its prime movers had, in any case, deteriorated, chiefly it would seem as a result of Antony's liaison with Cleopatra, queen of Egypt. The Senate declared war on her in 32 BC, thus providing Octavian's excuse for a showdown with Antony.

By then, both men had substantially increased their armies. Antony assembled a force of 23 legions on the west coast of Greece at Actium; others of his legions were absent in Cyrenaica. Octavian fielded about 24 of his 30 or so legions. While he harassed Antony by

The Roman empire ca. AD 100. Six legions were distributed along the Eastern frontier and two were based in the Nile Delta area, but the whole of North Africa lay under the control of a single legion. Another was based in Spain, and Britain's garrison numbered four, but the bulk of Rome's legions lay in fortresses along the Rhine and Danube. This imbalance became more pronounced throughout the second century.

BATTLE OF PHILIPPI

DATE 42 BC
CAMPAIGN Civil war, between the Liberators (Brutus and Cassius), and the Triumvirs (Antony, Octavian, and Lepidus)
DESCRIPTION The Liberators were encamped on either side of the Via Egnatia, Brutus to the north with his right flank resting on the mountains, Cassius to the south with his left flank against a large marsh. The camp of the Triumvirs sat astride the road itself, with a rampart and ditch running southward. Antony attempted to outflank Cassius by cutting a path through the marsh and, although thwarted, brought on the general engagement. Brutus's forces overran the opposing lines and captured the main camp; Antony, in turn, broke through Cassius's defenses, routed his soldiers, and took his camp, whereupon Cassius killed himself. Both sides then retired to their original positions and settled down for nearly three weeks. Octavian, meanwhile, shifted the axis of battle 90 degrees by constructing three camps on the northern fringes of the marsh, thus threatening Brutus's flank. To avoid encirclement, Brutus extended his lines east, but morale in his army was low. Finally, he bowed to pressure from his general staff and offered to engage in battle.
RESULT The Triumvirs won and the beaten forces fled.

land, his lieutenant Agrippa hemmed in Antony's fleet and cut his communications. At last, Antony staked all on a naval engagement in the Gulf of Actium (31 BC), but he and Cleopatra simply broke free of the blockade and eventually fled to Egypt, where they both later took their own lives. Antony's army surrendered, all time-served veterans were discharged, and the remainder were incorporated into Octavian's new order of battle.

Octavian was now effectively the ruler of the Roman world. He ensured his primacy by assuming all the key republican offices himself, taking the title of Princeps, "first citizen," and in 27 BC the new name of Augustus Caesar. His long reign (he died in AD 14) consolidated the position of emperor in the Roman world and the Republic was never restored. His position, and that of his successors, was guaranteed by a strong and loyal military.

After the battle of Actium, the swollen ranks of the army were reduced, perhaps over several years. By 25 BC, there were 28 legions under arms, although quite how Augustus arrived at that number, by what stages of reorganization, is not known. The incorporation of five of six complete Antonian legions (all, significantly, old Caesarian units) led to the duplication of numerals in their names, which persisted throughout the imperial period.

SERVICE IN THE AUGUSTAN ARMY

The conditions of service under the Principate differed significantly from those under the Republic. Augustus abolished the hitherto standard six-year stint, and by AD 5 new regulations required each soldier to serve for 20 years, with a farther 5 years as a reservist. This last distinction faded with time, and as discharges were made only every second year, some men served a total of 26 years. The rewards of service were regularized as well. Augustus founded the military treasury to meet the costs of the armed forces. Besides an annual salary, varying according to rank and pay grade, the legionary could look forward to a substantial gratuity on discharge. Furthermore, the custom arose whereby each new emperor paid the soldiers a bonus on his accession.

ROMAN NAVAL WARFARE

Rome's first fleet was built during the First Punic War (264–241 BC) to counter the Carthaginian mastery of the sea. Rome had the financial strength and the stocks of timber to maintain a large fleet, but after the defeat of Carthage and the crushing of the naval power of Syria and Rhodes (mid-second century BC) there was a general naval disarmament. Consequently, in the absence of adequate maritime policing, pirates were able to terrorize the seas unmolested until, at last, Pompey was given command over the whole Mediterranean (67 BC) and, in a lightning campaign, eradicated piracy. Roman naval power was never again allowed to fall into abeyance.

(Above) Auxiliaries stow equipment on a cargo boat, while legionaries man a two-banked liburnian, *the most common craft in the provincial fleets. The scene is the Danube River, ca. AD 100.*

During the civil wars, fleets proliferated just as the legions did; they were necessary for controlling trade routes and transporting armies. Ironically, it was one of Pompey's sons, Sextus Pompeius, who emerged as the scourge of the Mediterranean in 43 BC; Octavian and his lieutenant, Agrippa, finally defeated him in two battles off the Sicilian coast (36 BC). Mark Antony, too, relied on naval power in the eastern Mediterranean,

(Above) This ship was probably built and manned by Phoenicians employed by Sennacherib. It is a birene, with two rows of oars. (Top) Roman relief from Trajan's column showing a trireme, ca. 100 BC–AD 100. In earlier times, the topmost bank of oars was accommodated in the outrigger; here, all three banks clearly emerge from beneath the outrigger, which was perhaps retained as a bumper, protecting the rowers from buffeting and the oars from any attempts to shear them.

(Below) The Romans built two kinds of trireme: the cataphract *(or armored) and the lighter* aphract *(unarmored.) The vessel shown here is the former. There is a massive forecastle in the bows, and a cabin for the captain in the stern. The ram is single pointed, as opposed to the triple rams of earlier galleys.*

and the contest for control of the empire was, finally, settled by fierce a naval encounter in the Gulf of Actium in 31BC.

As part of his reorganization of the Roman Imperial Navy after Actium, Augustus concentrated his ships at Misenum on the Bay of Naples and Ravenna on the Adriatic. The *classis Misenensis* was the largest fleet: it has been calculated that, in the mid-first century, its manpower exceeded 10,000. The *classis Ravennas* was perhaps half as large. Both were commanded by high-ranking equestrian (that is, non-senatorial) officers (*praefecti classis*) who were responsible only to the emperor. Independent squadrons were soon established on all the major waterways—the Black Sea, the English Channel, the Rhine and Danube, and off the coasts of Syria, Egypt, and Mauretania. These provincial fleets were commanded by more junior *praefecti*, responsible to their respective provincial governors.

The standard warship of the republic had been the quinquereme, although galleys could be much larger in size. In the imperial fleet, however, the most prevalent warship was the trireme and, in the provincial fleets, the *liburnian* (a swift, two-banked galley); one *hexeres* (a double-bank galley with three men per oar) was retained in the Misenum fleet as the flagship, and there were a few quadriremes and quinqueremes.

The captain of each ship (*trierarch*) had a staff of petty officers and ratings; superimposed on this naval organization was a military one, whereby the entire crew, regardless of size, was organized as a *centuria* under the command of a centurion. On a trireme, for instance, the crew numbered about 200 and on a quinquereme, 300. The individual sailors were not slaves, as is often thought, but provincials who were granted Roman citizenship after 26 years' service. In peacetime, the galleys patrolled their own areas and despatched letters and orders; the riverine fleets escorted supply convoys and kept a watch on the frontiers. The personnel often acted as an onshore militia and, at sea, kept piracy at bay.

THE ARMY ON THE MARCH

A marching army comprised three main sections: the vanguard of light-armed troops, for screening and scouting; the main body of heavy infantry, including the baggage train; and the rearguard. Cavalry provided cover in advance and on the flanks. Behind the vanguard, pioneers cleared the route for the marching column, and a detachment of legionaries carried the tools for laying out the temporary camp, the army's overnight accommodation. Camps could range widely in size and form, but most were roughly rectangular with rounded corners. The perimeter was normally defined by a ditch and rampart, crowned with a palisade of stakes. Gates were often provided with earthwork defenses. The *clavicula* was a curving length of rampart and ditch projecting inward from the right, which forced any invader to expose his unshielded side when entering.

Camp at Masada, showing the clavicula *(bottom center), which exposed an attacker's unshielded side.*

After the death of the emperor Titus in AD 81, a marble arch was built to commemorate his capture of Jerusalem in AD 70. This sculptural scene portrays the triumph celebrated by him and his father, Vespasian. Legionaries carrying the spoils of the Temple are depicted in undress uniform and wearing olive wreaths. Their treasure includes the Table of Shewbread with incense cups, two silver trumpets, and the seven-branch candelabrum (the menorah.) The objects would have been noted on the placards that the soldiers carry.

Augustus retained three legions with the numeral III. Other legions, bearing the title *Gemina* ("Twin"), were clearly formed by the amalgamation of two existing units.

Augustus set about forging the far-flung conquests of the later Republic into an empire. Rome now controlled territories from Portugal in the west to the Euphrates in the east, from Belgium in the north to the Sahara in the south, but the interior was not wholly Romanized. Augustus secured the Alpine lands to the north of Italy, completed the long-overdue conquest of Spain, and annexed the regions south of the Danube, but his attempts to conquer Germany east of the Rhine were frustrated; three legions were lost in the process. Claudius (AD 41–54) was the next emperor to initiate a war of conquest by invading Britain, and in Nero's reign (AD 54–68) there was warfare on the eastern frontier. In AD 66, a revolt flared up in Judaea and quickly assumed major proportions. This was the so-called Jewish War, lasting until AD 73 or 74, when a pocket of resistance on the rock of Masada was finally crushed.

The power struggle following the death of Nero generated a new round of civil war. First Galba, then Otho became emperor. Then Vitellius, with the backing of the seven legions on the Rhine, decisively defeated Otho's army at Cremona. Meanwhile, the armies of the east had declared for T. Flavius Vespasian, the general conducting the Jewish War. His deputies won the empire for him: Antonius Primus stripped the Danube of troops and defeated Vitellius's army, again at Cremona. The subsequent revolt of Batavian auxiliaries on the Rhine had wider repercussions in the order of battle; whole legions were cashiered in the aftermath and new ones raised (or created by amalgamation). Legion V *Alaudae* probably disappeared at this time, but the overall complement was brought up to 28 once again.

Consolidation and civil war

Under the three Flavian emperors, Vespasian, Titus, and Domitian (AD 69–96), no great wars of conquest took place, but Roman forces continued to advance in Britain, and the German frontier was extensively remodeled. The accession of Trajan (AD 98–117) brought fresh annexations on the Danube and in the east, but few details of the warfare that must have accompanied them have survived. His successor, Hadrian, was more concerned with consolidating the frontiers than extending them, and in the Golden Age of Antoninus Pius (AD 138–61) there was very little major

PARTHIAN WARS

DATE AD 114–97

DESCRIPTION The Euphrates was the de facto boundary between Rome and the east. The only disputed territory was the kingdom of Armenia, sitting like a buffer between Rome's northeastern frontier and the Parthian vassals in Mesopotamia. Since the days of Augustus, the king of Armenia had been a Roman nominee; during the reign of Nero, however, the Parthians captured Armenia, but magnanimously allowed Rome to crown the Parthian-nominated king. Trajan decided to rectify the situation by annexing Armenia. In 114, he embarked on an invasion of Parthia and, by 116, Ctesiphon (the Parthian capital) had fallen without resistance, but revolts and a Parthian resurgence led to the rapid abandonment of all territories beyond the Euphrates.

An uneasy peace lasted until 162, when the Parthians suddenly invaded Armenia (where they installed a Parthian prince on the throne) and Syria. Marcus Aurelius sent large forces and capable commanders: Armenia was subjugated (163–64), Edessa and Nisibis seized (165), and Ctesiphon destroyed (166). Unfortunately, the returning armies brought plague to the west, but the eastern frontier was secured and substantially remodeled, taking in an area beyond the Euphrates. The fortress-city of Dura Europos received a Roman garrison. In 197, Septimius Severus launched an invasion of Parthia, the so-called Second Parthian War. (The First, in 195, was simply aimed at the Arab peoples of the north who had taken the opportunity of the civil war in the west to turn on the local Roman garrisons.) The Romans sacked Ctesiphon yet again, but Severus failed (as had Trajan before him) to capture the independent desert city of Hatra. It seems that he spent just 20 days besieging the city, during which time the defenders managed to destroy his siege machinery. A mutiny among his troops finally forced Severus to withdraw.

RESULT The net result of the eastern campaigns was the establishment of a new Roman province called Mesopotamia, but it covered just the northern area around Nisibis.

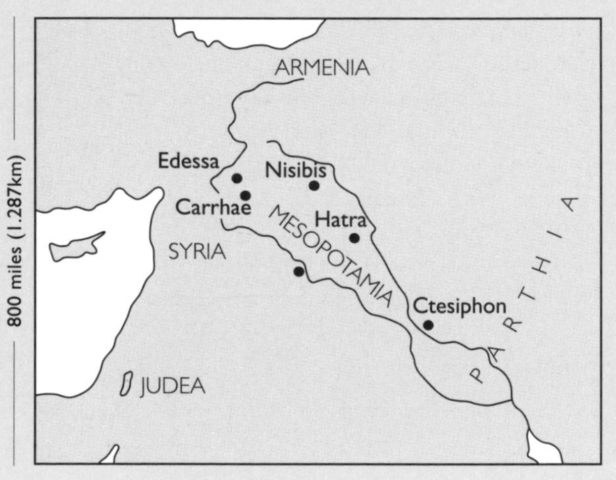

warfare. The unfortunate Marcus Aurelius (AD 161–80), however, was faced with a Parthian war, plague, and a full-scale invasion of northern barbarians; it seems that he intended to conquer territory north of the Danube, but failed. The Roman world was soon again convulsed by civil war, and the victor was Septimius Severus, who ruled from AD 193 to 211.

Throughout this period, the army comprised a number of different elements. In the later Republic, generals had enlisted the aid of irregular troops provided by friendly tribes and kings. These were usually cavalry and archers, making good the deficiencies of the legion. Augustus appears to have regularized such auxiliary troops into infantry cohorts (modeled on the legionary cohort) and cavalry *alae* ("wings"). Each *ala* comprised 16 *turmae* of 30-odd men, including three officers. A third type of unit, perhaps inspired by Caesar's German mixed cavalry, was the *cohors equitata*, an infantry battalion

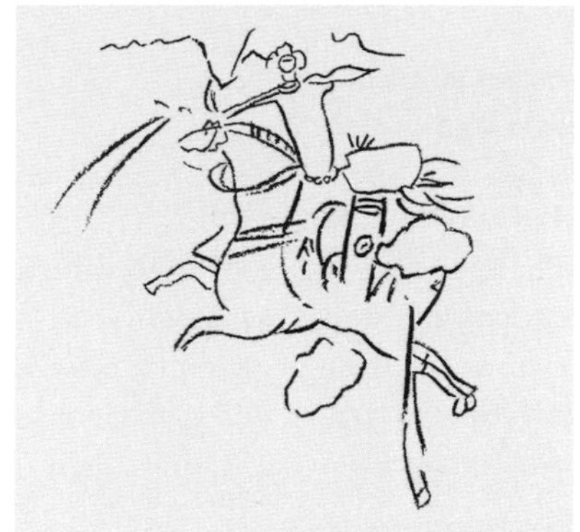

Copy of graffiti from Dura Europos on the Euphrates, depicting the two types of Parthian horsemen. The lancer and his horse are armored in mail and laminated plates; the archer is probably equipped with the gorytos, *a combination bowcase and quiver.*

with a cavalry element attached; in battle, the two were separated and each was brigaded with its fellows, instead of fighting as a mixed unit. All auxiliaries were normally noncitizens, in contrast to the citizen legions but, on discharge, they would receive citizenship.

There was considerable variation within the *auxilia*. At some time in the late 60s, double-size units (so-called *milliaria*) were introduced, and some units were composed entirely of archers (*sagittarii.*) From the time of Hadrian, there were units of heavily armored lancers (*cataphracti*) while, at the other end of the spectrum, units of North African bareback riders were completely unarmored. Many of the ethnic peculiarities of the specialized troops were gradually lost as the *auxilia* settled down to their role of frontier defense.

Extra duties

Of course, warfare was by no means the only occupation of the army. The daily routine demanded all kinds of tradesmen and specialists. In return for exemption from fatigues and, in many cases, extra pay, soldiers performed any one of over a 100 duties, from carpenters to medics. Promotions and transfers could carry a man from one branch of the service to another, and from one end of the empire to the other, in a military career often lasting a lifetime.

Legions and *auxilia* were not the only troops. Irregular units of ethnic origin were later introduced, perhaps to recapture the élan that had been lost with the standardization of the *auxilia*. There were also military and paramilitary forces in Rome, such as the imperial bodyguards (the Praetorian Guard and their cavalry equivalent, the *equites singulares Augusti*), and naval squadrons patrolled the major waterways. In time of crisis, the whole military machine worked in concert. But, from the time of Septimius Severus, fundamental changes were in store.

ROMAN SIEGE CRAFT

One of the earliest Roman siege operations was mounted at Agrigentum in Sicily in 262 BC. A twin line of fortifications, linking two camps, was constructed around the town, the inner line to confine the enemy, and the outer to repel any relieving force. After seven months, it was lack of vigilance that finally cost the Romans victory. The technique of bicircumvallation was basically sound, and was used again and again when there was danger of attack from the rear. Besieging an isolated enemy required just a single circumvallation. These sieges were essentially blockades, and depended upon the surrender of the enemy. More commonly, a Roman commander would mount an assault, with or without a blockade, involving the construction of a ramp to provide the siege machines with a gentle gradient and a smooth approach to the town walls.

The besieger's arsenal included a battering ram—a long, iron-tipped wooden beam suspended by ropes from a sturdy mobile housing called a "tortoise"; this was the classic means of breaching a wall. The Romans also used siege towers, which provided an elevated platform for missile attacks, either by archers or artillery; they often incorporated a battering ram at ground level. These machines had to be proofed against fire and bombardment, so they were often ironclad or covered with layers of wicker and hides.

One of the classic maneuvers of the Roman legionaries was the testudo, *or tortoise (depicted here on a relief from Trajan's column). This is described by many ancient authors with minor variations in size and form.*

Artillery

Each legion had a complement of artillery, useful in siege warfare, particularly for providing covering fire. Ancient artillery fell into two constructionally distinct groups—arrow-shooting *catapultae* and stone-throwing *ballistae*—although, around AD 100, a revolution in artillery design meant that both types were technically *ballistae*. By far the most common arrow shooter was the three-span variant—a machine about 5 feet (1.5 m) high, firing arrows some 25 inches (63.5 cm) long. Stone-throwers ranged up to monstrous machines 15 feet (4.5 m) high, capable of throwing stones weighing 110 pounds (45 kg).

During siege operations, personnel were protected by sheds and wicker screens. Legionaries moving up to the wall would adopt the *testudo* (or "tortoise") formation, with shields locked over their heads. At Jotapata in AD 67, the defenders broke up a *testudo* by pouring boiling oil over it, but the engineering skill and dogged determination of the Romans seldom failed. One conspicuous exception was at Hatra, the desert city that repulsed both Trajan and, on two occasions, Septimius Severus.

The remains of Roman siege works are preserved at several sites, but none is more spectacular than at Masada in the Judaean desert. Here, instead of filling a ravine, the Romans were obliged to build a ramp up the side of a mountain, and haul an ironclad tower with batteringram up the 1:20 incline. The ramp, circumvallation, and camps are still visible today.

(Right) Up until around AD 100, the Romans employed the arrow-firing catapulta *of the Greeks. The model shown here is a three-span (that is, medium caliber) catapult, which fired a 25 inch (63.5 cm) arrow.*

(Above) The basic weapon in the besieger's arsenal was the battering ram, housed within a mobile tortoise. The Roman model had a distinctively triangular cross section, with the ram suspended from the ridgepiece by long ropes. The tortoise itself was protected by boards and layers of clay or hide mattressing.

(Left) The stone-throwing engine of the Romans was the ballista*. The one shown here dates from around AD 230, and is of medium to small caliber, firing stones of 6 pounds (2.7 kg).*

Caesar's siege works at Alesia presented a formidable system of obstacles facing both inward and outward. The inner line (shown here in section) comprised a rampart and two ditches, the inner one of which was filled with water. Various booby traps inside the circumvallation ensured the security of the whole scheme.

4 ROME'S DECLINE AND FALL

When the emperor Marcus Aurelius (AD 161–80) died, the Roman empire declined, it was said, from a realm of gold to one of rust and iron. Military corrosion had already begun. Marcus' predecessors, by choosing to consolidate existing frontiers, risked losing the initiative. He inherited a prospect of war on two fronts: the Parthians destroyed a legion in Armenia, and the northern tribes threatened to cross the Danube. In the event, however, the eastern armies defeated the Parthians with the help of three legions from the Rhine and Danube, before the storm broke in the north. Here, at first, a Roman counteroffensive, spearheaded by the release of two lions across the Danube, as suggested by a quack oracle, ended in disaster; the German Quadi and Marcomanni seized the chance to cross the river from what are now the Czech Republic and Slovakia, and penetrated to the gates of Italy. One of Marcus' generals, Claudius Fronto, the man who raised two new legions, was honored posthumously with a statue "because he fell fighting bravely for his country after victories against the Germans." Then in a series of painful

VALERIUS MAXIMIANUS

In the winter of AD 179–80 Marcus Aurelius stationed 20,000 troops in the homeland of the Quadi and Marcomanni (modern Czech Republic and Slovakia) to force them to submit. One detachment, 855 men from the legion based in Aquincum, was posted to Laugaricio (Trencin) 80 miles (130 km) north of the Danube, where the soldiers cut an inscription on the rock face above the River Váh (Waag). Its commanding officer was Valerius Maximianus, a former cavalry officer whom Marcus had decorated for killing a German chieftain with his own hands. Maximianus came from what is now Slovenia, and had proved himself in administrative posts before being given the senatorial rank that qualified him to command a legion. He was a professional soldier, like the great "Illyrian" emperors of the third century from the Danubian provinces, whom he foreshadows.

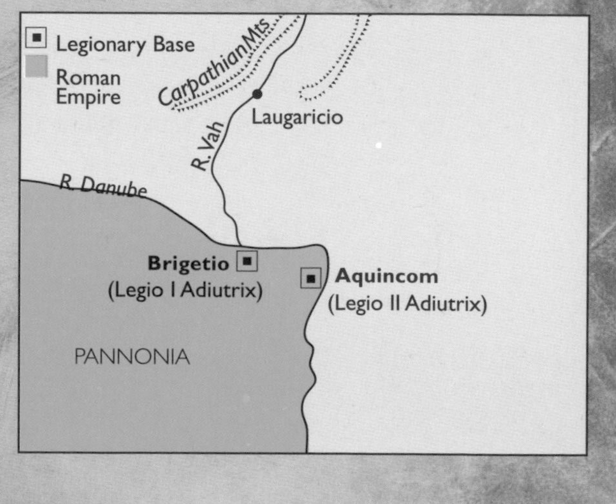

counterattacks in the 170s, Marcus carried the war into the enemy's homeland, murderous untidy episodes depicted in the carved reliefs of a stone column built to commemorate his victories. His glum, bearded face can still be seen, surveying not the tidy warfare of Trajan's Column, but what his modern biographer calls the "grim and sordid necessity" of it all. He was a devout philosopher, who equated military operations with a spider catching flies, forced by the logic of the military crisis to assume personal command. This would be true of his successors for the next two centuries; and they would die if they lost the army's confidence.

Marcus's unworthy son, Commodus (180–92), by abandoning his father's conquests, threw away the chance of dominating central Europe. Instead, he sought distinction as a gladiator, and he was lucky that the only major crisis of his reign was in northern Britain. Here, the tribes were defeated by Ulpius Marcellus, an eccentric disciplinarian who lived on (very stale) bread sent out from Rome, and convinced his men that he never slept by writing out his orders before he went to bed and having them issued at intervals during the night. Marcellus' successor, Publius Pertinax, a former schoolmaster whom Marcus had promoted for his military ability, as he did Valerius Maximianus, actually became emperor when Commodus lost the confidence even of his intimates and was murdered. But within a few weeks Pertinax, too, was dead, at the hands of the Praetorian Guard. The civil wars that followed proved what was said of the Year of the Four Emperors (69): "the secret of empire was out: emperors could be made outside Rome." The emperor was explicitly commander in chief, and once again the Danubian legions, now much the largest army group, imposed their nominee.

THE RAIN MIRACLE

The Column of Marcus Aurelius, still standing in a piazza in Rome, depicts Roman soldiers victorious under the wings of the god responsible for the rain miracle (AD 173–74). The story goes that a Roman army had been cut off in the land of the Quadi, and was suffering from heat and thirst, when a thunderstorm broke unexpectedly, and the soldiers were drenched in drinking water, while the enemy, the Quadi, were struck by lightning. Various people claimed the credit, including the Christians, who were being persecuted for refusing to worship the old gods. To prove they were patriotic, they retailed the legend of a Christian legion, the Twelfth *Fulminata* (Thundering) Legion. The rain miracle suggests a loss of confidence and hysterical relief. Stories of divine intervention would crop up all through the civil wars of the fourth century.

SEPTIMIUS SEVERUS

Since he lacked military experience, at first Septimius Severus (193–211) delegated to his generals. Their armies consisted of legionary detachments, a sign that it was no longer feasible to move whole legions. Significantly, too, the battles that overthrew the armies of Syria (193) and Britain (197) were both decided by the intervention of cavalry operating independently; this development thus foreshadowed the cavalry corps of the later third century.

Severus trusted the dreams that told him he would become emperor, but he remained emperor by paying attention to the army and its needs. "Enrich the troops and despise everyone else," he is supposed to have told his sons. He personally directed a successful

SIEGE OF BYZANTIUM

DATE AD 193–95
CAMPAIGN Civil war between Septimius Severus and Pescennius Niger
OBJECT To eliminate resistance to Severus
DESCRIPTION Byzantium was impregnably sited on the promontory defined by the Golden Horn, the Bosphorus, and the Sea of Marmara. It had massive walls with enfilading salients and towers, well equipped with artillery. In 193, it supported Severus's rival, the governor of Syria, and continued to resist a year after the governor's death. Only when reduced to cannibalism did the garrison surrender to a force from the legions of the lower Danube. In 324, Constantine refounded Byzantium as his new Rome. Constantinople, as it was soon called, was enlarged in the early fifth century, and given the elaborate walls that still survive in what is now Istanbul.
RESULT An end of the resistance to Severus in the east.

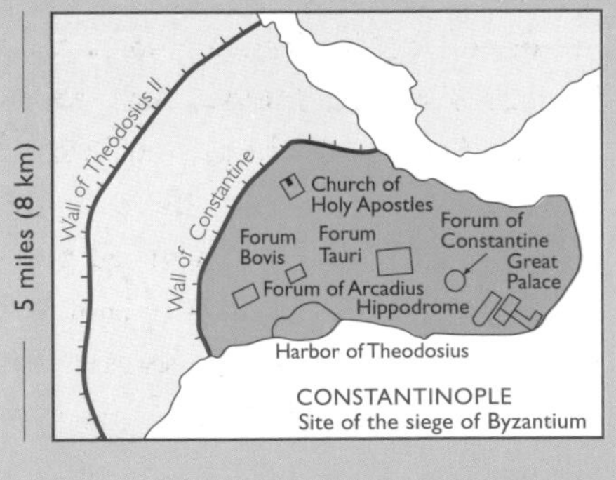

CONSTANTINOPLE
Site of the siege of Byzantium

invasion of the Parthian empire, in which northern Mesopotamia was annexed, the Roman empire's last significant conquest. Its garrison was two more new legions, commanded not by the usual senatorial legates, but by experienced officers who had twice been the senior centurions of a legion. A third new legion, II *Parthica*, was not committed to frontier defense, but was based just south of Rome. Here, the old Praetorian guard was disbanded and replaced by 10 cohorts at least 1,000-strong, recruited from experienced legionaries. These elite forces of heavy infantry, equivalent to at least three legions (when the largest provincial army was just two legions,) with the addition of cavalry guards seconded from the provincial armies, were the forerunners of the fourth-century "mobile army." They offered a determined emperor the solution to the military and political problems of war on two fronts: he retained a strategic reserve, first to protect himself from a rebellious general in the provinces, and then to reinforce the provinces against outside attack.

WAR ON TWO FRONTS

Severus, like Vespasian, believed that an emperor should die on his feet. So despite failing health, he directed a last campaign in Britain, where he died at York. His conquests in the north were abandoned by his son Caracalla (211–17), who turned his attention to a new enemy, the Alamanni. They were a coalition of tribes (the name means "all men") pressing against the linear defenses that linked the middle Rhine to the upper Danube. Their counterpart on the lower Rhine was another new coalition, the Franks. It was ominous for the future that in Europe the imperial armies, although they retained their qualitative superiority for another two centuries, were now being opposed by larger, better-organized tribal groups. The major threat was still on the Danube, where the Goths and Vandals were migrating southward, first pressing other peoples against the frontier and then breaching it themselves; in the mid-third century the Goths even took to boats and ravaged the coasts of Asia Minor. Farther east, the strategic balance tilted in the mid-220s when the loose-knit Parthian empire was overthrown by an aggressive Persian revival. The ensuing struggle lasted four centuries.

Two of Caracalla's successors, Alexander Severus (222–35) and Gordian III (238–44), campaigned against the Persians with limited success. The II *Parthica* accompanied them to Syria, as it had Caracalla; we know this from excavations at Apamea, where the walls incorporate its tombstones. The legionaries were mostly

KING SHAPUR OF PERSIA'S CAMPAIGN

DATES AD 241–44 and 250s
CAMPAIGN Persian invasions of the eastern Roman empire and Roman counterattack
OBJECT Rome and Persia competed for prestige in the Syriac-speaking world; Persia sought booty, prisoners, and Roman territories once part of the old Persian empire.
DESCRIPTION Shapur commemorated his triumph over three Roman emperors in a rock-cut relief: he holds Valerian with his hand, receives the submission of Philip (in 244), and tramples Gordian III. He also left a written account of his wars. Gordian was killed in a great battle; Philip sued for peace and paid tribute. In a second war, Shapur destroyed an army of 60,000 men and captured 37 Roman cities, including the capital, Antioch. In the third war, he invaded Roman Mesopotamia, and was attacked by Valerian with an army 70,000 strong: "There was a great battle, and we took Valerian prisoner with our own hands; and we captured his generals, and led them away prisoner into Persia; and we burned Syria, Cilicia, and Cappadocia" (there follows a list of 36 cities.) This account, inscribed on the wall of a Persian fire temple, provides a unique glimpse of the third-century crisis from the other side of the hill.
RESULT A stalemate costly to both sides.

Thracians, Romans only by courtesy, recruited from the hinterland of the lower Danube frontier. This was the milieu of Maximinus (235–38) "the Thracian," one of Alexander's most senior officers, who became emperor. When the army returned to Europe, and Alexander tried to negotiate with Alamanni invaders, it proclaimed Maximinus instead. He was the first emperor to rise from the ranks. Ruthlessly, he taxed the civil population to pay for the army, provoking an uprising that spread from Africa to Italy. While attempting to crush it, he was murdered in his turn by mutineers from II *Parthica*, anxious for the families they had left behind.

Turmoil reigns

The history of the next half century, until the accession of the great Diocletian (284–305), has been likened to "a dark tunnel, illuminated from either end, and by rare and exiguous light wells in the interval." We can only glimpse how Severus's army evolved into that of Diocletian and Constantine (306–37), a miracle of improvization on the cliff edge. From 235 to 284, there were at least 20 emperors recognized in Rome, and many more usurpers, most of them generals proclaimed by armies asserting the priority of their own front. This was the consequence of the long process that anchored the legions to the frontiers, where they recruited, the legionaries raised their families, and retired. If the legion were withdrawn, an invasion would follow. This surrender of the initiative has been compared to a failed blitzkrieg: the advancing spearhead halts and becomes a defended position, which is finally overrun. During this dark age, almost every emperor died violently, Decius (249–51) fighting the Goths, the others by assassination or in civil war. The exceptions are significant—Valerian (253–60), captured by the Persians; Claudius (268–70), dead of the plague after his defeat of the Goths; Carus (282–83) allegedly struck by lightning after his capture of the Persian capital Ctesiphon. This was in reprisal for the campaigns of the Persian king Shapur (241–72), whose conquests were halted only by a Roman protectorate, the caravan city of Palmyra. In the 260s, Palmyra usurped Rome's control of the eastern provinces, while in Italy Valerian's son Gallienus (254–68) lost the western provinces to a separatist "Gallic" empire, retaining only Africa and intermittently the Danubian provinces.

EARLY SWORDS

It was not until metalworking became possible that the sword became a practical weapon. Bronze and iron were the first sword metals, and both had their defects. Bronze is an alloy of copper and tin, and the proportions can be changed so that the resulting bronze can be of varying strength. Early iron was of relatively poor quality, as is shown by descriptions of the battle of Aquae Sextiae in 102 BC, when the Romans fought the Teutones and Ambrones; their swords needed to be straightened beneath the swordsman's foot at intervals during the battle. Gradually, as metalworking and the tempering of metals were better understood, the sword became a reliable and capable weapon.

In the first bronze swords—of perhaps 1500 BC—the hilt and blade were like the knives of the period, that is, two separate pieces riveted together. This made the sword adequate for thrusting but liable to come apart if used too enthusiastically as a slashing weapon. By about 1000 BC, the technique of forging the blade and hilt in one piece had been developed, and with that came the characteristic Bronze Age shape. The tang—the metal portion that formed the support for the hilt—broadened as it met the blade, which narrowed and then gradually increased in breadth to about two-thirds of the way down its length, after which it smoothly swept in to form a point. This was a practical shape for either thrusting or cutting. The whole blade is generally described as "leaf shaped." The tang would be enclosed in pieces of wood or bone, riveted in place, and shaped to provide a firm grip.

When iron came into use, the design of swords followed the pattern set by bronze. Indeed, for some time the use of bronze and iron overlapped. There are examples of swords with bronze hilts attached to iron

A group of Viking swords, probably from the ninth century, showing the typical hilt construction.

A sculpture from Byzantium shows typical Eastern swords of the fourth century, with angled grips and pommels shaped into bird's heads.

blades, where the iron tang is the foundation and the hilt is built up on it, and everything has been secured by hammering the tip of the tang in rivet fashion. The blade was made either in one piece, hammered on the edges to give a harder finish, or built up by hammer welding several layers of iron.

Having mastered the basic construction of swords, smiths now began to experiment with shape and form to arrive at various designs that suited the preferences of their customers. The original simple pointed and edged blade and the leaf-shaped blade were retained, but curved blades, which were more adapted to a slashing blow, became common, particularly in the Middle East. Roman legionaries, on the other hand, adopted a short, wide sword, which could be worn on the right side and drawn with the right hand—an asset in close combat.

Pattern welding

The principal technological difficulty in sword making was that forging a piece of iron hard enough to serve as a sword often meant that it was relatively brittle and could easily snap in battle. By the second century AD, Frankish smiths had developed a technique known as pattern welding, which involved layering hard and soft iron rods and twisting and hammering them into a homogeneous mass. Hardened rods were then laid along the edges and hammer welded to the mass to provide the hard cutting edge, the blade being more resilient and thus less liable to break. The whole was then heated and plunged into water, reheated, and allowed to cool naturally before being shaped and sharpened.

Pattern welding remained the preferred method of sword-making until about the tenth century, by which time the sword had generally assumed a slightly tapered blade in place of the earlier leaf shape. During the same period, the sword had become more than just a weapon; it had attained a certain mystical quality—which was doubtless due to the very high cost of a really first-class weapon. Swords were handed down in families and some were given individual names. The Vikings, for example, regarded their swords as having magical properties, and each warrior would give his weapon a suitable epithet, such as *Hvati* (keen) or *Langhrass* (long and sharp).

Dating from the period of the New Kingdom (ca. 1300 BC), this broad-blade Egyptian sword with a highly decorated gold hilt was unlikely to have been meant for use in battle. It was probably a symbolic weapon for ceremonial occasions.

A THIRD-CENTURY BRIGADE

This bronze disk, 6 ¾ in (17 cm) in diameter, belonged to Aurelius Cervianus, an officer in a third-century brigade formed by detachments from the two legions in southern Britain, the XX *Valeria Victrix* and the II *Augusta*; each parades under its own flag and legionary symbol. Instead of moving whole legions, expeditionary forces were assembled from such detachments, such as "the British and German legions with their auxiliaries" recorded near Belgrade in the reign of Gallienus. Gallienus honored the Rhine and Danube legions by name on his coinage in 259–60, which is found in northern Italy, where his "elite army" was based. These detachments operated independently and were the forerunners of the fourth-century mobile units.

Gallienus patronized Plotinus, the philosopher who made Platonism a rival to Christianity. Yet this cultured emperor also developed the weapon with which his "Illyrian" successors fought off Persians and Germans alike. This was what a contemporary calls the "elite army," a mobile force not committed to frontier defense, in effect the Roman army as it once had been. A medieval writer credits Gallienus with being the first to form cavalry units, "the Roman army having previously been largely infantry." This is an exaggeration, but we do now hear of *the* cavalry under its own general: it included Moorish light cavalry, mounted archers from the east, the legions' cavalry component (*promoti*), mounted legionaries (*stablesiani*), and detachments from frontier units. Mobile infantry Gallienus fought in the usual way: like Septimius Severus, he supplemented the Praetorian Guard and the II *Parthica* with detachments from the frontier legions, in Britain and on the Rhine and Danube. He was doing what modern armies have often done, forming units for special purposes by drawing on existing units.

Gallienus was later blamed for the disasters of his reign: "The memory of his vices will endure while there are cities to bear the mark"; but this libel came from the aristocrats whom he barred from a military career. Valerius Maximianus, had he lived now, would not have needed senatorial rank to qualify. Gallienus promoted professional soldiers, including the Thracian Traianus Mucianus, who enlisted in an auxiliary unit, transferred to II *Parthica* and then the cavalry component of the guard, before rising to command a series of cavalry units and legionary detachments. As other officers in the "elite army," he bore the title *protector*, used by Gallienus to distinguish his officer corps—not that he retained their loyalty. The defection of his cavalry general Aureolus was followed by a conspiracy involving Mucianus' patron, the commander of the guard, and the future emperors Claudius and Aurelian (270–75). They were the leaders of a virtual junta of "Illyrian" officers who had been born in the Danubian provinces, where so much of the Roman army was now recruited. In a relentless series of campaigns, Claudius defeated the Goths, Aurelian overthrew Palmyra and ended the "Gallic" empire, and Probus (276–82) cleared Gaul of the German invaders who poured in when Aurelian was assassinated. But

Detail of the arch erected by Galerius (293–311) in his capital city, Thessalonica (now Salonika in Greece), to celebrate his defeat of the Persians in 298.

although imperial unity was precariously restored, the Alamanni retained the territory they had seized in southern Germany, and the province of Dacia beyond the Danube was surrended to the Goths. Insecurity was felt in the heart of Asia Minor, and even Rome itself was given walls by Aurelian after he had defeated a German invasion of northern Italy.

DIOCLETIAN

These were the birth pangs of the late empire. The midwife was Diocletian (284–305), the genius who turned 50 years of improvization into a system. He shared power first with his fellow officer Maximian (285–305) and then with two more "Illyrians," Constantius (293–306) and Galerius (293–311). Four emperors now watched each other's back, in civil wars and on the frontiers. Thus, in 287, Maximian ravaged Germany, while Diocletian reasserted Roman authority in Armenia by a treaty with the Persians. Maximian made the mistake, however, of creating a naval command in the North Sea and English Channel for a Belgian officer, Carausius, who rebelled and could not be dislodged from Britain and northern Gaul. It took 10 years and several failures before Constantius was able to mount the seaborne expedition that reconquered Britain. Meanwhile, in 297, Diocletian was suppressing a revolt in Egypt, and Galerius was recovering from a humiliating defeat by the Persians in Armenia; the next year he achieved the regime's greatest success when he caught the Persian army off guard. King Narseh, son of the great Shapur, barely escaped with his life, and his harem fell into Roman hands. "By the kindly favor of the gods we have crushed the seething greed of barbarian peoples by slaughter of the same," proclaimed Diocletian in his Edict on Maximum Prices (301), which unsuccessfully applied the tactics of intimidation to the Roman economy. The energy that had reasserted Roman authority from Britain to Egypt, from Africa (where Maximian campaigned) to Armenia, is echoed in the record of his travels inscribed

LOGISTICS

Ancient authors, including Ammianus Marcellinus (and other surviving documents), tell us a great deal about Diocletian's reforms and how late-Roman units were fed, equipped, and moved to where they were needed. St. Ambrose, for example, describes the route march: food stockpiles, a day's rest every four days, with longer rests in cities with markets and good supplies of water (here they would be billeted on civilians). Papyrus fragments survive from the files of an Egyptian deputy governor, writing to local officials "so that by all means the most noble soldiers may receive their supplies without complaint."

by one of Diocletian's veterans on his wife's tombstone: Aurelius Gaius, a legionary cavalryman who rose to be a lieutenant (*optio*) in the imperial entourage, crossed the Rhine and Danube repeatedly, served in upper Egypt and almost every province from Mesopotamia to Mauretania, but never visited Italy or Rome.

Soldiers now speak of serving in the *comitatus*, the imperial entourage, from which comes the term for the mobile army, the *comitatenses*. Diocletian's was small by later standards. To the guard he added the famous *Ioviani* and *Herculiani*, legions formed from Danubian legionaries armed with the late-Roman weighted dart instead of the old javelin, and the *lanciarii,* such as Aurelius Gaius, legionaries armed with the lance; in cavalry we find the first *scholae* (mounted guards) and the crack *Comites* and *Promoti*, brigaded from detachments of the guards cavalry and the old cavalry guards. But expeditionary forces still consisted of temporary detachments from the frontier armies. Thus Galerius drew on the Danubian garrisons for his defeat of the Persians, and in Egypt a papyrus of 295 records the issue of fodder not only to the *Comites* but also to as many as 10 pairs ("brigades") of legionary detachments. Gallienus's cavalry corps was actually broken up into detachments, which were drafted into the frontier armies. Here, there is abundant archaeological evidence—new forts and extensive rebuilding—of Diocletian's emphasis on fixed defenses. An ancient writer says, with exaggeration: "By the foresight of Diocletian, the frontiers everywhere were fortified with cities, forts, and towers, and the whole army was stationed there." Many new units were formed—the 33 legions of Septimius Severus were increased to about 60—and the army's numbers may have doubled to more than half a million men. Food, clothing, horses, raw materials, even recruits, were levied from the civil population like taxation, under the supervision of an expanding bureaucracy. Diocletian's reforms gave the empire the means of survival, but at heavy cost.

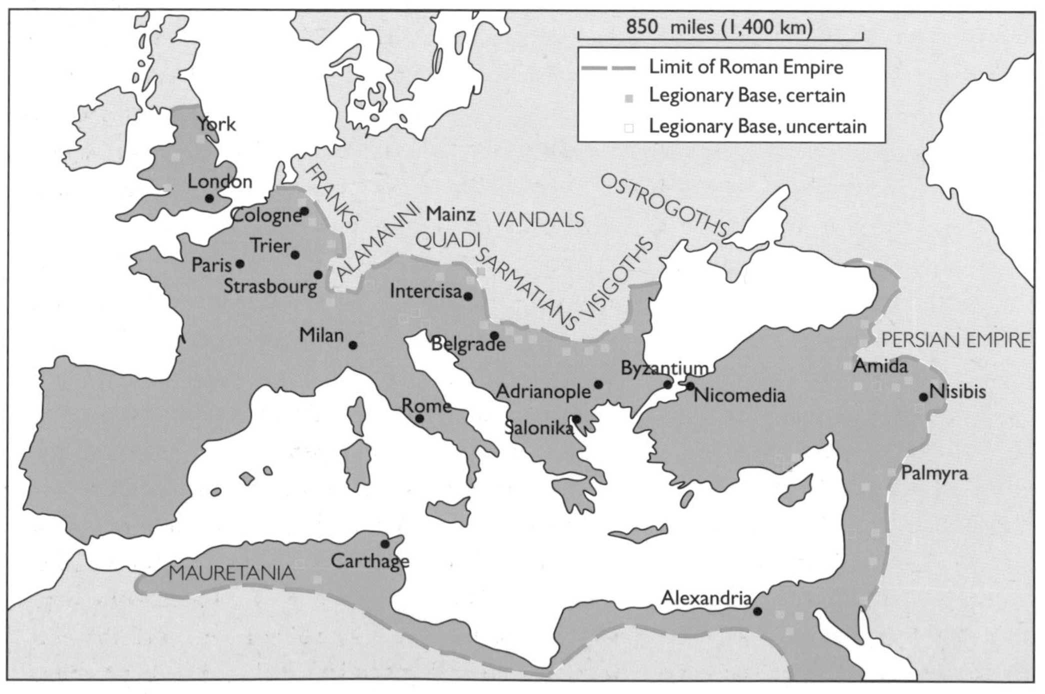

Map showing the extent of the Roman empire, ca. 300.

BATTLE OF THE MILVIAN BRIDGE

DATE October 28, 312
CAMPAIGN Constantine's invasion of Italy
OBJECT Overthrow of Maxentius and reinforcing claim to be western emperor.
DESCRIPTION At the Milvian Bridge, Constantine's new faith in the Christian god was confirmed. He had the deity's initials painted on his men's shields in consequence of a dream—in later years he claimed to have seen a cross of light in the sky. Constantine's rival, Maxentius, at first intended to defend the impregnable walls of Rome, and cut the Milvian Bridge on its northern approaches; then he changed his mind, crossed the Tiber on a pontoon bridge, and advanced. It was an error. Constantine's army was battle hardened and confident; Maxentius' army was thrown back in confusion and, as the soldiers retreated across the river, the bridge collapsed under their weight.
RESULT Maxentius and many of his armored cavalry were drowned, a scene depicted on the arch erected in Rome to commemorate Constantine's victory "by divine inspiration." At Maxentius's death, Constantine was accepted as ruler of the western empire.

CONSTANTINE

Diocletian abdicated in 305 and retired, appropriately, to a fortified palace on the Dalmatian coast near his birthplace. He had secured unity of command in a war on two fronts, but without lasting success, since Galerius was unable to dominate his colleagues as Diocletian had done. The disturbing influence was a general of genius, Constantius' son Constantine (306–37), who was proclaimed at York when his father died there. "Beginning in Britain by the sea where the sun sets," he told the people of Palestine in 324, "by the Almighty's power I abolished all existing evils, and finally reached the east." He is referring to the series of civil wars in which, supported by his new god, he eliminated first Maximian's son Maxentius (306–12) and then Galerius' lieutenant and successor Licinius (308–24). The campaign against Maxentius, which culminated in the battle of the Milvian Bridge, emphasizes the new strategy of mobility. Constantine used just a quarter of his available forces to surprise and overwhelm a numerically superior opponent. By the same logic, he enlarged the "elite army" by recruiting new units, especially from German volunteers and prisoners of war, and by withdrawing legionary detachments and cavalry from the provincial armies. The historian who praises Diocletian contrasts him with Constantine: the latter fatally weakened the frontiers by drafting most of the army to cities that did not need a garrison. (*Comitatenses* had no fixed stations, in fact, but were quartered where convenient.) Constantine's critic willfully misunderstands his strategy, which is that of Frederick the Great: "He who defends everything, defends nothing." While its neighbors retained the initiative, the empire could not hold every frontier against all attack. Instead, it could hope that the reduced garrisons would control minor raiding, and would even contain invaders passively by guarding stocks of food. In the time thus gained, the emperor would concentrate his mobile army—his insurance policy, incidentally, against rivals—and would mount a swift counterattack. His troops were better fed and equipped than their adversaries, better organized, trained, and disciplined, and could expect to win against numerical odds.

Constantine's last campaigns were on the lower Danube, where he briefly recovered part of Dacia, but he was planning war with Persia. This was inherited by his son Constantius II (337–61), a conscientious but ungifted general, who is said to have fought the Persians nine times without success. The war, which lasted until the mid-380s, was one of sieges and inconclusive field operations.

SIEGE OF AMIDA

DATE 359
CAMPAIGN Persian invasion of eastern Roman empire
OBJECT To cross the Euphrates and penetrate Syria.
NUMBERS Ammianus states that Amida was defended by 20,000 Romans, who were greatly outnumbered by the Persians.
DESCRIPTION The magnificently preserved sixth-century walls of Amida (Diyarbakir), founded on cliffs above the Tigris in southeast Turkey, give an impression of its strength in 359 when it was defended by seven Roman units and inflicted 74 days' delay and 30,000 dead upon the Persian invaders. The Persians raised siege mounds and iron-plated towers to command the walls, to which the Romans responded with stone-lobbing "scorpions" (mangonels). A band of Persian archers seized a tower by means of a secret passage (exploited again in the siege of 502), but were dislodged by bolt-firing catapults. The city fell when a Roman countermound collapsed, bridging the gap between the wall and a Persian mound, and the Persians surged across. Ammianus Marcellinus, an officer in the garrison, escaped; his superb history of the years 353–78 was published in Rome in the 390s.
RESULT Amida fell, but the Persians were unable to invade Syria, their primary aim.

Thus the Persians besieged the Roman fortress of Nisibis three times in 12 years without capturing it. Its massive defenses, in the words of a Syriac chronicle, made it as safe as "a rose behind thorns." In 359, Shapur II (309–79) changed his strategy at the suggestion of a well-informed Roman defector, and instead of crossing the Mesopotamian plain, where the Romans burned off the available fodder, he struck northward up the Tigris Valley, intending to invade Syria from the northeast. But even this initiative failed, when he halted to besiege the Roman fortress of Amida. The two months' siege is brilliantly described by a participant, the historian Ammianus Marcellinus, who tells us most of what we know about the late-Roman army in action.

Balancing act

Constantius could never concentrate on the eastern front. In the west, his brother Constans (337–50) was overthrown by the general commanding the *Ioviani* and *Herculiani*, and Constantius was forced to fight a civil war. His victory was remembered for its appalling losses: 30,000 dead, it was alleged, from an army of 80,000. Moreover, the Alamanni seized the chance to establish themselves in the Rhineland.

Constantius was unlucky in appointing his cousin Julian (355–63) to titular command in Gaul. Julian, a philosophy student, quoted Plato while he learned to drill ("If an ox can carry a knapsack, then so can I"), but his energy and enthusiasm appealed to the army. The military did not know, and would not have cared, that he had secretly renounced the Christianity forced upon him by Constantius. On a hot summer's day in 357, Julian, with a force of 13,000, confronted 35,000 Alamanni at Strasbourg on the Rhine. A surprising victory—the disciplined Roman infantry, especially the *Primani* legion, withstood a series of charges—gave Julian the initiative, which he exploited in campaigns of reprisal against the Alamanni's homeland. So when Constantius demanded reinforcements instead for the eastern front, where whole legions had been lost, the Gallic army mutinied and proclaimed Julian emperor. Another civil war was impending, when Constantius died of natural causes.

Julian had thus seen the difficulty of balancing the demands of two fronts, but as sole emperor, convinced that the gods had chosen him to restore paganism, he could decide priorities. He bungled the decision. Instead of campaigning against the Goths, as his staff advised, or of securing the Rhine, likewise the scene of major fighting after his death, he chose to invade the Persian empire. It was a disaster of logistics for which Julian atoned by his characteristically reckless death in a skirmish.

Julian was succeeded by the last great "Illyrian" emperor, Valentinian (364–75), who divided the empire with his submissive brother Valens (364–78) and reasserted the priority of the west, for the last time, by campaigning with fair success against the resurgent Alamanni. His brutal but efficient Spanish general, Theodosius, restored order in Britain and Africa with small mobile forces. Valentinian also directed the last reconstruction of the fixed defenses of the west, building forts along the Rhine and Danube. His death was dramatically appropriate.

Portrait of Julian the Apostate in bronze coin of Antioch, 360-363.

JULIAN'S PERSIAN EXPEDITION

DATE 363

OBJECT To restore Roman prestige after Persian invasions in the 340s and 350s, ideally by capturing the Persian capital of Ctesiphon, defeating the Persian field army, and deposing King Shapur II.

NUMBERS Roman armies of 18,000 (and Armenian allies) and 47,000; Persians not known, but greater.

DESCRIPTION Julian assembled 65,000 men and a fleet of at least 1,000 boats to carry supplies down the Euphrates. After detaching 18,000 men to make a feint towards the Tigris, he met only light resistance at first, bypassing fortresses or reducing them with siege artillery. The Persians flooded the approaches to Ctesiphon, but Julian reached it after a pitched battle, scoring a great tactical victory. However, he felt unable to assault the city and, after hesitation, he burned his boats instead and retreated up the Tigris. This was fatal, for the main Persian army confronted him, and all available fodder was burned in his path. The Romans retreated in good order but were desperately short of food and harassed by Persian attacks, in one of which Julian was killed. They only extricated themselves by accepting Persian terms of peace, which included the surrender of Nisibis.

RESULT The forced retreat of the Romans, with the death of Julian and heavy losses of men, material, and prestige.

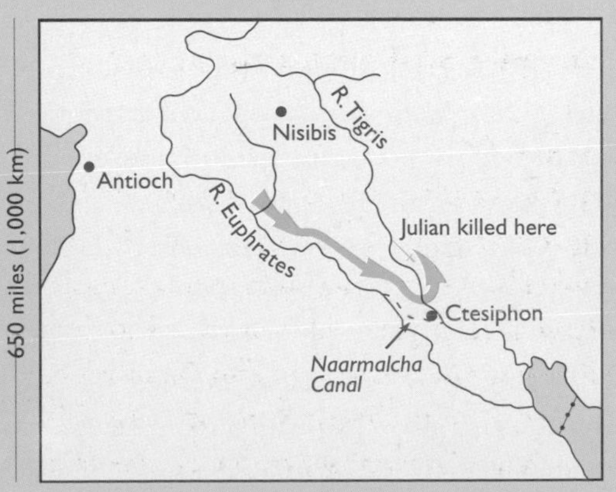

He suffered a stroke when the Quadi alleged that one of his new forts had provoked them into invading his native province of Pannonia. Within less than a year, Valens was confronted with a major crisis. The Goths had been dislodged by the sudden onset of the Huns from central Asia, and begged for permission to resettle south of the Danube. Valens agreed, not out of compassion, but to recruit them for the army and to reduce the burden of taxes on Roman civilians. It was a reasonable decision. Germans had been serving loyally in Roman units since the time of Constantine, if not before, and immigrant tribes under supervision had been absorbed in the empire for centuries. However, in 376 the operation was bungled—food ran short, Roman officials exploited the starving Goths, and they rebelled. Valens' generals made vain attempts to contain them; finally Valens mobilized his whole army and attacked the Gothic encampment near Adrianople. By sunset on August 9, 378, the Black Day of the late-Roman army, Valens and two-thirds of the eastern mobile army were dead.

THE COLLAPSE OF THE WESTERN EMPIRE

The western empire never recovered from the blow. The surviving western emperor, Valentinian's son Gratian (375–83), made Theodosius' son Theodosius eastern emperor (379–95), and between them they tried to limit the damage. The desperate shortage of trained soldiers, however, made it impossible to defeat the Goths; instead, they were allowed to settle south of the lower Danube, their social structure intact, in return for providing contingents for service *with* the Roman army. The preposition is important: these contingents were commanded by their own chieftains, they were cobelligerents who had little cause to like or trust the Romans. They marched with Theodosius, to the embarrassment of his apologists, in both the civil wars he fought against western usurpers after the death of Gratian. The defeat of Magnus Maximus (383–38) enabled Theodosius to draft mobile units to the east. In 394, he overcame the second usurper in a two-day battle; the first day ended in defeat, the brunt of it borne by his Gothic allies, 10,000 of whom are said to have been killed. "To lose *them*," commented a Christian admirer, "was a victory in itself."

The western empire was thus weakened by civil war and by replacing eastern losses, and was outflanked by the collapse of the Danube frontier. By contrast, the eastern empire in Asia Minor, Syria, and Egypt had much stronger natural defenses, the sea,

BATTLE OF ADRIANOPLE

DATE August 9, 378
CAMPAIGN Roman attempt to contain and defeat Gothic invasion
OBJECT To impose terms upon the Goths with or without defeating them in a pitched battle.
DESCRIPTION It was a very hot day, and the Gothic wagon laager was eight hours march from the Roman base at Adrianople. The Roman army advanced in column and deployed awkwardly to assault the laager, infantry in a crescent, cavalry on the wings, by which time men and horses were tired, thirsty, and hungry. The Goths were waiting for their cavalry to return from foraging. Roman cavalry units, apparently part of the left wing, attacked prematurely and were forced to retreat. At this moment the Gothic cavalry appeared "like a thunder bolt," fell upon the Roman left wing, and drove into the unprotected flank of the advancing infantry. The infantry was trapped between the Gothic cavalry and the Gothic infantry in the wagons, and fought crammed together until it broke. The fugitives were pursued until darkness fell. The emperor Valens and two-thirds of his army were killed.
RESULT A major defeat of the Roman army, with heavy losses of infantry units and consequent inability to coerce the Goths.

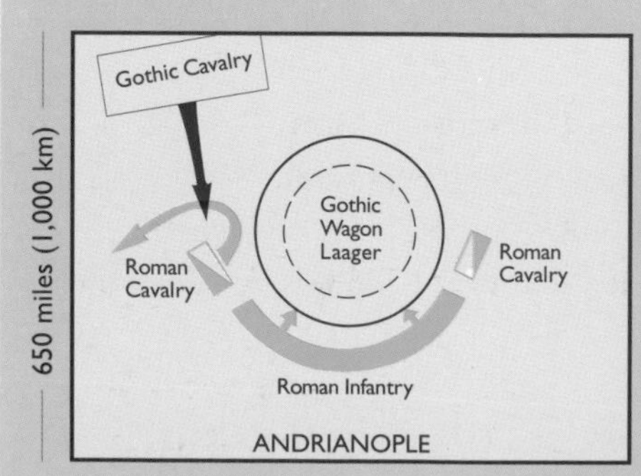

SACK OF ROME

DATE 410
CAMPAIGN Gothic invasion of Italy
OBJECT To force the Roman government of the western empire to negotiate.
DESCRIPTION The Porta Salaria is the gate by which the Goths entered Rome on August 24, 410. Three days of pillage followed. The walls of Rome were a massive obstacle, 11 miles (18 km) of brick-faced concrete nearly 13 feet (4 m) thick and 67 feet (20 m) high, with 381 enfilading towers and 18 gates. The Goths' commander, Alaric, had blockaded Rome twice, in the winter of 408–9 and again in 409, to force the government of Honorius in Ravenna to give his people land. When negotiations failed once more in 410, Alaric returned to Rome and soon broke in.
RESULT The "fall" of Rome; some material damage, a great loss of prestige, and shock; no immediate political settlement between Romans and Goths.

mountains, and desert; it was much richer than the west, and its logistical base was almost intact. It shared the same internal weaknesses, the "idle mouths" of army, bureaucracy, and Church, for example, and the aspects of its social structure loosely called "corruption," but externally it was under far less pressure. It was unfortunate that Theodosius died five months after his victory, and that the empire was divided once more, between his incapable sons Honorius (395–423) and Arcadius (395–408).

Invasion by northern tribes

In north Italy, Honorius' court was dominated by his father's general Stilicho, the son of a Vandal-born officer, who bravely tried to make economical use of the shrinking western army. The *Notitia Dignitatum* (see pages 64–65) credits him with almost 50 mobile units in Italy alone, but in the crisis of 405 when Italy was invaded, he mustered just 30, which seems to be a more realistic index of his resources. The Goths were on the move once more, many of them under a dynamic new leader, Alaric. Stilicho was unable or unwilling to defeat him decisively, yet he might have controlled him, but for a new disaster. On December 31, 406, the Vandals and other German peoples crossed the frozen Rhine, and in their wake came the Franks and Alamanni.

These tribes were never expelled. In a kaleidoscope of wars and alliances they entrenched themselves in the western provinces, the Roman government finding itself cast in the role of the moujik pursued by wolves: whom next to throw off the sled?

In Britain, the garrison proclaimed emperor a common soldier, Constantine III (407–11), who invaded Gaul and briefly controlled Spain, but Britain rebelled from him and Roman rule was never restored. In Italy, Stilicho fell from power (408), but his successors were even less able to control the Goths; after inconclusive negotiations, Alaric carried out his threat to sack Rome. The next year (411) he died, and the Goths remained dangerous nomads, devastating the tribes in Spain on Roman orders, before they were allowed to settle by treaty (418) in southwest Gaul.

The survivors of this devastation in Spain, the Vandals, succeeded where other invaders had failed—in 429 they crossed the Strait of Gibraltar. When the western empire's last intact provinces were replaced by an aggressive Vandal kingdom, its decline was irreversible. In 444, the western emperor, Theodosius' grandson Valentinian III (425–55), admitted economic and military bankruptcy. The taxpayers were exhausted, the soldiers were cold and hungry. The eastern empire would survive for centuries, but the western empire was bleeding to death.

NOTITIA DIGNITATUM AND THE LATE-ROMAN ORDER OF BATTLE

THE *NOTITIA*, to translate its full title, was the late-Roman "List of all high offices, civil and military" in the east and west, dating from the division of the empire in 395. Several indirect copies survive, made in the fifteenth and sixteenth centuries from a unique Carolingian copy preserved at Speyer, but long since disappeared. One of these copies, now in Munich, includes a second set of illustrations traced from the Speyer manuscript, which are the closest to the late-Roman originals; some of these are reproduced here. The purpose of the *Notitia* is unclear, but it is possible that it was used as an aide-mémoire by the office staff of the western commander-in-chief, whose incomes derived from issuing letters of appointment. The western list was certainly updated for a few years, perhaps until the fall of Stilicho in 408. The *Notitia*, whatever its purpose, is divided into chapters, each one devoted to a high official or army commander, with a schematic picture of his duties and a detailed list of his subordinates and other responsibilities. Generals commanding mobile armies are thus represented by the shield devices of their units listed by unit type and seniority, frontier generals by a picture of their sector and a list of garrison units with their stations.

The *Notitia*, although it is a civil document as well, pays most attention to military matters; in theory at least, it lists every military unit in the empire, and thus embodies the order of battle of the Roman armies at the end of the fourth century. Many details are corroborated by literary sources, including Ammianus Marcellinus (names of units, for example, and "brigades"), or by other documents, such as laws, inscriptions, and papyri, but there are some puzzling

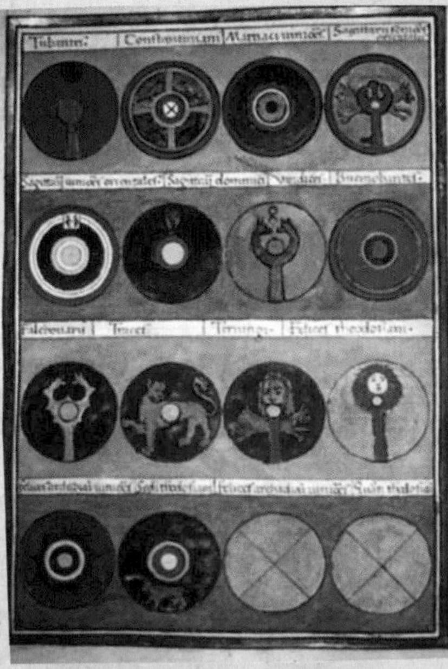

Illustrations from the Notitia Dignitatum. *The page on the left is depicting shields of Magister Militum Praesentalis II, a late Roman register of military commands. On the right is the entry for Vadomarius one of the top kings of Alamanni and an early opponent of Constantius II.*

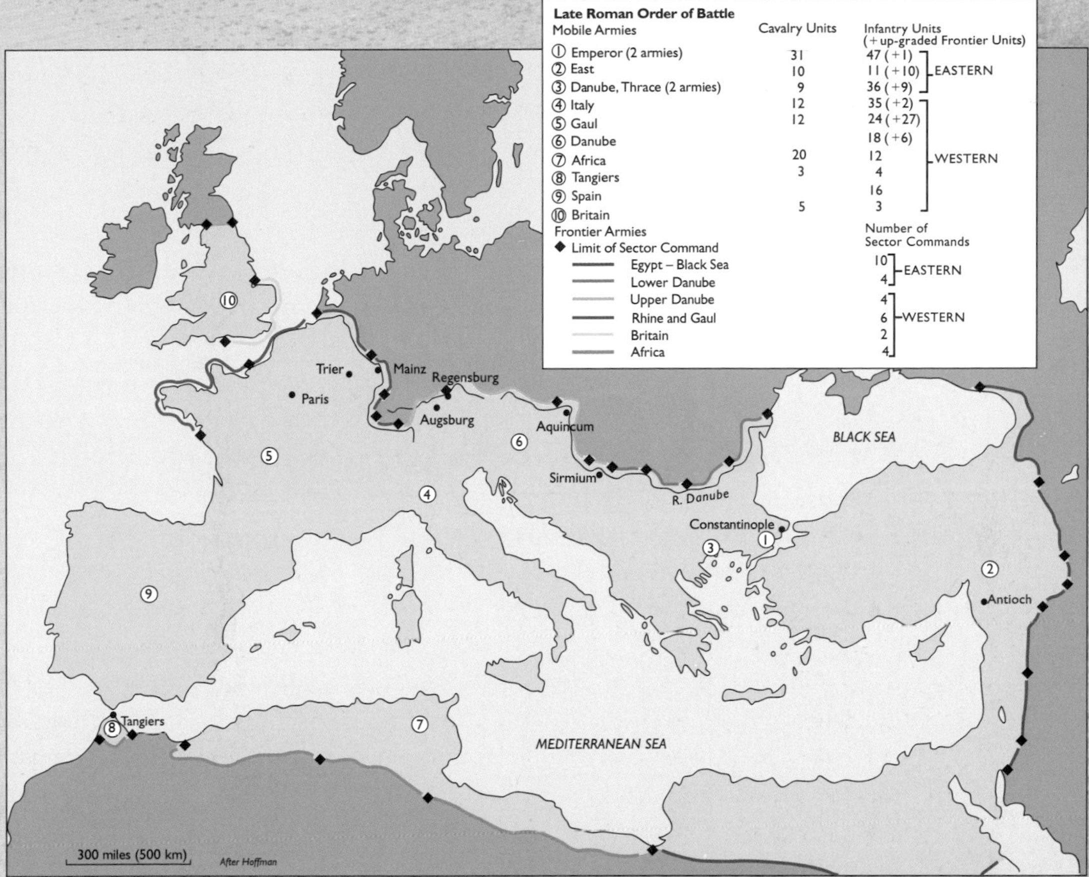

discrepancies. Thus the garrison of Hadrian's Wall seems to have remained unchanged for more than 150 years; there was no sign of the *Notitia*'s alleged 16 mobile units when the Germans overran Spain in 409; and Stilicho when Italy was invaded in 405 mustered only 30 units, although the *Notitia* credits him with almost 50, not to mention many more in Gaul. Moreover, the *Notitia* says nothing about a unit's establishment, one of the outstanding problems in late-Roman army studies, although it lists four types of cavalry unit and at least six different types of infantry. In any case, we do not know whether units were up to strength. (Other evidence suggests they were rather small by earlier standards and so not at full capacity.) The *Notitia* has its theoretical and schematic aspects, such as the charming illustrations, but there is no doubt it preserves the broad features and many details of late-Roman strategy and military organization.

Many units in the *Notitia*'s order of battle (*above*) can be dated, and since mobile units are listed by seniority, it is possible to unpeel "layers" in the *Notitia*; to see the effects of invasions and of Adrianople, and also of the military reforms of Constantine and Diocletian, even the history of Gallienus' cavalry corps, and the survival of units from the armies of Septimius Severus and Marcus Aurelius. The enhanced importance of cavalry is obvious, both in the high proportion of units and the practice of listing them before infantry in the frontier armies and in the eastern mobile armies. This is part of the premium set on mobility, seen most of all in the distinction between mobile armies held in reserve and the armies of the frontiers. This is the strategy of Constantine and his successors, but its origins can be seen in the third-century crisis, and indeed as early as the second century.

5 THE DARK AGES

The phrase "dark ages" is applied to a period in European history stretching from about AD 400 to around 1000, a time otherwise known as the Early Middle Ages. The era is "dark" in that there is a shortage of historical evidence. Central and eastern Europe are emerging into the historical light for the first time by 1000, but for western Europe the years after the end of Roman rule are, in fact, better served by documentary evidence than those before. Where evidence is sufficiently detailed it reveals that the conduct of war in barbarian Europe often reached a sophisticated level, even if the literary evidence frequently obscures it with its emphasis on heroic deeds and individual actions.

RECRUITMENT AND ORGANIZATION OF ARMIES

The military system of the Roman empire was in decline long before the western empire ceased to exist. By the fifth century, western Roman armies consisted of barbarian war bands serving under their own leaders, paid from taxation. The East, too, relied heavily on such mercenaries. Long before 500, in the West the central administration responsible for collecting taxes and allocating resources to armies had withered away in Gaul and Spain; only in Italy did it continue to function under barbarian rulers until the devastating wars and invasions of the next century. The central feature in the military organization of the barbarian kingdoms was the war band or retinue of kings, princes, and aristocrats (including ecclesiastics), made up of adolescents and young men of noble birth, who lived in permanent attendance upon their lords in return for their sustenance, gifts of treasure, and ultimately in the expectation of land. Among the Franks they were called *antrustions*, in Lombard Italy *gasindii*, and *thegns* in Anglo-Saxon England. The nucleus of a royal army was the king's household, supplemented by nobles' retinues.

These were not the only sources of soldiers. Where town life survived, south of the Loire in Gaul, in Italy, and in Spain, levies from the cities and their districts were available at least for defense and local wars. In Gaul, Spain, and Italy, military service was initially limited to the barbarians, but it was a fiction that the Roman population was entirely demilitarized. Roman aristocrats soon began to behave like barbarians, recruiting their own retinues and participating in warfare. In exceptional circumstances in the sixth century, in Visigothic Spain and Ostrogothic Italy, slaves were armed and they may have formed a significant source of military manpower.

In theory, all free men, or at least those who possessed sufficient property to equip themselves, were subject to military service, but the numbers should not be overestimated, since the majority of the population was not free. Moreover, the costs of campaigning made such soldiers of limited military value. By the eighth century, in some areas steps were taken to reduce the number of men performing service by requiring poor free men to join together to equip one of their number. The most famous example of this comes from the reign of Charlemagne (768–814), king of the Franks and founder of the Carolingian empire, but at some time a similar system was introduced into England where it was still in force in the eleventh century.

This helmet was found in the ship burial at Sutton Hoo in East Anglia, England, possibly the tomb of King Redwald, who died between 616 and 627. The workmanship is Swedish, but this is a Germanic version of a late Roman parade helmet—a symbol of authority rather than practical armor.

THE GROWTH OF FEUDALISM

Limiting the amount of service owed by free men was one reason why military service increasingly (but never exclusively) became the preserve of the aristocracy. Another was that kings granted to their nobles estates, in part to reinforce their loyalty, in part so that they could better equip themselves and their military followers. Such grants of benefices or fiefs were conditional on the performance of military service. In eighth-century Francia, the ties between king and follower were reinforced by oaths of vassalage. In this lies the origin of the military feudalism of the Middle Ages. So long as the king was active and successful, he could keep control over his nobles, but by the late ninth century, Frankish monarchs were losing control over many counts and their lands.

Military and political power became fragmented in much of Francia and Italy, and this fragmentation continued in many areas as lesser nobles who controlled castles established their independence. However, this process did not occur everywhere. In Normandy, Flanders, and Anjou, for example, counts successfully retained control over their vassals and built powerful states, while the kings of West Francia (which would become France) found their power increasingly restricted and localized around Paris. In England and Germany, tenth-century kings kept control over their nobles, helped by the prestige of military success against Viking and Magyar (Hungarian) invaders.

Paid standing armies were unknown in the West during most of the Middle Ages. In the surviving eastern Roman (Byzantine) empire, a standing army financed from taxation continued to exist. However, the armies with which Justinian's generals conquered Africa and Italy (530s–50s) depended heavily on the recruitment of bands of barbarians and prisoners of war. The disastrous losses of territory suffered in the seventh century forced the Byzantine

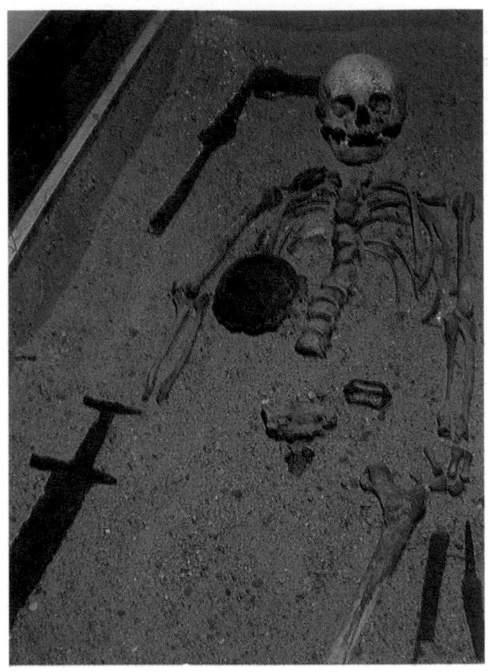

Weapons from pagan graves are a major source of evidence for Dark Age equipment. This warrior from tenth-century Norway had sword, spear, and ax (seen above) as well as arrows and knives. His shield boss and belt buckle also survived. Either he did not possess helmet and body armor, or his relatives could not afford to bury them with him.

rulers to settle many military units on the land and to recruit from the resulting military districts (*themes.*) It was in the Muslim world that the only true standing armies were to be found. The vast Arab expansion in the seventh and eighth centuries led to the recruitment of armies of slaves (*mamelukes*), consisting largely of Turks in the East, and of Christian and Slavonic captives, many purchased from the Vikings, in Spain.

The *housecarls*, who appear in England after the Danish conquest by Cnut (1016), have been interpreted as a paid standing army, perhaps of a few thousand men. Evidence shows the *housecarls* to have been the military household of Cnut, similar to those maintained by kings and aristocrats throughout the Early Middle Ages. From 1012–50, English rulers did maintain a permanent, mercenary *fleet*. Such household bands continued to form the nuclei of armies in the eleventh century, as well as serving as castle garrisons, especially in frontier regions.

WEAPONS AND MILITARY EQUIPMENT

In the Early Middle Ages, iron weapons and armor were almost prohibitively expensive. Full sets of military equipment were the prized possessions of kings and aristocrats, who gave them as gifts to their followers. Military success depended to a great degree on a plentiful supply of these costly and frequently beautiful weapons. The main sources of information for weapons in the fifth to seventh centuries are pagan graves in which they were deposited. Conversion to Christianity caused this practice to end and information comes instead from chance finds, manuscript illustrations, and sculptures.

Defensive weaponry consisted of helmets, shields, and shirts of mail, or metal or horn scales sewn to leather jerkins and shields. The seventh-century royal burial at Sutton Hoo in East Anglia contained a highly decorated helmet, round shield, and the remains of mail. Greaves have been found in Frankish burials and formed part of the best-armed warriors' equipment. An eighth-century helmet found at York has nose guards and cheek guards, and a mail curtain protecting the neck. Its style is paralleled on a sculpted stone at Aberlemno in Scotland, probably erected to commemorate the Pictish victory over a Northumbrian host at Nechtansmere in 685.

The Bayeux Tapestry (see page 80) depicts the armor current in England and northern France in the eleventh century. English infantry and Norman cavalry both wear conical helmets with noseguards, and hauberks, which reach to the knees and elbows, and carry round and

The Aberlemno stone no. 2, from Scotland, celebrates the defeat and death of the Northumbrian king Ecgfrith at Nechtansmere. The Picts (on horseback) have helmets, shields, swords, and spears; the English (on foot) are similarly equipped. The helmets depicted here parallel the one found at Coppergate in York, England, in 1982. Previously, Viking artifacts had been discovered at Coppergate during archaelogical excavations.

oblong or kite-shaped shields. This equipment provided a high degree of protection. Offensive weapons consisted of long swords, short swords (*scramaseaxes,*) throwing axes (*franciscas,* a characteristic weapon of the Franks), spears (for example, the Frankish barbed *ango*, and the English *aetgar*), and the Viking battle-axe, the use of which by the English is also depicted on the Bayeux Tapestry. Bows and arrows were used in war, but their penetrative power is not known.

While complete sets of arms and armor remained the province of the wealthy, successful warfare led to the acquisition of weapons and armor by fighting men, and no race was so successful at war from the fifth to the early ninth centuries as the Franks under their Merovingian and Carolingian rulers. From the late eighth century on, some rulers took steps to improve how well their soldiers were equipped, instead of relying on the spoils of war. Around 800, Charlemagne laid down that the infantry were to equip themselves with spear, shield, and bow. The traditional armament of the cavalry was lance, shield, and long sword (*spata*), to which was added the bow. But some of the Carolingian cavalry were much better equipped. The armored knights, for example, the striking force of Frankish armies of the time, included among their armament mail shirts, helmets, and even metal leg guards.

Charlemagne laid specific emphasis on the possession of this equipment by his most important subjects. The war-horse was a major cost, having a value equivalent to 18 to 20 cows. Thus this equipment was limited to the wealthiest free men and royal vassals, and such of their companions as they chose to arm with it. Export of such weaponry was prohibited at the end of the eighth century.

Men "made of iron"

In the tenth century, the rulers of Wessex and the Ottonian kings of Germany, soon to be emperors, increased the quality and quantity of their military equipment. The success that these kings enjoyed over internal rivals and neighbors was due in large measure to this improvement. Their conquests were achieved by men who, to their victims, were "made of iron," and who practiced a form of blitzkrieg. By the middle of the tenth century, the West Saxon descendants of Alfred the Great had succeeded in creating a single kingdom of England. The armament of their warriors is indicated by the death duties that nobles paid, consisting of horses, coats of mail, helmets, swords, spears, and shields. The greatest landowners occasionally added warships to their bequests. In 1008, Æthelred II (975–1016) collected a tax in the form of helmets, and an indication of how much war gear he amassed is the belief of a contemporary German writer, Thietmar of Merseburg, that Æthelred had 24,000 coats of mail stored in London.

THE RISE OF HEAVY CAVALRY

How medieval warfare came to be dominated by heavy cavalry is not easy to establish. The defeat of a Roman army at Adrianople (378) and the death of the emperor Valens at the hands of a Gothic-Hun army has been seen as a turning point, after which the Imperial government abandoned its traditional reliance on infantry and turned instead to heavy cavalry. But Adrianople was largely an infantry battle and the role of barbarian cavalry has been overestimated. Anyway, the Romans had been increasing their armored cavalry units since the third century. Among the barbarian invaders heavy cavalry did not predominate either. The expense of armor, war-horse, and weapons meant this style of fighting was restricted to kings and nobles.

Another turning point in the rise of heavy cavalry took place in the eighth century. At one time it was argued that the Frank Charles Martel used church lands to build up a heavy cavalry force after his clash with the Arabs at Poitiers in 732 convinced him of the need for one. Another theory was that the introduction of the stirrup in western Europe in the early eighth century made possible "mounted shock combat" by giving the rider a firmer seat. The benefits conferred by the stirrup are indisputable, but there is no evidence that knowledge of it reached the West precisely in the first half of the eighth century. Cavalry was certainly not unknown in Frankish armies before this time, but it did not become the dominant element before the end of the century.

The reasons for the Carolingian dynasty's successful wars of conquest, which continued for almost a hundred years, lay in its methods. Its armies operated with a destructiveness and sheer savagery that destroyed the ability and desire of opponents to resist. This is not to deny the significance of heavy cavalry in the armies of Charlemagne. Estimates of the total numbers available around 800 vary from 5,000 to 35,000. What is certain

(Above) The backbone of Roman armies was the heavy legionary infantry, but from the later third century onward, the use of cavalry of all types was increased, especially after the reforms of Constantine (324–37), in response to new threats.
(Below) Germanic cavalry fight with Roman legionnaires. Woodcut after bas-relief from the Column of Marcus Aurelius in Rome, published in 1880.

Cavalry came to play a greater role in the Byzantine empire during the Dark Ages. Many of its enemies—including the Bulgars shown here—were Asiatic cavalry.

is that the Franks possessed a formidable heavy cavalry. Charlemagne paid careful attention to the equipment of his armies—light cavalry and infantry, as well as heavy cavalry—and to logistics on campaign. The great men of the realm were given estates from which they were required to provide well-equipped horsemen. The incentive was participation in profitable and glorious campaigns of conquest.

Although pitched battles were rare in these wars, when they did occur, the Frankish armored cavalry had a great advantage over their more lightly armed opponents. Their tactic was a disciplined close-order charge, and they relied on swords in the mêlée, but they were quite capable of dismounting when the occasion required it. Superior equipment made them irresistible—as long as they remembered their discipline. At the battle of the Süntel Mountains against the Saxons in 782, and in 891 at the battle of the Dyle against the Danes, the Frankish cavalry were overconfident and forgot their discipline. In consequence they were defeated.

Ottonian success

The ninth-century divisions of the Carolingian empire left the East Frankish (German) kingdom short of well-equipped Franks to draw on. When the Saxon Duke Henry the Fowler became king (918–36), he converted the Saxon nobility, hitherto used to fighting as light cavalry, into a force of armored horsemen. He turned them into disciplined, professional "men of iron," who gave his dynasty (the Ottonians) the edge over its enemies in Germany, the Magyars (Huns), Slavs, and opponents in Italy. Like the Franks, they relied on a close-order charge. Before the battle of Riade (933) against the Magyar horse archers, Henry reminded his men to maintain their line, to use their shields to deflect the first discharge of arrows, and only then to spur their horses to close contact. Ottonian success in the tenth and eleventh centuries was founded on Henry's foresight.

The emergence of armored horsemen as a significant force had already occurred by the year 1000. It was due to gradual evolution, not revolution. In the eleventh century, the major development was the effective deployment of the lance through the technique of "couching" it firmly under the arm. By then, among western Europeans, only the English did not fight on horseback. Although their military equipment closely resembled that of, for example, the Normans, they rode to battle but dismounted to fight. Yet it is important not to exaggerate the dominance of heavy cavalry. Medieval armies consisted of infantry, spearmen, and archers, too, whose role was well appreciated—this is clear whenever detailed evidence is plentiful, as for the battle of Hastings (1066) and the First Crusade.

Viking ships were technologically advanced. The combination of oars and sails gave them the mobility to terrorize the coastal regions of western Europe.

SIZE OF ARMIES

It is impossible to calculate the size of early medieval armies; indeed, the historian is frequently unable to say anything on this matter. Dark Age and medieval writers do sometimes give figures for armies, of the order of tens or even hundreds of thousands, but historians are unanimous in agreeing that these are gross exaggerations and of no use. There is also general agreement that armies were normally no more than a few thousand strong, and often just a few hundred. The contrast with the notion that in barbarian society all free men were liable to military service is striking, but can be explained. The cost of equipment limited swords and armor to a few warriors, but their military effectiveness was out of all proportion to their numbers. A few hundred well-equipped men were capable of great deeds.

A prominent example of this is the activities of the Vikings in western Europe during the ninth century. These pagan raiders from Denmark and Norway (the Swedes tended to operate in Russia) demoralized and terrorized their enemies, and subsequently made substantial conquests and built settlements in England and Francia. Not surprisingly, it was assumed that large hosts were needed to achieve this. However, an examination of the chronicle evidence led historian Peter Sawyer to conclude that even the "Great Danish army" (*magnus exercitus* in Latin, *micel here* in Anglo-Saxon), which conquered and settled three of the four ninth-century Anglo-Saxon kingdoms, was less than 1,000 strong at any one time. Nicholas Brooks has subsequently made a convincing case for numbering the great army of 865, and its successor, which came to England in 892, in thousands, while accepting that no precision is possible. These two forces were led by Danish kings, and were the focus of Viking activities in the West. In short, they were coalitions of the small personal war bands of hundreds that normally launched hit-and-run raids.

There is similar difficulty in establishing the size of the forces that invaded the Roman empire, or the armies of

Charlemagne. From his vast empire he might have been able to field a force of 5,000 to 35,000 armored cavalry, depending on whose calculation is used, supplemented by hordes of lighter cavalry and infantry. But only a fraction of these would have been assembled at any one time, and the most significant factor in Carolingian military successes was not quantity but quality and organization.

COMMAND

In the Dark Ages and long after, one of the chief attributes of kingship, and of nobility, was leadership in war. To a great extent, this was the justification for monarchy, and success in war was vital for successful rule. Only in the Muslim world did military and political leadership become separated, but in outlying areas, such as Spain, military governors were able to establish their independence from the center.

The largest armies were led by kings in person, although it made sense for them to avoid actual combat. The death of a king in battle, as at Hastings in 1066, brought resistance to an end. At a lower level, members of the nobility led hosts, either on their own account or at the command of their king. In England *ealdormen,* often of royal blood themselves, led the warriors from their shires, while in Francia this was performed by counts and, in border districts, dukes who had responsibility for several counties. Similar noble officers are met with in Italy and Spain. But the delegation of military power was not without its dangers. If central authority weakened, these noble office holders were likely to become independent, which is what happened in the Carolingian empire in the tenth century.

Ecclesiastical commanders

Bishops and abbots were prominent as military commanders in the Carolingian empire, by virtue of their noble birth and the great landed wealth of the Church. This is found, too, in late Anglo-Saxon England and in Germany. Ecclesiastics may have been powerful but they could not establish their own dynasties. The military power of their estates was at the disposal

THE CAMPAIGNS OF CHARLEMAGNE

DATE 768–812

CAMPAIGNS These demonstrate Charlemagne's abilities and Frankish military effectiveness

OBJECT To eliminate threats, win lands and treasures with which to reward his followers, gain renown, and to please god (as he saw it).

DESCRIPTION His first task was to finish the subjugation of Aquitaine in 769. The campaign reveals the hallmarks of his generalship: swiftness, concentration of force, building of strongholds, and use of terror. The conquest of Saxony, begun in 772, occupied much of the next 33 years. Charlemagne's biographer, Einhard, described it thus: "no war ever undertaken by the Frankish people was more prolonged, more full of atrocities, or more demanding of effort." All the methods of colonial warfare were employed—ravaging, hostage taking, massacre, construction of strongholds, plantation of Frankish settlers, and conversion to Christianity. But geography and the Saxons' primitive political organization made them resilient, and there were many revolts.

Charlemagne's second great feat was the destruction of the Avars (Huns,) after gaining control of Bavaria in 787. Due to Saxon revolt he led just one campaign in person (791) in eight years, and it was left to lieutenants to break into the Avar "ring" and carry off immense plunder. In 773–74 Charlemagne conquered Lombard Italy, confounding his opponent by campaigning over winter. He led armies into Spain, against the Slavs across the Elbe, and into Italy beyond Rome. Up to 800 he led in person and after retiring from active campaigning he directed armies to all frontiers. In 810, at the age of nearly 70, he led his last host against an expected Danish invasion.

Charlemagne created an empire that stretched from the Atlantic to Hungary, from Denmark to the Ebro in Spain, and south of Rome in Italy. This was the achievement of a master of strategy and logistics, yet he fought only two pitched battles, both in 783. Although Charlemagne's empire did not long survive him as a political entity, he shaped the future of Europe.

VIKING GREAT ARMY IN ENGLAND

DATE 865–79

OBJECT To plunder and reduce defeated Anglo-Saxon kingdoms to tributary status; then to settle conquered areas.

NUMBERS Numbers on both sides are impossible to calculate. The Anglo-Saxon kingdoms probably fielded a few thousand warriors each. The great army, led by several kings, included most Danish bands hitherto raiding in the West, and so probably numbered a few thousand. Elements settled in 875 and in 877, but the remainder was able to overrun part of Wessex and settle East Anglia (878–80). Wastage due to casualties and retirement was offset by the arrival of new bands.

DESCRIPTION When West Frankish resistance became too stiff, the Viking bands operating in the West joined up to concentrate on England. The Vikings of the great army adopted a new strategy. Each fall they moved to a new district and seized a royal center, usually with existing fortifications, to serve as winter quarters and a secure base while the bulk of the host was plundering. Initially, there was little the Anglo-Saxon kingdoms could do other than pay tribute in order to ward off farther plundering. Alfred, king of Wessex, fought eight battles in 871, but he too came to terms. He was more successful in 875–77 when he kept a close watch on the invaders, making it difficult for them to forage or plunder. But in January 878, he was taken by surprise at Chippenham and driven into the Somerset marshes until he could raise another army, blockade the Danes in Chippenham, and enforce surrender on terms.

RESULT In 879, the leaders of the great army accepted that West Saxon resistance would not be overcome; the army split again, part settling East Anglia, the remainder returning to the Continent.

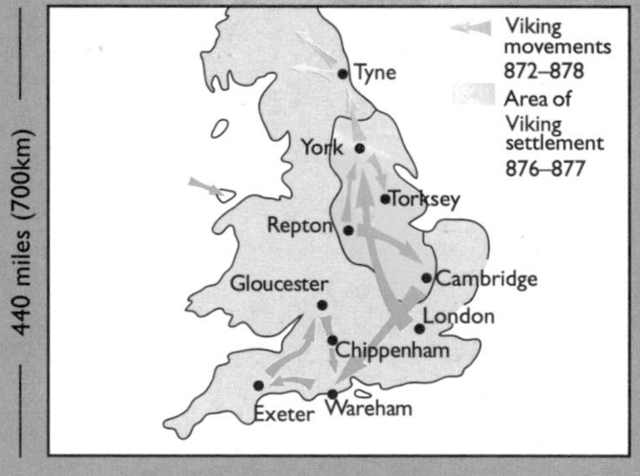

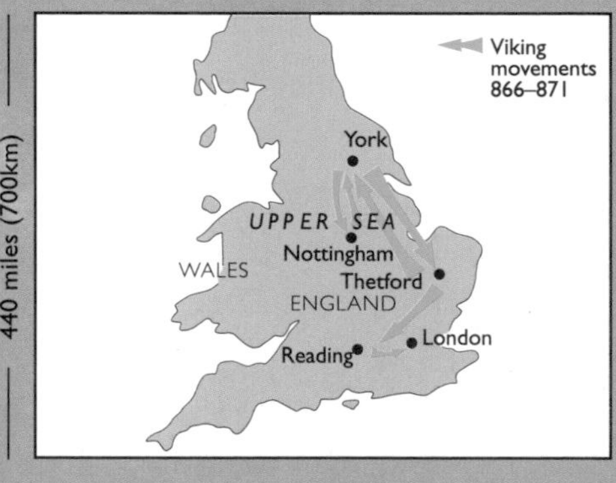

of the Crown (they did not fight in person.) In the arts of war, as in peace, their experience, literacy, and lands made them indispensable royal servants.

Below these levels of command little is known. After the county or shire came an individual lord's following, commanded by a noble or his delegate. The military household reinforced by a lord's leading tenants was the chief tactical unit of medieval armies.

STRATEGY

War in the Middle Ages was almost constant in many regions, whether it was public war between states, or private war between neighbors or rivals. Much of it was small-scale raiding. Grand strategy is frequently difficult to distinguish, but this does not mean medieval generals were incapable of executing operations on the grand scale. As in so much else the clear example is Charlemagne. On several occasions, we meet the use of multiple invasions, which would split the defenders' strength as well as easing problems of movement—two columns invading Italy (773) and crossing the Pyrenees (778), and three hosts sent into Bavaria from three points of the compass (787).

In 791, two armies advanced into Hungary, one on each bank of the Danube, with a supply fleet linking them. This arrangement made possible the outflanking of the Avar (Hun) defense lines on the south bank of the river. For the next campaign Charlemagne ordered the construction of a pontoon bridge, but it was never put to use as rebellions caused the king to be called away.

The Viking great armies certainly followed a coherent strategy, consisting of seizing a fortified base on a major river and exploiting the region around it before moving to another region. The first great army followed this strategy in Britain from 865 until 879, by which time many of its surviving members had become settlers. The army was reinforced and left England, where West Saxon resistance had become too stiff, for Francia where this second great army campaigned until 892. Again the West Franks organized effective resistance and so the whole army migrated back to England. But the Saxon king of Wessex, Alfred (871–99), had prepared for this and in 896 the great army broke up.

The strategy adopted against the Viking great armies in West Francia and Wessex is noteworthy. Its main feature was the mobilization of labor to reconstruct Roman walls and build new fortresses, and to construct fortified bridges to impede the movement of Viking fleets inland. Both the West Frankish Charles the Bald (840–77) and Alfred employed this strategy with success. In England, the fortress strategy was adapted by Alfred's successor, Edward the Elder (899–924), for the conquest of the Danish settlements in the Midlands and East Anglia. He extended his control by building one or more fortresses after each campaign, from which to bring more land under military domination. This process resulted in the conquest of the land between the Thames and Humber in just a decade. At about the same time, the German king Henry the Fowler (911–36) was establishing a similar network of fortresses with permanent garrisons in Saxony to defend and extend the frontiers against Slavs and Magyars.

(Left) King Alfred the Great of Wessex reigned from 871 to 899, a very successful king noted for not only his military successes against Danish Vikings but also for his great learning. Taken from A History of England *published ca.1855–1860.*

BATTLE OF MALDON

DATE August 10 or 11, 991
OBJECT Olaf Tryggvason's fleet came to Folkestone to raid the coast of southeast England, moving north to Sandwich and Ipswich, before establishing a base on Northey Island in the Blackwater estuary.
NUMBERS English numbers are unknown. Their commander was Ealdorman Brihtnoth, whose army included his household and retainers and the Essex militia (*fyrd*). Olaf's fleet was put at 93 ships, a possible 7,000 warriors, but probably considerably fewer.
DESCRIPTION Viking raids on England were renewed in 980 and Maldon was the first serious English setback. A contemporary poem is the only detailed record of an Anglo-Saxon army in battle. Ealdorman Brihtnoth drew up his host opposite Northey, where a causeway joins the island to the mainland, and permitted the Vikings to cross and form battle order. Why did he take this risk? A century of successes had probably made the English confident of the outcome of battle. The English dismounted, sending their horses to the rear, and formed the traditional shield wall. The Vikings were in a similar formation. Battle opened with an exchange of spears and archery before the two shield walls engaged in close combat with spears and swords. The turning point came when Brihtnoth was wounded and then cut down. Panic set in. Many of the English ran to the horses and fled. As portrayed in the poem, the conflict had been a simple one—indeed, it is likely that the shield wall was not capable of more than rudimentary maneuver.
RESULT This battle looks like the turning point in the reign of Æthelred II ("the Unready"), although it took 20 years before the Danish king Swein could aim at conquest, and another five years before it was achieved by his son Cnut.

Two viking longships engaged in battle, an engraving from the 1830s.

Planned raids

The most widely employed and medieval strategy was "ravaging"—a form of economic warfare, which was generally more productive than a battle-seeking strategy. Pitched battles carried too many risks when strategic objectives could usually be achieved by organized raiding. Ravaging operated at all levels of warfare and fulfilled several functions. At the highest level, the systematic destruction of the means of production, as practised by the Carolingians in Aquitaine in the middle decades of the eighth century, destroyed the material base and will to resist. Conquest could thus follow on the heels of ravaging. At the operational level, pillaging supplied armies—although commanders did not ignore the need for large armies to carry supplies with them—and enriched the participants, and so provided a major incentive to fight. The standard counter to a raiding strategy was to assemble a field army in the vicinity of an invading force. Then it could either be forced to desist from pillaging or defeated in detail. This method of active defense was used with success by, for example, Alfred against the Viking great army in the late 870s and again in the 890s. In regions of strong fortified sites, that is where Roman town walls remained defensible, in southern France and Italy for example, a passive defensive strategy involved taking refuge until the invader withdrew. The disadvantage of this strategy was that it did not prevent considerable damage being caused to economic resources, nor would it work against determined and well-equipped invaders, such as the eighth-century Carolingians.

TACTICS

Where fortified sites were few, the defender was constrained to give battle or suffer dangerous loss of resources and prestige. However, it's difficult to know what tactics were used when battles did occur due to the inadequacy of narrative sources. Descriptions of battles are few, and they give fewer details of tactics, being largely concerned with the heroic deeds of individuals. This is not the same thing as saying that Dark Age battles were undisciplined. The discipline required for the Frankish cavalry charge from the late eighth century onward is described in the feature on heavy cavalry (see pages 70–71).

For an indication of the degree of tactical sophistication that early medieval armies were capable of, the historian has to wait until the battle of Hastings in 1066. This reveals the coordination of infantry and cavalry, and a high degree of discipline. This is true not only of Duke William's army, which was recruited widely in France, but to a lesser extent of the English shield wall. Although this formation seems to have been incapable of more rudimentary maneuvers, it was a tough nut to crack as long as it maintained its formation. One countermeasure against cavalry not employed by the English in 1066 was the digging of traps; their use is recorded from the early 6th century, when the Thuringians broke up a Frankish cavalry charge in this way.

Nevertheless, in general, it seems to be true that early medieval battles tended to be brief and relatively unsophisticated, and that for much of this period the most elaborate tactics were those of the Byzantine armies. This did not, it should be noted, protect the Byzantine empire from severe setbacks and losses of territory at the hands of Persians, Muslims, Asiatic, and Slav invaders in the Balkans and Germanic enemies in Italy. The Byzantine empire survived, and in the sixth and tenth centuries it expanded again, but it would be unsafe to attribute this to a permanently superior military system.

A brief survey such as this cannot do justice to the multiplicity of military systems and methods of the Dark Ages. There have always been inadequate military systems and incompetent commanders. Moreover, the nature of the evidence for warfare in the Early Middle Ages often defeats analysis. There is sufficient evidence, however, to show that this period was not barren of military innovation, discipline, and application of the science of war.

A HANDBOOK FOR GENERALS?

The most popular military handbook of the Middle Ages was *On War* (*De re militari*) by the late-Roman Flavius Vegetius Renatus. Vegetius commented on all aspects of war. Some principles could not be applied to medieval armies, but two were relevant. One concerned supply: the army that was not carefully provisioned courted disaster. The second concerned laying waste enemy territory, which enriched the soldiers, making them enthusiastic to fight, and reduced enemy resources. More than 300 copies survive; this large number is testimony to the book's relevance throughout the Middle Ages.

6 MEDIEVAL WARFARE

The medieval period was one of technological innovation. Fortifications grew from simple towers to great concentric castles and eventually became artillery-proof bastion forts. Siege weapons both led and responded to these developments: the twelfth century produced the trebuchet and the fourteenth century gunpowder artillery. Ships grew from low-lying galleys to towering galleons. Protection improved from ring-mail coats to complete suits of plate armor. Missile weapons, in the hands of English bowmen or French arquebusiers, eventually transformed the "hosts" of horsemen into armies of foot soldiers.

CAVALRY AND CASTLES

It is a myth that warfare in the Middle Ages was dominated by the mounted warrior, the knight. This is no more true than to say that the tank is the sole battle winner today. Their tactical roles are not dissimilar, but we should not translate one into the other too literally. Cavalry is the spiritual ancestor of the armored fighting vehicle, but the mounted arm has always played a part in cooperation with, rather than in isolation from, the rest.

In contrast, fortification, expressed in the form of the castle, was central to the conduct of war ca. 1000–1400. The link between the mounted warrior and the castle was a social one; lords and their retinues lived in and around their fortress. This conjunction was a product of a social and political change seen in continental Europe and West Francia (France) in the two centuries ca. 800–1000 following the reign of the Emperor Charlemagne. A combination of factors, including the attacks of the Vikings, Muslims, and Magyars and the decline of central, monarchical authority, led to power descending to local level in western Christian Europe. Any lord with a castle and following of knights was a force to be reckoned with and to be wooed by princes.

The result was a military development that proved to be an efficient vehicle for expansion and conquest under the leadership of Frankish rulers. The knight, a mail-clad and shielded cavalryman carrying sword and lance, proved more than a match tactically for most opponents. The Westerners' competence at the related arts of fortress building and siege techniques meant that they could take and hold fortresses, so riveting their rule on the land.

This military success is usually associated with the Normans. William the Conqueror won a decisive victory at Hastings in 1066, and consolidated his hold over England and much of northern France in the next two decades. A little earlier, the Norman Hauteville family had begun to carve out an empire in southern and central Italy. Robert Guiscard

BATTLE OF CIVITATE

DATE June 17, 1053
CAMPAIGN War between Pope Leo IX and Norman lords
OBJECT To prevent Leo from joining up with his Byzantine allies.
NUMBERS Papal—several thousand men, including a strong force of Swabian infantry. Norman—reckoned at 3,000 cavalry by the later chronicler Geoffrey Malaterra, but probably less than 1,000 knights.
DESCRIPTION Robert Guiscard commanded the Norman left wing, Humphrey the center, and Richard of Aversa the right. Spying disorganization in the Italo-Lombard forces, Richard charged and dispersed them. In the center, the Norman horsemen could make no headway against the Swabian foot. With Guiscard's force in reserve and the return of Richard's wing, the Pope's forces were eventually overcome.
RESULT The Papal army was destroyed and Leo taken prisoner.

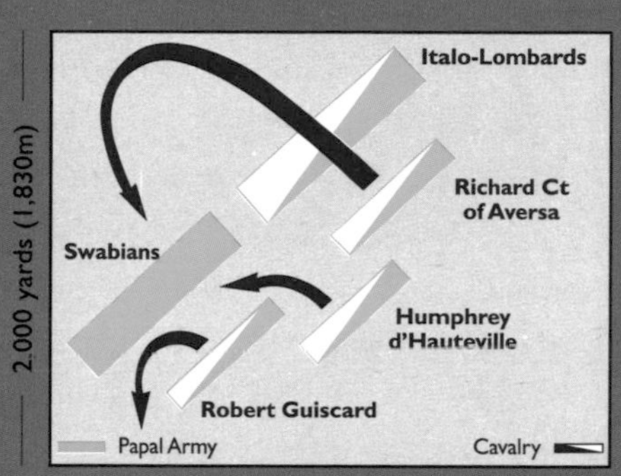

even led forces against Byzantium following his conquest of Bari in 1071. Ten years later he defeated the emperor Alexius at Durazzo (in modern Albania). The emperor's daughter described the charge of the Frankish knights as "able to pierce the walls of Babylon," whose thickness was legendary.

This might seem to support the idea of the invincible knight, but in fact the victory was due to cooperation with missilemen. At Hastings, the Norman archers wore down axe-wielding foot soldiers until the knights could charge in. At Durazzo, Italian crossbowmen performed the same role. When the Varangian guard seemed about to win the battle, the bowmen pinned them down and broke up their formation until the retreating knights could regroup and counterattack. Significantly, the campaign was won through the capture of the fortress port of Durazzo and a naval victory by the Venetians, rather than the battle alone. Western technological advantages and all-arms cooperation was the winning combination. It is no coincidence that sons of both William the Conqueror and Robert Guiscard, respectively Robert Curthose and Bohemond, were leading figures on the great military expedition known as the First Crusade. But it was not just the Normans who employed knight and castle as a weapon for conquest. It was a technique employed by all the Frankish rulers in Anjou, Flanders, and Aquitaine.

The German emperors also relied upon the military service of knights by the end of the eleventh century. Pope Gregory VII, in his dispute with the emperor Henry IV, declared Henry excommunicate and dissolved his vassals' obedience to him. The result was civil war and the destruction of the emperor's military forces. The only way successive emperors could assert themselves over the popes was to campaign in Italy. This involved taking armies of knights south over the Alps from Germany, but little could be achieved by even such a powerful ruler as Frederick Barbarossa (1154–90) without the siege equipment to overwhelm the cities of northern Italy.

This is often seen as an example of something "new"—the defeat of an army of knights by foot soldiers. But once again the true reason was the combination of Italian cavalry with the stolid holding power of infantry found throughout the Middle Ages. The Anglo-Norman rulers had already expressed their awareness of this.

THE BATTLE OF HASTINGS

The Bayeux Tapestry, the Anglo-Saxon Chronicle, and Duke William's biography by the soldier turned chaplain William of Poitiers, provide unusually detailed evidence for the campaigns of 1066. Harold (crowned January 6, 1066) faced threats from his brother Tostig, King Harald Hardrada of Norway, and Duke William of Normandy. Tostig, first off the mark in the spring, was easily driven off. Harold defended the south against the Normans, leaving the northern earls Edwin and Morcar to face the Norwegians. The response of the three leaders to the problems of seaborne invasion and defense demonstrate the high degree of military organization of eleventh-century states. During the summer, both Harold and William kept their armies supplied, avoiding the danger of epidemics. In one sense Harold's achievement was greater because his men had no prospect of plunder to motivate them.

The main fighting was crammed into one hectic month. The northern earls were defeated by the Norwegians at Gate Fulford (September 20) and Harold, already on his way, took the invaders completely by surprise at Stamford

(Above) The site of the battle of October 14, 1066. The ridge on which the English position was formed gave them a considerable advantage—Harold fell on the right of the picture.

In this section of the Bayeux Tapestry the start of battle is illustrated. The Norman assault was opened by infantry, followed by cavalry. Neither could make any impression on the English shield wall. It was the combination of archers and cavalry that was decisive in winning the battle, and it can already be seen in the depiction here.

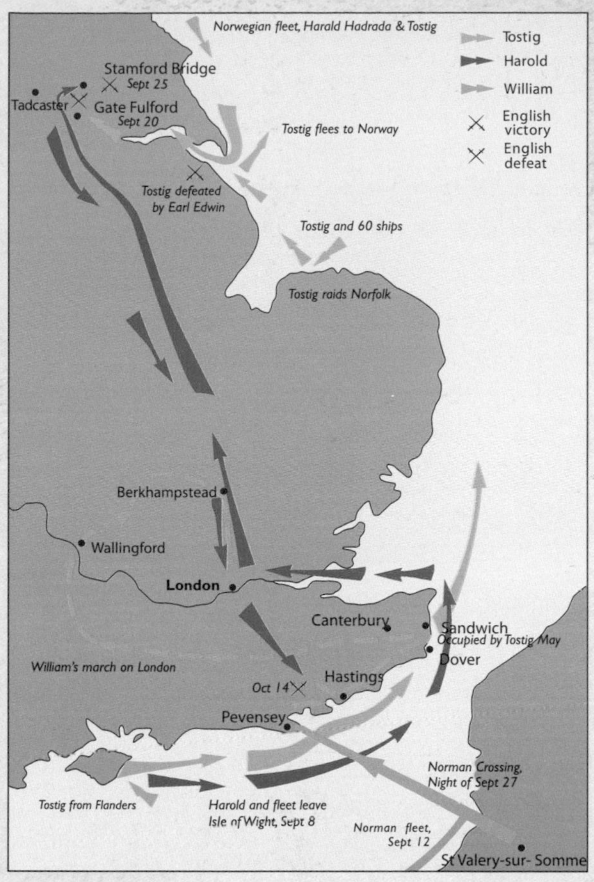

(Left) Harold of England was caught between two fires. His march north took the Norwegians by surprise, and the return 250 miles (400 km) south was even more impressive. (Below) Harold, forced to give battle, was in a superb defensive position—on a sharp ridge with well-protected flanks. Moreover, William had to attack if he was to win England. The slope negated the effect of the Norman cavalry, and English axes inflicted fearsome wounds. William's tactics reveal a high order of generalship.

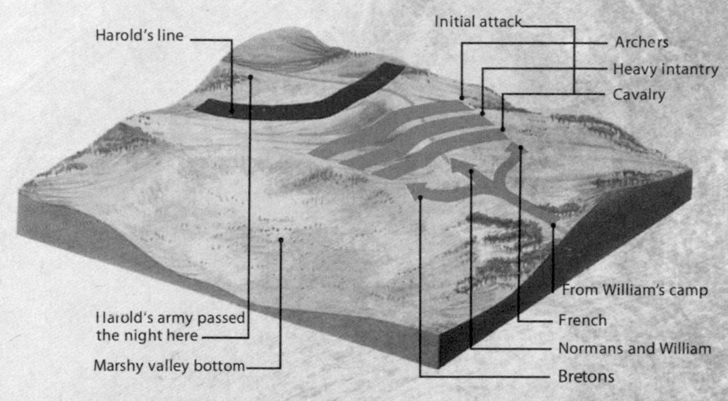

Bridge (September 25). King Harald and his ally Tostig were among the dead. This was Harold's first pitched battle. Meanwhile, the winds in the Channel changed, allowing the Norman fleet to sail on the night of September 27. William landed at Pevensey, moving on to Hastings , from where he plundered for supplies, and to provoke Harold.

By the night of October 13, Harold was within 10 miles (16 km) of Hastings. His actions have been criticized as reckless, and he probably did fight before all his strength was mustered. The maxim "courage is worth more than numbers, and speed is worth more than courage" may explain his strategy. The Normans stood to during the night of October 13–14, fearing a surprise attack, but William's scouting enabled him to seize the initiative. He marched to confront the English on the morning of October 14. The risk he took was great: the English were in a strong position, and William had to attack.

The English fought on foot in the customary shield wall. Battle opened about 9 a.m. Two lines of Norman infantry failed to break the English position, as did the Norman heavy cavalry. The rumor spread that William was dead, the Bretons on the left fell back, and rout threatened. In this crisis William rallied his men. Now William altered his tactics. The cavalry used the feigned flight to lure some of the English to destruction. Combined attacks by infantry, especially archers, and cavalry reduced English numbers. Toward the end of the day Harold was struck in the face (clearly shown on the Bayeux Tapestry) and as the English at last began to crumble, he was cut down by a party of knights. With his death, English resistance ceased. It took William most of the day to crack the English position, but his generalship, and the discipline of his army were of the highest order. The battle was won, but not yet the war—English rebellions continued until 1070.

Illustration celebrating the 700th anniversary of the victory of Philippe Auguste and the French at the Battle of Bouvines (July 27, 1214), from French newspaper Le Petit Journal, *July 26, 1914.*

In a series of battles in the first half of the twelfth century commanders had actually *dismounted* their knights in order to win battles. English king Henry I did this at Tinchebrai (1106) against his brother Robert, whose cavalry charges could make no headway against them, and then won the battle with a mounted flank attack. He also defeated the French king at Brémule in 1119, with a combination of archery, dismounted knights, and cavalry. In 1124, one of Henry's professional soldiers, Odo Berleng, led a tiny garrison force of archers and dismounted knights against the rebel Waleran of Meulan. An impetuous cavalry charge by the Waleran was simply shot down by the archers, unhorsing the knights, and leaving them to be rounded up for ransom by the royalist foot. Finally, in 1138, at the Battle of the Standard, an English army defeated the Scots led by their king David I. Many English knights were dismounted and placed in the front rank alternately with archers, so that their lances protected the missilemen.

All rulers were aware of the importance of good infantry. Henry II of England, the most powerful ruler in mid-twelfth century Europe, employed Flemish and Brabançon foot. At Bouvines in 1214, such men fought in the army of his son John's ally, the emperor Otto. Their success against the French cavalry meant that the eventual victory of Philip II of France was long in doubt.

CASTLE WARFARE

Battles were, in any case, often secondary to fortress warfare. It was remarkable that the conquest of England was achieved without long, drawn-out sieges. A Norman chronicler pointed out that this was because the English did not use castles. Two generations later, after sustained castle building, the civil war between the king Stephen and the empress Matilda dragged on for two decades (1138–53). Castle building had long been known on continental Europe. Fulk Nerra, count of Anjou (987–1040) and a "pioneer in feudal government" had based his campaigns of expansion upon the construction of stone castles in the Loire Valley. In Germany, Duke Frederick of Bueren did the same along the Rhine.

The Battle of Nicopolis took place on 25 September 1396 and is often referred to as the Crusade of Nicopolis. It was the last large-scale crusade of the Middle Ages and resulted in the rout of an allied army of Hungarian, Wallachian, French, Burgundian, German and assorted troops (assisted by the Venetian navy) at the hands of an Ottoman force, raising of the siege of the Danubian fortress of Nicopolis and leading to the end of the Second Bulgarian Empire.

How did castles control the land? They could not interdict the passage of an enemy (except in the narrowest passes) before the development of gunpowder artillery. Essentially, they were bases for supplies, refuges in case of defeat, and jumping-off points for raids and sallies. The building of such a fortification in, or on the borders of, enemy territory, was a declaration of hostile intent. Farther, the garrison, although not the castle itself, could threaten lines of communication. Only if the castle was taken did it cease to become a threat. It could then be removed (razed) or turned against its previous owner.

The conquest of England provides a most instructive example of castle strategy. The first thing William did on landing was to raise a castle at Hastings, made from timber and earth, as the Bayeux Tapestry shows. He did the same at Dover on a magnificent natural site. Once in control of London, he ordered the construction of a tall, square stone building, still known as the Tower. This he matched at the strategically important site of Colchester. When faced with rebellion at Exeter and York in the following year, he built new castles as strongpoints after capturing the cities. As the king did, so did his barons, staking claims to the English countryside with hastily raised "motte-and-bailey" constructions. On the dangerous Welsh border, literally hundreds of these sites are still visible.

In the twelfth century, many castles were rebuilt in stone, and some were abandoned. The Anglo-Norman realm produced some of the best stone castles, including Dover (Kent), Castle Rising (Norfolk), and Durham in England; Falaise and Château Gaillard in Normandy.

THE MEDIEVAL CASTLE: IT'S CONSTRUCTION AND USE

The castle was the fortified residence of a lord, someone who exercised political and judicial authority over territory. It used to be supposed that the timber and earth "motte and bailey" was the earliest form, but stone towers were already being built in the Loire region of France in the 10th century, for example Doué-la-Fontaine (ca. 950) and Langeais (ca. 994). Timber castles were much favored by the Normans in the early stages of their conquest of England, because they were quick to construct, but they obviously relied upon plentiful supplies of wood. This is why they were not an option in the Holy Land away from the coast.

In the twelfth century, wherever castles were sited, there was a tendency to rebuild in stone. Castle Rising, in Norfolk, is a fine example of such a tower keep, with each floor reserved for a different function. Fortifications began to become more complex as well. Curtain walls surrounded the tower, and barbicans (outworks) protected the main gate. The castles of the Crusader states and Edward I's Welsh fortifications represent the highest form of the art. Of course, they became enormously expensive, taxing the revenues of kingdoms. In the Crusader states, only the wealthy military monks—Templar, Teutonic, and Hospitaller—could afford their upkeep.

Even the largest castles usually had very small garrisons. They were intended as residences, storehouses of food and supplies, places of refuge for dependent peasantry, and bases for attacks into enemy territory. This is what made them such a good investment for their owners. A handful of men, often commanded by their lord's lady, could hold large forces at bay until relief arrived. Until the development of gunpowder artillery able to breach walls quickly, investing a castle meant a great commitment of men, material, and time for an attacker.

(Above) The motte and bailey consisted of a mound (motte) furnished with a wooden tower and an attached defended enclosure (bailey) wherein lay the chapel, storehouses, and living quarters for its inhabitants. Such a castle could be built in a week. (The Bayeux Tapestry shows the Normans achieving this at Hastings, in 1066.)

(Below) A plan of Harlech castle in Wales. Set on a huge crag above the estuary of the Dwyryd River, and farther secured by a rock-cut ditch from the landward side, this concentric castle has four great drum towers at each corner, and a powerful gatehouse. Built between 1283 and 1290, Harlech is one of Edward I's finest achievements.

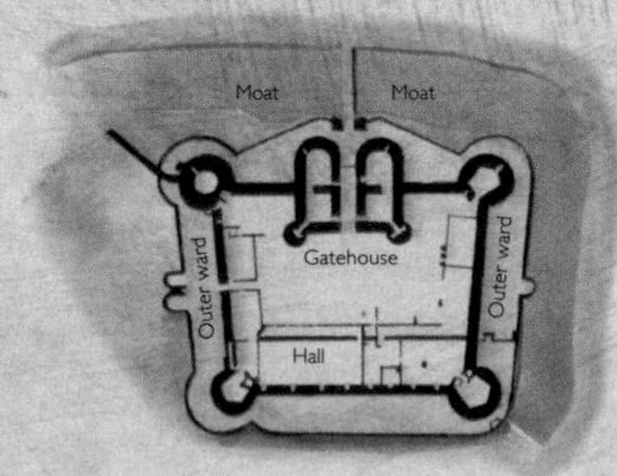

(Below) This cutaway drawing shows something of the layout and internal arrangements of a twelfth-century castle where stone has replaced timber. The defended gateways were vital to its security. Invulnerable to fire, unlike its timber predecessor, the stone keep could only be defeated by undermining. Even then, at Rochester in 1215, the defenders fought on after a corner tower had fallen, secure behind an internal dividing wall.

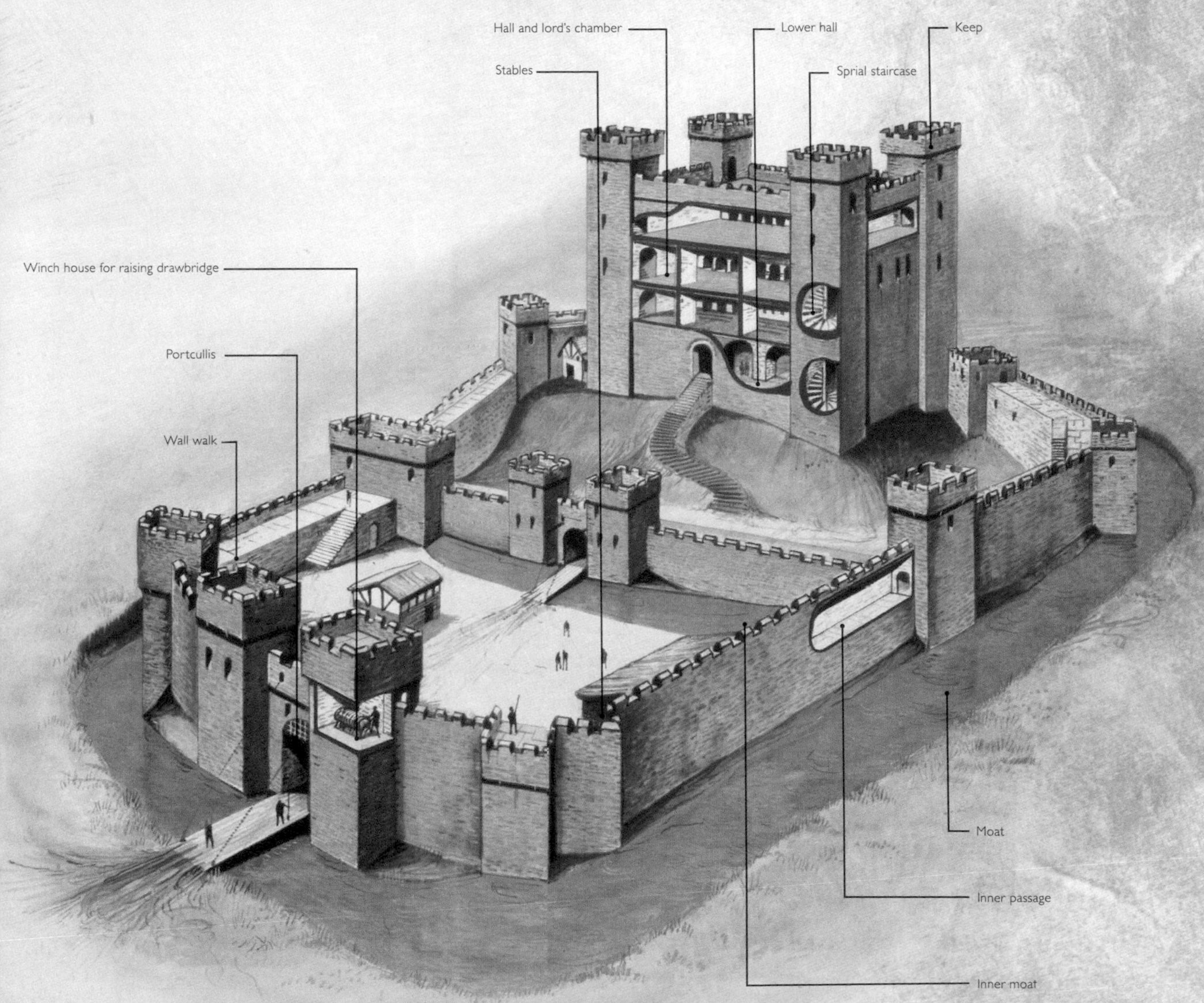

THE CRUSADES

In November 1095 at Clermont in central France, the pope Urban II, himself a Frenchman from the knightly class, preached that it was necessary for military men to march east to recover Jerusalem from the Turks—or, at least that is what many understood him to mean. The result, the Crusades, entailed 500 years of conflict between the Christian and non-Christian world. It was not just Muslims, or Saracens as the Crusaders called them, who were the enemy; the pagan tribes of Lithuania and Prussia were also legitimate opponents. As it turned out, the conquest of the Holy Land, although brilliantly achieved with the capture of Jerusalem in 1099, was the shortest lived. The *Reconquista* in Spain and the "Drive to the East" from Germany brought new lands permanently under Christian rule.

The First Crusade took perhaps 20,000 knights and 100,000 others (not all combatants) from all parts of western Europe to Asia Minor and Syria. They resembled hordes of locusts to the Byzantines, who were happy to let them pass on to do battle with the Turks because the Turks had terrorized their empire for half a century. In 1097, the Crusaders captured Nicaea and then marched across waterless Asia Minor. It was here they first encountered the Eastern way of war. Instead of charging hand to hand, the Turks skirmished at a distance with their powerful bows in the classic nomad manner. This was to be the model for countless battles of the Crusader era. In the battle fought at Dorylaeum under a burning June sun, the Westerners hit on the tactical response. Almost beaten by the heat, dust, and arrows, which dropped the knights' horses, they fell back on their camp, where bows and crossbows held the Turks at bay. Then a second Crusader column arrived and took the enemy in the rear.

Antioch is taken by surprise during the First Crusade (1098–99). Bohemond, a Norman leader, bribed a tower commander to let the besiegers in. Illustration from a late medieval manuscript.

ANTIOCH AND JERUSALEM

The next test was the great city of Antioch, fortified by 6 miles (10 km) of tall walls. Storming it was impossible and it took 10 months, including the harsh Syrian winter, which almost destroyed the besieging army, before the city fell by treachery. A Turkish relieving force arrived too late and was fought and beaten just a few days later. At Jerusalem, which was reached in the summer of 1099, Western siege technology was employed to the full. The Crusaders constructed three great siege towers and from one of them gained the foothold that caused the city's fall.

Victory in battle against the forces of the Egyptian caliphate at Ascalon in southern Syria consolidated the Crusaders' position. Four states were established based on the cities of Edessa, Antioch, Tripoli, and Jerusalem. The first generation following 1099 was one of expansion at the expense of the Muslim powers, but a series of great commanders reconquered the lands of Islam. At the battle of the "Bloody Field" in 1119, Roger, Duke of Antioch, carelessly led his men into an ambush, pursuing a feigned flight by Turkish troops. In 1140, the Atabeg Zengi recaptured Edessa and pressure was increased on the other states. A series of counterattacks into Egypt led by the energetic King Almaric was eventually frustrated by the Turkish general Shirkuh. But it was his protégé, a Kurd known as Saladin, who proved the ablest commander. He lured the Christian army under its impetuous commander King Guy into a trap at the Horns of Hattin, near Lake Galilee in 1187.

Loosening grip

The Crusader states were always short of manpower and now their king, barons, and almost all their knights fell into enemy hands. There was no one to defend the castles or cities and they all fell under Muslim control, except for strongly fortified Tyre.

The loss of Jerusalem had a profound effect in the West and the three most powerful monarchs, Richard of England, Philip of France, and emperor Frederick Barbarossa all took the cross. The Third Crusade (1189–92) achieved little apart from the capture of the important port of Acre. Frederick died en route, Philip defected, and Richard had to leave before he could exploit his victories over Saladin. The movement never again achieved such heights. The Fourth Crusade was diverted to, and conquered, Christian Constantinople in 1204. Successive Crusades to Egypt in 1219–21 and 1248–50, while initially successful, eventually floundered in the swamps of the Delta.

SIEGE OF ACRE

DATE August 1189–July 11, 1191
CAMPAIGN Third Crusade of western rulers against the Muslim forces of Saladin
OBJECT Crusaders besieging the city were, in turn, surrounded by Muslims attempting to relieve it.
DESCRIPTION Guy, King of Jerusalem, set out to capture the most important port in the Holy Land with a few hundred men. He dug in on a nearby hill. Reinforcements allowed a Christian blockade of the city by April 1190. In April and June of 1191 respectively, Philip II of France and Richard I of England led their forces into the besiegers' camp. There followed a period of intensive assaults on the city and attacks by Saladin's forces on the Crusader camp. The armies had risen to number tens of thousands on both sides; this was the climax of the war, but Saladin was unable to drive off the besiegers.
RESULT Fall of Acre to the Christians.

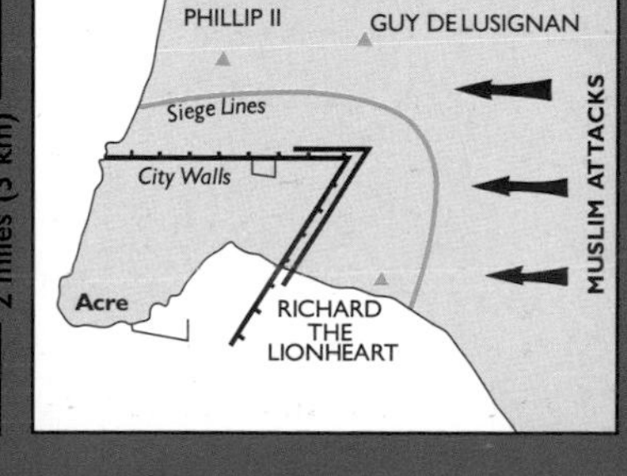

RICHARD "THE LIONHEART"

Richard "the Lionheart," King of England (1189–1199), was the embodiment of the perfect knight, physically brave and robust, a fine fighter, and with the charisma to make men want to follow him. Even when critically ill during the siege of Acre and when the Crusaders were themselves besieged by Saladin's vast army, he held his motley force together. He was also a tactician of genius, and inflicted two decisive defeats on the Muslims, at Arsuf and Ascalon. His control and the discipline he instilled enabled the knights and crossbowmen to work in unison. He knew the importance of fortifications and how necessary it was to both build and capture them. He died of a crossbow wound at Chalus in the Limousin, while besieging the castle there.

King Louis of France was actually captured with all his army on the latter expedition. A combination of fleets and siege weapons achieved more than battle, and the Christians ran the risk of being defeated. In fact, it was not military action but diplomacy that won back Jerusalem for a short period from 1228–40.

LEGACY OF THE CRUSADES

The Crusader states left a remarkable architectural heritage. Their castles were the largest and most sophisticated of the time. In northern Syria, Saône stands just inland from Lattikiah, between two gorges, a 98-foot (30-m) rock-cut ditch farther protecting it from attack. Farther south, standing against Muslim Homs is Krak des Chevaliers, the most perfect example of concentric fortification in the East. The "Knights" from which it takes its name were the Templars, an order of military monks founded in 1128. Along with the Hospitallers, or Knights of St. John, they provided a large proportion of the knightly cavalry for Crusader armies. They were so feared by the enemy that Saladin had all captured brothers executed after Hattin. These military orders became immensely wealthy due to donations of property in Europe and, in the case of the Templars, through banking. Only they had the resources to take on the expense of the vast stone castles necessary to defend the Holy Land. This they did successfully until there were no more men to man the walls. This was the fate of Krak, which finally surrendered in 1271.

Other orders were instrumental in religious wars elsewhere. They played a part in the Spanish *Reconquista,* although this was carried out by the Christian kings of the Peninsula rather than by crusade. In central and northern Europe, the Teutonic Knights carved out an empire for themselves after they transferred their headquarters to Prussia in 1229. Their huge castle complex at Marienburg represented their military might. Although checked by the Russians at Lake Peipus in 1242, the Teutonic Knights were an important power, rivaling kingdoms, until they were finally humbled by defeat at Tannenberg in 1410 by a coalition of states.

NOMADIC WARFARE

Eastward from the Hungarian plains into central Asia and from Egypt to Persia, the main weapon was the bow. Unlike in the Western world, it was wielded from horseback. The main protagonists of this style of warfare were nomadic steppe dwellers, traveling peoples who roamed over great areas of grassland in order to feed their flocks and herds. The primary exponents of nomadic warfare were the Turks and Mongols of Central Asia, and it was from here that waves of invasion rolled west into the Christian and Arab world and east into China.

BATTLE OF ARSUF

DATE September 7, 1191
CAMPAIGN Third Crusade of Western rulers against the Muslim forces of Saladin
OBJECT Saladin was trying to prevent Richard I of England (the Lionheart) from reaching Jerusalem.
DESCRIPTION Richard led his army south along the coast from Acre toward Jaffa, in defensive formation. His knightly cavalry were kept covered up behind the infantry to protect their precious horses from archery. The infantry was divided in half and alternated in position between the landward and seaward side, to rest them. Muslim harassing attacks meant that the Crusaders' march was very slow, but their morale held. They continued to march even while their padded *gambesons,* or protective tunics, bristled with the shafts of Muslim arrows. Eventually, Saladin was forced to deliver an all-out assault on the Crusader army. Richard kept his men well in hand despite the frustrations of thirst and constant archery attack. His counter thrust with his knights was well timed, and in three successive charges the Muslims were thrown back and fled.
RESULT A reverse for Saladin which enabled Richard to develop his strategy unhindered.

In the mid-eleventh century, nomadic Turks invaded the Middle East. They established a dynasty, known as the Seljuks, in Asia Minor, in old Byzantine lands, and other groups established themselves in Iran, Iraq, and Syria. Their disruption of the Muslim world was one reason for the success of the First Crusade. However, they came not only as conquerors but also as mercenaries, selling their skills to established regimes. The Byzantine emperor and the Baghdad caliph alike took them into their service. In fact, states living on the edge of the nomadic world had long experience of absorbing such military peoples. It was normal practice to form regiments of invading tribes and use them to keep others out. In the eleventh and twelfth centuries, the Byzantines employed Normans, Varangians (Viking and English), and Turks, while the Cairo caliphate relied on Berber and Bedouin cavalry and on Nubian foot soldiers.

The Turkish nomads were such good warriors that they were soon recruited for their skills with bow and horse. Their traditional style of fighting was that of a cloud of skirmishers, but there was another tradition of fighting in the Middle East, known as the "cataphract," and for this, man and horse were both draped with flexible scale armor. Used primarily as shock troops, this cavalry fought in regular ranks and preferred the bow to the lance. Rulers also had bodyguards of this type bound to them as slaves—slavery did not have the same stigma attached as in the Christian West.

SALADIN

Salah al-Din, Sultan of Egypt 1169–93, served his military apprenticeship under Nur-ed Din, a leader who strove to unite the Muslims against the Crusaders. Saladin was thus able to base his power on Egypt, but it still needed his great strength of character to keep the forces of the disparate emirs in the field. He showed both strategic vision and tactical ability in handling his armies. If not quite the chivalrous opponent of Western legend, he was a shrewd politician, devoted to Islam and more merciful in his reconquest of Jerusalem than his Christian opponents. Although he suffered a succession of setbacks at the end of his life, Saladin had lived just long enough effectively to thwart the objectives of Richard I's Crusade.

BATTLE OF AYN JALUT

DATE September 3, 1260
CAMPAIGN Invasion of Syria by Mongols under Kitbugha against Mameluke Sultan Qutuz
OBJECT To conquer Syria and Egypt.
NUMBERS Mongols—two "tumans" at half strength, 10,000 horsemen, and a large proportion of non-Mongol subject troops; Mamelukes—12,000 cavalry, including elite guard troops and an unknown number of infantry.
DESCRIPTION Sultan Qutuz's dispositions concealed his greater strength. Baibars' feigned flight drew the Mongols into contact. Mongol allies fled on their left wing, while their right was overwhelmed by greater Mameluke numbers. As Qutuz and Kitbugha clashed, the Mamelukes achieved a double envelopment.
RESULT The Mongol force was destroyed and Kitbugha captured and executed.

Success of the Mamelukes

To be a ruler's slave-bodyguard was a way of reaching the highest position in a state. Such soldiers had been known for a long time in the east as *ghulams*, and in the thirteenth century, under an alternative name of Mamelukes, a group seized power in Egypt, ousting Saladin's dynasty. This happened at a time of political crisis, the invasion of Egypt by Louis of France and his Crusaders (1250). The results were enduring. The regime lasted until the Ottoman conquests in the early sixteenthth century, and as late as 1798 Mameluke cavalry fought Napoleon's army at the Battle of the Pyramids.

As a military dynasty, the Mamelukes trained carefully for warfare. Their *furusiyas,* or training manuals, still exist showing how a Mameluke had to be a complete warrior with bow, sword, and lance, both on horseback and on foot. They proved to be the only force in the Muslim East that could defeat the ferocious Mongols. This they did in 1260 after the destruction of Baghdad and the murder of the caliph there. The Mamelukes were expert in siege warfare. Their second and greatest sultan, Baibars, traveled on campaign with an artillery train of siege engines. The last castles of the Crusader states could not hold out against them and by the early fourteenth century, the Christians were driven back to Cyprus and Rhodes. The Mamelukes pressed on into Asia Minor, extinguishing the Christian Kingdom of Armenia in 1375. Here, they faced their eventual conquerors—the Ottomans.

THE OTTOMANS

The Osmanli dynasty grew from one of the small confederations of nomadic Turkish tribes in northeast Asia Minor around 1300. It was a "ghazi," or frontier state of Islam, pledged to conquer lands for the faith. In 1326 the Ottomans captured the important Byzantine city of Bursa, and then crossed over into Europe. In 1361, they took Edirne and began to conquer Greece and the Balkans. Their victory over the Serbs at Kosovo in 1389 reduced the Serbs to vassal status, and the noose began to close around their main goal—Constantinople. Defeat at the hands of Tamerlane, the Mongol conqueror in 1402, at Ankara, set back Ottoman expansion for half a century; but once recovered, the city's conquest was inevitable.

The reason for Ottoman success lay in their ability to combine all types of forces in their armies. Many of these were made up of Christian subjects fighting under their *voynik* lords. They also relied upon traditional nomadic Turkish cavalry for raiding and ravaging an enemy's territories and forcing him back into towns and fortresses, which could then be stormed or starved into submission. There was a strong element of religious fervor in Ottoman forces, spearheaded by the Dervish religious groups they sponsored and including *delis* (madmen), extravagantly costumed and fanatical warriors.

The army was largely a cavalry force based on the nomadic horse archer, but included more heavily armored *spahi* (soldier) cataphract types, raised along feudal lines. Infantry played an important role, both the ordinary Azab bow or spearmen and the elite Janissaries. Originally formed from prisoners of war, in 1438, the *devshirme,* or round up of young Christian boys, was instituted. Brought up as Muslims, they became fanatically loyal to their masters. They were better equipped than most infantry, specialists in the bow, crossbow, and later arquebus, and wore distinctive tall white caps.

The Ottoman army included skilled technicians in siege warfare and artillery. The successful sieges of Constantinople (1453) and Rhodes (1480) bear witness to this. Artillery was also used in the field. Guns and wagons defeated the Mamelukes at Chaldiran in 1515, while chained guns and a solid Janissary line gave victory over the Hungarians at Mohacs in 1526. The Ottomans spelled the end of the crusading movement. Impetuous Western cavalry were defeated by Bayezit at Nicopolis (1396) and by Murat II at Varna (1440), and Kosovo (1448). This combination of tactical and technical superiority made the Ottomans the greatest military force in the Mediterranean and Middle East until the end of the sixteenth century.

The art of fortification was not neglected in the East either. The Arab citadels of Cairo and Aleppo and the Rumeli Hisar, built by the Ottomans north of Constantinople on the Bosphorus, bear witness to this.

SIEGE OF CONSTANTINOPLE

DATE April 5–May 29, 1453
OBJECT Conquest of Constantinople by Turks
NUMBERS Turks—100,000 including 12,000 elite Janissaries and many cannon; Byzantines—7,000 men of which only Giustiniani's 500 Genoese were of good quality.
DESCRIPTION After establishing a blockade, the Turks made a naval attack, which was repulsed, on April 12. Superior Venetian vessels also defeated the Turks on April 20. But by the brilliant plan of transporting ships overland into the Golden Horn, Mehmet outmaneuvered the defenders. Meanwhile, Ottoman cannon blasted holes in the 1,000-year-old walls. Assaults on May 7 and 18 were repulsed, but eventually the Janissaries stormed the city.
RESULT Fall of Constantinople; death of Constantine amid the ruins.

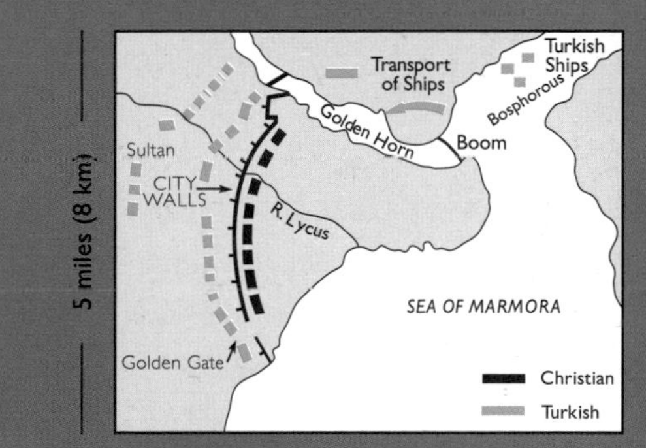

MEHMET II "THE CONQUEROR"

The conquest of Constantinople set the tone for Mehmet's reign (1452–80). The Ottoman empire had recovered from the humiliation of Ankara in 1402, when Bayezit was captured. Mehmet's personal slave troops numbered 7,000—just the elite of vast armies. Between 1458 and 1460, Greece was overrun. In 1459 Serbia and in 1463 Bosnia submitted, although Hungary held out under the leadership of John Hunyadi. War against Venice steadily reduced the Republic's territories and forced her to sue for peace in 1478. Mehmet won control of all the Black Sea, the Adriatic, and the eastern Mediterranean. In Anatolia, an army of 100,000 men was mobilized to defeat his Karaman enemies by 1474. Mehmet was a fanatic, pursuing religious, *ghazi* warfare to its logical conclusion, and this earned him the title "Conqueror."

ARMOR FROM 1100

From the First Crusade (1095–99), the Norman knight, in his chain-mail coat, or hauberk, encountered the armored horsemen of Byzantium and the Arabic Middle East. On the battlefields of Sicily, the Balkans, Asia Minor, and Palestine, two styles of warfare—Eastern and Western—clashed. The Normans relied on the mighty Frankish-style cavalry charge. The Byzantines and Arabs used lightly equipped, bow-armed cavalry, supported by heavily armored horses and riders carrying short spears and lances for the charge. This style of fighting was ancient. It dated back to the Persians who fought Alexander the Great in the fourth century BC. Like the Eastern heavy cavalry, they, too, wore scale armor (small metal plates attached to a cloth garment in the manner of fish scales,) chain mail, and lamellar armor (small strips of iron or toughened leather laced together to form a continuous flexible sheet.) Despite all this protective armor, the Norman knights' charge was very effective, and there are stories of Arabs in the early twelfth century delightedly adopting the armor captured from their western enemies.

Over the next three centuries, the knight became more and more heavily armored, as smiths grew increasingly adept at fashioning the studs that made the rings of mail, and at producing steel plate in larger and larger pieces. The knights of the Third Crusade (1189–92) wore mail "pants", carried smaller shields, and had rounded helmets—better for warding off blows—with noseguards. By the time of the Fall of Acre (1292), a well-equipped knight would have had an all-

(Left) Chain mail—so called because it was composed of thousands of tiny interlocking rings—was the most consistently popular form of protection in the Middle Ages. The torso was protected by the hauberk and the head by a coif, the two parts often being made in one piece. It would have required a fairly substantial cloth shirt to be worn underneath to prevent the metal from chafing the skin, and would probably have had a surcoat on top to keep the iron dry in bad weather and also to carry the wearer's blazon or coat of arms.

(Left) Henry VIII's foot armor. By 1400, plate armor had developed to such a degree that it covered the entire body in a flexible shell. It was not as heavy as is popularly supposed. A full field armor weighed between 45 and 55 pounds (20 and 25 kg), less than a modern infantry pack and better distributed over the body.

metal helmet that covered his entire head, with just a couple of slits for the eyes. The shield had become smaller still and was triangular instead of kite shaped. Small plate reinforcements protected the knee.

At the battle of Nicopolis in 1396, the knights' helmets had visors to see through, which could be raised up or down to cover or uncover the face. The knights also wore gauntlets on their hands, a cuirass on the chest and back, and frontal leg and foot protection, all of which were made of steel plate. A hundred years later, during the French invasion of Italy in 1494, the knights were covered in steel plate from head to foot and were virtually invulnerable in single combat. They often dispensed with the shield altogether.

Yet while all this development was taking place, the knight's role on the battlefield was becoming less and less significant. During the fourteenth and fifteenth centuries, the foot soldier equipped with long bow, hand gun, or halberd triumphed repeatedly over the mounted knight, who increasingly found himself obliged to fight on foot, after his horse had been felled. Protection for the horse could never be made as comprehensive as protection for the rider. The last great mounted charge by fully armored cavalry was made at Pavia in 1525. However, helmets and cuirasses were still worn by cavalry until the end of the nineteenth century.

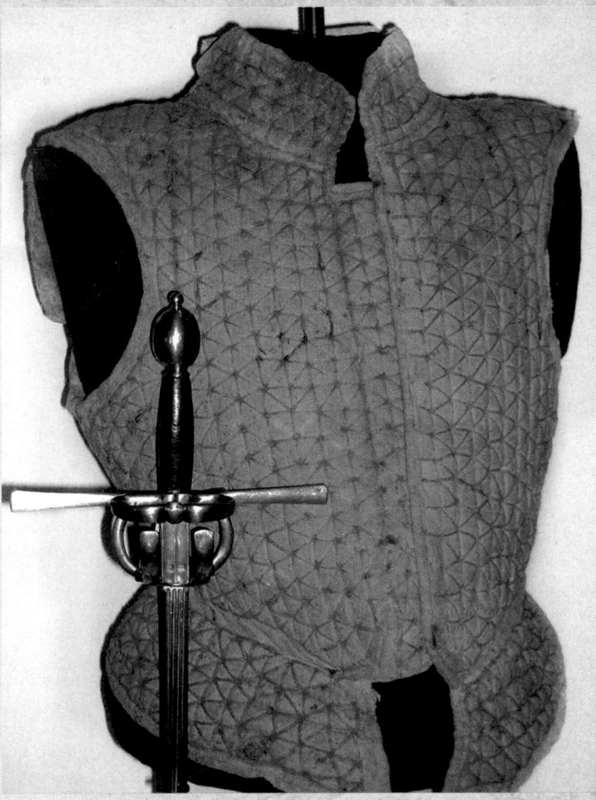

Jack of plate armor with iron plates sewn between layers of felt and canvas. The jack is similar to the brigandine that had the plates riveted into place in an overlapping pattern to give protection with some degree of suppleness.

THE ARMORED INFANTRYMAN

Mobility was as important to the foot soldier as it was to the cavalryman. He therefore wore lighter armor than the mounted soldier. A succession of snapshots of a medieval infantryman would show, as in the case of the knight, the gradual development of more thorough protection. Initially, non-metallic materials were worn, in the form of a quilted linen tunic stuffed with cotton or old rags. Known to Arabs as *al-Qutun*, which is the word for "cotton," westerners called it an akheton or gambeson. Gradually, the linen outer cover was replaced by leather, and small metal plates or scales were substituted for the cotton stuffing. This was called the "coat of plates" or "brigandine." A third form of protection, one also worn by knights, was a treated leather known as cuir-bolli. The leather was boiled and beaten into shape, then allowed to dry. Wealthy foot soldiers could afford mail shirts and, by the end of the fourteenth century, plate cuirasses and plate armor for the arms and legs.

During the sixteenth and seventeenth centuries armor tended to be discarded. However, it never disappeared entirely, as the gorget of the eighteenth-century noncommissioned officer or, more recently, the flak jackets and helmets of the World War II have shown. Since 1945, it has undergone a revival in the shape of lightweight body armor—the bulletproof vest—made from materials such as Kevlar, a synthetic fiber developed in the 1960s and worn by armies since the 1980s.

BOWS AND PIKES

Although infantry had always been important in medieval armies, there is no doubt that their significance grew in relation to the knights from ca. 1300 onward. The battle of Courtrai in 1302 is often taken as a decisive moment in the contest between cavalry and infantry. Flemish townsmen wielding long spears and *goedendags* ("good days," an ironically named ironbound club with a sharp spike) and crossbows saw off the flower of French chivalry, inflicting great loss. It should not be forgotten, however, that the Flemings were positioned behind dykes and ditches, and it was the tactical incompetence of the French, whose commander, Robert, Count of Artois, delivered frontal charges against this strong position, which led to the disaster. In the following year, faced with a hedgehog formation of spears, the French attempted nothing more than piecemeal assaults by small groups. Scottish *schiltrons* of spearmen similarly withstood English cavalry at Bannockburn in 1314. In a defensive position, good foot soldiers were as impregnable as the British squares at Waterloo were to the French cuirassiers, but they had the same weakness—they could not advance in the face of well-handled cavalry.

There was nothing new in the use of bodies of spearmen or pikemen, but the English contribution to warfare was to be the exploitation of mass archery fire. Already the armies of Edward I had employed large numbers of Welsh bowmen. They carried a weapon usually called a longbow, a simple stave 5 to 6 feet (1.5 to 1.8 m) long with an effective range of more than 200 yards (180 m). Unlike the slow-firing crossbow, an expert archer could release 6 to 12 shafts a minute, depending on his needs. This put down a concentrated barrage of missiles that few could penetrate. Edward II's defeat at Bannockburn was largely due to his inability to bring his battle-winning force into action; something Robert the Bruce maneuvered to prevent. At Halidon Hill in 1333, the Scots met defeat at the hands of well-deployed archers. This was the first of many victories to be won by English archers in the fourteenth and fifteenth centuries. They became the most sought-after troops in Europe.

They were put to good use in the long-running series of wars between England and France known as the Hundred Years War (1338–1453). What started as a legal dispute between Edward III of England and Philip VI of France over Edward's possessions in Gascony

An English force, headed by archers, drives away a Scottish army. Although of lower social standing than men-at-arms, trained archers were recognized as the best all-round soldiers. In the foreground, others engage in a favorite activity: pillaging.

became a struggle for the throne of France itself. The war began with French aggression—raids and the burning of towns on the southern English coast. This ended with the destruction of the French fleet at Sluys in 1340. Here, too, the archers had a part to play. Sluys was fought very much like a land battle, with ships packed together, allowing the withering storm of arrows to sweep enemy decks. The English fought the war on land by the method known as *chevauchée,* which meant a ride through enemy territories, often sacking and burning town and countryside alike. This had the dual purpose of undermining the political allegiance of an area to the French crown, and, when it suited the English, of challenging the French to do battle.

Crécy and beyond

This is probably what Edward III intended in the campaign of 1346. He marched his army of 11,000 men, three-quarters of whom were archers, toward Paris and then withdrew north. The French pursued and nearly trapped the English at the Somme, but Edward slipped across the fords of Blanchetacque near the river's mouth and took up position at Crécy. He dismounted all his men-at-arms, supported them with the archers, and had pits dug to protect the battle line. When the French arrived, they hurled themselves into battle piecemeal, in a series of cavalry charges, and suffered a humiliating defeat.

Ten years later, his son Edward the Black Prince, who had won his spurs at Crécy, scored another great success. Following a very lucrative *chevauchée* south from Bordeaux to the Mediterranean in 1355, Edward decided to march north the following year. He was supposed to have met up with another English force on the Loire, but this did not transpire and the Black Prince led his army and its wagon loads of booty back to just south of Poitiers. Here, John of France caught up with him. The French had 13,000 men, about double Edward's small force. Dismounting, the French came on toward the English position behind a small hedge and the hand-to-hand fighting was long and hard. An English mounted counterattack won the day, and John and most of his nobility were captured.

Such victories as this won for the English the reputation as the foremost military nation in Europe and made their archers the most desirable as mercenaries. John Hawkwood's White Company won great renown in Italy, where city-states employed large numbers of such troops. Companies of mercenaries serving no one except themselves terrorized much of France at the time. They won the name of *Ecorcheurs,* or "flayers," for the devastation they wrought. The peasantry, who were already suffering from the ravages of the Black Death, had no choice but to join together themselves to attack such bandits. Mercenaries had now become an integral part of warfare.

BERTRAND DU GUESCLIN

Du Guesclin rose from a family of Breton minor nobility to be Constable of France, the highest military position in the kingdom, from 1369 to 1380. With Charles V, he reversed the trend of the war with England. He had cause to know and rue English skill in war, being captured and ransomed several times, once at the battle of Auray in 1364. He led another army to defeat at the hands of English bowmen at Nájera in 1367, during the Black Prince's Spanish expedition. But he then replaced the battle-seeking strategy of the 1340s and 1350s with "scorched earth" and the harrying of English *chevauchées.* In 1370, Sir John Knollys, and in 1373 John of Gaunt, both struggled home with their armies in tatters and no booty to show for it. Du Guesclin died fighting English mercenaries in Languedoc.

BATTLE OF AGINCOURT

DATE October 26, 1415
CAMPAIGN Invasion of France by Henry V of England against the armies of Charles VI
OBJECT To show that an English army could march unhindered to Calais across French territory.
NUMBERS English—1,000 men-at-arms and 5,000 archers led by Henry; French—20,000 to 25,000 men-at-arms plus large numbers of unengaged foot under joint and confused command by French nobles.
DESCRIPTION Forced to fight vastly superior French forces, Henry was able to put them at a disadvantage on a cramped battlefield between two woods, where the superiority of the enemy numbers was nullified. As the French chose not to attack, Henry seized the initiative and advanced into bowshot. Now his deadly archers, protected by stakes, shot down a cavalry charge and threw the dismounted knights' attack into confusion. The tiny English army then charged and routed the French. Late in the day, fears of French recovery persuaded Henry to massacre some of his prisoners.
CASUALTIES On the English side a few hundred men, including such notables as the Duke of York; the French lost 5,000–6,000 killed and many thousands of captives, including their greatest nobles.
RESULT A huge blow to French military prestige, which meant that the French were unwilling to offer battle for many years.

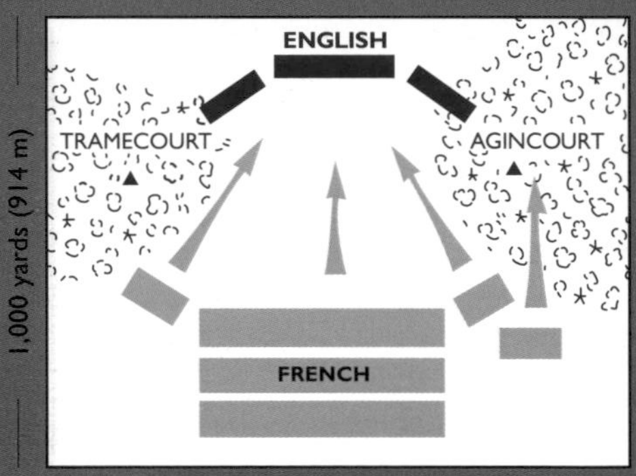

Rulers who wanted to raise troops for a campaign recruited paid soldiers rather than calling upon feudal obligation. In England, this system was known as indenture. Men of all stations from prominent lords to local squires contracted with the government to bring along their retinues. Some men, such as Sir John Fastolf, made a fortune from such contracts, receiving both money and grants of land in payment. Troops were divided between "lances" (that is to say men-at-arms and their body servants) and archers. An increasingly large proportion of archers were mounted. This gave the force great mobility, suitable for *chevauchée*. Indeed, such bowmen were very like the later dragoons, who took their firepower to where it could be used most effectively. The effectiveness of archery is shown by the increasing proportion of archers in English armies from 2:1 to men-at-arms in the mid-fourteenth century to 10:1 in Edward IV's planned expedition of 1475.

The increasing importance of missile weapons had another result: the development of more sophisticated armor. Pieces of plate armor had been added to mail from the mid-thirteenth century, first at the knee, elbow, and shoulder and then as a coat of plates not unlike a modern flak jacket. In the mid-fourteenth century developments in metalworking produced articulated coverings for the limbs and a heavy, visored helmet. By the early fifteenth century, a complete suit was achieved, known as "white armor", because the entire body was covered in polished steel. It was still possible for arrows to penetrate plate, but only because arrows had developed as well, with bodkin heads that bored their way through the metal like modern armor-piercing shells. At Agincourt, the English archers were able to shoot into the heavy French helmets at short range. But already, on the battlefields of Europe, a weapon was appearing that was to supplant the deadly longbow—the gunpowder handgun.

GUNS AND FOOT SOLDIERS

While the longbow dominated tactics in the Anglo-French wars, developments in central and southern Europe pointed in another direction. These were as a result of wars of independence from feudal overlords in Switzerland and Bohemia.

In 1315, at Mortgarten a small force of Swiss infantry had attacked and routed superior numbers of well-equipped Austrians. Admittedly, this was an ambush—the Swiss attacked a marching column in a narrow defile, and broke the Austrian ranks by rolling down rocks and logs—but their ferocious follow up attack with halberds tore the knightly opposition apart. In 1339, at Laupen, the Swiss faced Burgundian cavalry and infantry, but the combination of pikemen and archers was more than enough to beat this force. The problem faced by many armies was the coordination of infantry and cavalry on the battlefield. One solution, as we have seen, was to dismount the knights and attack on foot. This is what the Austrians attempted at Sempach in 1386. The heavily armored knights did force the Swiss phalanx back, but they had no response to a Swiss counterattack. Contemporaries commented on the Swiss bravery and discipline, which gave them victory.

The wagon fort

The idea that infantry should possess these virtues came as something of a surprise to these writers, conditioned as they were to associate military values with the knightly classes. The events in Bohemia following the death of Jan Hus, condemned as a heretic at the Council of Constance in 1415, were to shake these assumptions still farther. Bohemia rose in revolt against the Holy Roman emperor, and under the leadership of Jan Ziska, a new method of fighting was developed. He took the ancient idea of the wagon fort and equipped it with artillery, handguns, crossbows, and infantry carrying various vicious pole arms. The most primitive of these was the flail, which symbolized the peasant nature of the revolt against authority. This was a good defensive formation, as his victory at Prague in 1419 proved, but Ziska then developed mobile wagons, which allowed him to attack at Kutna Hora in 1422. The Hussites defeated the emperor's forces many times, even after Ziska's death in 1424. They were inspired by reformist religious fervor and even the sound of their hymns was enough to persuade the enemy to flee. They were irresistible in the field for two decades, but, like many revolutionaries, they were destroyed by internal dissension when the moderate Ultraquists defeated the radical Taborites at Lipani in 1334. However, the artillery-equipped wagon fort had made a permanent contribution to warfare. John Hunyadi (1437–56) and his son Matthias Corvinus (1456–90) were able to defend Hungary from the Turks by its use.

HENRY V

Henry V, King of England from 1415 to 1422, was the foremost commander of his age. He had had a long military career before his invasion of France in 1415. From the age of 15 he fought Owain Glyndwr for the control of Wales (1402–5). In 1403, he commanded the left wing at the Battle of Shrewsbury against the Percy rebels. Having learned the hard lessons of warfare, he prepared meticulously for the siege of Harfleur in 1415 and took the town in five weeks. His *chevauchée* to Calais was nearly disastrous, but tactical cunning saw him through. The mature general emerged in the conquest of Normandy from 1417–20. By determined sieges, he subdued the duchy and forced Charles VI into the Treaty of Troyes, recognizing Henry as his heir. Henry died at the siege of Meaux in 1422.

LONGBOWS AND CROSSBOWS

The bow is simply a spring by which an arrow can be launched with far greater speed than can be accomplished by the unaided arm, so increasing range and velocity. It also allows for greater accuracy and penetrative ability. The bow appears to have originated in North Africa in the Paleolithic era, and spread throughout the Mediterranean area and into Europe and Asia; and it seems to have evolved independently in the Americas, Australia, and Tasmania. It was in use throughout the world by at least 8000 BC and has appeared in an enormous number of forms.

(Left) An early Bronze Age arrowhead dating from ca. 1800 BC bears witness to the use of flint even after the discovery of metal. The skilled crafting of the barb ensured the head stayed in the wound.

LONGBOWS

Simple bows are made from a stave of springy wood, to one end of which a strong cord is permanently attached. The other end of the cord is formed into a loop, and to use the bow, the stave is bent into a curve and the looped end of the cord slipped over the other end into a prepared notch. Staves have been made of virtually every kind of strong, resilient wood. The English longbow was made of yew, although elm was sometimes used when yew was not available.

The arrow could be fashioned from almost any straight piece of wood, keeping in mind that its stiffness affected its accuracy. The arrow was prepared with a notch—or "nock"—at the rear end into which the bowstring fitted, and a head at the other end, which could be anything from the tip of the wood (fire hardened) to complex and ornate shapes of stone, bone, petrified wood, ivory, jade, or metal. Stability in flight was provided by "fletching" the arrow, that is, fitting stabilizing "flights" at the tail end. These were usually two, three, or four feathers, arranged symmetrically around the shaft and attached by gluing or binding. Some arrows, notably those used by Bushmen and other indigenous peoples, are without flights, but these can be used with accuracy at only short ranges. For the maximum range, flights are essential, giving a degree of aerodynamic lift to the arrow as well as ensuring that it flies straight.

Japanese and Burmese bows often had far more bow above the shooter's hand than below it. This odd shape allowed the use of a large bow without it fouling the ground, useful for mounted archers.

Where suitable wood was not readily available, compound bows were developed, usually consisting of a wooden stave as the supporting structure to which were added other materials to provide springiness. Eskimo archers attached a number of strings of sinew to the back of the stave to provide the desired tension. Other systems

This depiction of the Battle of Agincourt (1415) from Froissart's "Chronicles" records the importance of the longbow in that battle. In reality, the French army was approximately three times larger than the English.

included the use of horn or sinew as a laminate, or both on opposite sides of the bow stave. One result of these constructions was to change the simple shape of the bow from a plain curve into a double reverse curve, a shape particularly common among Turkic nomads and indigenous Americans.

CROSSBOWS

The crossbow appeared in China around 500 BC. How it arrived in Europe is a matter of some conjecture—possibly with the Byzantines, Saracens, and Huns—but by the twelfth century, it had become a popular weapon throughout Europe. At its simplest, the crossbow is a conventional bow mounted upon a shoulder stock, but the mechanizing of the bow produced an exceptionally powerful weapon, which had a maximum range of about 350 yards (320 m), comfortably outranging the longbow's 200yards (183 m). Its principal defect was its slow rate of fire. A heavy crossbow could fire one shot per minute, the lighter crossbows perhaps four shots per minute, whereas a skilled long bowman could release 6 to 12 shots in a minute. In medieval warfare, where the target was generally massed ranks of men, rate of fire counted for more than precise accuracy.

The matter of drawing the crossbow also caused problems. The simplest way was to fit a stirrup to the forward end of the stock, place this on the ground and put one foot into it, then seize the string with both hands and draw it up until it could be lodged in its catch. The "claw" was a simple hook attached to the man's belt; he stood on the stirrup, bent forward, and hooked the claw onto the string, then straightened up, and so drew the bow. Another method was the "goat-foot" lever, a claw-like contrivance that hooked onto pivots on the sides of the stock and, by means of a hinged hook, levered the bowstring back.

Once drawn, the string was retained by a catch, and the projectile, generally known as a bolt or "quarrel" (from the French *carreau*—the square section of the tip), was laid in a groove in the stock. Pressing a trigger released the string, and the strength of a compound bow propelled the quarrel at high velocity, sufficient to pierce chain mail at a 100-yard (90-m) distance.

A compound crossbow made of horn, sinew, and wood needed a small windlass to draw the bowstring back. The windlass was hooked onto the bow and the pulley hooks engaged with the cord. The archer stood on the stirrup, at the end of the bow stock, and wound the handles to draw the cord back until it could be held by the catch.

First standing armies

Meanwhile, in Western Europe a development was taking place that was to set the scene for the standing armies of the modern world. In France and Burgundy permanently maintained forces called ordinance companies were established. Initially, this may have been an expedient by Charles VII to control the excessive numbers of professional soldiers in his kingdom in 1445 as a result of the war with England. He declared that there should be 1,800 men-at-arms, 3,600 archers, and 1,800 lightly armed horsemen. As well as providing a standing army this was an attempt to create a balanced force, combining the strike power and mobility of knightly cavalry and the missile impact of the archers. His successor, Louis XI, recruited 8,000 Swiss foot to provide a solid infantry.

In Burgundy, in 1472, Charles the Bold's ordinance Companies comprised 1,200 men-at-arms, 600 mounted crossbowmen, 3,000 mounted archers, 2,000 pikemen, and 1,000 foot archers. This was a balanced all-arms force, and Charles also experimented with light field artillery drawn on wheeled carriages.

English forces continued to contain large numbers of archers until the mid-sixteenth century. During the latter stages of the Hundred Years War, they delivered victory as long as they were properly employed. The rashness of Thomas, Duke of Clarence pointed the moral at Baugé in 1421. Rushing on ahead of his archers, he met defeat and death at the hands of the Armagnacs. The English had their revenge at Cravant in 1423 and at Verneuil in the following year. This battle was interesting from a tactical point of view because the French employed archers, too—Scotsmen—who conducted a bloody shooting match with the English. The battle was eventually won by the English reserve, also bow-armed.

French revival began with Joan of Arc, whose inspiration led to the relief of the siege of Orléans and to victory at Patay in 1429. Even then, English archery defeated the French at Beauvais in the following year. Recognizing the importance of archery, Charles VII instituted a native force of "free archers" as part of his army reforms.

Effect of heavy artillery

The defeat of England in the Hundred Years War is often related to the development of gunpowder weapons. This is true insofar as the heavy siege artillery with which the Bureau brothers provided Charles VII assured the capture of English-held towns and fortresses, but not at a tactical level. At Formigny in 1450, when Sir Thomas Kyriell's *chevauchée* was trapped and annihilated by the French, artillery was present, but the arrival of a flanking force decided the issue. At Castillon in 1453, Sir John Talbot's hot-headed charge against entrenched

BATTLE OF NANCY

DATE January 5, 1477

CAMPAIGN Charles the Bold's attempt to create a Burgundian empire, against René, Duke of Lorraine, and Swiss cantons

OBJECT To take Nancy, besieged on October 22, 1476.

NUMBERS Burgundians—7,000, including 1,136 mounted men-at-arms, 1,788 mounted archers, 2,463 infantry; allies—14,000 plus 6,000 veteran Swiss.

DESCRIPTION The Swiss cantons did not want to campaign in winter, but René persuaded them to provide a relief force. The allies cut Charles's supply lines in early December. He marched to meet the relief force and barred the way with his artillery. Marching through terrible conditions of ice and snow, the Swiss managed to outflank the Burgundian position. Then, coordinating their attack with the main body by horn blasts, they charged and routed the enemy.

CASUALTIES The Burgundian army was destroyed, and Charles was killed in the rout.

RESULT The end of independent Burgundy.

artillery, both large pieces and 700 handgunners, led to an English disaster, rather than any intrinsic superiority of gunpowder weapons. More important to France's eventual victory was the end of the Anglo-Burgundian alliance in 1435, and Charles VII's effective royal control in contrast to the pathetic Henry VI's command.

Wars of the Roses

Henry's weakness and the resulting noble faction-fighting led to civil war in England, usually called the Wars of the Roses, because the protagonists were the Houses of York (white rose emblem) and Lancaster (red rose). There were 16 major engagements between St. Albans in 1455 and Stoke in 1487, when the Tudor Henry VII finally consolidated his rule. Tactically, they were unexceptional, often decided by the defection of an important noble and his following in the course of battle. This was the case at Northampton in 1460, where it enabled the Yorkists to storm an entrenched position defended with artillery; in the second battle of St. Albans in 1461, a Lancastrian victory; and famously at Bosworth in 1485, where Lord Stanley's late intervention led to the death of Richard III and Tudor victory. Edward IV, Yorkist king 1461–70 and 1471–83, was a commander of real genius. Returning from France (after his temporary deposition), he won a victory at Barnet on April 14, 1471. Just three weeks later (May 4), he had force marched his army west to Tewkesbury, where he won another decisive victory and secured his throne.

Swiss dominance

However, the wars that pointed the way to the armies of the sixteenth century were fought not in the British Isles but in Central Europe. Charles the Bold had created a military force with which to turn his collection of possessions into an empire. This brought him into conflict with the Swiss cantons and their victory over the Burgundians assured the dominance of the pike for the next 200 years. In fact, the Swiss infantry was still largely composed of halberdiers, although the proportion of pikemen had increased throughout the fifteenth century.

The crossbow and the halberd were popular infantry weapons. Used in combination by the Swiss, they were battle winners. Unlike the longbow, the crossbow did not need years of training to acquire expertise, nor great strength to use.

It seemed that Charles's "modern" army of cavalry, archers, and mobile field guns would be invincible, but at Grandson on March 2, 1475, he was unable to coordinate these elements in the face of a determined Swiss attack. Their infantry blocks, supported by smaller units of crossbows and handguns, unnerved Charles's mercenaries, who fled. The blow was to Burgundian prestige rather than any great physical loss.

The next clash came before the walls of Murten, which Charles was besieging, on June 22. The Burgundians had established a defensive entrenchment designed to be manned by guns and archers, but the Swiss surprised Charles's army. Three great columns of infantry maneuvered with discipline to overwhelm the piecemeal attacks of the enemy, who suffered heavy loss.

The final act was played out at Nancy six months later, when Charles lost his army, his empire, and his life. The Swiss went on to become the most popular soldiers and mercenaries in Europe for another three centuries.

SIEGE TECHNIQUES AND ARTILLERY: 1100–1480

The importance of fortifications in medieval warfare ensured that careful attention was paid to the art of taking them. It was an area where techniques and technology made great advances throughout the period. In the eleventh century the advantage lay with the defenders. It took William, as the young Duke of Normandy, two years to reduce the castle of Brionne, secure in the middle of a river. He had to employ the most ancient, although eventually successful, approach of blockade.

William was not so patient later in his career, overwhelming Exeter in 1067 in short order. In this case, the choice was to go over or under the defenders' walls—or to use a combination of the two. Mining was used throughout the Middle Ages but it was dependent on suitable conditions (a water barrier was the most difficult to overcome) and also the presence of the necessary specialists. Miners had to be brought from all over England for King John's siege of Rochester castle in 1215.

In order to go over the walls, attackers built huge wooden siege towers moved up on wheels or rollers. The towers had bridges suspended from their upper stories to carry storming parties. This is how Jerusalem was captured in 1099.

Any attack was preceded by a battering from artillery. This consisted of *mangonels* or *petraries* (stone throwers), which were torsion-powered wooden engines. By the mid-twelfth century, as a result of contact with the Arabs, the Crusaders had developed the *trebuchet*—a counterweighted machine that could hurl huge boulders 200–400 yards (180–360 m). Such artillery was in use at the siege of Acre by the Crusaders in 1190. During the thirteenth century trebuchets were the foremost siege weapon.

By 1330, the weapon that was eventually going to transform warfare—the gun fired by exploding powder—made its appearance

(Below) A huge trebuchet, its heavy counterweight suspended between the massive uprights, the missile slung from the firing arm.

in the West. The Mongols had been using rockets and other incendiary weapons a century earlier, but it was the development of the technology of cast metal pots and tubes, based upon bell founding, that produced a powerful artillery. These weapons had the advantage of containing the force of the explosion and so increasing its propulsive force. Edward III used such artillery when he besieged Calais after his great victory at Crécy in 1346, but the town was eventually taken by starving out its defenders.

Heavy siege artillery took time to develop. Henry V terrorized France with it from 1415–22. Charles VII of France recovered his kingdom with an irresistible train in the 1440s. The possession of heavy guns by an attacker was enough to make most defenders surrender without a fight before their walls were shattered. In the East, only the Ottomans paid attention to developing gunpowder artillery at this time. Employing Western experts, they used it successfully in the sieges of Constantinople in 1453 and Rhodes in 1480.

(Left) The fortress's attackers are assaulting the main gate using a combination of battering ram and mining to make a breach for storming. Trenches and wooden fences protect the attackers.

(Right) Calais was besieged by the English in 1346–47 resulting in Calais fealling under English control, remaining as such until 1558, providing a foothold for English raids in France.

7 THE GUNPOWDER REVOLUTION

Although gunpowder and guns were to change the entire concept of warfare during the Renaissance, both had been in existence for a very long time. The first definite reference to gunpowder and its potential use in the West occurs as a cryptogram contained in a manuscript written in 1242 by the friar and alchemist Roger Bacon. From this it is clear that Bacon was aware of its explosive properties and that these could be controlled. His recourse to secrecy stems from the attitude of the Church, which, the previous century, had laid an anathema upon any who made fiery substances for military purposes; this may refer to such products as Greek Fire, which had been known for many centuries, but equally its intention may have been to include black powder in the overall context of prohibited materials. Be that as it may, it is apparent from Bacon's text that some degree of development and experiment had taken place prior to 1242. It is thought gunpowder actually originated in China.

BLACK ARTS

The suggestion that the gun was invented accidentally by a German monk named Berthold Schwarz does not bear serious examination because there is some doubt that he ever existed, and the first documentary evidence of artillery in action appears in a manuscript of 1325 showing a primitive cannon firing at the walls of La Rochelle, predating the period in which he is supposed to have worked. The first authenticated use of cannon in open warfare was at the Battle of Crécy in 1346, where Edward III employed three. The first handgun had been developed by 1388.

Although presented with a *fait accompli,* the Church still did not like guns and warned those involved in their use that they were dabbling in the Black Arts. These early weapons were extremely expensive to produce and dangerous to friend and foe alike. Terrible accidents were frequent. During their training, gunners were told that it was "unseemly" to trample on powder that had been spilled around the gun, not because this was considered unmannerly, but because the unstable compound could ignite and cause a major explosion. Rather than become involved in the heavy cost of establishing their own artillery park, kings setting out on campaign would rent their guns and gunners from contractors, much as a present-day construction company rent its plant.

Nevertheless, the quality of guns and the skill of artillerymen improved with the passing of time. At the battles of Formigny (1450) and Castillon (1453), the formidable English archers were defeated by artillery, which outranged them. Moreover, as the fifteenth century drew to its close, the feudal system was replaced by strong central administrations across Europe. Thus, for the first time national instead of private funds were available for the development and comparatively large-scale manufacture of artillery and other firearms, and this impetus produced the revolution in methods by which land and sea warfare were conducted. By modern standards, the revolutionary process was slow, taking almost two centuries to complete, and its application was uneven, changes occurring at different times and in different places. Taken as a whole, however, the period is extremely important in the history of warfare, covering as it does the difficult transition from medieval to modern methods. At Bosworth Field (1485), men thought and fought in the medieval manner; at Blenheim (1704), their thinking and actions were recognizably modern.

COMPARATIVE RANGES

LONGBOW: accurate to 200 yards (183 m)
PISTOL: accurate to 10 yards (9 m)
MATCHLOCK ARQUEBUS: accurate to 50 yards (46 m)
FLINTLOCK MUSKET: accurate to 75 yards (68.5 m)

LIGHT CANNON (SAKER) firing 5-pound shot:
accurate to 350 yards (320 m)
maximum range 1,700 yards (1,554 m)
MEDIUM CANNON (CULVERIN) firing 17-pound shot:
accurate to 400 yards (366 m)
maximum range 2,500 yards (2,286 m)
HEAVY CANNON (CANNON) firing 60-pound shot:
maximum range 2,000 yards (1,829 m)

BATTLE OF BOSWORTH FIELD

DATE August 22, 1485
CAMPAIGN Wars of the Roses
OBJECT The Yorkist king, Richard III, was attempting to intercept the Lancastrian claimant to the throne, Henry Tudor, who was marching on London.
NUMBERS Yorkists—12,000, plus a small number of guns; Lancastrians—10,000.
DESCRIPTION Richard's army was drawn up with its pikemen and billmen in the center, flanked by cavalry, with an extended "forward" of archers and billmen in front; the position of his guns is unknown, but it is almost certain that they were aligned with the "forward." The majority of Henry's troops were cavalry, formed behind a "forward" of archers. On Ambion Hill, to the north of both armies, was a third and as yet uncommitted body of troops under Sir William Stanley. Henry had been promised their support, but Richard was fully aware of the Stanley family's sympathy for the Lancastrian cause and was holding Lord Stanley's son as hostage. For the moment, therefore, Sir William Stanley preserved a neutral stance. The battle began with an exchange of arrow flights, and Richard's guns fired a few rounds. The two armies then closed in a general mêlée. Richard led a personal attack on Henry but was killed in the process. At this point Sir William Stanley launched an attack on the Yorkist flank and the remainder of Richard's army fled. While small in scale, the battle was extremely important because the new king, Henry VII, restored stability to England and established a strong central administration.
CASUALTIES Yorkists—900; Lancastrians—100.
RESULT A decisive victory for the Lancastrians, which established the Tudor dynasty and ended the Wars of the Roses.

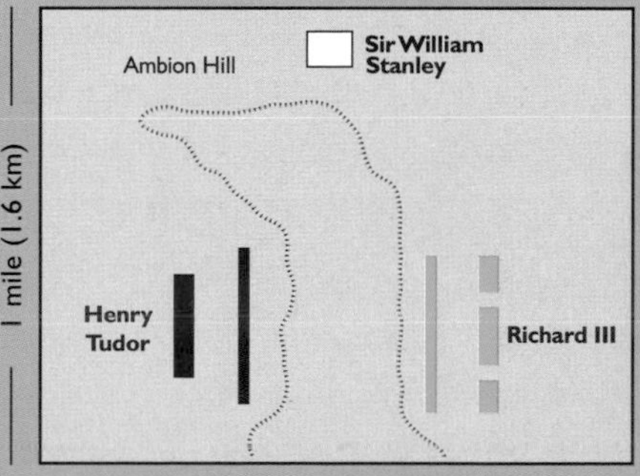

The Battle of Pavia 1525, one of a tapestry suite woven at Brussels ca. 1528-31 after cartoons by Bernard van Orley (ca. 1491–1542). A The Imperial army is shown breaking into the walled park on the French flank, with the French mounting their counterattack. In the background are the defenses of Pavia and the French siege lines, and the field works erected to block the, original advance of the Imperialists.

ARTILLERY AND LAND WARFARE

As the use of guns became commonplace, and exchequers were able to support the cost of their purchase, the possession of artillery began to reflect the status of monarchs and the old practice of hiring guns and gunners for campaigns and sieges was abandoned. For the moment, gun manufacture remained in private hands, although the business was international in its scope. Many of the guns purchased in this way were given individual names; Henry VIII, for example, bought a great deal of ordnance from the Low Countries during the early years of his reign, including a dozen matched guns, each of which was named after one of the apostles. Normally, gunmakers also provided powder, ammunition, and draft animals as part of the transaction. Once royal armies had been expanded by the addition of a permanent artillery park, it was entirely logical that the responsibility for this should rest with a corps of regular artillerymen, administered by master gunners and their assistants.

The roles performed by artillery in land campaigns were siege warfare, which employed the heaviest weapons, and field operations, in which lighter guns were used. The one problem that was never satisfactorily resolved during the period was the relative immobility of the arm. This was caused partly by the great weight of the weapons themselves, which, in turn, demanded heavy, cumbrous carriages from which they could be fired, and partly by the contemporary state of the roads, the best of which were little better than miry lanes. An additional complication was the fact that, while the professional status of the artilleryman had been recognized, the transport of the guns was still the responsibility of civilian contractors, who supplied oxen or horse teams and drivers. Needless to say, if a situation developed that was not to the contractors' liking, they were quite likely to make off with their animals and leave the guns stranded. Thus, the best speed at which artillery could be moved was walking pace, with the gunners trudging alongside, or even slower if oxen were employed. Munitions were carried separately, as part of the artillery train, and everything depended on the powder and ammunition wagons reaching the right place at the right time. It has been calculated that a siege train of 100 guns and 60 mortars required the support of 3,000 wagons, the whole pulled by 15,000 horses, occupying 15 miles (24 km) of road and traveling at about 2 mph (3 km/h).

This immobility was less of a disadvantage in siege warfare, unless the siege was broken, as at Pavia in 1525, when the guns could not be got away. On the battlefield, however, once the guns were emplaced they remained in position, the tide of battle ebbing and flowing past them, and because of this, their capture came to be regarded as tangible proof of victory.

Contemporary commanders were, of course, aware of the problem. Several attempts were made in the sixteenth century to standardize guns and, in the process of evolutionary development, somewhat lighter weapons and carriages were produced. The Swedish king Gustavus Adolphus introduced small battalion guns, which could be manhandled by infantrymen; and toward the end of the period, light galloper guns, drawn by a single horse, made their appearance.

During the seventeenth century, trail wheels were fitted to the carriages of some guns, and by 1680 these had evolved into the limber, which was simply a pair of wheels onto which the trail could be hooked, thereby spreading the load between four wheels instead of two; the concept of the limber as an ammunition carrier lay 100 years in the future.

Field-artillery tactics for much of the period were very simple. The guns were drawn up in front of the army's battle line and their first task was to silence their opposite numbers. Once this had been accomplished, they could set about firing into the packed ranks of the enemy army. By the end of the seventeenth century, however, a more scientific approach had begun to prevail, with guns being grouped to support other arms during specific phases of the engagement.

BATTLE OF PAVIA

DATE February 25, 1525

CAMPAIGN War between Francis I of France and Hapsburg Emperor Charles V.

OBJECT To break the French siege of Pavia.

NUMBERS Imperialists—total of 23,000 men under the Marquis of Pescara, including 12,000 German pikemen, 6,500 Spanish–Italian infantry and arquebusiers, 800 men-at-arms, 1,500 light cavalry, and 17 guns, plus the 6,000-strong besieged garrison of Pavia; French—total of 22,000 men under Francis I, including 4,000 Swiss and 5,000 French pikemen, 6,000 French and 3,000 Italian infantry and arquebusiers, 1,200 men-at-arms, 2,000 light cavalry, and 53 guns.

DESCRIPTION The Imperialist army approached Pavia at the end of January and entrenched; both sides engaged in an inconclusive bombardment across an unfordable stream. Under cover of a storm and artillery fire, Pescara broke the deadlock on the night of February 24-25 by marching north to cross the stream and penetrate a walled park on the French left, leaving a few men in his trenches to create the illusion that they were still occupied. Francis, taken by surprise, led a cavalry charge against the Imperial left center, while the rest of his army slowly changed front. His attack was at first successful, but the French horsemen were routed when a force of Spanish arquebusiers and pikemen fell on their rear while the Imperial cavalry counterattacked from the front. The French infantry, entering the battle piecemeal, were destroyed by superior numbers of halberdiers and arquebusiers. The French artillery played little part, the unexpected redeployment masking the fire of the few guns that could be brought up in time. The garrison of Pavia made a sally and destroyed those units that Francis had left in the siege lines. The battle, in which the use of small-arms firepower had played a major part, lasted a mere two hours.

CASUALTIES Imperialists—about 500 killed and wounded; French—about 13,000 killed and wounded, 5,000 captured and all artillery lost.

RESULT The French army was destroyed, Pavia relieved, and Francis I captured.

GUNS AND GUNPOWDER

The first picture of what is indisputably a gun appears in a manuscript of 1325 and shows a soldier applying a red-hot iron to the vent of a bulbous container from which a large arrow is being propelled by an explosion of the contents. It was soon apparent that a tube shape would be more effective and at first this was made by arranging red-hot iron bars around a mandrel and hammering to weld them together; white-hot iron hoops were then shrunk onto the tube to give it strength. Another method was to make short iron tubes shaped like bobbins, then join them together to form a barrel and reinforce the joints.

Bar and bobbin guns were difficult to seal at the breech end of the barrel, so most early guns were breechloaders, the breech consisting of a removable powder chamber closed at one end, secured by hammering a wedge between it and the rear of the gun cradle. Unfortunately, the major disadvantage of breechloaders was a backblast of gas and flame, which progressively reduced the weapon's efficiency the longer it was in action. For this reason, large caliber siege guns were muzzle-loaders, the chamber being fitted into the rear of the barrel by means of a screw mechanism or lugs.

By the second quarter of the fifteenth century, muzzle-loaders were being cast in one piece, using bronze. Shortly after that, trunnions were cast with the barrels. This permitted the latter to be secured to wheeled carriages by cap-squares, and, thus, increased the mobility of artillery, enabling it to accompany armies in the field. Trunnions also permitted gunners to elevate or depress barrels and so obtain variation in range.

By 1600, the number of guns in service was rising dramatically. They began to be classified by size and given generic names, such as cannon and culverin. The

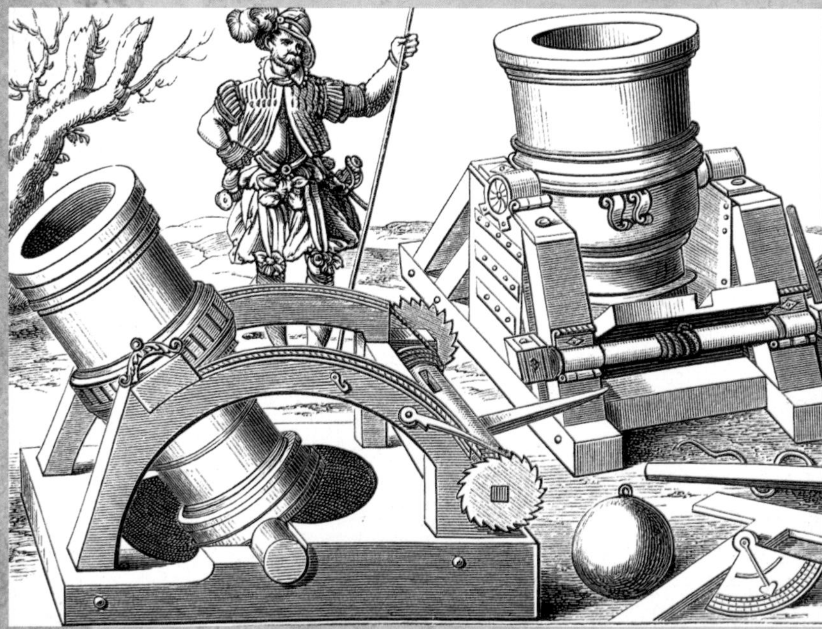

A mortar (ca. 1400) designed to generate high-angle fire. A shell would be fuzed to burst above the defenses.

A sixteenth-century gun located at Gripsholm castle, England. By the 16th century, cannon were made in a great variety of lengths and bore diameters, the longer the barrel, the longer the range.

ARTILLERY WEAPONS OF THE 16TH AND 17TH CENTURIES			
	Weight (lb)	Caliber (in)	Shot (lb)
Falconet	400	2.25	1.125
Falcon	750	2.75	2.5
Minion	1,100	3.25	4.75
Saker	1,900	3.75	6
Demi-Culverin	3,000	4.5	11.75
Culverin	4,300	5.25	16.25
Demi-Cannon	5,600	6.5	32
Cannon	8,000	8	64
A number of intermediate classifications also existed. By the end of the 17th century, guns began to be classified by their weight.			

short-barrel mortar, capable of high-angle fire, was also introduced during this period, and was joined in the seventeenth century by another high-angle weapon, the howitzer. The difference between the two was that while the mortar's elevation was fixed and variations in range were obtained by adjusting the charge, the howitzer's charge was fixed and its elevation could be altered. Once the blast furnace had been brought into use, it became possible to cast sound iron guns, which were cheaper to produce and more robust. Breechloading was eventually abandoned and the gun assumed the form it was to retain for 400 years.

Treated powder

Equally important to the new science of gunnery was the quality of the gunpowder. This varied widely and traveled badly until, early in the fifteenth century, someone hit on the idea of mixing the components in a wet state, allowing the result to dry and then passing it through a fine strainer to achieve a standard size of grain. The result, known as corned powder, was more powerful, traveled well, and was resistant to damp. Despite this, it took a very long time for it to be brought into common usage, partly because it was extremely expensive, and partly because the older guns could not withstand the increased pressure.

An arquebusier. His powder charges, measured and ready for use, were slung in a bandolier across his back, and one can be seen just below his left forearm; a small horn of priming powder is suspended from his neck. He carries a sword and pistol for his own defense during close-quarter fighting.

INFANTRY

At the end of the fifteenth century, the infantry element of most armies consisted of pikemen, halberdiers, and archers. The pikemen and halberdiers—the latter armed with a spear incorporating an ax blade just below its head, and sometimes a hook for dragging an opponent out of his ranks—wore helmet, breastplates and backplates, and flexible thigh pieces for protection during hand-to-hand fighting. The archers were more lightly equipped. This medieval array, rooted in centuries of feudal warfare and as yet not seriously compromised by cannon, was forced to adapt to changing conditions very quickly by the development of the arquebus, which evolved from a light antipersonnel gun normally mounted on the walls of fortifications.

Early versions of this weapon were tucked under the right arm and fired from an inclined rest spiked into the ground; later and somewhat smaller models were held against the chest and gripped with both hands. Both had very limited range and accuracy, but as early as 1503 Spanish arquebusiers under Gonzalo de Cordoba inflicted a convincing defeat on a conventional Franco–Swiss army at the battle of Cerignola. Cordoba preferred to position his arquebusiers in trenches or behind barricades, which not only provided a degree of protection but also increased accuracy. Units of pikemen and halberdiers were positioned nearby to repel enemy attacks. In open country, however, the arquebusiers were clearly vulnerable and were forced to rely on pikemen for their defense. The system adopted by the Spanish, and copied by the majority of European powers, was to form integrated units known as *tercios,* in which the arquebusiers were stationed in front of or on either flank of the pikemen, supporting the advance of the latter with their fire or retiring under the long pikes if they were attacked.

Farewell to arms

Two types of soldier, the halberdier and the archer, had no place in the new scheme of things. The halberd was too short to be of use in the changed conditions, and although halberdiers were present in considerable strength during the early battles of the period, their numbers declined steadily until, by the end of the sixteenth century, the use of the weapon was confined largely, but not exclusively, to the ceremonial role. The demise of the archer is more difficult to explain, because the protagonists of the longbow could claim, correctly, that the weapon had a much higher rate of fire, greater accuracy, and longer range than infantry firearms. This remained true as late as the middle of the nineteenth century. The arrow, however, was less effective against plate armor than it had been against chain mail, whereas the kinetic energy stored in an arquebus or musket ball, which was far larger and heavier than a modern small-arms round, enabled the missile to penetrate plate with ease and knock man or horse flat with its impact. In consequence, while archers continued to be employed both on land and at sea, their numbers also declined, and in 1595 a Royal Ordinance decreed that henceforth the English trained bands would arm themselves with firearms instead of the traditional longbow. Ironically, the introduction of firearms led to the reduction of infantry armor to helmet and breastplate, worn only by pikemen for protection during close-quarter combat.

Muskets and firing mechanisms

From the arquebus the musket was evolved, a more convenient weapon that could be fired from the shoulder, although at first a rest was still needed to support its 25 pounds (11-kg) weight. Normally, arquebusiers and musketeers fought in ranks 10 deep, the front rank discharging its weapons and then filing to the rear, where they reloaded as they made their way forward again by rotation, a system that enabled a continuous if proportionately narrow front of fire to be maintained.

The earliest firing mechanism was the matchlock, requiring the insertion of a burning slow match into the priming pan. The later wheel lock incorporated a toothed wheel, which, when activated by a trigger, struck sparks from a flint within the enclosed priming pan, thereby reducing the chances of an accidental discharge. The flintlock, in which a spring-loaded hammer containing a flint, again activated by a trigger, struck sparks into the pan, was less complex in its construction and less expensive to make. All three types of mechanism were used during the period, although by the end of the seventeenth century, the matchlock had all but disappeared and the flintlock, because of its simplicity, had been generally adopted for military use, witness the Brown Bess musket, the basic design of which was to serve the British soldier well for over 150 years.

MATCHLOCK AND WHEEL-LOCK MECHANISMS

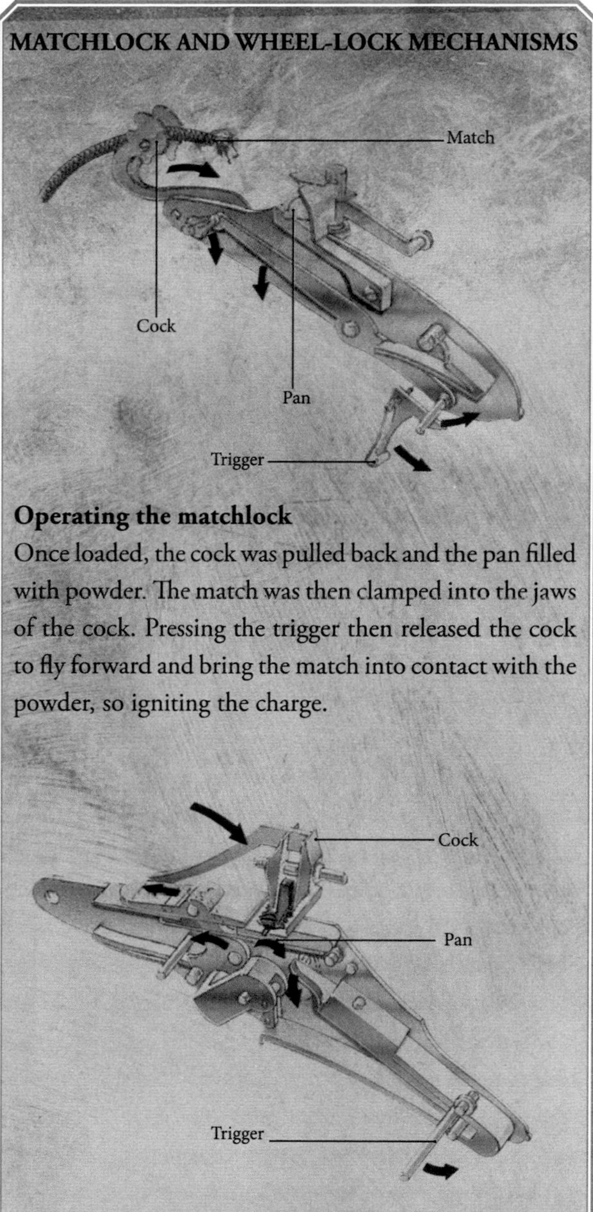

Operating the matchlock
Once loaded, the cock was pulled back and the pan filled with powder. The match was then clamped into the jaws of the cock. Pressing the trigger then released the cock to fly forward and bring the match into contact with the powder, so igniting the charge.

Operating the wheel-lock
The cock was pulled forward to the full cock position, the pan loaded with powder and the cover closed. The striking wheel was then wound uop.On pulling the trigger the pan cover slid away, the wheel spun, the cock fell and brought the pyrites into contact with the serrated edge, and the sparks flew into the pan to ignite the charge.

BATTLE OF BREITENFELD

DATE September 17, 1631
CAMPAIGN Thirty Years War.
OBJECT Gustavus Adolphus and the Elector of Saxony sought to recover Leipzig from the Imperialist–Catholic faction.
NUMBERS Protestants—total of 40,000 Swedes and Saxons, including 248 infantry companies, 170 cavalry squadrons, and 60 to 70 guns; Imperialists—total of 32,000 men under Tilly, including 21,000 infantry, 11,000 cavalry, and 30 guns.
DESCRIPTION Tilly's army was drawn up with 14 *tercio* blocks in the center and cavalry on either flank. The Swedish army also had infantry in the center and cavalry on the flanks, but its smaller units were deployed in two lines with detachments of musketeers supporting the cavalry, and the infantry had the support of 42 two-man battalion guns. The smaller and less flexible Saxon contingent was drawn up on the Swedish left. The battle began at noon with an artillery exchange. Tilly's intention was a double envelopment of the Protestant army. After about two hours the cavalry on the left of the Imperial army attempted to turn the Swedish right, but the Swedes extended their line by taking units from elsewhere, alternating musketry volleys with countercharges by their own cavalry. Meanwhile, the *tercios* attacked, routing the Saxons. The Swedish left immediately mounted a counterattack, driving some of the Imperial cavalry back into the *tercios*. The Swedes extended their flank, their combination of firepower and shock action compressing the pikemen until their weapons were useless. Advancing steadily, the Swedes recaptured the Saxon artillery, then took Tilly's own guns, turning them upon the struggling *tercios*. Gustavus Adolphus attacked on the right flank and the wreckage of the Imperial army was swept from the field. Tilly, wounded, had already been led away.
CASUALTIES Protestants—4,000 killed and wounded; Imperialists—7,000 killed and wounded, 6,000 captured, 8,000 surrendered subsequently in Leipzig.
RESULT Leipzig was taken, Tilly's army destroyed, the future of German Protestantism was assured.

Musketeer on the march, musket over his left shoulder and match burning at both ends in his left hand.

The first major changes in infantry tactics were introduced by Gustavus Adolphus. The weight of the musket was reduced to 11 pounds (5 kg), so that it could be fired from the shoulder without a rest, and the fixed cartridge, incorporating charge and ball, was introduced. These measures increased the musketeer's efficiency to the point that his dependence on the pikeman was reduced and the proportion of musketeers to pikemen was, therefore, increased. Simultaneously, it was possible to reduce the musketeers' ranks from 10 to a maximum of 6, so that units held a wider area of front than hitherto. The overall effect was to give the Swedish infantry a flexibility and firepower that the *tercios* lacked, amply demonstrated during the decisive Battle of Breitenfeld in 1631.

Bayonets and grenadiers

The introduction of the bayonet spelled the end of the pikeman. Legend has it that some time around 1640, possibly at Bayonne, a body of musketeers, lacking pikemen for their defense, solved the problem by plugging long knives into the muzzles of their weapons. The plug bayonet was in widespread use by the 1660s, but its obvious disadvantage was that the musket could not be fired while it was fixed. The answer to this was to fit the bayonet with a ring that could be slipped over the muzzle and then held in place by studs, leaving the musket free for firing and reloading. Ring bayonets first appeared in 1678, and their use quickly became general, eliminating the need for pikemen.

With the pikemen went the last vestige of infantry armor, which would not reappear until the twentieth century, and then for very different reasons from hand-to-hand combat. Instead, the infantryman wore a uniform coat of national color, ornamented with distinctive facings and buttons intended to give his unit an *esprit de corps.*

As one type of infantryman began leaving the battlefield another, the grenadier, had already entered it. The function of the grenadier, as his name suggests, was to hurl grenades, which were then small spheres packed with gunpowder and fuzed by a length of burning slow-match. Because wide-brim or tricorn hats interfered with the swing of the arm, grenadiers wore a cap with trailing bag similar to a nightcap, but by 1700, several armies had begun to stiffen these to the shape of a bishop's miter, ornamented with the regimental insignia or royal cypher. This work was performed best by the tallest and strongest men, and grenadiers, therefore, came to be regarded as being elite. Each battalion possessed a grenadier company, although in the field the practice was to brigade grenadiers together and employ them as assault infantry.

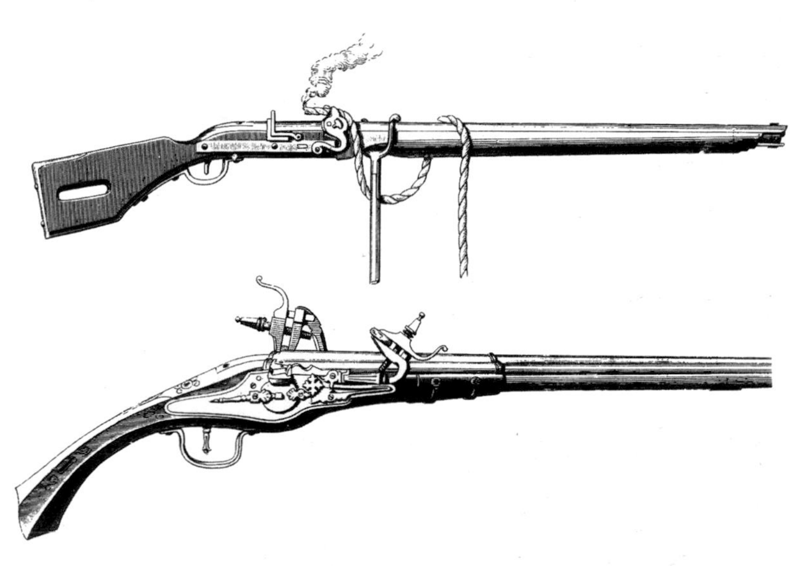

(Top right) The matchlock musket, here on firing rest, was fired with the musketeer's left foot forward, his left hand steadying the rest, and his right hand encircling the small of the butt, pulling it in toward his shoulder to absorb as much of the recoil as possible. When the trigger was activated, the serpentine lowered the burning match into the priming pan. (Bottom right) Wheel lock arquebus. Smaller and lighter than the matchlock, the arquebus could be fired with both hands on the weapon; some were fired from the chest, some from the shoulder, and others held under the right arm. This example is somewhat advanced in that it is fitted with a second dog containing a flint (iron pyrites,) which can be brought into use if the first fails.

Cavalry trooper's armor at the time of the English Civil War, 1642–1651. The helmet, known as a pot, was unlike the cuirassier's in that it relied on bars to protect the face and was fitted with a peak and a lobster tail neck guard. The cumbrous tassets (plate armor designed to protect the upper legs) were often discarded.

CAVALRY

The demise of the knight, already apparent during the previous 150 years in his encounters with English archers and Swiss pikemen, became a reality with the introduction of gunpowder, the great leveler; in fact, for much of the gunpower revolution, the mounted arm in general was in decline, despite the emergence of the professional cavalryman.

The essence of the problem was that cavalry was unable to perform its traditional role of shock action against infantry, being simultaneously vulnerable to the fire of arquebusiers and musketeers and kept beyond striking distance by massed pikes. In such circumstances the lance merely became an encumbrance and, except in Eastern Europe, had been discarded by the end of the sixteenth century, although the Scottish cavalry was still employing lancers some 50 years later.

An apparent answer was presented by the pistol, the type adopted at first being a wheel lock, the matchlock mechanism being clearly unsuited to mounted action. Each trooper was equipped with two or three pistols and attacks were delivered at walking pace or, at best, the trot, in 10-deep formations. At point-blank range the front rank would discharge its pistols and then wheel to the rear to reload and move forward by rotation, in the manner of contemporary musketeers, this type of cavalry maneuver being known as the caracole. Only when gaps began to appear in enemy ranks did the troopers attempt to close with the sword. Once the pistol had been accepted as the principal cavalry weapon, the caracole was also employed against hostile cavalry, with the result that for many years the entire concept of shock action disappeared altogether, the only maneuver performed at the gallop being the pursuit of a broken enemy. Thus, the contribution made by cavalry during the sixteenth and the early years of the seventeenth centuries was rarely decisive.

Once again, it was Gustavus Adolphus who rationalized the situation. Forbidden to perform the caracole, his cavalry attacked at a fast trot in four ranks, later reduced to three. Having fired their pistols, the two leading ranks closed immediately with the sword, followed by the remainder, who reserved their fire for the subsequent melee. Naturally, the effect of such a radical departure from the accepted drill was devastating. Furthermore, each Swedish cavalry regiment had the direct support of a 200-strong company of musketeers and light artillery, the fire of which created further gaps in enemy ranks to be exploited by the horsemen. During the English Civil War, the achievements of Oliver Cromwell's Ironsides confirmed the return of decisive cavalry shock action to the battlefield and also demonstrated the critical importance of rallying after a successful charge.

The heavy cavalry of the period were *cuirassiers*. At first their armor differed little from that of the medieval knight, although they wore long boots in place of lower leg armor. However, thigh and arm pieces were discarded so that by the middle of the seventeenth century, armor had been reduced to helmet, breastplate, and backplate. The dragoon, armed with a short musket known as a dragon, bayonet, and sword, also appeared around this time.

A cuirassier *performing the caracole. Apart from the boots, his appearance is very similar to that of the medieval knight. Such expensive equipment could not be justified once the efficiency of firearms increased.*

BATTLE OF NASEBY

DATE June 14, 1645
CAMPAIGN English Civil War.
OBJECT Royalists, under Charles I, and Parliamentarians, under Cromwell and Fairfax, sought a decisive action.
NUMBERS Royalists—4,000 infantry, 5,000 cavalry, and 12 guns, total 9,000; Parliamentarians—7,000 infantry, 6,000 cavalry, and 13 guns, total 13,000.
DESCRIPTION The two armies were drawn up with infantry in the center and cavalry on the flanks, plus a reserve behind. Cromwell deployed a regiment of dragoons along the hedges to their left. The battle began with both armies' right-wing cavalry mounting successful attacks, but while Royalists pursued their enemy until repulsed by musketeers, Cromwell exercised tighter control. He led his second line against the Royalist infantry, which was pushing back the Parliamentarian center. The king could have launched a decisive counterattack into Cromwell's flank, but the reserve was not committed and the chance was lost. Cromwell's dragoons, who had fired a dismounted volley into the flank of the Royalist charge, now mounted their horses and joined in the attack on the king's infantry. Outnumbered and beset from three directions, most of them surrendered. The remnant of the Royalist army fled, abandoning guns and baggage train.
CASUALTIES Royalists—about 6,000 including numerous prisoners; Parliamentarians—probably less than 1,000.
RESULT The battle destroyed the king's cause in the Midlands. The north had been lost at Marston Moor (1644). The few troops loyal to the king in the south and west were unable to halt the advance of the Parliamentary army.

BATTLE OF ROCROI

DATE May 19, 1643
CAMPAIGN Thirty Years War, campaign of 1643 in France and Belgium.
OBJECT The French army under the Duc d'Enghien was attempting to relieve Rocroi, which was besieged by a Spanish army under Don Francisco de Melo.
NUMBERS French—18 infantry battalions, 32 cavalry squadrons, and 12 guns, total 23,000; Spaniards—20 infantry *tercios*, 7,000 cavalry, and 28 guns, total 27,000.
DESCRIPTION Approaching Rocroi, d'Enghien discovered that the roads to the town were undefended. Pushing through a narrow defile flanked by woods, he deployed his army on a ridge overlooking Rocroi. His infantry was in the center of the line and the cavalry on the flanks. Melo's army formed up in similar fashion between the city and the ridge. The two armies encamped overnight and battle was joined the next morning, May 19. Immediately, the Spanish infantry, fighting in close-packed squares (*tercios*) gained the upper hand. On the left, the French cavalry launched a charge over marshy ground, which was blocked by the opposing cavalry and driven from the field in a counterattack. The victorious Spanish cavalry attacked the French infantry but was checked when the French infantry reserve was moved up. On the right things went better for the French, whose cavalry, supported by musketeers, routed the Spanish cavalry and then took the infantry in the flank and rear. The redoubtable *tercios* continued to resist but were pounded by artillery and subjected to a succession of cavalry charges.

At 10 a.m., d'Enghien offered the *tercios* terms of surrender similar to those offered a besieged garrison. These were accepted and the Spanish were permitted to quit the field with their colors and weapons.
CASUALTIES Some 4,000 French dead and 7,000 Spanish dead and wounded and 8,000 taken prisoner.
RESULT Rocroi was the first Spanish defeat in a significant land battle in nearly a century. It was also the beginning of the end of the *tercio* as a decisive fighting formation. Subsequently, linear formations were increasingly favored.

The dragoon's only armor was a helmet, generally discarded by 1700, and his role was that of a mounted infantryman who rode to the battlefield but could fight mounted or dismounted. Properly employed, he provided a valuable asset with the return of tactical flexibility. His contemporary, the carabineer, was a cavalryman armed with a lighter musket known as a carbine, pistols, and sword. There was also a brief fashion for horse grenadiers.

The backbone of the line cavalry, however, consisted of regiments of horse, armed with sword and pistols. In continental Europe the light cavalry roles, including scouting and "screening" (covering the army's movements), were at first performed by mounted irregulars recruited in the Balkans and Eastern Europe, but toward the end of the seventeenth century, the first regular hussar regiments were formed for this purpose.

The last 50 years of the period, therefore, witnessed a restoration of the cavalry's ability to perform shock action. The French cavalry, in particular, acquired a reputation for dash, although during the War of Spanish Succession (1701–14) this was often eclipsed by Marlborough's ability to handle cavalry en masse at the higher level of command (see pages 118–19). Nevertheless, while cavalry had recovered its purpose on the battlefield, it had lost its former dominance and was now simply one of several arms that, of necessity, were forced to cooperate to achieve success. Indeed, the ratio of cavalry to other troops, already falling, continued to fall throughout the next century.

In 1538 this monastery at Tynemouth was disbanded by Robert Blakeney, the last prior of Tynemouth. The priory and its attached lands were taken over by King Henry VIII who granted them to Sir Thomas Hilton. New artillery fortifications were built from 1545 onwards, with the advice of Sir Richard Lee and the Italian military engineers Gian Tommaso Scala and Antonio da Bergamo. The medieval castle walls were updated with new gunports.

FORTIFICATION AND SIEGE CRAFT

Unless it was situated on an inaccessible crag or surrounded by a wide body of water, no medieval fortress could hope to survive a siege conducted with artillery support, although as late as the English Civil War some castles were able to offer remarkably tough resistance. Equally, medieval siege methods were useless against a fortress armed with guns, which could destroy siege towers and other impedimenta at long range. Thus, gunpowder induced a major revolution in the opposed skills of fortification and siege craft, just as it did in other forms of warfare.

For the fortress builder, it was necessary to sink most of his defenses into the earth, with only fighting parapets and gun embrasures visible above ground, sited to sweep the approaches with their fire. Henry VIII constructed a series of defense works along the southern coast of England, against attack by France or Spain, designed specifically for all-round defense by artillery. The basic format of these castles was a circular central keep surrounded by interconnected semicircular bastions mounting tiers of guns, the whole complex being encircled by a wide ditch.

GREAT CAPTAINS: GUSTAVUS AND MARLBOROUGH

Gustavus Adolphus came to the throne of Sweden in 1611, at the age of 17, and was almost immediately involved in a protracted series of local wars that established Sweden as the major military power in the Baltic. Sweden was poor and had limited manpower resources. Therefore, while Gustavus's standing army was national in character, it needed to make up for small numbers with efficiency. It was raised by selective conscription, given uniforms for *esprit de corps*, humanely disciplined, paid regularly, and, above all, trained. The key to improved tactics lay in weapons. Gustavus reduced the weight of the musket, so that it could be fired from the shoulder, and introduced a fixed cartridge. This increased the rate of fire and the musketeers' ranks could be reduced from 10 to 6.

The flexibility of the Swedish infantry was provided by the internal organization of its units. A company had 72 musketeers and 54 pikemen; four companies formed a battalion; eight battalions formed a regiment; and two to four regiments formed a brigade. Gustavus trained his cavalry to charge knee-to-knee and engage with the sword, so restoring shock action to the battlefield. Each cavalry regiment had the support of a musketeer company and light artillery, which would be employed prior to and between charges.

The Swedish artillery assumed an importance equal to that of the infantry or cavalry. The most important development was in the field of regimental guns. Those in use were replaced by conventional 4-pounder guns firing fixed grape or canister ammunition one-third as fast again as a musketeer. Each infantry and cavalry regiment was equipped with one or two such guns.

By 1630, Gustavus had spent about half his revenue on his armed services, and it was the financial inducement offered by Cardinal Richelieu of France that prompted his direct involvement in the Thirty Years War. The superiority of the Swedish system was clearly demonstrated at Breitenfeld in 1631, but at Lützen in 1632, while the Swedes were again victorious, Gustavus was killed. His contribution to military science had been immense and his methods were quickly copied by every army in Europe.

(Above) Gustavus Adolphus, King of Sweden 1611–32. He is credited as the founder of Sweden as agreat power, leading to Swedish military supremacy during the Thirty Years War, helping to determine the political as well as the religious balance of power in Europe.

The Duke of Marlborough

John Churchill was born in 1650 and served as a junior officer in Tangier, at sea against the Dutch, and for a while with the French army. He was responsible for defeating the Duke of Monmouth's rebellion in 1685. On the outbreak of the War of the Spanish Succession, William III appointed him Commander in Chief of the Allied armies and Ambassador to the Dutch United Provinces. He concluded the treaty that established the Grand Alliance of the United Kingdom, Holland, and the Austrian Empire. When Anne succeeded to the crown the following year, she added the appointment of Captain General to that of Master General of the Ordnance, which he already held, and made him a duke.

Marlborough was both an excellent strategist and a master of tactics. He increased the pace of the cavalry charge to a canter. This proved most effective against French cavalry, who were still performing a version of the caracole, and was followed by deep penetration and prompt rallying. He also personally ordered the deployment of artillery, massing his guns on a critical sector or sending them forward to provide close-quarter support during a general advance.

Above all, Marlborough was an inspiring leader. He recognized that most men were soldiers because they had no alternative and made officers responsible for the welfare of their men. The men responded. Marlborough was always quick to detect any flaw in his opponents' dispositions and to concentrate overwhelmingly against their weaknesses. It was thus that he won his spectacular victories at the battles of Blenheim (1704), Ramillies (1706), and Oudenarde (1708), and was able to force his way through the formidable Ne Plus Ultra lines in 1711.

The War of the Spanish Succession ended in 1713. Marlborough had been recalled in 1712, but as a result of the alarm generated by the Jacobite Rising of 1715, he was again appointed Master General of the Ordnance and, prior to his death in 1716, was able to place the artillery on a permanent footing. He was one of history's outstanding captains. Under Marlborough, the prestige of the British army reached a level unequaled since the longbow dominated the battlefield.

(Above) John Churchill, Duke of Marlborough (1630–1716). A great strategist and, like the Duke of Wellington, a commander born to get the best out of a coalition army.

TERMS USED IN FORTIFICATION

BANQUETTE—fire step behind a protecting parapet

BASTION—work consisting of two faces and two flanks, forming part of the main defenses

CASEMATE—vaulted chamber within a rampart, containing an artillery port

COUNTERSCARP—exterior wall of a defensive ditch

CURTAIN—rampart connecting bastions

DITCH—excavation in front of ramparts

EMBRASURE—opening in parapet to permit artillery fire

GLACIS—clear slope on the enemy side of a ditch, covered by fire from parapets

PARADOS—embankment behind a defensive position, protecting it against fire from the rear

RAMPART—thick wall of earth and/or masonry forming the main defenses

RAVELIN—work beyond the curtain consisting of two faces meeting in a salient, closed at the rear by counterscarp; protected gates and flanks of bastions. Sometimes called a demilune

SCARP—inner wall of a ditch, leading upward to the rampart

The problem with circular bastions was that, although less vulnerable to cannon fire and able to provide a degree of support for each other with their cross fire, this still left areas of dead ground, which could be exploited by the enemy. This was not true of wedge-shape bastions, which could be sited to provide mutual support covering every angle of approach. From this discovery, the star system of fortification was developed, so called because the overall design of a fortress, consisting of bastions linked by curtain walls, resembled a star. From their outer edge, the permanent defenses consisted of a sloped glacis, counterscarp, ditch, scarp, and ramparts. To protect gateways and vulnerable sections of the curtain, ravelins and other outerworks could be added, each with its own counterscarp, ditch, and scarp, so producing an extremely complex ground plan. Very little detail of the defenses was visible to an attacker because even the parapets were covered with a deep layer of earth, which cushioned the impact of cannon balls and so reduced the danger from flying stone splinters.

Arrival of military engineering

To launch an assault on such a fortress without adequate preparation was to invite crippling casualties. Mining offered an alternative if the ditch was dry, but this involved tunneling through the foundations of the counterscarp, then under the ditch, and finally through the thickness of the scarp. Even if the attempt was successful and a charge was laid and fired, the stone-fronted earth ramparts could absorb the effects of the explosion far better than could the walls of a medieval castle.

The only method likely to guarantee success was to concentrate artillery fire against what was considered to be a weak sector of the defenses, and then dig a sap toward it. The batteries would be emplaced 600 yards (548 m) from the walls and then connected by a trench, which became known as the First Parallel. From this zig-zag, saps would be pushed out and guns brought forward to establish a Second Parallel 300 yards (274 m) from the defenses. This would be repeated until a Third Parallel existed within musket shot of the ramparts. Once the defenses had been battered into silence and a breach in the walls effected, the garrison might surrender, or an assault might be launched if it rejected terms.

The master of this type of warfare was Sebastien le Prestre de Vauban, who received his commission as an engineer in 1653 and in 1687 became the French army's Director of Engineering. Vauban

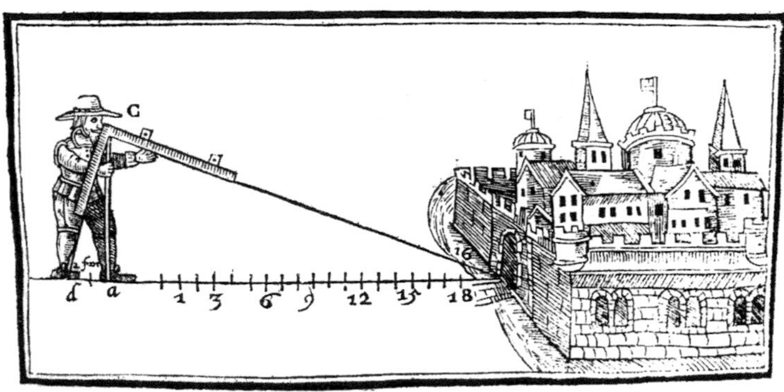

The growth of military engineering during the seventeenth century fostered more sophisticated surveying techniques, as shown above. This in turn resulted in more accurate maps.

NICCOLO MACHIAVELLI

Prominent among military theorists of the day was Niccolo Machiavelli (1469–1527), author of *The Prince and The Art of War*. In many respects, Machiavelli drew erroneous conclusions, notably in underestimating the effectiveness of firearms, but he condemned the mercenary system and advocated the Roman legion as a model for infantry formations, a direction in which the Spanish were already moving with their *tercios*.

consolidated the experience of the previous 100 years' fortification and siege craft, applying mathematics to the former and logical progression to the latter. He built more than 100 fortresses and conducted some 40 sieges, some of them against fortifications of his own design. His systems of attack and defense were so precise that, given the number and type of guns employed, and the construction of the fortress, it was possible to predict with reasonable accuracy how long one might be capable of offering resistance. In such circumstances, there was no disgrace in a garrison agreeing to march out with honor, provided it had done its utmost.

The complexities of fortification and siege craft led to the establishment of permanent bodies of military engineers, whose duties, in addition to the construction of defense works, also involved building bridges and roads. Military engineering had barely existed in 1485, yet as a result of the gunpowder revolution, it had attained the status of a science within 200 years.

CONDUCT OF OPERATIONS

Applying the new technology to the battlefield presented contemporary commanders with the kind of difficulties posed by mechanization in the interwar years, 1919–39, in that no precedents existed and there was no experience on which to draw. At first, even forming the battle-line was a slow and complicated process, because it required deploying pikemen and arquebusiers or musketeers to the mutual advantage of both, emplacing the artillery in the most favorable position, and deciding how best the cavalry was to be employed.

The battles themselves tended to be fought in slow motion, with ritual formality, generally beginning with an artillery duel, which might last an hour or two before the armies came to grips. The musketeers would fire in ranks by rotation, the pikemen would perform their cumbrous drill, culminating in the deadly "push of pike" with their opponents, and the cavalry would perform the caracole until one side or the other broke.

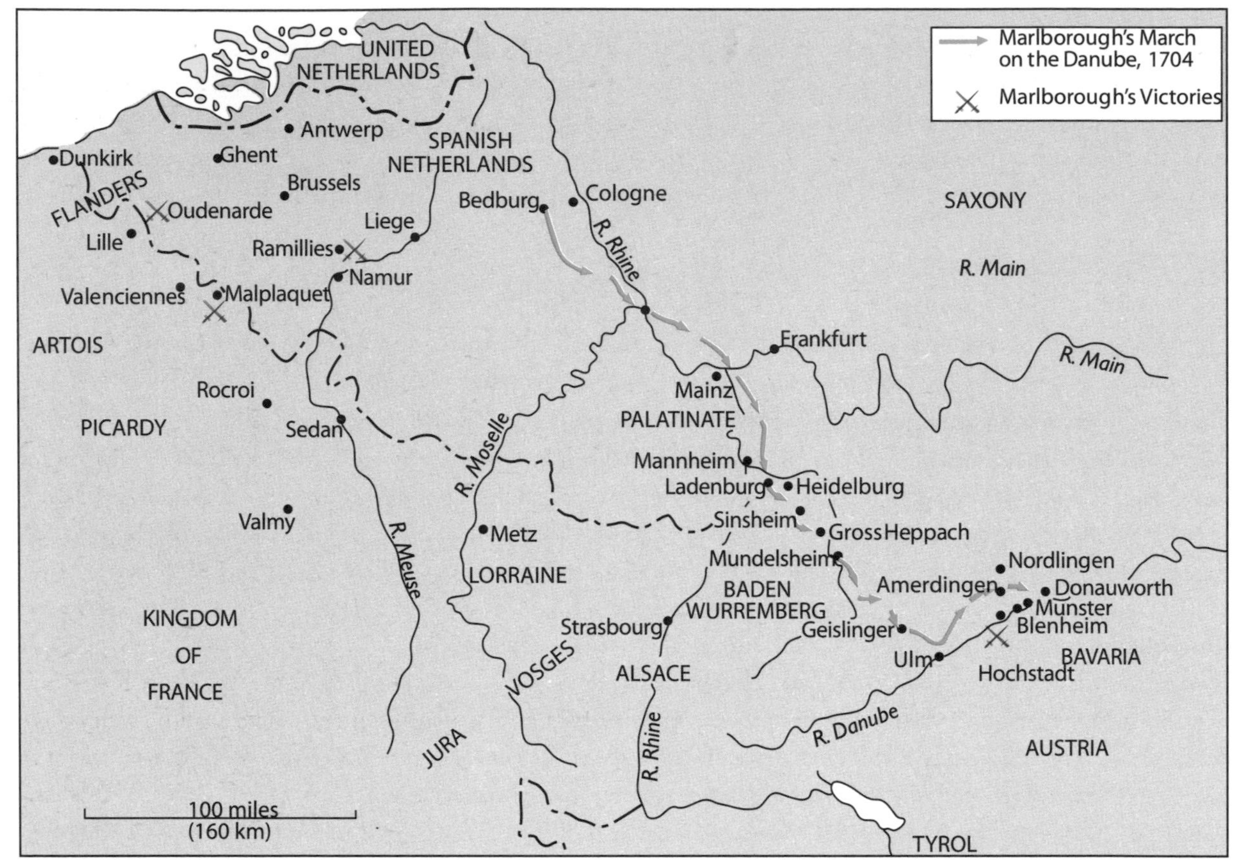

Marlborough's campaigns. His great strategic march of 1704 was a masterpiece of planning and deception. The French were at first convinced that he intended advancing up the Moselle, then that he planned an invasion of Alsace, whereas his real intention was to effect a junction with Prince Eugène of Savoy's Imperial army and break the deadlock on the Danube front. This he succeeded in doing at Blenheim.

Before planning a campaign, a commander had to be sure that his troops could be properly fed and supplied—living off the land was never a viable proposition, except in the very short term—and for this he usually relied on civilian contractors. During the winter months, when the roads degenerated into mud wallows, armies tended to retire into billets to await better weather.

Composition of the troops was another cause for concern. Although armies might be nominally French, Spanish, Dutch, or Imperialist, the national element was comparatively small. The ranks were filled with contingents from other countries and bands of mercenaries. Some mercenaries, notably the Swiss, gave value for money, but the loyalty of others belonged to whoever paid best. The German *Landsknecht* and *Reiter* (mounted pistoleer) bands accorded a rough loyalty to their own captains, provided they could deliver pay and plunder, but acquired a reputation for brutality. Even worse were the *Condottiere,* employed by the Italian city-states to fight their wars; they had no intention of becoming involved in anything as dangerous as a battle and, offered suitable incentives, would change sides at the drop of a hat.

The reforms instituted by Gustavus Adolphus changed the face of the battlefield. Infantry were still deployed in the center with cavalry on the flanks, but linear rather than columnar formations were adopted by both, a support line being formed behind the battle line. Individual units were smaller and more flexible, enabling them to be moved quickly where they were needed. This, in turn, placed greater emphasis on the role of the junior officer. Overall, the result was to accelerate the tempo at which operations were conducted.

War had now become a matter for professionals. Officers and men alike needed to be trained in tactics and the most efficient use of weapons. By the latter half of the seventeenth century, the concept of the nation state was firmly established and national standing armies were formed, providing regular pay, arms, uniforms, and rations under the proprietary system, in which colonels were paid a sum of money by central government to raise and equip their regiments and maintain them year by year. Officers purchased their commissions, which could be sold on, as could the proprietary interest itself. By and large, the system worked well enough in its time, although it was open to abuse. The need for foreign mercenaries was largely removed, although the reliable Swiss were still recruited by several monarchs for internal security and for their personal guards, including the Papal Swiss Guard, which still exists. The internal efficiency of armies was improved by such matters as ordnance, engineering, and procurement being administered centrally, and the establishment of permanent supply depots enabled greater numbers of troops to be maintained in the field.

Under Marlborough, two centuries of painful transition from medieval to unmechanized modern warfare were consolidated. For infantry and artillery, the emphasis was on firepower, and for cavalry it was on shock action. The brigade, consisting of two or more regiments, became the tactical unit. Gone was the old formal array, replaced by a more flexible system of battle in which infantry, artillery, and cavalry were deployed according to the terrain and the commander's intentions. The pattern was set for the next 150 years.

BATTLE OF BLENHEIM

DATE August 13, 1704
CAMPAIGN War of the Spanish Succession.
OBJECT To break the impasse on the Danube front.
NUMBERS Allies—65 infantry battalions, 160 cavalry squadrons, 60 guns, total strength 52,000; Franco-Bavarians (under Marshal Tallard)—79 infantry battalions, 140 cavalry squadrons, 90 guns, total strength 56,000.
DESCRIPTION Tallard's flanks were protected by the Danube on the right and wooded hills on the left, and most of his infantry was positioned in three villages along his front—Blenheim on the right, Oberglau in the left center, and Lutzingen on the left. Between Blenheim and Oberglau was a large area of undefended water meadows. Marlborough attacked and masked the villages on the enemy left while his main force crossed the Nebel stream to the meadows. Aware of the danger, Tallard ordered his cavalry to charge them and for a while the issue was in doubt. It was resolved when Marlborough personally brought up a brigade of cuirassiers, defeating the counterattack. The British infantry and cavalry advanced and by 5:30 p.m. had smashed through the weak French center. Tallard was captured and the Elector of Bavaria withdrew, pursued by Eugène. At 11 p.m., the French garrison in Blenheim surrendered.
CASUALTIES Allies—12,000 killed and wounded; Franco-Bavarians—20,000 killed and wounded, 14,000 captured, 6,000 desertions, and 60 guns lost.
RESULT Two-thirds of the Franco-Bavarian army were destroyed, the French threat to Vienna was removed, and the Allies overran Bavaria.

BATTLE OF POLTAVA

DATE June 28, 1709
CAMPAIGN Great Northern War
OBJECT A Russian army under Peter the Great had come to relieve Poltava (in modern Ukraine), which was besieged by the Swedes under Charles XII.
NUMBERS Swedes—18 infantry battalions, 12 cavalry squadrons, and a few guns, total 17,000; Russians—30 infantry battalions, 30 cavalry squadrons, and 40 guns, total 80,000.
DESCRIPTION Peter established himself in an entrenched camp covered by a series of advanced redoubts. Charles, short of supplies and ammunition, wanted to secure a quick victory and launched a night attack, which was intended to pass between the redoubts and then assault the Russian camp. He had been wounded in the foot some days earlier and was unable to exercise effective control of the battle from his litter. Thus, while his center and left columns succeeded in passing through the redoubts at dawn and repulsing a covering force of cavalry beyond, the column on the right fell behind when, contrary to his intentions, it became embroiled in a fight for the redoubts themselves. Spotting its isolation, Peter despatched a force of 10,000 men, which quickly surrounded and eliminated it. The rest of the Swedish army reformed after some time-consuming wrangling among commanders, and the infantry launched a series of attacks on the entrenchments, but were shot to pieces by superior Russian firepower. By the end of the day, the Swedish infantry had virtually ceased to exist. The cavalry managed to leave the field but was overtaken and surrendered two days after the battle. Charles escaped into Turkish territory.
CASUALTIES Swedes—7,000 killed and 2,600 captured; Russians—1,300 killed and wounded.
RESULT Swedish domination was destroyed and Russia established as a European power. Although the war continued until 1721, Sweden was forced onto the strategic defensive. Peter himself commented that the foundation stone of St. Petersburg was laid at Poltava.

NAVAL WARFARE

At the end of the fifteenth century, the most important class of naval vessel in the Mediterranean was the galley, the basic design of which had not altered since classical times. Fitted with lateen sails for normal cruising, in action the vessel was propelled by banks of oars manned by criminals or prisoners of war, who were chained to their benches. Galleys might attempt to sink or disable their opponents by ramming, but they also carried a large number of soldiers and their normal tactics were to board after an exchange of missiles, which often included incendiary devices.

In rougher Atlantic and northern waters, to which such narrow-hull vessels were unsuited, the principal warship was the square-rig carrack, with a beam approximately half its overall length, fitted with high fighting platforms known as castles fore and aft. These were manned by archers and men-at-arms whose task was to capture the enemy vessel by boarding. Engagements at sea, which rarely took place beyond sight of land, were therefore simply land battles afloat. The most important participants were soldiers rather than seamen.

Design revolution

This changed very rapidly with the advent of cannon and the growth of national exchequers, which permitted a revolution in warship design. The galley, its narrow beam occupied by oarsmen, could mount just a few light guns forward, and was unable to adapt further. The carrack, on the other hand, could be employed as a gun platform, particularly after the hinged port was invented about the beginning of the sixteenth century, beacuse this enabled cannon to be mounted broadside in tiers within the hull.

Thereafter, warship design followed two schools. The first envisaged the vessel as a floating fortress that used her guns as a preparation for boarding, and was adopted mainly but not exclusively by the Spanish. The result was the galleon, distinguished by its towering aftercastle, and such Great Ships as Henry VIII's *Henry Grâce à Dieu* of 1514, displacing more than 1,000 tons and armed with 151 light and heavy guns.

The Battle of Lepanto was the last major decisive action fought between fleets of galleys. Although cannon were used extensively by both sides, the issue was decided by ramming and hand-to-hand fighting on the enemy's decks.

The second, supported by such great seamen as Sir John Hawkins, Sir Francis Drake, and Sir Walter Raleigh, saw the warship as a weapon system complete in itself, capable of disabling and sinking opponents with its own gunfire. To this end, slimmer vessels with trim lines and a more scientific sail plan were produced, their better sailing qualities enabling them to fight at ranges of their own choosing. When, during the defeat of the Spanish Armada, the two concepts clashed, the latter emerged the undisputed victor and evolved into the ship of the line, the design of which remained essentially unchanged until the advent of steam propulsion, armor plate, and turret guns in the nineteenth century.

The technical problems facing the designers of the new warships were formidable. Because of the great weight of the guns carried, coupled with soaring top hamper, the need to preserve a low center of gravity was essential, particularly in heavy weather or strong beam winds. Failure to recognize this led to the sinking of the *Mary Rose* (1545) and the loss of the Swedish *Vasa* in Stockholm Harbor in 1629. Gunpowder itself posed a terrible hazard to wooden ships; in 1512, off Brest, the English *Regent,* close-grappled with the French *Marie la Cordelière,* was burned out when the latter's magazine exploded.

Gun mountings

At first mountings were fixed, and the weapon's recoil contained by a stout timber baulk or heavy ropes. This system produced difficulties in handling sponge and rammer staves and for this reason primitive breech-loaders were used; unfortunately, the backblast of gases made them inefficient and dangerous and this area of development was abandoned for 300 years. By the middle of the sixteenth century, it had been decided to let the recoil forces work for the gun crew. Guns were mounted on small four-wheeled trucks, which rolled inboard on recoil, producing sufficient room in which to sponge, reload, and ram, and were then run out by means of tackles.

THE SPANISH ARMADA

DATE July 19–30, 1588
CAMPAIGN Naval war between Elizabeth I of England and Philip II of Spain.
OBJECT The Armada, commanded by the Duke of Medina Sidonia, was to transport the Duke of Parma's invasion army from the Netherlands to England.
NUMBERS The Armada—20 galleons, 44 armed merchant vessels, 23 transports, 35 smaller vessels, four galleasses, manned by 8,500 seamen and 19,000 soldiers; 2,431 guns: 1,100 heavy, including 600 culverins, the rest light anti-personnel weapons. The English fleet—about 50 warships, including 5 of over 600 tons and 11 of 400–600 tons, manned by 6,000 men (three-quarters were seamen); more than 1,500 heavy cannon, the majority being long-range culverins. A number of auxiliary vessels and supply ships, some privately fitted out, sailed in support.
DESCRIPTION The Armada left Corunna on July 12 and was sighted by English scout vessels off the Lizard a week later. The English fleet, commanded by Lord Howard of Effingham with Sir Francis Drake as his vice admiral, sailed from Plymouth on July 20. The next day the Spanish formed a defensive crescent, the rear of which was harried by the English, setting the pattern of the battle as the fleets moved up the Channel. The gunnery of the English ships, their better sailing qualities, and knowledge of local tides and currents, enabled the English to inflict the greater damage. With the exception of their culverins, the heavy guns aboard the Spanish ships were more suited to siege warfare than to a naval engagement and the English fought beyond the range of the antipersonnel weapons.

Heavy engagements took place off the Dorset coast and the Isle of Wight. Medina Sidonia abandoned his plan to effect a landing on the latter and proceeded to Calais in order to replenish his dangerously reduced stock of ammunition. Howard followed and, during the night of July 27–28, sent fireships among the anchored Spanish vessels, many of which cut their cables in panic. A major engagement took place off the Flanders coast on July 28, strong winds pushing the fleets steadily northeastward. These winds prevented the Spanish from entering

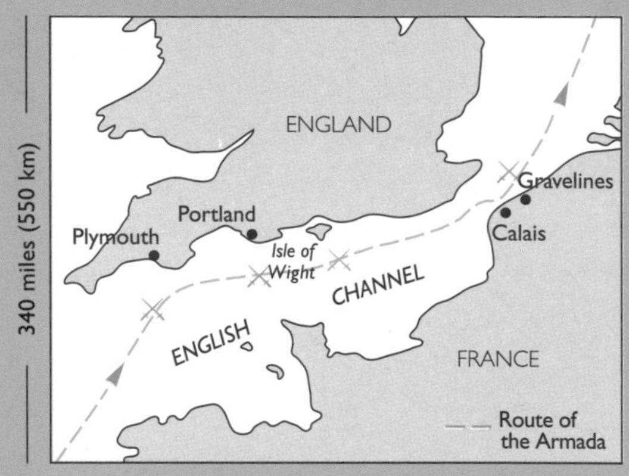

Dunkirk or Bruges, where a junction with Parma might have been effected. On July 29, the Armada was almost driven onto the lee shore of Zeeland, and Medina Sidonia, his ammunition exhausted, decided to return to Spain by sailing around Scotland and Ireland. Howard followed him northward until lack of provisions forced him to return to port on August 2.

The Armada had lost 11 ships. In the Atlantic, another 19 were wrecked on the Scottish and Irish coasts in severe gales; the fate of 33 more remains unknown. The survivors, their crews dying from hunger and thirst, straggled into Spanish ports in September. The defeat of the Spanish Armada involved the most protracted sea battle ever fought and established the gun as the principal weapon of naval warfare for the next 350 years.
CASUALTIES Of 63 Spanish vessels, 63 were lost from various causes during the engagement and its sequel, with personnel casualties in proportion; no English vessel of importance was lost and personnel casualties were light, given the protracted nature of the fighting.
RESULT The Armada failed in its purpose and Spanish naval prestige never fully recovered. The prestige of the English Royal Navy was now firmly in the ascendant. In overall terms, the battle vindicated those who favored the fighting ship as gun platform rather than as floating fortress, and had an immediate effect on warship design throughout the Western world.

Meanwhile, the galley continued to soldier on. On October 7, 1571, a fleet of Christian galleys commanded by Don John of Austria inflicted a crushing defeat on a similar Turkish fleet off Lepanto. During this, the most decisive galley action since Salamis, ships were sunk by gunfire for the first time. It was, however, generally realized that flimsy galleys were no match for the new warships, except in the rare circumstances where the latter were completely becalmed, enabling the galleys to stand off their vulnerable quarters and pound them at will.

Despite this, enthusiasts produced an intermediate design—the galleass—combining oars with sail and mounting broadside guns. Most navies showed interest in the idea, but by 1600, it was clear that the galleass could not be regarded as a first-line warship because the concept was inherently flawed. On the one hand, heavy guns had to be mounted deep in the hull, so that the oars had to be shipped when they opened fire, thereby reducing the vessel's speed and maneuverability; on the other, lighter guns could be mounted above the oars, but this reduced the weight of metal that could be thrown. The galley itself continued to serve in the Mediterranean and, later, in the Baltic, until the nineteenth century.

By 1600, the nature of sea power had become clear. It could be used to prey on an enemy's mercantile interests, as England regularly did against Spain's, using warships or privateers—privately fitted out vessels given official status by letters of marque—or it could be used to blockade the enemy's home ports, or to mount heavy and destructive raids. The naval aspects of the English Civil War introduced a new element, namely the often-disputed right of maritime powers to intercept neutral vessels trading with the enemy.

The three Anglo-Dutch wars fought between 1652 and 1673 stemmed from trade rivalry and took place entirely at sea, producing the first major fleet actions since the Armada. They set the pattern of naval warfare for the next 150 years. Whereas fleets had formerly approached each other in line abreast, they now did so in line ahead, a formation that enabled their commanders to exercise maximum possible control. To increase efficiency, the English produced a system of prearranged tactical maneuvers, which could be signaled by fleet commanders. Known as the *Fighting Instructions,* they first appeared in 1653 and, with appropriate modifications, remained in use in Britain for two centuries. Although intended as a guide, some commanders chose to interpret them as strict rules, with the result that individual captains were often unable to exercise their initiative when favorable opportunities arose. Before an engagement commenced, both sides sought to position themselves upwind of the enemy, which gave them freedom to maneuver as they wanted. Whenever possible, the English sought to break the enemy's battle line, separating his ships into small groups, which could be overwhelmed in turn.

Dutch Attack on the Medway, June 1667 by Pieter Cornelisz van Soest.

The period that had begun with seamen possessing little or no status in warfare witnessed such radical change that by its end standing navies and their supporting services were firmly established as instruments of national policy. From 1688 onward, the United Kingdom and France were to be at war, more or less continuously, for the next 128 years, during which the Royal Navy achieved an ascendancy at sea that was seldom lost and was not seriously challenged until the twentieth century.

FROM FLOATING FORTRESS TO SHIP OF THE LINE

The recovery of the Mary Rose off the coast of southern England in 1982 was the result of one of the most important marine archaeological operations ever conducted. It led to the preservation of a ship that provides a vital link between the converted merchantmen of the medieval era and the ships of the line of the ensuing three centuries.

Built at the behest of Henry VIII in 1509–10, she was designed as a floating fortress that would first batter her enemies and then send over soldiers to board. A four-mast carrack with orlop, main, and upper decks, she had fore- and sterncastles and fighting tops on each mast. She was square-rig on the fore and main masts with lateens on the mizzen and bonaventure. Her displacement (700 tons) was given in "tuns burthen," which is a contemporary measure of cubic capacity. When launched, her armament consisted of 43 guns and 37 antipersonnel weapons.

In 1536, the *Mary Rose* was extensively refitted. Compromises had to be reached between the designers of the ship and her users—soldiers. Their requirements and so their ideas differed. The ship's fore- and sterncastles may have been raised and the armament was increased, leading to a larger crew of 215 sailors and soldiers.

Her trim was dangerously affected by these alterations. Shortly before she sailed to do battle with the French off the Isle of Wight on July 19, 1545, her crew was swelled by a further 300 soldiers, most of whom were placed on the upper decks, above her center of gravity. The fleet left harbor in a light breeze, but this freshened as the *Mary*

The Sovereign of the Seas, *the largest ship in the world when she was launched in 1637, possessed a sail plan a century ahead of her time. In 1660, following the restoration of the monarchy, she was renamed* Royal Sovereign.

Mary Rose *as she might have appeared after her refit, her center of gravity dangerously high. Note the contrast between the great bulk of the hull and superstructure above the waterline and the small proportion below it.*

Rose entered the Solent. She heeled over to starboard, water poured in through the open lower gunports, and she sank like a stone.

Sovereign of the Seas was the pride of Charles I's navy. She was launched in 1637 and cost £66,000, raised through the hated Ship Money tax. Characteristic of a ship of the line (a warship designed to fight in the line of battle), her primary weapons were her guns, boarding being seen as secondary. *Sovereign of the Seas* was then the largest ship in the world, displacing 1,700 tons, and the first to carry 100 guns. She served as the prototype for every British ship of the line until 1860.

She had three gun decks flush throughout the hull, with extra guns on the beak, forecastle, half deck, and quarter deck; gun crews on the upper decks were protected from falling debris by stout gratings. The upperworks of the hull were ornamented with gilded decoration known as gingerbread work. Her sail plan was unique, including royal sails above the fore and main topgallants and a topgallant on the mizzen. In 1651, she was refitted by Peter Pett, the son of Phineas, her designer. Her forecastle and after superstructure were lowered to improve her weatherliness. In 1660, she was renamed *Royal Sovereign* in honor of the Restoration.

Nelson's *Victory* best embodies the concept first expressed by naval designers in the *Sovereign*. Appropriately, she is preserved within a short distance of the *Mary Rose* at Portsmouth on the south coast of England.

8 THE BIRTH OF MODERN WAR

During the century that followed the end of the War of the Spanish Succession in 1714, many important developments in military science took place, and a number of characteristics emerged that might be ascribed to modern warfare. It also produced several of the greatest military commanders in history.

Certain factors remained constant for the first three-quarters of this century. Until the beginning of the Industrial Revolution in the later part of the eighteenth century, economies were based largely upon agriculture, which was so labor intensive that it was impossible to divert large numbers of workers into military pursuits without affecting radically the capability of a state to feed itself; thus armies remained small, and were drawn from the least productive members of society. This necessitated the imposition of the strictest discipline to control what the British Secretary at War in 1795 termed "men of a very low description," and led to the employment of mercenaries. These reinforced the fact that because wars were fought for the dynastic or personal motives of the monarchs who controlled the states, there was little overt "nationalism" beyond a personal loyalty to the monarch.

The conduct of wars was determined both by practicality and by ethical considerations. It is easy to overstate the latter, but the concept of limited war arising from the philosophy of enlightenment had an effect. (However, it is interesting to note that the most intellectually minded of the great captains, Frederick II of Prussia, while probably considering himself the model of the philospher-king, was capable of a degree of ruthlessness that hardly accorded with his love of music, literature, and philosophy.) Some elements of eighteenth-century warfare that corresponded to the theories of enlightenment were adopted for reasons of practicality. For example, in general, armies were not allowed to subsist by foraging off the countryside but were dependent upon the provisions held by supply depots and magazines. This was not to protect the civilian population, although that was the effect, but because the agricultural economies could not support such ravaging, and armies could not support the indiscipline that would have resulted. (This is not to imply that civilians did not suffer; the passage of an army frequently brought with it violence and desolation.) While enlightenment might suggest that the expending of human life was unjustified unless a specific goal was in view, it also made financial sense in that trained soldiers were so valuable that they should not be hazarded unless an action had a reasonable chance of success. Such quasiethical considerations extended throughout the period; as late as the Napoleonic Wars a considerable body of opinion held that killing the enemy was unjustified unless a specific object could be attained by it.

(Above) Frederick the Great, the dominant military figure of the mid-18th century. Frederick established Prussia as the fifth and smallest European great power.

In the first half of the eighteenth century there were few technological innovations in military weaponry. The musket remained basically unchanged to the end of the Napoleonic Wars, once the more substantial iron ramrod and socket-bayonet had been introduced at the beginning of the century. The musket could then be fired while the bayonet was fixed, making the pike redundant as a means of defense. Armies remained small, professional, and drilled to fight in rigid lines, with maneuver in action generally slow and limited. Few organizational developments were made, although the French Marshal Maurice de Saxe (1696–1750) experimented with legions composed of all arms (infantry, cavalry, and artillery,) which adumbrated the later concept of *corps d'armée* in producing autonomous formations capable of acting without support. Although Saxe was the finest general since Marlborough and Eugène of Savoy, his greatest influence was felt after his death with the publication of his book *Mes Rêveries*, which was still being quoted as a manual even after the Napoleonic Wars.

THE AGE OF FREDERICK THE GREAT

The dominant character of the middle of the eighteenth century was Frederick II of Prussia (1713–86). An immense influence upon military theory and one of the greatest generals of all time, Frederick the Great, as he was known, enjoyed two distinct advantages over many of his rivals: as a sovereign prince he was free of any strictures imposed by a superintending monarch or government; and he inherited from his father an extremely professional army and a state that was both prosperous and totally subservient, with a proficient internal organization, which allowed his wishes to be enacted with a minimum of difficulty.

Prussia first became an influential state in northern Europe under Frederick William of Brandenburg (1620–88), "the Great Elector," whose financial reforms and creation of a professional army laid the foundations for the reforms of his grandson Frederick William I, who molded a state that was ultimately both prosperous and strong, and possessed of the finest army in Europe. He did not, however, commit this army to war. It was left to his son, Frederick II, who succeeded to the throne in 1740, to prove that the Prussian army was capable not only of automaton-like drill on the parade ground but equally of stoic performance on the battlefield.

Frederick's first campaign arose out of the conflict over the rights of succession to the Holy Roman Empire following the death of the emperor Charles VI. Charles had no male heir, and had decreed that his successor should be his daughter, Maria Theresa, now the age of 23.

The Battle of Fontenoy (May 10, 1745), shown in this painting by Vernet, was a major combat during the Second Silesian War. Advancing into Flanders, the French army of Marshal Maurice de Saxe was opposed by an Allied army of British, Austrian, Dutch, and Hanoverian troops, commanded by William Augustus, Duke of Cumberland. Despite heroic efforts by the British and Hanoverian troops, Cumberland (shown here on the white horse) was defeated, but withdrew in good order.

This was disputed by other claimants, the Elector of Bavaria, Philip V of Spain, and Augustus III of Saxony. In November 1740, six months after succeeding to the throne of Prussia, Frederick declared that he would support Maria Theresa's claim, but that in return for this unrequested aid he would occupy Silesia, pending the settlement of an old Brandenburg claim to this province of the Empire. On December 16, 1740, he invaded, precipitating the First Silesian War, which in turn led to the War of the Austrian Succession.

In the early part of 1741 Frederick consolidated his grip on Silesia, but in the spring an Austrian army moved to reoccupy the province and on April 10 engaged Frederick at Mollwitz. Early Prussian reverses caused Frederick to quit the field, only to return upon receiving news that the magnificent Prussian infantry had held firm and driven the Austrians from the field. In the aftermath of this, Frederick's first victory, the war expanded with Bavaria, France, Saxony, and Savoy opposing Austria, while Britain and Holland supported Maria Theresa.

Following another Prussian victory at Chotusitz (May 17, 1742), Austria ceded Silesia to Prussia, which caused Frederick temporarily to leave the conflict.

Austrian fortunes improved in the following year, with George II of Britain winning a considerable victory with his Anglo-Allied-Hanoverian army against a French force at Dettingen (June 27, 1743), thanks largely to the discipline and spirit of the British and Hanoverian infantry. Similar successes for the Austrian camp led Frederick to reenter the war in August 1744, initiating the Second Silesian War. This finally turned the balance against Austria. Following Saxe's victory over an Anglo-Allied army at Fontenoy (May 10, 1745), which resulted in the French conquest of Austrian Flanders, Frederick shattered an Austrian army at Hohenfriedberg (June 4, 1745), and farther Prussian victories (notably at Sohr, September 30, 1745) led Maria Theresa to confirm Frederick's possession of Silesia by the Treaty of Dresden (December 25, 1745). Although campaigning continued in the Netherlands until 1747, to all intents the War of the Austrian Succession was ended, and hostilities were closed officially by the Treaty of Aix-la-Chapelle in October 1748.

Frederick the Great's infantry was the mainstay of his army, and became the model for the armies of Europe. The regiment of Prussian infantry numbered as the 6th (shown here, ca. 1759) was Frederick's Guard regiment, and composed entirely of grenadiers. All Prussian infantry wore blue uniforms, but the metal fronted miter cap was a unique distinction of the elite status of grenadiers.

THE ART OF WAR IN MID-CENTURY

Frederick's creative urge produced not only outpourings of musical and literary work, but also two military treatises of immense significance, his *Military Instructions* to generals of infantry and cavalry (1748). Initially secret documents, they were soon published and translated, and were of such great importance that even after the supersession of "Frederickian" methods by those of the Napoleonic era, they remained important references; a new edition was published in Britain as late as 1818. The *Instructions* contain much (but not all) of Frederick's military thought and, as befitted an enlightened monarch, emphasized the merits of limited war: "terminate every business prudently and quickly ... it is better one man perish than a whole people." "To shed the blood of soldiers when there is no occasion for it, is to lead them inhumanly to the slaughter." The cornerstone of Frederick's military system was the rigid discipline and precise drill that became synonymous with his army, which was necessary to hold its members in the ranks and discourage desertion. In contrast to the somewhat sterile characteristics of conventional tactics, where linear formations dominated and which relied upon slow-moving advances and measured volley-fire, Frederick practised offensive actions of maneuver.

FREDERICK THE GREAT'S "OBLIQUE ORDER"

The "oblique order" of attack was one of the most important of Frederick the Great's developments. It required an army to be well disciplined and capable of executing maneuvers under the most difficult of conditions. Initially, the army advanced toward the enemy line behind a strong advance guard, which engaged or occupied the attention of the enemy army; ideally, the maneuvers of the Prussians would also be screened from view by features of the terrain. The Prussian main body then deployed in echelon, or "oblique order," to engage the enemy's flank. Increasing pressure was put on the enemy's flank as each successive unit came into action. If all went according to plan, the enemy's flank would buckle, and the Prussian cavalry, stationed to protect the oblique attack, would then exploit any collapse of the enemy's position.

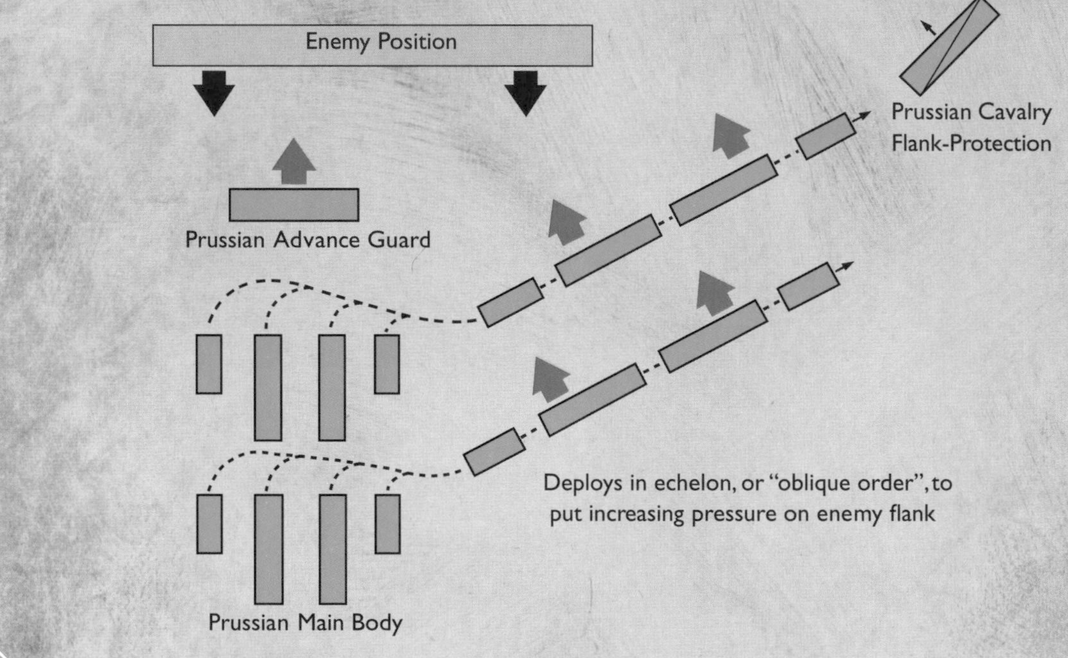

By emphasizing that wars were decided by success in battle, he made a conscious effort to defeat his enemies in the open field, thus hastening the demise of fortress warfare, which had been prominent in the preceding era. Frederick's most important development was the so-called "oblique order," adopted to counteract the disadvantage of disparity in numbers under which the Prussian army often fought, and to utilize the discipline and ability to maneuver of the superb Prussian infantry. The tactic was designed so that a portion of the enemy force would be outnumbered and defeated before the remainder could assist. Frederick reasserted the importance of the shock effect in cavalry tactics, and although the earlier practice of intermingling infantry and cavalry was still employed by the French as late as Minden (1759), in general Frederick's lead was followed, and cavalry employed in concentration, their principal tactic being the charge with the sword. There was also a development in the classification of cavalry into heavy regiments used primarily for such shock action, and light regiments, epitomized by Frederick's hussars, with the additional skills of skirmishing, reconnaissance, and raiding. Frederick devised the first truly mobile horse artillery, able to keep pace with and provide fire support for cavalry. Most significant was Frederick's recognition of the importance of supplies. As a consequence, he paid great attention to the provision of supplies for his own troops and to the disruption of his enemies' lines of communication.

A development of this period not influenced by Frederick was the increase of light infantry, troops skilled in skirmishing, scouting, and operating in "open order," that is not in the rigid line of battle. The most effective light infantry at this period were those maintained by Austria, mostly "irregulars" recruited from the Hungarian borders and using their indigenous skills of scouting and woodcraft. Although the Prussian army maintained some such units, Frederick never liked them, maintaining the belief that there was something faintly dishonorable about the tactics of such troops.

LIGHT INFANTRY

Originating in the middle of the eighteenth century, most notably in Austrian service and in the campaigns in North America, light-infantry tactics were the period's nearest equivalent to, and precursor of, modern tactics. Light-infantry service demanded a level of initiative greater than that of the automaton-like drill of the line, skill to take advantage of natural cover, and a higher level of marksmanship. As stated by the British *Volunteer Manual* of 1803: "Vigilance, activity, and intelligence, are particularly requisite ... a light infantry man ... should know how to take advantage of every circumstance of ground which can enable him to harass and annoy an enemy, without exposing himself ... To fire seldom and always with effect should be their chief study ... Noise and smoke is not sufficient to stop the advance of soldiers accustomed to war; they are to be checked only by seeing their comrades fall ..."

SEVEN YEARS WAR

The war, which began in 1756, utlimately raised Frederick to a position of preeminence, but in the course of making his military reputation unassailable he almost destroyed his kingdom. Such were the demands made upon the Prussian state in repelling the coalition against Frederick that not even his genius could have saved the day had it not been for the superb quality of the troops he led: the campaigns proved the validity of what he had written in his *Instructions*, that "with troops like these the world itself might be subdued ..."

The Seven Years War arose principally from the perceived threat of a militant Prussia. Austria allied with France, Russia, and others; Frederick's only ally was Britain, whose financial aid was essential. Seeing the threat of a coalition against him, Frederick invaded Saxony in late August 1756, taking possession after his defeat of an Austrian army at Lobositz (October 1, 1756). Frederick temporarily occupied part of Bohemia, defeating the Austrians at Prague (May 6, 1757) before having to retreat after a repulse at Kolin (June 18, 1757). In the second half of 1757, Frederick was forced onto the defensive in the face of invasions by Austrian, French, and Russian armies; from necessity, he was forced to revert to a reliance upon fortifications instead of the pure offense of his earlier career, perhaps demonstrating that, despite his tactical innovations, he was more a perfecter of accepted methods of war. He was aided greatly by his ability to use interior lines of defense, that is, he could operate in a more restricted area than the opponents who surrounded him, his lines of communication were shorter, and he was able to concentrate at different points more quickly than his enemies. Although the Prussian army had increased from 80,000 in 1740 to almost double that number by the early 1760s, the multiplicity of threats against Frederick meant that his resources had to be divided widely, and thus his field army was generally greatly inferior to that of his opponents: 21,000 against 64,000 at Rossbach, 35,000 against 65,000 at Leuthen, for example. Such disparity makes his eventual success the more amazing, and confirms that he was a military genius of the first rank.

MUSKETS AND ARTILLERY

Although improvements were introduced into the weaponry of 1714–1815, the capabilities of armaments remained to a large extent unchanged. The principal weapon was the smooth-bored musket or "firelock." Its accuracy was generally poor, so that although a maximum range of 700 yards (640 m) might be attainable, at anything over 100 yards (90 m) the chance of hitting a specific target was small. As George Hanger, a noted British marksman, wrote in 1814: "as to firing at a man at 200 yards (180 m) with a common musket, you may as well fire at the moon and have the same hope of hitting your object." Under the conditions of warfare of the era, however, it was not necessary to hit a single man at this distance. Troops maneuvered in packed formations, so all that was needed was to register a hit at any point on a block of men many yards long.

Infantry continued to maneuver in lines and columns; against cavalry, the universal defense was to form a square, all sides facing out, presenting an impenetrable hedge of bayonets on each side. The bayonet was carried by all troops armed with muskets, but was very rarely used except in the storming of fortified places or in isolated skirmishes. Its merit was almost entirely psychological. Bayonet charges were made only when the enemy was already wavering as a result of artillery fire or musketry.

Cavalry utilized the impetus of the charge, the sabers of the heavy regiments usually being straight but those of the light regiments often imitating Hungarian or central European design by having curved blades. From the later eighteenth century, the lance was reintroduced in a number of armies; generally a disadvantage in a cavalry mêlée against an enemy armed with sabers, against infantry the lance was a lethal weapon of execution.

Artillery remained smooth bored and muzzle loading. The principal ammunition was the solid iron cannonball or "roundshot," with explosive "common shells" generally

Musket drill: Present arms, first motion (top); present fire (middle); prime (bottom), when the ignition powder was poured into the pan. These prints are from Thomas Rowlandson's Loyal Volunteers of London & Environs, *published in 1798.*

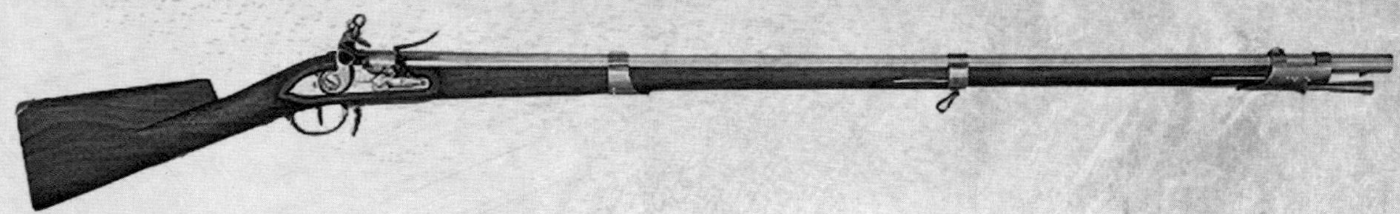

One of the most famous flintlock muskets was the French "Charleville". The musket was loaded via the muzzle with a lead ball and gunpowder in a cartridge, and ignited by the flintlock mechanism. When the trigger was depressed, the flintlock struck a spark, which was sent to the propellant charge via the touch hole in the barrel.

being restricted to howitzers, which were short-barrel guns designed for high-angle fire. These were the only weapons capable of "indirect" fire; ordinary cannon had so low a trajectory that they could not fire over the heads of friendly troops, and they had to be positioned among or in advance of the army's front line. Other projectiles included "canister" or "case shot"—musket balls packed into tin canisters, which ruptured upon leaving the muzzle, turning the cannon into a giant shotgun; and grapeshot—similar but using iron balls larger than musket shot.

The mechanics of targeting were improved greatly by the end of the eighteenth century with the invention of the "tangent sight" and the screw elevator, but a practicable rate of fire remained at two or three shots per minute. Projectiles could carry over a mile, but gunners generally reserved their fire until the target was within about half that distance. Canisters were restricted to short range, rarely beyond about 500 yards (460 m).

(Above) British infantry at Fontenoy. Smooth-bored muskets delivered volley fire. Bayonets were seldom used. (Below) French Gribeauval fieldpiece and coffret (ammunition chest.) Ordnance was improved with a lessening of weight but not of hitting power. Most effective was the French artillery designed by Jean-Baptiste de Gribeauval (1715–89). The light "battalion guns" of infantry units went out of use by 1800 and guns were employed in larger concentrations.

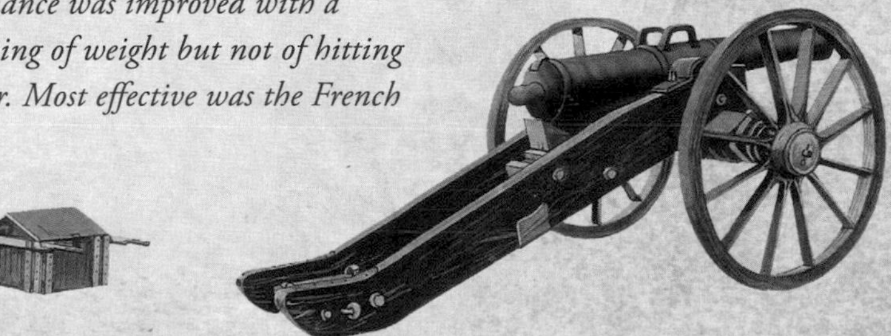

As the Allies converged on Berlin, Frederick won two victories of immense significance: at Rossbach (November 5, 1757) against a combined Franco-Austrian army, and Leuthen (December 6). Having repelled this threat, Frederick had a brief respite until the middle of the following year, when he was again assailed, this time by Austrian and Russian armies. The two main actions of 1758 (Zorndorf, August 25, against the Russians) and Hochkirch (October 14, against the Austrians) were inconclusive slaughters, but served to secure Frederick's position for another year. In 1759, Frederick's camp had a major success when Prince Ferdinand of Brunswick, with an Anglo-Prussian army, defeated a French army of twice their strength at Minden (August 1), another triumph for the resolute British infantry. In other respects it was a bad year for Frederick. His offensive against an Austro-Russian army broke down at Kunersdorf (August 12), a defeat that cost him more than one third of his army.

In 1760, Frederick continued to defend himself, outmaneuvering his opponents and defeating an Austrian army at Leignitz (August 15). He just won a desperate action at Torgau (November 3) when his original offensive miscarried. By the end of 1761, Frederick was on the verge of defeat, able to assemble only about 60,000 troops. His sustained resistance was almost in vain, until the death of Empress Elizabeth of Russia in January 1762 removed that state from the alliance against him. With Ferdinand of Brunswick continuing to hold off the French threat, Frederick was at last able to concentrate upon just one enemy, Austria, and after a farther victory at Burkersdorf (July 21, 1762)

BATTLE OF PLASSEY

DATE June 23, 1757

CAMPAIGN Anglo-French War in India

OBJECT The battle of Plassey arose out of Anglo-French rivalry in India, both nations endeavoring to exploit the riches of the subcontinent. The Nawab (prince) of Bengal, Siraj-ud-dowlah, with French assistance, opposed the operations of the British East India Company. In response to his temporary capture of the British base of Calcutta, the young British general Robert Clive (1725–74) marched against the nawab, who was encamped by a bend in the Bhagrathi River, at Plassey.

NUMBERS British—3,000 men, including about 700 Europeans; 10 small guns. Indians—50,000 men; 53 heavy guns. General Mir Jafar had been intriguing with Clive against the nawab.

DESCRIPTION Clive drew up his army before the Nawab's camp, but retired to the cover of mango groves when the artillery opened fire. In response, Clive's light guns were ineffectual, but the nawab's loyal general, Mir Madan, was mortally wounded. When a rainstorm soaked their gunpowder, the Nawab's forces began to retire. Clive advanced, driving back the nawab's small French contingent. Mir Jafar remained uncommitted, allowing Clive to storm the camp. The nawab fled and was later murdered, to be replaced as ruler by Mir Jafar.

CASUALTIES The nawab lost some 500 men, Clive lost 65.

RESULT The action was small but its effect was immense, opening India to Britain, and demonstrating that small bands of disciplined Europeans, resolutely commanded, could defeat huge native forces.

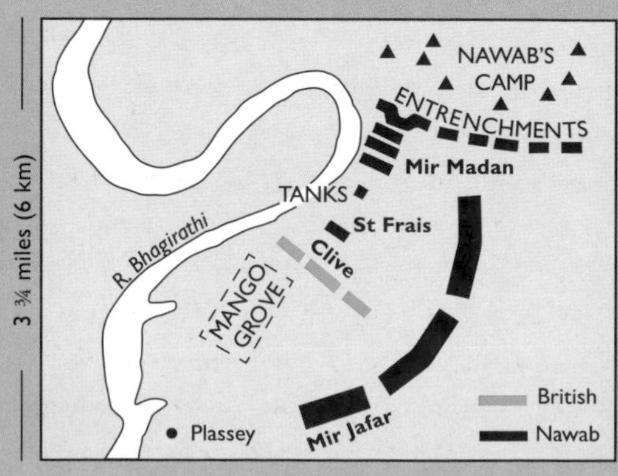

Frederick the Great and officers of his army: (Left to right) dragoon officer in the light blue uniform adopted in 1745; general of cuirassiers, with the light blue facings of the 5th and 11th regiments; Frederick, in the uniform of his guard grenadiers; General Hans Joachim von Zieten in the dress uniform of his 2nd Hussars, including eagle-wing plume; officer, guard grenadiers. Frederick himself was careless of his appearance and dressed very plainly.

all participants were too exhausted to continue. The Seven Years War ended with an armistice in November 1762 and a treaty in February 1763. The result of so great an effusion of blood was that little had been achieved beyond the survival of the Prussian state, Frederick retaining Silesia. It did, however, guarantee Frederick's place in the pantheon of military geniuses, his survival against overwhelming odds and assaults on all fronts being little short of astounding. It is hardly surprising that in the following years his army was imitated by almost every European state, except France.

CONFLICT IN THE COLONIES

The Seven Years War (or the French and Indian War) spilled over into the existing confrontation between Britain and France as colonizing powers in North America and India. These campaigns emphasized the increasing importance of seapower, no longer simply a matter of the protection of trading routes but now the defense of a line of communication in support of the increasing military operations in distant colonies.

In India, Anglo-French rivalry was played out against a background of tribal and factional warfare within the subcontinent, with much of the French effort being maintained by allied Indian rulers. The interests of both major European powers were channeled through trading agencies, the most powerful of which was the British East India Company, which had many of the powers of a sovereign state, including the right to declare war and to maintain its own army. Thus the British war effort was run almost by proxy and at less expense to the treasury than if the entire venture had been run by the government. The most decisive action of the period was the victory of the young Robert Clive, originally an East India Company clerk, over the immense army of the Nawab of Bengal at Plassey (June 23, 1757).

The extinction of French interests in India was assured by the British victory of Wandewash (January 22, 1760) and by the surrender of the main French base at Pondicherry (January 15, 1761), the fall of which was inevitable after the French navy was unable to overcome the squadrons supporting the British presence in India, confirming the importance of maritime supremacy. Although Pondicherry was restored to the French by the Treaty of Paris (February 10, 1763), the French trading organization, the *Compagnie des Indes*, was dissolved in 1769, leaving Britain with no serious European rival for the colonization and exploitation of the resources of India.

BATTLE OF QUEBEC

DATE September 13, 1759
CAMPAIGN Seven Years War
OBJECT British Prime Minister William Pitt the Elder wanted to expel the French from Canada; British attempts to capture Quebec, a principal French stronghold, were frustrated by the city's near impregnable position.
NUMBERS British–4,800; French–4,500.
DESCRIPTION Quebec, "the battle which won Canada," was one of the most audacious operations of the period of the Seven Years War. The British army commander of the expedition to Quebec was the young and dynamic General James Wolfe, one of the most outstanding British soldiers of the period. Transported by a British fleet, Wolfe landed below Quebec in late June 1759 but was unable to establish an effective foothold near the city to engage the French defenders, until a precarious path was discovered up the cliffs just north of the city. On the night of September 12–13, Wolfe led an amphibious landing along the St. Lawrence River and up the steep cliff path. By first light, his men were drawn up in front of the city, on the Plains of Abraham. The French commander, Louis Joseph, Marquis de Montcalm, immediately marched his men from his camping ground to oppose Wolfe. The armies being arrayed in opposing lines, the excellence of the British musketry drove the French away in moments; both commanders were wounded mortally, Wolfe dying on the battlefield and Montcalm that night.
CASUALTIES 58 British killed, 572 wounded; about 1,400 French killed or wounded.
RESULT Five days later Quebec capitulated, and although almost a year passed before the French rule of Canada was ended, the battle on the Plains of Abraham was the decisive action that ensured British possession of Canada.

North American battles

Anglo-French rivalry in North America had involved some considerable operations in King George's War (1740–48, contiguous with the War of the Austrian Succession), including the British-American capture of the French fortress of Louisbourg (1745), which was restored to France upon the conclusion of peace. The conflict was renewed before the outbreak of the Seven Years War, or the "French and Indian War." Campaigning in North America involved very different skills from those required in Europe, the terrain being most suited to what were described as "irregular" operations, that is, those involving the skills of scouting, skirmishing, and woodcraft, associated with light infantry, rather than line and volley fire. The two methods came into contact at the battle of the Monongahela (July 9, 1755), when General Edward Braddock's British army was ambushed and more than half were killed by a numerically inferior force of French and Indians.

At the beginning of the Seven Years War, the British ministry determined to drive the French from Canada and extend British rule throughout the whole of colonized North America. In July 1758, one-third of the British expedition recaptured Louisbourg (the second expedition had failed in 1757), but an attack on the French defenders of Fort Ticonderoga (held by the French commander in Canada, the Marquis de Montcalm) was a costly failure. Ticonderoga eventually fell in July 1759, but attempts to capture the French stronghold of Quebec were frustrated until the young General James Wolfe led an amphibious British landing, which surreptitiously established itself upon the Plains of Abraham, before Quebec, on the night of September 12–13, 1759. In the battle that followed, both Wolfe and Montcalm were mortally wounded, but the total defeat of the French led to the surrender of Quebec, and in September 1760, to the complete capitulation of the French in Canada. British domination of North America was confirmed by the Treaty of Paris, and the merits of light infantry tactics were henceforth unchallenged by most forward-thinking military experts.

Cornet Thomas Boothby Parkyns in the uniform of the British king's light dragoons, 1776–81, painted by John Boultbee. The uniform of light troops exhibited similar features in many armies, often including short coat tails and helmets. Uniforms similar to this, featuring the traditional red coat of the British army, were worn by the British light dragoons who served in the American War of Independence.

THE AMERICAN WAR OF INDEPENDENCE

Barely a decade after the victory in Canada, Britain faced a new challenge to their domination of North America. The rebellion of the 13 American colonies was the culmination of years of political dissent between the colonists and the home administration. The war, which began on April 19, 1775, with skirmishes at Lexington and Concord, was to have important implications for military developments in Europe, not least in the renewed confirmation of the value of proficient light infantry and the use of skirmish tactics in terrain that rendered European-style maneuver difficult. However, it is not correct to view the War of Independence as exclusively a conflict between backwoodsmen armed with rifled muskets against the less enterprising, solid formations of redcoats.

The emergence of the rifled musket was by no means a new development. The greatly enhanced accuracy attained by a rifled (internally grooved) barrel, which imparted spin to the bullet, had been recognized at least from the early sixteenth century, but had been neglected in most armies. With the light infantry tactics used in North America, the rifle was an ideal weapon.

In the hands of trained marksmen, the rifle was very effective. The colonists' military forces, however, based on the existing militia organization and the so-called "minute men" (capable of assembling at a moment's notice), while making limited use of rifled firearms, evolved into an army organized, equipped, and trained upon European lines, with the predominant weapon being the smooth-bore musket as carried by the vast majority of their British opponents.

A farther factor to emerge in the War of Independence was the growth of what might be termed a "national army." The men, even if enrolled under a degree of compulsion, felt an enhanced attachment to their cause, greater than if they had been simply professional soldiers who had enlisted for a livelihood.

Finally, the War of Independence differed from European conflicts in the lack of cavalry used by both sides, conditions and resources not being favorable for the deployment of large mounted formations; and it demonstrated the difficulties of attempting to direct and supply an army from the opposite side of the Atlantic.

Washington's army

From the unpromising material of haphazardly organized and poorly equipped militia, the Continental Congress at Philadelphia announced the establishment of a "Continental Army"—one comprising units not controlled primarily by their own states. George Washington (1732–99) was appointed commander. A Virginian landowner who had previously served the British (he had escaped from Braddock's disaster), Washington was the chief creator of the army that emerged from the original rabble, and he was certainly the most able general who served in the war. Washington's organizational skills were considerable, as was his ability to recognize the salient features of the strategic situation. He was loath to fight unless his chances of success were good, and his introduction of foreign professional soldiers to provide an experienced cadre was instrumental in perfecting the American army. The most significant of the foreign recruits was the Prussian Baron von Steuben, trained in the school of Frederick, who produced the first American drill manual.

BATTLE OF YORKTOWN

DATE September–October 1781
CAMPAIGN American War of Independence
OBJECT To defeat Charles, Earl Cornwallis, commander of British forces in Virginia, who in August had retired to Yorktown and Gloucester, each side of the York River, to await reinforcements.
NUMBERS British—7,500 men; 65 mostly light guns; provisions were not abundant and the army was sickly. American—about 9,000 men plus about 7,000 French; 92 guns in all.
DESCRIPTION On September 28, the Allied forces of North America and France began the investment of Yorktown. Cornwallis abandoned his untenable outer defenses on September 30, allowing the Allied artillery to bombard the whole of the Yorktown position. With his communications severed by the French fleet, Cornwallis was unable to receive help or evacuate his forces. The Allied siege lines pushed closer, two British redoubts being stormed on October 14; a spirited counterattack by the British was repelled two days later. Almost out of ammunition and supplies, with nearly 2,000 sick, Cornwallis was compelled to surrender (October 19), the British marching out to lay down their arms to the appropriate tune of "The World Turned Upside Down."
CASUALTIES American–French about 400; British 600, with the rest captured.
RESULT Although the war continued for more than a year, to all intents Yorktown secured the independence of the American colonies, and demonstrated the crucial importance of the control of the sea.

The first major engagement of the war was fought on June 17, 1775, at Bunker Hill, overlooking Boston Harbor. An entrenched American position was carried by the British at the third attempt, confirming yet again the steadiness of the British infantry under intense fire, and demonstrating the determination of the American colonists.

The value to the Americans of Washington's presence in command became obvious in 1776, when his small army escaped entrapment and inflicted two sharp reverses upon the British at Trenton (December 26, 1776) and Princeton (January 3, 1777), which probably saved the revolution from extinction.

Most actions in the American War were on a small scale, but nevertheless the results could be profound, such as the surrender of Sir John Burgoyne's outnumbered British army at Saratoga (October 17, 1777). This not only put new heart into the American camp, but was followed by French recognition of American independence, leading to a French declaration of war on Britain (June 17, 1778). This effectively turned the tide of the war. American fortunes were depressed in 1780, with serious reverses and unrest within the army; but Washington's appreciation of the strategic realities saved the day. With the help of the French fleet and the Comte de Rochambeau, commander of the French army, he outmaneuvered the British, and by isolating them from support, compelled the surrender of the army of Earl Cornwallis at Yorktown (October 19, 1781). Although this did not mark the end of hostilities, it was the final major action of the war. The Treaty of Paris (November 30, 1782) ended the American War, with the independence of the United States guaranteed and all British holdings evacuated.

THE ERA OF THE FRENCH REVOLUTION

The two decades and more of conflict that followed the French Revolution of 1789 resulted in radically new methods in the conduct of war. Some of these were farther developments from what had occurred in previous years, some were deliberately innovative, and some arose from necessity.

The deposition of the French monarchy by the French revolutionary movement, and its declared intention to export revolution to other states, caused the formation of a coalition, led initially by Austria and Prussia, determined to restore the *status quo ante* in France. The Revolution had left the French army in a parlous state. Its officer corps had been almost exclusively aristocratic, and it was decimated by the emigration of fugitive nobility, so that only the experienced cadre of the exroyal army was left as a nucleus for the formation of the large army that was required to repel the coalition gathering to invade France. Although this core of disciplined troops were of great value, the mass of volunteers and conscripts swept into the army in the early years of the revolutionary wars could not be trained in conventional methods, mainly because of a lack of time but also because some political radicals equated established practice with subservience and inequality. The early French revolutionary armies, however, had one great advantage over their opponents, in their nationalistic and patriotic fervor, which extended even to those conscripted compulsorily by the *Levée en Masse* of August 1793. This, enacted at a time when the French state was on the point of collapse, provided for the conscription of the entire male population, and thus produced the first truly "citizen army" of modern times. Although the first assault on France was repelled by the remnants of the old army, by the middle of the following year, France was in chaos, riven by "the Terror," stricken by Royalist risings within as well as assailed from without, and controlled by the Committee of Public Safety, whose political commissars frustrated the plans of those generals who escaped execution.

Discipline and fervor

The reorganization that followed not only saved France but set the style of tactics for the following 20 years. Lazare Carnot (1753–1823), war minister for the Committee of Public Safety, presided over the enactment of the *Amalgame*, decreed in February 1793 and enacted in January 1794, by which each regular battalion of exroyal infantry was allied to two volunteer or conscript

BAYONETS

The bayonet stems directly from pole arms, such as pikes, spears, and poleaxes. It was obviously inappropriate to have a firearm-bearing soldier encumbered by a pike, yet there was need for a pole arm to stand off cavalry, and for hand-to-hand encounters when ammunition was gone or when there was no time to go through the complicated process of reloading.

The original "bayonette"—the name came from the town of its supposed origin, Bayonne in France—was introduced into the French army in 1647. This was a plug bayonet, a spear like blade to which was attached a long conical steel plug that was inserted directly into the muzzle of the musket. A collar lodged against the barrel to prevent it from sliding in too far. This was serviceable enough, but had certain defects. The musket obviously could not be fired once the bayonet was fitted, and during the act of fitting, the soldier was virtually unarmed. Misfortune overtook an English army at Killiecrankie in 1689, when a sudden rush of Scottish Highlanders overwhelmed soldiers as they were attaching bayonets.

As a result of these defects, the socket bayonet was developed. This had the blade cranked and attached to a hollow sleeve, which

(Left) An English plug bayonet of 1688. The wooden handle was pushed into the muzzle of the musket to convert the weapon into a rudimentary pike. (Below) The 28th of Foot (the Gloucestershire Regiment) form a square at the Battle of Waterloo (1815) to resist a French cavalry attack. The front ranks kneel and brace their muskets against the ground, the blades angled up to disembowel any horse getting close.

slipped over the muzzle of the musket. The blade lay below the axis of the barrel and left sufficient clearance to permit the weapon to be loaded and fired while the bayonet was attached. The bayonet was firmly secured by a slot in the socket engaging with a stud on the barrel, requiring a half turn to fit or remove it.

The bayonet was originally a defensive weapon. Steady infantry standing two or three deep and adopting a "square" formation could defend their position against a sudden rush of cavalry; the combined length of the musket and bayonet was sufficient to permit a standing soldier to reach a man mounted upon a horse. It was this that led to the standard form of blade, a triangular reed-shaped section, which remained in use until the nineteenth century.

The idea of using a short sword as a bayonet was tried from time to time, but the first regular users of the sword-type blade appear to have been the British rifle regiments in the early 1800s. However, the advent of breech loading and then magazine arms provided infantry with a firepower capable of beating off cavalry, at which time the bayonet turned from being primarily defensive to being a personal offensive weapon. For this ,a knifelike blade was of more use than a spike blade, and so from the middle of the nineteenth century, the knife or sword blade became common, although a few armies still retained spike blades.

The difficulties of attaching bayonets in the heat of the battle led some armies to adopt permanently attached bayonets, which folded above or below the barrel of the weapon and could be released and locked into place very quickly. A singularity of the Imperial Russian army, which carried over into the Soviet army, was the permanently attached bayonet.

ATTACHING THE BAYONET

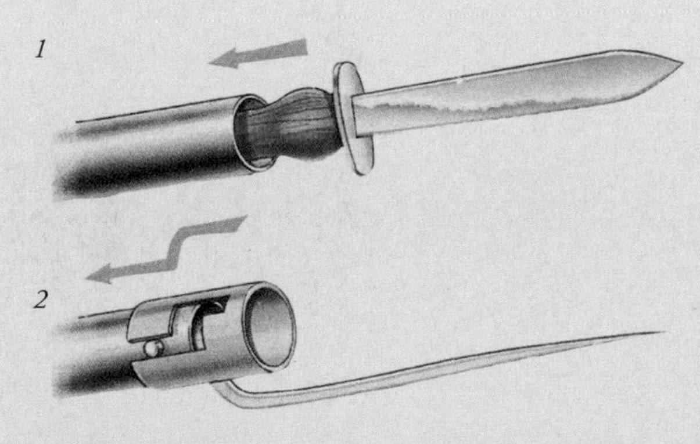

1. Plug bayonet—pushed directly into the muzzle of a musket.

2. Socket fitting— a sleeve attached over the muzzle by a push, a half turn, and another push.

3. Ring fitting—a spring catch in the handle engages with a stud on the rifle.

4. Folding bayonet—lies back under the fire end of the rifle, until swung forward for action and locked by a spring catch.

LINE VERSUS COLUMN

The diagram below, although a considerable simplification, illustrates the relative merits of the two principal battle formations of this period, line and column. Infantry in line (1.), usually two or three ranks deep, was able to bring every musket to bear simultaneously. An attack in column (2.) was capable of much more rapid movement, but unless it was deployed into line before battle was joined, it was at an immense disadvantage over the line because only the first two or three of its ranks were able to fire. (This weakness could be offset by preceding the attack with hordes of skirmishers, but this did not always occur.) The line might protect itself by stationing cavalry on its flanks or "refusing" the flank (throwing it back at an angle; 3.); and when the column had been engaged, part of the line could swing forward to enfilade the unprotected flank of the enemy column (4.).

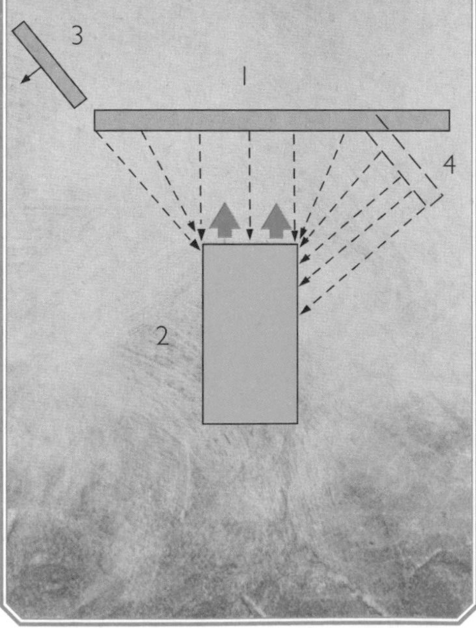

battalions. The plan was calculated to utilize the disciplined firepower of the regulars and the nationalistic fervor of the new battalions. By arraying the new battalions on either flank of the regular battalion in line, both qualities could be utilized simultaneously.

Two other tactical principles characterized the French revolutionary armies. The first was attack in column. Columnar formation (actually a succession of lines) could maneuver much more quickly than line formation, and although only the muskets of the first two or three ranks could be brought into play, the impetus of a charging column could burst through opposing lines of infantry. The second principle was associated with the column, and was the ultimate development of light-infantry tactics. To protect the column from the enemy's view and to gall the enemy line, it was usual for vast hordes of sharpshooters or skirmishers (*tirailleurs*) to be deployed. Although the French army included units designated as light infantry, the difference between them and the ordinary line regiments was minimal. All French troops were capable of fighting in "open order," and while some had enhanced skirmishing skills, it was possible for entire brigades to be deployed as skirmishers. In this, the French possessed great superiority: the Austrian army's light troops declined in effectiveness, and the British army, which had been so proficient in skirmish tactics in North America, ignored these troops in favor of Frederickian-style drill to such an extent that mercenaries had to be employed as light troops in the early campaigns of the French Revolutionary War. Not until the early nineteenth century did Britain possess a small, light infantry arm, which was superior even to that of France. The other main Napoleonic combatants, Prussia and Russia, were never as proficient in skirmish tactics despite the tradition of rifle shooting prevalent in Germany.

Another critical factor that emerged from the revolutionary period was the French method of supply. At first, the French republic was simply unable to provide enough food for its rapidly enlarged armies, so that troops had to resort to "living off the land" or foraging, and although they frequently went hungry, almost by chance this situation provided a great strategic advantage—by not being tied to supply depots, and not needing to guard lines of communication at all costs, French armies attained a freedom of movement totally surpassing that of their opponents, whose retention of the old system of supply lines and whose frequent halts to bake bread put them at an immense disadvantage. Such was the effect of this rapidity of movement that even when conventional methods of supply were possible, the French army retained the system of foraging until it totally broke down in the winter of 1806–7. In the face of his army's literal starvation, Napoleon was obliged to reintroduce a more effective means of supply.

THE RISE OF NAPOLEON

Having repelled initial attacks, the French made such progress that a number of their enemies (including Prussia) were forced to make peace in mid-1795. France occupied the Netherlands and directed her operations against Austria, one of the two most persistent opponents of the French throughout the period. The other was Britain, which had entered the coalition against France in 1793. Only Britain remained at war with France continually, except for the brief Peace of Amiens, 1802–3.

From 1796 the war was waged on two principal fronts, in Germany and northern Italy. The campaigning in Italy gave rise to the dominant military personality of his generation, Napoleon Bonaparte. He first came to prominence in 1793 when, as an obscure officer of artillery, he was instrumental in ejecting an enemy expedition that had occupied Toulon. After that, his connections with the Directory (the new French government established in August 1795) led to his appointment to command the ragged and ill-disciplined French armies opposing the Austrians in Italy. Operations hinged around Austrian attempts to relieve their beleaguered garrison at Mantua, and by a combination of his military skill and the way he was able to galvanize his troops by the force of his personality, Bonaparte was able to defeat greatly superior Austrian armies with regularity, most notably at Lodi (May 10, 1796), at Castiglione (August 5, 1796), Arcola (November 15–17, 1796), and at Rivoli (January 14, 1797). Having compelled Austria to make peace and then established French satellite republics in northern Italy, Bonaparte attempted to create the foundation of a French Middle Eastern empire by his optimistic expedition to Egypt.

BATTLE OF FLEURUS

DATE June 26, 1794
CAMPAIGN French Revolutionary Wars
OBJECT An Austro–German army, under Saxe-Coburg, came to relieve Charleroi, which had been captured the previous day by the French, under Jourdan.
NUMBERS Jourdan commanded some 75,000 men; Saxe-Coburg about 52,000.
DESCRIPTION Jourdan believed his army to be greatly inferior to that of Saxe-Coburg, so decided to hold a partly entrenched and widely spread position to the north and west of Charleroi. Saxe-Coburg made an error in his tactical deployment by attempting to attack all along the French line, instead of concentrating upon a single sector; consequently, five main columns attacked the French simultaneously. Jourdan was able to combat all the Austrian attacks (he was aided by the use of an observation balloon, the earliest example of aerial reconnaissance), so that an Austrian breakthrough was prevented. Saxe-Coburg made a number of territorial gains, but French counterattacks drove him back, and after six hours' fighting, the Austrians retired.
CASUALTIES The Austrians lost about 2,300 killed and wounded; Jourdan about 4,000.
RESULT Saxe-Coburg did not renew his attack; the French continued to advance and expelled the Austrians forever from the southern Netherlands, securing the northern frontier of France.

BATTLE OF MARENGO

DATE June 14, 1800
CAMPAIGN War of the Second Coalition
OBJECT To establish French dominance over northern Italy.
NUMBERS Napoleon had divided his forces and was encamped with 24,000 men and 23 guns at Marengo, near Alessandria; the Austrians had 31,000 men.
DESCRIPTION Austrian General Michael Melas succeeded in surprising the French in the early hours of June 14. Napoleon sent a frantic request for help to his scattered divisions, but by midafternoon the French had been driven back by three Austrian columns, and so confident of victory was Melas that he handed over the pursuit to his deputy, General Zach. Napoleon's luck changed with the arrival of his subordinate, General Louis Charles Desaix, who without waiting for orders had begun to march his division toward Napoleon as soon as the cannonade was heard. Arriving at about 5 p.m., after a forced march, Desaix declared that although one battle was lost, there was still time to win another, and attacked. He was seconded by a crucial cavalry charge led by General François Etienne Kellermann. Despite Desaix's death at the head of his troops, the weary French mounted a counterattack, which turned the expected Austrian victory into a complete rout.
CASUALTIES French about 7,000; Austrians about 7,000 and 7,000 prisoners.
RESULT Next evening Melas signed an armistice, and although the war lasted until February 1801, Marengo was the decisive blow. Napoleon made much of his victory; but credit should have gone to Desaix and Kellermann.

Although he defeated the Mameluke and Ottoman armies sent against him, the crucial nature of the command of the sea was demonstrated again when the French fleet was annihilated by the British admiral Horatio Nelson at Aboukir Bay (August 1, 1798), isolating the French from resupply. Their army was eventually defeated by a British expedition (1801), but Bonaparte had returned to France in late 1799 to establish himself as the country's leader with the title of "First Consul," the three-man Consulate having replaced the corrupt and ineffective Directory by a coup d'état.

During Bonaparte's absence in Egypt, a Second Coalition had been formed against France, and Austro-Russian forces had driven the French from Italy. Assembling a new army, Bonaparte made an audacious advance through the Alpine passes into northern Italy, and defeated the Austrians convincingly at Marengo (June 14, 1800). Farther defeats on the German front compelled Austria once again to make peace, and for a brief period, even France's most intractable enemy, Britain, agreed to a cessation of hostilities, ending the French Revolutionary War.

Bonaparte's star was now fully in the ascendant, and he was proclaimed "Consul for Life" on August 2, 1802. From there, it was merely a short step to his coronation as Emperor of the French (December 2, 1804). He styled himself Napoleon I, from which the era takes its title. This meteoric rise was proof of the validity of Napoleon's remark that, under the social conditions that arose from the French Revolution, if the talent were present, every soldier carried a marshal's baton in his knapsack.

NAPOLEON'S ART OF WAR

In assessing the reasons for Napoleon's successes, his own abilities are of paramount importance. His military capabilities are beyond question, to which were joined a capacity for unceasing hard work, ruthlessness, a grasp of political realities, and an ability to engender not only respect and admiration among his followers but adoration verging upon idolatry. He also had the great advantage of "unity of command": he had no political masters to obey, both foreign and military policy being entirely in his hands.

Although he inspired and led the army that achieved his great victories, he was not a great innovator, but rather he refined the elements that were already in existence, including the reforms and reorganizations of Carnot as well as earlier ones. The artillery, for example, one of Napoleon's most effective arms, had been modernized radically from 1765 by Jean-Baptiste de Gribeauval, whose artillery system remained the finest in Europe until well into the nineteenth century. Artillery employment changed during the period in a manner common to several armies, with the realization that, where sufficient guns were available, a concentration of artillery fire was more than the sum of its parts. This led to the general discarding of so-called "battalion guns"—lighter fieldpieces that accompanied individual battalions to provide immediate fire support—and the assembly instead of larger formations, "massed batteries," which became an offensive arm. They could blast a hole in the enemy line for infantry or cavalry to exploit, instead of, as previously, acting basically as a support for the other arms.

Napoleon's cavalry attained great significance, but although the French cavalry at the outset of the revolutionary wars was wretched, the basic tactics and classifications were established before Napoleon's time.

A grenadier of Napoleon's Imperial Guard, shown in a contemporary print by Pierre Martinet. The imperial guard was perhaps the most famous military formation of the Napoleonic era, originating as a bodyguard and increasing in size until it became the army's most valuable reserve in the later campaigns. The Grenadiers of the Guard—mostly part of the "Old Guard" of stalwart veterans—were known by the nickname grognards *(grumblers.)*

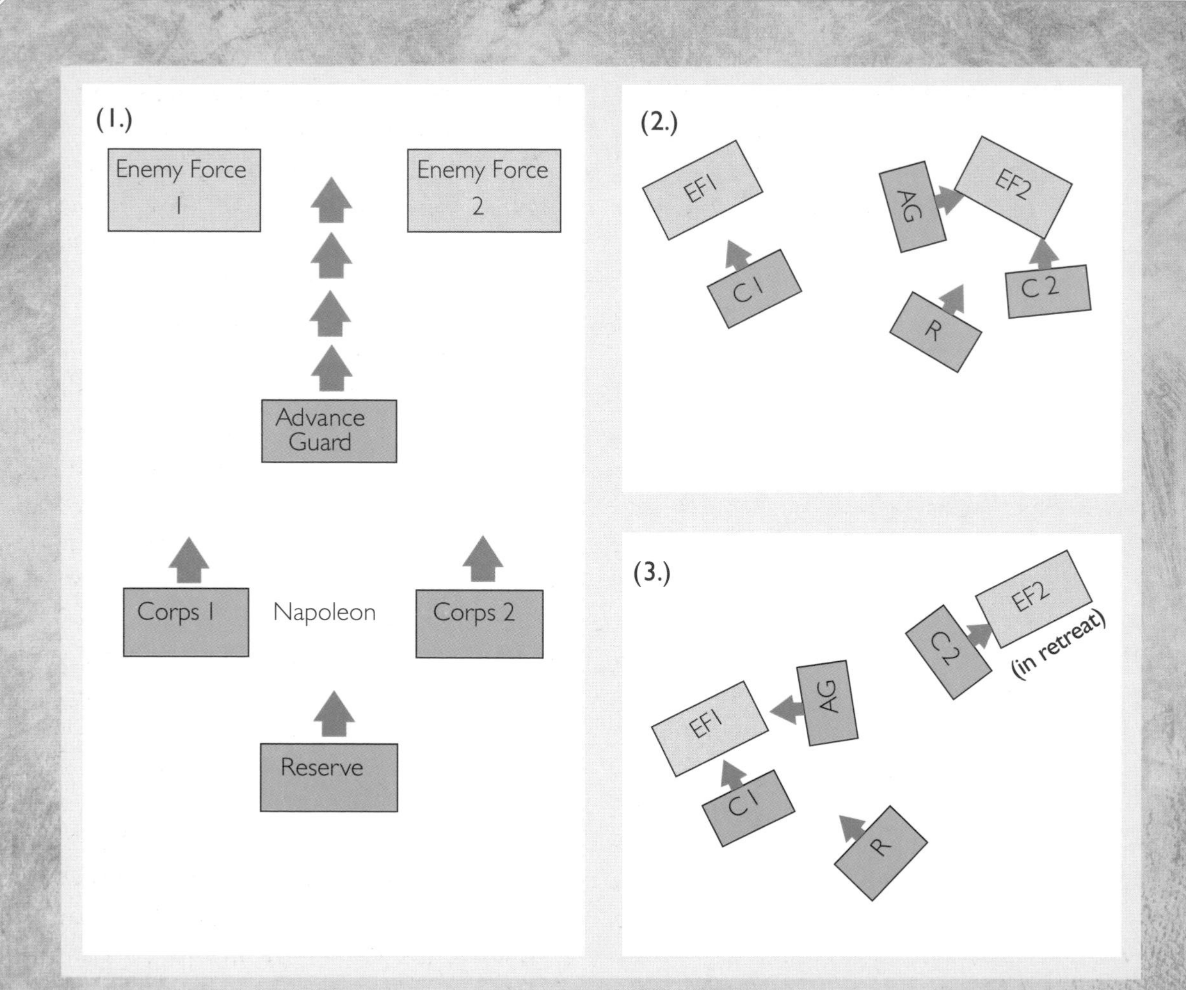

NAPOLEON'S TACTICS

Napoleon's method for defeating one or more enemy forces whose combined strength was greatly superior to his own consisted of seizing the so-called "central ground," and depended upon the ability of each of Napoleon's *corps d'armée* to be able to operate without support for a considerable length of time. Initially (1.), a rapid march would establish Napoleon's force between the two enemy bodies, hence the "central ground." One autonomous corps would then fight a holding action against one of the enemy forces (2.) while Napoleon concentrated the rest against the second enemy force, enabling him to defeat it by achieving local superiority of numbers. When this enemy force was in retreat, just one French corps would be assigned to pursue it (3.), while Napoleon marched the remainder to the assistance of the corps fighting the holding action. He would then defeat the second enemy force, again by achieving local superiority of numbers.

At the beginning of the nineteenth century, another development took place of crucial significance in the creation of semipermanent higher formations. Previously, the largest tactical unit had usually been the regiment, or sometimes a temporary association of two or more in a brigade. Although some nations were remarkably slow in introducing permanently organized brigades, these units were soon followed by the organization of two or more brigades into divisions, which usually included their own cavalry detachment (for reconnaissance), artillery, and supporting services. The existence of such formations greatly facilitated the transmission of orders, so that with the establishment of a "general staff" of trained administrative and command officers, the general's orders could be enacted very much more rapidly than orders transmitted to each regiment from one central source.

Equally, the organization of supply was facilitated, a factor vital to the management of armies of ever-increasing size. Napoleon took this one stage farther with the creation of autonomous *corps d'armées* of two or more divisions, each complete with all its supporting services and each capable of fighting a battle unaided. Allied with the capacity for rapid marches made possible by the practice of "living off the land," this was perhaps the most important feature of Napoleon's system of war. Its efficacy was demonstrated by his advance upon Austria in 1805, which completely outmaneuvered the Austrians and led to the surrender of a large part of their army, and his advance upon Prussia in 1806.

Master of strategy

Aspects of the French system were copied by many of Napoleon's enemies, but rarely with equal success. For example, Austrian attempts to institute a system of partial foraging were disastrous. Austria, Prussia, and Russia all adopted a system of *corps d'armée*, but only Britain devised an effective counter to the French method of attack, in Wellington's use of the "reverse slope" tactic. By concealing his troops on the reverse slope of a low ridge and behind proficient light infantry, they were shielded from both the fire and the view of the attacking French; thus when the British advanced in line to the crest just as the French attack approached, their appearance was a surprise, the French were unable to deploy, and their columns were defeated by a brief burst of British musketry followed by a controlled bayonet charge upon the wavering French ranks. Despite the success of the tactic, it was not adopted by other nations opposed to Napoleon.

As a strategist, Napoleon was the nonpareil of the age. His aim was always to destroy the enemy's field army instead of to embark upon protracted campaigns based upon the occupation of territory; the French capacity for rapid movement permitted the most audacious maneuvers and resulted in a number of speedily decided campaigns. Against numerically superior enemies, he maneuvered his opponents into two bodies, concentrating first against one and then against the other, each time achieving "local superiority" of numbers and defeating each one in turn. Alternatively, he would engage the enemy with a minority of his army and swing around the opposing flank with the bulk of his force, the so-called "strategy of envelopment," cutting the enemy's communications and forcing him to fight upon Napoleon's terms. As a strategist, Napoleon's only real failing was his inability to grasp the significance of sea power.

NAVAL WARFARE

Warships in the eighteenth century were divided into two basic categories. The larger vessels, "ships of the line" (originally "of the line of battle") were two- or three-decked craft, essentially floating gun-platforms designed to batter the enemy with their heavy armament. They were classified according to the number of guns they carried, which varied according to nationality and period. Typically, "first raters" would have 110 guns or more, "second raters" 98 guns, "third raters" 64 to 80 guns, and "fourth raters" from 50 to 64 guns. Naval artillery was generally heavier than that used on land; cannon firing a 32-pound (14.5 kg) shot were the standard arm. The carronade was introduced in the later eighteenth century (named from the place of its original manufacture, Carron Ironworks at Falkirk, Scotland). This was a short-barreled gun used for close-quarters action, so terribly efficient that it gained the nickname "the smasher."

The smaller warships were the frigates of 32 to 44 guns—"fifth raters"—and the smaller sloops, brigs, and gunboats, which were "sixth raters" of up to 28 guns.

Naval tactics were determined by the fact that a ship could discharge its guns from only the sides, producing "broadsides." Thus originated the "line of battle" in which opposing fleets would assemble in line astern and batter each other with broadsides, often at extremely close range. When locked together, a boarding party might be sent on to the enemy ship, the crews fighting hand to hand. In general, the "line of battle" was a sterile formation, which precluded decisive victory.

Admiral George Rodney used this tactic at the Battle of the Saints, April 12, 1782. The French flagship Ville de Paris is shown in the center of this painting in ean ngagement with the HMS Barfleur.

A typical "ship of the line," these were the most effective naval vessels, with between 50 and 110 guns. The larger ships had three gun decks. The smaller ships, especially frigates, were equally useful for such duties as reconnaissance and raiding. Probably the most famous ship of the line of the era is HMS Victory, *which was built at Chatham in 1765. A 100-gun "first rater,"* Victory *served as Lord Nelson's flagship at the Battle of Trafalgar in 1805.*

For a decisive action, a revised tactic was necessary, which took advantage of the comparative helplessness of a ship attacked from bow or stern, where its gunnery could not respond. The application of this tactic in a major action was postulated by a British writer, John Clerk, who printed privately a treatise on naval tactics, which advised that the fleet should deliberately break the enemy's line, overwhelming that part astern of the break before the remainder were able to change their course and return to help. The theory was perfected by Horatio Nelson, who at Trafalgar broke the enemy line in two places by attacking in two columns. Once the line of battle had devolved into a number of close-quarter, ship-to-ship actions, superior discipline, ship handling, and gunnery were the deciding factors, in which the British navy at this period surpassed all others.

A farther factor was the conflicting theory of targeting. The French aimed to destroy the enemy's rigging and masts, to render them incapable of pursuit, in accordance with the French policy of seeking combat only when a definite objective was in view. For the British, the destruction of enemy ships was sufficient in itself to justify combat, and their gunnery was thus targeted on the enemy's hull, with the objective of destroying guns and killing the crew, and so rendering the ship incapable of farther operation.

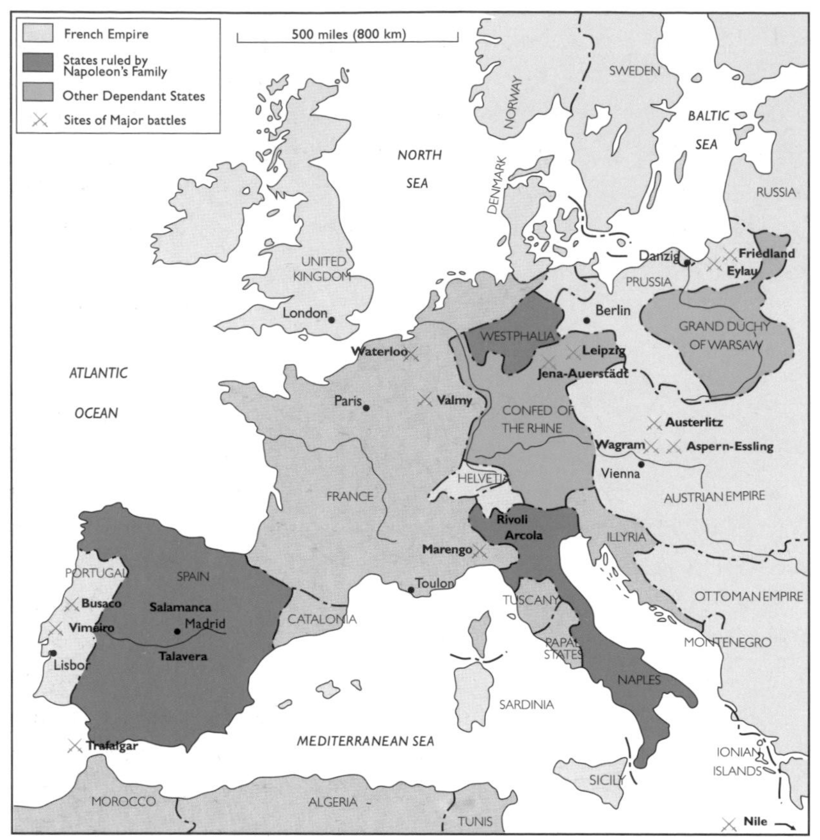

Napoleon's Europe exhibited the results of successful French campaigns from the mid-1790s. Military conquest expanded the borders of the French empire into the Netherlands and northern Italy, with client states located between France and Napoleon's enemies. Most significant of these was the Rheinbund, *or "Confederation of the Rhine." Ultimately, the attempt to impose his brother Joseph as king of Spain, and the continued conflict with Britain, undid him. This map, showing Napoleon's empire, demonstrates his strategic problems. Napoleon was unable to supervise more than one campaign in person, and the conflict in the Iberian peninsula was a constant drain on his resources.*

THE NAPOLEONIC WARS

The war between France and Britain resumed in 1803. Napoleon's initial aim was an invasion of England, to which end he had to divert as much of the British navy as possible to allow him temporary domination of the English Channel. His plan to decoy the British fleet to the West Indies failed, and a considerable proportion of his fleet and that of his ally, Spain, was destroyed at Trafalgar (October 21, 1805), which ensured that the plan of invasion could never be resurrected.

Even before the Battle of Trafalgar, however, Napoleon had postponed the invasion and turned instead upon Austria, who together with Russia had joined Britain in the third coalition against France. In one of the most brilliant operations of his career, Napoleon made a lightning march to the Danube, enveloping a large part of the Austrian army, which was forced to capitulate at Ulm (October 20, 1805), a strategic victory without parallel. He completed his most successful year by smashing the main Russo-Austrian field army at Austerlitz (December 2, 1805), which led almost immediately to Austria's exit from the war.

In 1806, Napoleon turned upon Prussia, which had finally decided to join the allied opposition to France, partly from disquiet over Napoleon's establishment of an organization of French satellite states in Germany, the *Rheinbund,* or Confederation of the Rhine. Undertaking another advance of amazing swiftness, Napoleon destroyed the main Prussian army at Jena and Auerstädt (October 14, 1806), removing Prussia from the war in little over a week.

He followed this by engaging the Russians at Eylau (February 8, 1807) and, much more decisively, at Friedland (June 14, 1807). The peace terms that

Napoleon dictated to the czar at Tilsit in the following month made him master of almost all of western and central Europe.

This left Britain alone in opposition to France, and in an attempt to strangle British trade Napoleon devised his "continental system" by which British goods were prohibited from all the states over which Napoleon exerted influence. Due to the British domination of the sea, this had hardly any economic effect on Britain, whereas the British naval blockade and actions against French trade wrecked the French maritime economy.

The Peninsular War

In an attempt to impose the continental system throughout Europe, Napoleon invaded Portugal (Britain's last supporter) via his ally, Spain, following which he decided to depose the ineffectual Spanish monarchy and replace it with a Bonapartist regime under his brother Joseph, who became king. This had two important consequences. First, it inflamed the Spanish population in a widespread revolt, a farther example of the new concept of "patriotic war." Although the caliber of the Spanish army was low, popular risings resulted in a most brutal guerilla war that occupied vast numbers of French troops.

Second, it led to British intervention in the Iberian peninsula, turning the war into a "Spanish ulcer," which ultimately bled Napoleon's empire to an insupportable degree. Napoleon intervened in the Peninsular War only briefly in person, being otherwise occupied in eastern Europe. Although he had many capable subordinates, command in Spain was never unified under a general approaching Napoleon's stature, and the French defeat proved that Napoleon's possessions were too widespread for a war to be waged successfully on more than one front simultaneously.

The Peninsular War also produced the other dominant general of the age, Arthur Wellesley, Duke of Wellington. Wellesley came to prominence in India in a number of successful campaigns that had taught him the basics of his art, his most important victory being at Assaye on September 23, 1803, against the Marathas.

BATTLE OF AUSTERLITZ

DATE December 2, 1805
CAMPAIGN War of the Third Coalition
OBJECT Napoleon wanted to break the Allies' coalition.
NUMBERS Napoleon—73,200 men, 139 guns; Alexander I of Russia and Francis I of Austria—85,400 men, 278 guns. Russian General Mikhail Kutuzov was inhibited by the overbearing presence of the two rulers.
DESCRIPTION Napoleon had moved rapidly to isolate the Austrian army and compell its surrender at Ulm on October 20. Then, by feigning weakness, he persuaded the Allied commanders to advance against him before they had been reinforced. The armies met at Austerlitz, near Brunn in Moldavia. The Allied army maneuvered exactly as Napoleon had hoped: General Peter Bagration's secondary attack to the north was contained by the French Marshal Lannes, and as the main Allied force advanced, Napoleon counterattacked with Marshal Soult's corps. The Allied army was split in two, and as Napoleon reinforced Soult and drove back an attempted counterattack by the Russian Guard, it disintegrated.
CASUALTIES French losses were almost 9,000; Allied losses were 26,000.
RESULT The battle's consequences were immense: Austria capitulated two days later and the Russians retired to their own territory. Austerlitz was a tactical masterpiece, and ranks with the greatest victories in history. It was a product of Napoleon's genius and the magnificent quality of his army.

Two members of Wellington's infantry wearing the British army's traditional redcoat. The soldier on the left is a private of the 23rd (Royal Welsh) Fusiliers, and the soldier on the right is a private of the 6th (1st Warwickshire) Regiment. Both are wearing their campaign uniform of 1812, as depicted by Charles Hamilton Smith in his Costume of the Army of the British Empire (1812–14).

Although Wellesley learned his trade on a continent where the most successful tactic was rapid attack by a small European force against immensely more numerous but ill-disciplined Indian armies, the limited nature of his resources in the peninsula resulted in his adoption of a defensive mode of warfare until he was strong enough to take the offensive, from 1812. He also demonstrated his mastery of tactics, which, although his strategical skill was probably not as great as that of Napoleon, firmly established him as one of the greatest commanders of his or any other age. The British army's preeminent reputation was confirmed by these campaigns. As Wellington observed, the force that he molded and commanded with such genius was for its size probably the most complete military machine then in existence.

Despite the evacuation of one British army (that of Sir John Moore, killed in the battle of Corunna on January 16, 1809) from the peninsula in the face of enormous odds, Britain retained a foothold at Lisbon, through which port her army was supplied, farther confirmation of the enormous advantage accorded by British command of the sea. Wellesley attempted an offensive into Spain, winning a hard battle at Talavera (July 28, 1809), but the impossibility of cooperation with the ineffectual Spanish forced him onto the defensive. He retired behind the Lines of Torres Vedras, a fortification he devised to secure the Lisbon peninsula. By the British operation of a scorched-earth policy in front of the Lines, the French were starved into retreat, a major triumph for the most effective fortification of the period.

By 1812, Wellesley (now the Duke of Wellington) was sufficiently powerful to mount an offensive against the French forces, weakened by the diversion of resources to the east and the continual harassment by Spanish guerrillas. Wellington won a major victory at Salamanca (July 22, 1812), advanced again in the following year, destroyed King Joseph's army at Vittoria (June 21, 1813), crossed the Pyrenees, and invaded southern France before the war ended. British financial aid to

The Battle of Polotsk, August 17–18, 1812, during Napoleon's disastrous Russian campaign. The French Marshal Oudinot and General St. Cyr with their French and Bavarian corps drove back General Wittgenstein's Russian army. Taking command after Oudinot was wounded, St. Cyr was rewarded with a marshal's baton. Wittgenstein was defeated again, on November 14, 1812, in the second Battle of Polotsk, fought near the same location.

others of Napoleon's opponents was crucial, but the Peninsular War was of major significance in Britain's contribution to Napoleon's downfall.

Napoleon's personal efforts in Spain ended in early 1809, when he had to return to Germany to face a renewal of the war by Austria. He was not immediately successful, for although he captured Vienna, the main Austrian army eluded him, and in an attempt to engage them by bridging the Danube, Napoleon suffered his first serious reverse at Aspern-Essling (May 21–22, 1809). A renewed and better-organized attempt at crossing the Danube was successful, and the French inflicted a comprehensive defeat upon the Austrians at Wagram (July 5–6, 1809), ending the war.

In 1812, in the face of renewed Russian hostility, Napoleon assembled an immense *grande armée* drawn from all the states under his influence, a multinational force of quite exceptional size, with which he invaded Russia in June—more than 450,000 men took part in the invasion, not including supporting formations. Unable to win a decisive victory over the Russian army, despite an immensely bloody battle fought at Borodino (September 7, 1812), Napoleon advanced to capture Moscow but, with much of the city burned by Russian incendiaries, he had to retreat in the late fall and winter. A combination of severe weather and Russian harassment practically destroyed his army. From this point Napoleon's fall was inevitable.

He gathered a new army in 1813, but the Russian success led to Prussia rebelling, encouraged by a vociferous German nationalist movement, and the "war of liberation" began. Austria and Sweden joined the forces closing in around Napoleon, resulting in the "Battle of the Nations" at Leipzig (October 16–19, 1813).

BATTLE OF LEIPZIG

DATE October 16–19, 1813
CAMPAIGN Napoleonic Wars
OBJECT After Napoleon's defeat in Russia in 1812, he was assailed by a coalition of Russia, Austria, Prussia, and Sweden, intent on driving the French from their client-states in Germany. Having failed to defeat the Allied forces in detail, Napoleon concentrated around Leipzig, upon which the four allied armies advanced.
NUMBERS Napoleon's army, numbering about 120,000 on the day before the battle, was reinforced to about 195,000 with 700 guns. The Allies' original force of 250,000 increased to 365,000 men and 1,500 guns.
DESCRIPTION Napoleon intended to hold a defensive perimeter around the city of Leipzig, while the allies attacked in four main columns. Their first attack was made on October 16, but the key action took place on October 18, when a massive allied attack was mounted upon all parts of Napoleon's line. Hopelessly outnumbered, Napoleon had no option but to order a retreat westward. Although he managed to extricate much of his army, the defeat he had suffered was of major proportions.
CASUALTIES Napoleon sustained about 73,000 casualties (killed and wounded) and the Allies about 54,000.
RESULT The defeat at Leipzig cost Napoleon control of Germany—his Saxon allies actually deserted him during the battle—and laid France open to invasion in 1814.

Napoleon was fortunate to escape with part of his army. With Germany lost and his erstwhile satellites turned against him, Napoleon prepared to defend France in the following year. He had been suffering from worsening ill health from at least 1812, but for a time in 1814 his old skill and vigor returned. However, his skillful maneuvers against the converging allied forces served only to postpone the inevitable. Assailed on all fronts and with his resources collapsing, Napoleon abdicated on April 11, 1814.

At the same time as the later Napoleonic campaigns were being waged, another conflict occurred in North America between the United States and Britain, the "War of 1812." Although its actions were small in comparison with the huge actions fought in Europe, it was significant in diverting considerable British resources from the war against Napoleon, and for the series of remarkable "frigate actions" in which the Americans were successful, denting the prestige of the British navy for the first time in the period. American attempts to invade Canada were repelled, as were British landings in the United States, although a considerable success was the burning of Washington's public buildings (including the White House) by a British expedition. The last and most famous action of the war, the repulse of a British force at New Orleans (January 8, 1815), was fought before news of the signing of peace was received by the opposing armies.

Peace in Europe was short lived. Exiled to the Mediterranean island of Elba, Napoleon brooded for some months before returning to France. He reestablished control quickly and determined to take the offensive immediately to endeavor to achieve one major victory to strengthen his bargaining position before he was overwhelmed by the coalition again formed against him. He invaded the Netherlands, intending to defeat the Anglo–Netherlands and Prussian armies under Wellington and Blücher respectively; but although he defeated the latter at Ligny (June 16, 1815), Blücher extricated his army and, determined to support his ally at all costs, marched to support Wellington's position at Waterloo. The battle fought there on June 18, which destroyed the French army and ended Napoleon's career, is probably the most famous of modern times, and was a climactic end to an era in which the nature of warfare changed radically and in which many aspects of modern warfare can be recognized.

BATTLE OF WATERLOO

DATE June 18, 1815
CAMPAIGN The Hundred Days of Napoleon's restoration
OBJECT Napoleon escaped from his exile on Elba on February 26, 1815, and very quickly reestablished his rule in France. It was imperative for him to score an early victory to improve his bargaining position.
NUMBERS Napoleon—105,000 men; Wellington—68,000 Anglo-allied troops; Blücher—89,000 Prussians.
DESCRIPTION Napoleon advanced rapidly, sending a minority of his force under Marshal Michel Ney toward the Anglo–allied outposts at Quatre Bras, while he led 80,000 men against Blücher's Prussians. Stubborn British defense and an uninspired performance by Ney left the Anglo–allies at Quatre Bras undefeated, but Blücher was severely mauled at Ligny and the Prussians withdrew. Napoleon detached a portion of his army under Marshal Emmanuel Grouchy to pursue the Prussians, while he joined Ney and moved upon Wellington, who retired from Quatre Bras to a position at Mont St. Jean, near the village of Waterloo, on June 17.

Despite his defeat, Blücher determined to support his ally and retired to Wavre. By the evening of June 17, Wellington's 68,000 Anglo-allied troops and 156 guns awaited Napoleon's attack at the head of 72,000 men and 246 guns. Blücher left 17,000 men and 48 guns to engage Grouchy's 33,000 and 80 guns, and marched with 72,000 and 44 guns to Wellington's relief. Wellington's position was upon a low ridge, anchored by the fortified château of Hougoumont and the farm of La Haye Sainte.

At around 11:30 a.m. on June 18, Napoleon launched a furious assault against Hougoumont, hoping to compel Wellington to commit his reserves and weaken his center for a breakthrough; but Hougoumont held throughout the day, and successive French attacks were beaten off by Wellington's beleaguered army. Not even a concentrated bombardment by the French artillery and repeated massed cavalry charges could break through, despite the loss of La Haye Sainte. By about 4 p.m., Blücher's leading elements were in action on Napoleon's right wing, diverting an increasing amount of his strength. The crisis came when Napoleon launched his reserve, part of the fabled Imperial Guard, at Wellington's center; its repulse was the signal for the complete disintegration of the French army.
RESULT Blücher's Prussians pressed on with the pursuit of the routed French; Wellington's army was in no state to move, having suffered so severely for so long. The most famous battle of modern history ended Napoleon's long career. Although victory was a result of allied cooperation, the chief reasons for its outcome were the skill of Wellington and the dour determination of his British contingent.

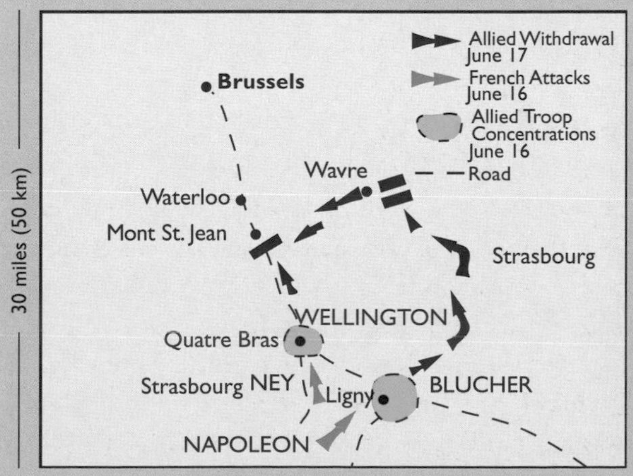

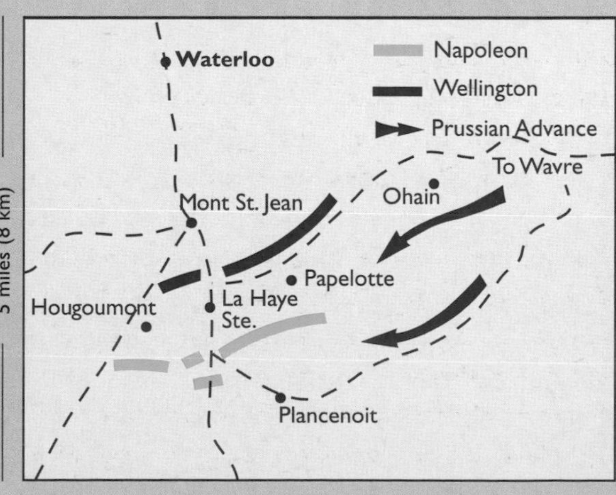

GREAT COMMANDERS

FREDERICK II OF PRUSSIA

Frederick the Great, undisputedly the greatest commander of his generation, did not look like a soldier. Slight of build, he suffered a wretched childhood at the hands of his boorish father, Frederick William I, who attempted to beat out of Frederick the artistic and intellectual qualities that were his natural characteristics. Frederick remained absorbed with music, literature, and philosophy—he had a long and ultimately acrimonious association with Voltaire—but despite these ideals, he was openly aggressive as a politician and a commander. His early campaigns in particular relied heavily upon offense, and only in later years did circumstances force him to operate in a more defensive mode. Frederick had exceptional qualities as a commander, although his inventiveness declined as years of attritional warfare reduced the abilities of his troops. Both king and army became the models for much of the remainder of Europe as a result of his outstanding victories.

Four of the most outstanding commanders in history, shown in contemporary portraits:
(I) Napoleon Bonaparte (1769–1821)
(II) Frederick the Great (1713–86)
(III) Arthur Wellesley, 1st Duke of Wellington (1769–1852)
(IV) Horatio, 1st Viscount Nelson (1758–1805)

NAPOLEON BONAPARTE

Born in Ajaccio, Corsica, of minor and impoverished aristocracy, Napoleon was an obscure officer of artillery in the French army until his plan for evicting the Anglo-Spanish-French expedition to Toulon brought him to public notice. His rise was amazingly rapid. After his "whiff of grapeshot" saved the national convention from a royalist mob, his connections with influential people and his own immense talent secured his future. He had made an exhaustive study of his profession, and this together with an appetite for relentless labor and a belief that he was destined for greatness, led to his astonishing successes in Italy. A coup d'état established him as dictator of France and ultimately emperor. He was a strategist of the highest order, formulating a method of warfare against which his opponents initially had no answer. Among his greatest talents was his ability to motivate his men, although much of his apparent concern for them was artifice, concealing his ruthless nature. Later, he overreached himself with the invasion of Russia in 1812. Eventually, he was marooned by his enemies on the Atlantic island of St. Helena, an embittered and lonely fate for a man who had been master of half Europe.

In this painting by Antoine Charles Horace Vernet (1758 - 1836) and Jacques François Swebach (1769-1823) Napoleon surveys the battlefield of Wagram, where he defeated the Austrian archduke Charles (1771–1847). The Battle of Wagram (July 5–6, 1809) concluded the last campaign in which Napoleon was victorious.

DUKE OF WELLINGTON

Arthur Wellesley was the greatest British soldier since Marlborough, and arguably the greatest of all time. The offspring of Irish nobility, his family connections eased the early stages of his career, but his progress was due to his own immense talent and a selfless attitude to public service. Winning his early reputation in India, he led the most successful British army for a century when given command in the Iberian peninsula. Beset with immense difficulties and unreliable allies, and sometimes hindered by political considerations at home, the successful conclusion to the Peninsular War, and the final defeat of Napoleon at Waterloo, were due entirely to his genius and the solid, reliable character of the British troops he led. Sometimes criticized as being a defensive commander, he showed his talent for offense when circumstances allowed, and his organizational skills were no less extensive than his tactical ability. Appearing cold and austere, he engendered no real affection among his army but instead had their total trust, inspiring loyalty to "Our Arthur." His later career encompassed every office of state, including prime minister, which duties he discharged with the same diligent concern for the public good that had marked his military career, so that upon his death he was mourned as the nation's greatest servant, "the Iron Duke."

HORATIO, 1ST VISCOUNT NELSON

Horatio Nelson was the greatest British sailor of the age, and probably the most innovative naval commander in British history. Born into minor Norfolk gentry, he entered the Royal Navy as a boy and rose to command a ship of the line at the outbreak of the French Revolutionary Wars. In 1794, he lost the sight of an eye in Corsica; in 1797 he was largely responsible for the victory of St. Vincent by his audacious maneuvers, and later in the year he lost an arm at Tenerife. He wrecked Napoleon's attempt to create an Middle Eastern empire by annihilating the French fleet at Aboukir Bay, and in 1801 destroyed the Danish fleet at Copenhagen. In 1805, he commanded the fleet at Trafalgar in the battle that ended the prospect of a French invasion of Britain, tragically dying at the moment of his victory. His influence was not simply as a tactical innovator—he refined the theory of "breaking the line" to its ultimate—and a strategist of the first rank, but as a quite exceptional character who imbued a reverence among his followers. In that, he was matched only by Napoleon, although he had none of Napoleon's dissembling or lack of sincerity. The mutual affection between Nelson and his subordinates, whom he styled his "band of brothers," was an important factor in the successful execution of his plans.

9 INDUSTRY AND WAR

As the glare of Napoleon's comet sunk over the horizon toward St. Helena, Europe sought to come to terms with the events of the past quarter century. The peace settlement that followed the Napoleonic Wars, which was largely the work of the Congress of Vienna, was essentially conservative, setting much store by the principle of legitimacy. The Quadruple Alliance (Britain, Austria, Russia, and Prussia) underwrote the peace, agreeing to future joint action should it be needed to preserve "the Concert of Europe."

THE LEGACY OF NAPOLEON

However, there were good reasons for the peace to prove fragile. The French Revolution had unleashed, across the whole of Europe, enthusiasms that could never again be quelled. The new French constitution declared that: "Frenchmen are equal before the law, whatever their titles or ranks." The unequal distribution of political and economic power, in France as elsewhere, helped inspire revolutionary upheavals. Conservative powers intervened to suppress the revolutions that threatened to disturb the peace of Europe in the 1820s, although in 1830 the restored Bourbons were ousted by the "July Monarchy" of Louis-Philippe.

In 1848, which became known as the "Year of Revolutions" because of the general upsurge of rebellion, there were serious outbreaks in Paris, Berlin, Vienna, and elsewhere. The Prussian and Austrian dynasties survived, but in France Louis-Philippe was removed to be replaced first by a republic and then by the Second Empire of Napoleon III. Even Russia, that most conservative of states, was the scene of a failed revolt in the winter of 1825, although this was an attempted coup by upper-class army officers, the Decembrists, instead of a genuinely popular outburst.

The widespread disturbances of 1815–48 reflected something more than resentment at economic exploitation or political inequality; they also bore testimony to the growing strength of nationalism. Two geographic areas were especially vulnerable to the joint pressures of liberalism and nationalism. The Austrian empire, huge and unwieldy, stretched from the Carparthian Mountains to the Mediterranean and from the Balkans to the Alps: the centrifugal tendencies of its national minorities threatened to pull it apart in 1848, and for the remainder of the century its instability was to have far-reaching consequences. Germany, in contrast, enjoyed greater national identity, but little in the way of political unity. Prussia was the most important of its numerous states, but in 1848–50 Prussia failed to assert her dominance of the German-speaking world.

Thus, despite the conservative settlement of 1814–15, European stability was to be threatened by the combined effects of liberalism and nationalism. By mid-century, these forces had already brought about marked political change in France; they had rocked the Austrian empire, and had fueled demands for German unity, creating pressures that, as the century wore on, were to pit the rising power of Germany against the waning strength of France. In short, the Vienna settlement was to prove less durable than its authors had expected. As has so often been the case, the world arising from the ashes of one war was all too soon to be scorched by other conflicts.

Conscription was one of the most potent legacies of the Napoleonic period. The French *levée en masse* of 1793 established a principle of universal military service, which was to make possible the mass armies of the nineteenth and twentieth centuries. True, its application was by no means universal. It was often politically convenient to stress the theory of universal obligation and the practice of generous exemptions. Prussian victory in the Franco–Prussian war of 1870–71 was what proved, beyond dispute, that the effective mobilization of a nation's manpower played a leading role in the quest for victory.

General Antoine Henri Jomini (1779–1869), a shrewd analyst of the genius of Napoleon Bonaparte, about whom he wrote a biography. Jomini's mindset was backward looking, to the age of small armies and limited wars. Like Frederick the Great, he was an advocate of "interior lines" which enabled a well-positioned army to deal in turn with a succession of threats.

JOMINI AND CLAUSEWITZ

Some military theorists harked back to the Napoleonic age. General Antoine Henri Jomini, although Swiss by birth, had served in the French and Russian armies, and in the *Précis de l'art de la guerre* (1836) he analyzed Napoleon's conduct of operations. Jomini was heavily influenced by eighteenth-century theorists, such as Lloyd and Bülow, and looked back with affection to an era of small armies and controllable wars. He identified the importance of applying mass to the proper point at the decisive moment—the quintessence of Napoleon's style—and in his concern for the geometry of operations, he deduced the importance of "interior lines," which enabled a centrally placed army to deal with external threats in turn.

General Karl Maria von Clausewitz (1780–1831) served as the Prussian chief of staff and saw action at Waterloo before becoming director of war studies at the military school in Berlin. Clausewitz was a keen student of the "friction of battle" and emphasised the role of the defensive in battle, foreshadowing the carnage of World War I. His key work was The Art of War.

Although he recognized the value of genius among leaders and robust morale among the led, Jomini's great strength was his ability to make war seem dependent on principles that could be distilled and taught. He was enormously influential, not only in Europe but also in North America, and as late as 1914 the commander in chief of the British Expeditionary Force was dissuaded from embarking on a potentially suicidal course of action by remembering a line from a book written by a disciple of Jomini.

General Karl Maria von Clausewitz, on the other hand, enjoyed fewer plaudits in his lifetime. He had served in the Prussian and Russian armies in the Napoleonic wars, and been chief of staff of a Prussian corps at Waterloo. Although he became director of the Prussian

Kriegsakademie after the war, he had little impact on the school's syllabus or teaching, and died of cholera in 1831 while serving as chief of staff of a force sent to put down Polish insurgents. His great work *Vom Kriege* (*On War*) was published after his death, and many of its defects stemmed from the fact that its author never had the opportunity to revise it properly.

Clausewitz saw war in quite different terms from the structured, measured conflict described by Jomini. It was the realm of physical exertion, chance, and danger, characterized by constant friction, which made even the simplest things difficult. Clausewitz placed war firmly in its political context, emphasizing that it was the continuation of state policy by other means, and the business of three distinct elements: the people, the army, and the government. The people injected violence and passion. Armies had to cope with the uncertainty that overshadowed war, and politics was the business of the government. He saw the defensive as the stronger form of war and described a vigorous defense—"a shield of blows"—as the defender fell back until his opponent had outrun himself, when the culminating point of victory was reached and the counterattack—"the flashing sword of vengeance"—was unleashed.

Linking eras

Jomini enjoyed far more influence than Clausewitz for most of the nineteenth century. It was not until after the Franco-Prussian War that Clausewitz was discovered by a Europe eager to find the touchstone of Prussian success. Yet Jomini and Clausewitz, in their very different ways, link the Napoleonic era with World War I. Jomini codified the experience of the past, while Clausewitz looked forward to the age of total war. His writings were all the more relevant because, alongside the heady passions of liberalism and nationalism, which were to provide the emotional mainsprings of conflict, the onrush of industrialization was to fill the arsenals of Europe and North America with weaponry the quantity and effectiveness of which was, quite literally, to change the face of war.

THE IMPACT OF TECHNOLOGY

Industrialization was the essence of nineteenth-century war. Up to that time, the pace of military change had been slow. The "Brown Bess" musket carried by Wellington's infantrymen at Waterloo was not markedly different from that used by their grandfathers under Marlborough; and the Swedish king, Gustavus Adolphus, killed at Lützen in 1632, would not have found the armies of 1832 totally strange. Infantry, the most numerous arm, delivered massive short-range firepower from dense formations. Under ideal circumstances a soldier might hit a man-size target at 80 yards (75 m), but the conditions were rarely ideal. The dense and stinking smoke that shrouded the battlefield reduced visibility, the fouling of burned powder clogged musket barrels and locks, and the unreliability of the flintlock mechanism meant that perhaps one-quarter of all shots were misfires.

Artillery had remained a direct-fire weapon. Most of its killing occurred at well below 1,000 yards (900 m). Gustavus might have been impressed by the fact that some field guns now fired bursting shells, but he would have observed that these were very much in the minority and that round shot, or multiple rounds, such as grape or canister, still enjoyed pride of place. The cavalry retained its two old roles. Light horsemen carried out scouting and reconnaissance, and joined in the pursuit of a beaten enemy, while heavy cavalry, often part armored in cuirass and helmet, undertook shock action on the battlefield.

Between Waterloo in 1815 and Mons 99 years later, technology intervened to transform this time-honored picture, and much else besides. The process had started in the eighteenth century, when numerous innovations—most notably James Watt's development of the first commercially viable steam engine in 1776—had improved coal-mining and iron founding. Iron production increased enormously over the period; in Germany it rose from 85,000 tons in 1823 to more than 1,000,000 tons in 1867 and a staggering 15,000,000 tons on the eve of World War I. The Bessemer Converter enabled a fourfold increase in steel output in Britain and Germany between 1865 and 1879.

CONCENTRATED ESSENCE OF INFANTRY: THE MACHINE GUN

The idea of producing multiple shots from a single weapon had existed almost as long as the firearm itself. The first mention of ribauldequins, or "Organ Guns," occurs as early as 1339. These had a number of barrels laid side by side, and could be sited to command entrances or defiles or, if mounted on wheeled carriages, brought into an army's battle line. Yet, their real value was decidedly limited. They could deliver just a single volley, for it was usually impracticable to reload each barrel in turn in the heat of battle. James Puckle's machine gun, patented in 1718, worked on the revolver principle, with a single barrel fed from a revolving chamber. It was neither a technical nor a commercial success.

The first militarily useful machine guns appeared in North America in the mid-nineteenth century. In 1861, during the Civil War, the Union army bought a small number of Agar machine guns, but these were never fully tested in action. Chicago dentist Richard Gatling developed his revolving machine gun in 1862, and in 1866 the U.S. army placed a large order. The following year, the British army did the same.

The French adopted a machine gun of their own. The *Mitrailleuse* was developed in the artillery workshop at Meudon, and in 1865 it went into mass production: 215 guns were available by January 1, 1870. The weapon looked like a conventional fieldpiece, mounted on a wheeled carriage. Its bronze tube contained twenty-five 13mm barrels, which were loaded simultaneously with a block containing 25 rounds, fired in a *rafale,* or burst. The gun's performance in 1870 was disappointing. *Mitrailleuse* batteries were often mishandled, being held back with the artillery where superior Prussian guns could deal with them. This was in part because few *Mitrailleuse* battery commanders had received training on the weapon, which had been kept scarcely less secret from its friends than from its enemies.

The Gatling, like many early machine guns, was multibarreled. As the barrels were rotated, each in succession came level with the magazine, where a cartridge dropped into its loading tray. The cartridge was then forced into the chamber by a rammer, fired, and had its spent case extracted as the barrels turned (see inset).

Ship's Gatling gun and its crew posed on deck of USS Enterprise *(1877-1909), circa spring 1890.*

As long as machine guns relied upon gravity feed and black-powder cartridges, they remained unreliable. With the advent of the metallic cartridge and smokeless powder, new developments were possible. The American Hiram Maxim hit upon the idea of using the recoil of one round to load and fire the next. Cartridges were contained in a fabric belt, which was cranked automatically into the action. The Maxim was a genuine machine gun in that it did not depend on the firer operating its mechanism, merely in keeping the trigger pressed. Maxim demonstrated his gun in England in 1884 and went into partnership with Vickers the same year. The British army adopted the Maxim in 1891, and many others followed suit.

Maxim's design established the pattern of machine guns for the next 30 years. His fellow countryman John M. Browning made his own contribution by using some of the gas that fired the bullet to assist the loading process, and the Vickers, adopted by the British army in 1912, incorporated this addition. The Vickers was water cooled, with a water-filled jacket surrounding its barrel. In 1914 a British battalion usually had two Vickers guns. In the German army, a three-battalion regiment had six guns, forming a machine-gun company, which put strong centralized firepower at its commanding officer's disposal. The standard German weapon was the 1908 Spandau, a belt-fed, water-cooled 7.92 mm gun. As World War I went on, the number of machine guns grew rapidly, and there was a tendency to group medium machine guns in special units. The British Machine Gun Corps was founded in 1915. Light machine guns were developed. Some, such as the Lewis, were purpose-built. Others were developed from existing weapons. In 1915, the Spandau was modified to become the 08/15 by the addition of a wooden stock and the replacement of the heavy mount by a small bipod.

The machine gun made unsupported assault suicidal, and helped drive the infantryman into the troglodyte world of trench warfare. Well might the Machine Gun Corps' memorial at London's Hyde Park Corner proclaim:

Saul has slain his thousands
But David his tens of thousands.

A contemporary print shows Union infantry of the 63rd Ohio Volunteers at the battle of Corinth, Mississippi, in October 1862. Well-entrenched Union troops were driven back by a Confederate assault, but rallied to mount a victorious counterattack. The firepower of muzzle-loading rifles, the chief infantry weapon of the war, gave a marked advantage to the determined defender.

New production methods marched alongside burgeoning iron and steel output. In the eighteenth century, small arms were produced by techniques that had changed little since the Middle Ages. Individual craftsmen in small workshops or larger factories assembled weapons, filing a lock here, straightening a barrel there. Despite the existence of official specifications, no two weapons were exactly alike, and the system's dependence on skilled labor made rapid increases in production difficult to achieve.

ARRIVAL OF THE MASS-PRODUCED RIFLE

During the nineteenth century, this process was transformed. First, government arsenals, such as Enfield in England, Harper's Ferry in the United States, Chatellerault in France, and Tula in Russia, devoted themselves to arms production, and at the same time a number of commercial companies—Krupp and Vickers prominent among them—applied the full entrepreneurial zeal of the age to the manufacture and marketing of weaponry. Second, the techniques used by government arsenals and private manufacturers alike made possible the swift production of standardized weapons with interchangeable parts. Precision machine tools made for finer manufacturing tolerances, and the beginnings of industrial automation meant weapons and spares came clattering off the new production lines. One case points up the general trend. In 1866, France decided to equip her army with the "Chassepot" infantry rifle. By the time the Franco–Prussian War broke out four years later, more than a million of these rifles, hundreds of millions of rounds of ammunition, not to speak of bayonets, cleaning kits, and cartridge boxes, were ready for use.

In parallel, improvements in medical science, with Lister's work on antiseptics, Pasteur's on bacteriology and vaccination, and Jenner's experiments with smallpox vaccine, all helped improve life expectancy. The population of Europe grew rapidly, from 187 million in 1800 to 266 million in 1850, 401 million in 1900, and 468 million in 1913. The picture was not altogether rosy, however, for despite advances in medicine, disease remained more deadly than the bullet. It was not until the twentieth century that the soldier was more likely to die from enemy action than from illness. In the American Civil War, the Union army lost 96,000 men in battle, while 183,000 died of disease, and for the 4,285 British soldiers who were killed or died of wounds in the Crimea, another 16,422 died of disease or exposure.

Technology affected war in three main areas. It increased the range and lethality of weapons; improved transport and communications—from railroad to steamship to electric telegraph; and, finally, it strengthened defenses, from the armored turret to the concrete fortress carapace.

Improvements to weapons in the first half of the century showed the way ahead. In 1805, Alexander Forsyth, a clergyman with an interest in wildfowling and chemistry, had developed a lock that used fulminate of mercury, instead of a flint, to ignite a weapon's main charge. The percussion lock was improved over the next 30 years, and, by 1840, all major armies were replacing their flintlock muskets with the more reliable percussion weapon. If the percussion lock enhanced the reliability and simplicity of infantry weapons, it did nothing for their accuracy. That depended on the adoption of rifling. It had long been understood that cutting spiral grooves in a weapon's barrel imparted spin to the bullet and greatly increased accuracy; riflemen had performed creditably in North America during the American War of Independence and in Spain during the Peninsular War. But problems with early rifles prevented their widespread introduction. It was important to have a tight fit between bullet and rifling, but what was tight with a clean weapon became difficult or impossible as fouling clogged the rifling.

The problem of having a bullet that was tight fitting on firing but could be loaded easily was solved in France, where a series of experiments resulted in the projectile known, from the name of its inventor, as the Minié bullet. This was conical, with a hollow base—early patterns contained an iron or wooden plug—and flanged rim.

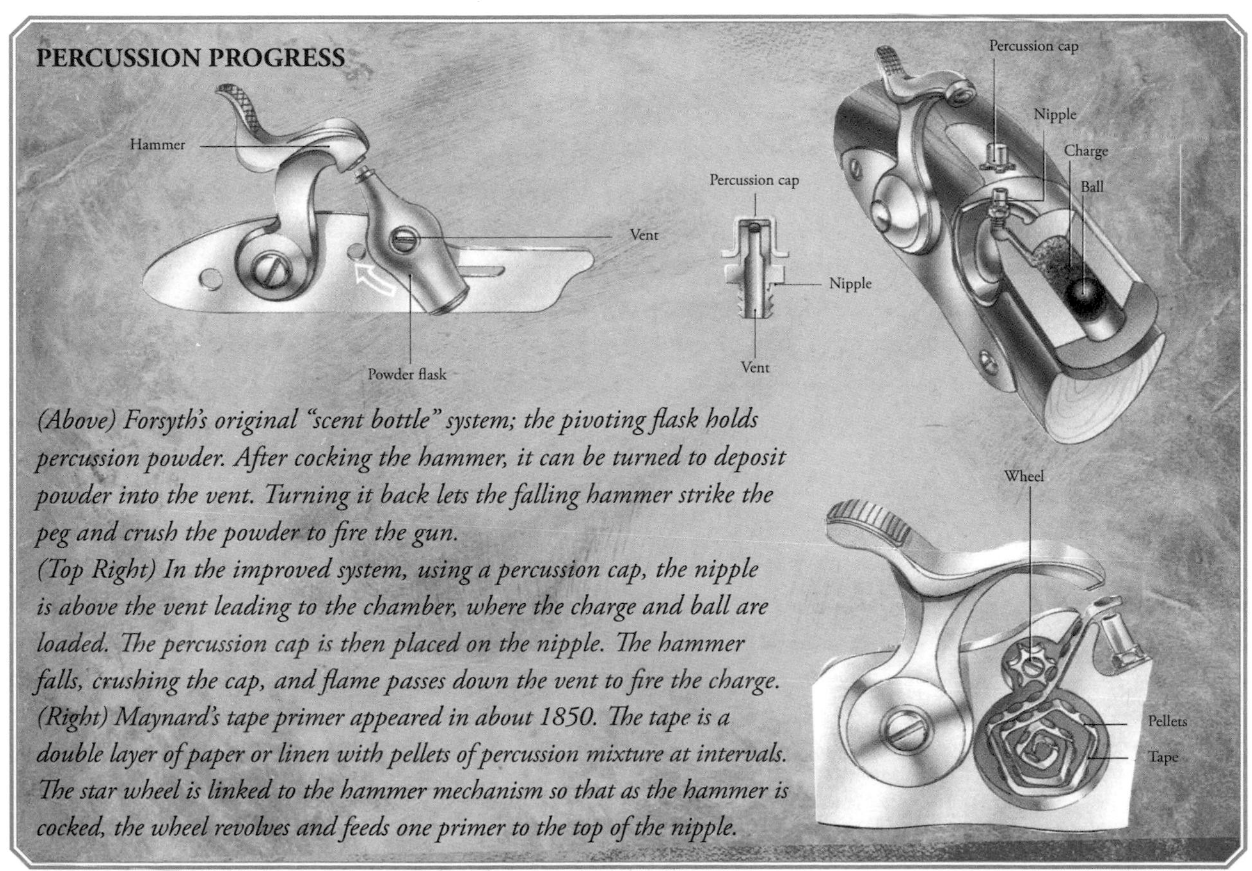

(Above) Forsyth's original "scent bottle" system; the pivoting flask holds percussion powder. After cocking the hammer, it can be turned to deposit powder into the vent. Turning it back lets the falling hammer strike the peg and crush the powder to fire the gun.
(Top Right) In the improved system, using a percussion cap, the nipple is above the vent leading to the chamber, where the charge and ball are loaded. The percussion cap is then placed on the nipple. The hammer falls, crushing the cap, and flame passes down the vent to fire the charge.
(Right) Maynard's tape primer appeared in about 1850. The tape is a double layer of paper or linen with pellets of percussion mixture at intervals. The star wheel is linked to the hammer mechanism so that as the hammer is cocked, the wheel revolves and feeds one primer to the top of the nipple.

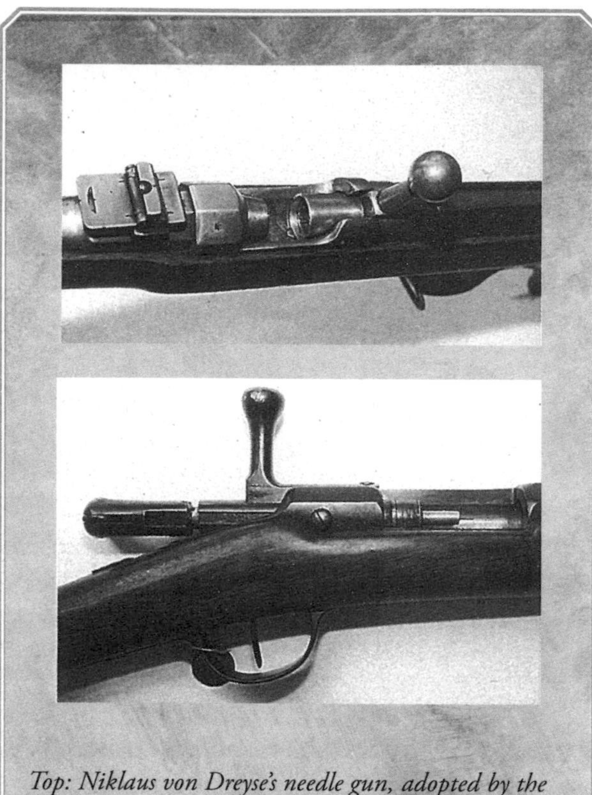

Top: Niklaus von Dreyse's needle gun, adopted by the Prussian army in 1840, finally showed that breech loading was a viable system. Its success pioneered the way for all subsequent bolt-action rifles.
Above: The French Fusil Mle, designed by Antoine Chassepot in 1866, was a distinct improvement on the Dreyse gun. The simplified firing mechanism had the needle as a fixture inside the bolt, and automatically cocked as the latter was closed.

It slipped easily down even a heavily fouled barrel and, on firing, the gases of the explosion drove into the hollow base, forcing the flanges to bite into the rifling. In the 1850s, the Minié became the first rifle issued to the infantry as a whole, and, corrupted as "minny," was the characteristic infantry weapon of the American Civil War.

Advent of the breech loader

Between 1830 and 1860 infantry weapons had at least doubled in reliability, and their effective fighting range had increased to 300–400 yards (275–355 m). Over the next 30 years, the pace of change was to be no less rapid. The disadvantages of loading a weapon from the muzzle had long been recognized. For one thing, it was extremely difficult to accomplish while lying down. Some militarily useful breechloaders had been produced earlier, but it took the nineteenth century's industrial developments to make the breechloader feasible on a large scale.

Prussia led the way. In the 1840s, she equipped her infantry with the Dreyse bolt-action needle gun, so called because of the needlelike firing pin, which entered the base of the cartridge to strike the primer and fire the round. Although the Dreyse suffered from numerous defects—short range, and a poor gas-tight seal at the breech among them—it gave a startling demonstration of its prowess in the Austro–Prussian War of 1866, when its sheer rapidity of fire cut swathes through the Austrian infantry. Thereafter all major armies sought to reequip with breechloaders.

The French "Chassepot" was infinitely better than the needle gun. A rubber obturating ring diminished the problem of gas leakage at the breech, and the weapon's effective fighting range was some 600 yards (550 m). At St. Privat on August 18, 1870, the Prussian Guard launched an ill-conceived frontal attack on the French 6th Corps, and lost some 8,000 men, mainly to "Chassepot" fire, in 20 minutes.

The enormous success of the "Chassepot" increased the speed of change. Several armies converted their muzzle-loaders to breechloaders as a temporary expedient (the

British Snider was a classic case in point) while the search for the most effective breechloader went on. The hunt was no simple one and led down a number of blind alleys. The single-shot breechloader, with either a falling breechblock, such as the Martini-Henry, or a turning one, such as the Remington rolling block, was able to cope with the radical reduction in caliber made possible by the development of the metallic cartridge and cupro-nickel bullet. But it could not be modified to permit rapid fire, and so it was the bolt-action rifle, with a box magazine at the breech or a tubular magazine below the barrel, that eventually became the standard infantry weapon across the world.

Bolt-action infantry rifle

In the 1880s, the bolt-action magazine rifle, with a caliber of around .303 inches or 7.92 mm, was universally adopted. Most were known from the arsenal where they were developed or produced, such as the U.S. Springfield; from the name of their inventor, such as the French Lebel; or from a combination of both, such as the British Lee-Enfield. The introduction of smokeless powder—the way was led by France, with *Poudre B* in 1885—set the seal on the process, and by the turn of the century, the infantry rifle had attained the form it was to retain through one world war and well into a second. Mass-produced, accurate, and reliable, it had an effective fighting range of up to 1,000 yards (915 m) against a mass target. Its magazine held 5 to 10 rounds and permitted very rapid fire. The average British infantryman, a regular soldier with thorough training, could get off 15 rounds a minute, and some of his more experienced colleagues could do even better. Alongside this went the perfection of what Captain Sir Basil Liddell Hart, English soldier and miliary historian, was to call "the concentrated essence of infantry"—the machine gun.

IMPROVEMENTS IN ARTILLERY

Artillery had developed along lines similar to small arms, with the introduction of breechloading rifled weapons as the crucial line of departure. But the scale of the technical

Chassepot armed French infantry defend a street during the Franco-Prussian war. The figure with the baggy red pants is a zouave, from a unit raised among European settlers in the French colony of Algeria.

problems to be solved, the importance attached to the projectile as well as to the weapon itself, and the difficulty of absorbing recoil—so simply accomplished by the firer's shoulder in the case of the rifle—meant that the development of artillery often lagged behind that of infantry weapons.

Advances in metallurgy solved the first problem facing artillery manufacturers. Bronze was costly. Cast-iron gun barrels, a cheaper alternative, were unmanageably heavy if thick and dangerous if thin. Wrought iron, hammered into shape around a mandrel, and sometimes with strengthening bands shrunk on at points of maximum pressure, was an improvement.

MAGAZINE RIFLES

The idea of a magazine rifle was to give the individual soldier more firepower. There were, of course, arguments against this. Given a full magazine, said the opposition, the soldier will simply fire off all the ammunition as soon as he sees an enemy a mile away. But the siege of Plevna (1877) showed that this was not necessarily so. At Plevna, the Turkish defenders, each with 500 rounds, were armed with Winchester magazine carbines, and they repulsed several Russian attacks with withering, disciplined firepower. This showed that any army without a magazine rifle was at a disadvantage.

Despite its success at Plevna, the American Winchester was rarely used as a military weapon, but it introduced the tubular magazine, in which a row of ammunition was carried in a tube beneath the barrel. Individual rounds were pushed back by a spring and fed up to the chamber by working a lever that also cocked the hammer. This was satisfactory with soft-nose bullets, but the small-caliber jacketed bullets that the military were contemplating using risked firing the cap of the next cartridge in front under the shock of recoil, and accordingly the tubular magazine was not trusted.

Nevertheless, the French adopted the tubular magazine for their 0.3-inch (8-mm) Lebel rifle (1886), as did the Germans for their Commission rifle (1888), because it provided a quick solution. The British and other nations preferred to test various options before selecting a system, and the only practical solution was the box magazine.

The bolt-action rifle

James Paris Lee, a Scot who emigrated to North America, had developed a bolt-action rifle. Beneath the bolt was a metal box into which cartridges were placed on top of a spring. As the bolt was opened, the spring forced the cartridges up against a stop; the bolt pushed the top cartridge into the chamber as it closed. After firing, the opening of the bolt extracted the empty cartridge case,

(Left) A French marine with a Kropatschek magazine rifle of 1878, which had a tubular magazine under the barrel.

(Below) Adopted by the U.S. army in 1892, the Krag-Jorgensen was a Norwegian design, which used a similar bolt to the Lee, but the ballistics were poor. After exposure to the Mauser in the Spanish-American War, the Krag was abandoned for the Springfield, which used a bolt and magazine system licensed from Mauser and a more powerful cartridge.

(Top) The short Lee-Enfield. The Lee bolt action, allied to either the Metford or Enfield barrel, armed the British empire from 1888 to 1954, and until the l980s as a sniping rifle. Although theoretically less accurate, due to using locking lugs at the rear end, than the Mauser, it was sufficiently accurate for combat shooting and had the advantage of far smoother and faster action than any other bolt action before or since. Sergeant Snoxall of the Small Arms School fired 38 shots in one minute in 1914, and at 300 yards (275 m), range put every shot into the inner ring of the target, a record never surpassed. (Above) The Mauser of 1898, this "Karabin 98k" was to remain the standard infantry rifle until 1945.

(Above) A sectioned drawing of the Lee action—the bolt has just been opened extracting the empty case. The simple trigger mechanism, and the folded spring, which forces the cartridge up in front of the bolt as it closes, can be seen.

and the return stroke loaded a fresh round. The box could be detached for refilling, and the rifle was provided with a spare magazine for quick reloading in action. Lee had produced a few sporting rifles on this principle, and after severe testing, the Lee bolt and magazine were adopted by the British army in the Lee-Metford rifle, Metford being the designer of the barrel. Another innovation was the adoption of a jacketed bullet of .303-inch (7.6-mm) caliber, a considerable reduction from the .45 caliber, which was usual for military rifles of the day.

The small jacketed bullet was developed by Major Rubin of the Swiss army. It had high velocity—giving better accuracy—and, due to its metal jacket, did not leave a coating of lead in the rifle barrel. The French took the same course but used a solid brass bullet with their M1886 rifle, as did the Germans with their M1888 rifle.

The Germans realized that their tubular magazine weapon had been a mistake, and applied to the arms manufactureres Peter paul and Wilhelm Mauser for something better. They adapted the box magazine idea, producing a rifle with a five-shot box magazine concealed inside the stock. The rifle's bolt action was improved, locking into the chamber of the barrel. Mauser rifles sold worldwide.

In Austria, Count Mannlicher designed another magazine rifle, similar in some respects to the Mauser but eventually adopting a "straight-pull" bolt and a rotating magazine, still concealed inside the butt. The straight-pull bolt relied upon cam action: the bolt handle was pulled straight back, withdrawing a sleeve, which drew a stud through a curved cam path in the bolt body, causing it to rotate. Some people said it was quicker than a turn bolt, but it was generally more fragile. The Swiss adopted a straight-pull design, while the Japanese and Italians copied Mauser. Only the Scandinavians and the Americans tried something different, in the Krag-Jorgensen rifle, which had an odd side-mounted magazine fed through a trapdoor.

The changing face of war. Canadian troops, dressed in utilitarian khaki uniforms and armed with long Lee-Enfield magazine rifles, climb a rock-strewn kopje during the Boer War of 1899–1902. This regiment took the standard British pith helmet as part of the uniform; other Canadian troops adopted the Stetson hat, which had been popular with the North West Mounted Police (the Mounties) since 1895. Many of the Canadian troops came from the Mounties. After the Boer War, in 1903, the Stetson became the Mounties' official headgear.

During the American Civil War the smooth-bore 12-pounder "Napoleon" was the mainstay of Union artillery, supported by a variety of rifled cannon, notably 10- and 20-pound "Parrots," their cast-iron barrels reinforced by wrought-iron bands. But the real answer had already been found. The German manufacturer Krupp exhibited steel cannon at the Great Exhibition of 1851. Originally, their barrels were made up of several components, but they were soon machined from solid steel.

The second difficulty, producing a gas-tight breech, was half overcome once guns were made of steel and manufacturing tolerances could, therefore, be finer. Several workable solutions were produced, among them Krupp's sliding breechblock and the "interrupted thread" perfected by the French engineer de Bagne. The superiority of German artillery in the Franco-Prussian War encouraged swift imitation and, although the British army briefly switched back from breechloaders to muzzle-loaders, rifled breechloaders were in general use by the 1880s. Producing a shell that would take the rifling without wearing out the barrel had caused problems similar to those experienced in small-arms design. The eventual solution was to add a copper driving band, flexible enough to mold to the rifling, ensuring a gas-tight seal without abrading the inside of the bore.

This left just the question of recoil unanswered. As long as the barrel was fixed directly to the carriage, the shock of firing was transmitted through the whole weapon, causing it to spring backward. The gun's detachment of soldiers had to manhandle it back into position and relay it before firing again. The "recuperator" system interposed a hydraulic buffer—with a plunger working inside an oil-filled chamber—between barrel and carriage. Although the barrel still leaped back sharply, the recoil was absorbed by the recuperator, and the carriage scarcely moved. The famous French 75 mm, the *soixante-quinze* of 1897, used not only the recuperator but also "fixed" ammunition—projectile and cartridge joined in a brass case—and could hammer out an unprecedented 20 rounds a minute.

Union heavy guns in Fort Brady, Virginia on the James River. The piece in the foreground, the reinforcing band on its cast-iron barrel clearly visible, is on a fortress mount. The two guns immediately behind it are on field carriages. Shells are stacked in the left foreground, and handspikes, to help the gun's detachment to traverse the weapon, stand ready.

Better projectiles

Advances in the gun were paralleled by improvements in the projectile. New propellants and burster charges gave better performance and less smoke. Shells could be fitted with percussion fuzes to burst on the ground, or with time fuzes to burst in the air. The shrapnel shell, named after its inventor, Lieutenant Henry Shrapnel of the Royal Artillery, was intended to explode above enemy infantry, showering them with small balls, while high explosive—HE in military shorthand—ripped holes in buildings or ground and turned woods to debris.

Some high-explosive shells were very large indeed and were intended for use against fortifications. The sloping glacis in front of a fortress, and the armored turrets that began to sprout from the top of the building, offered obdurate targets to guns that fired directly at them. However, they were more vulnerable to heavy howitzers, which fired shells that rose high on steep trajectories to drop with devastating force on top of the fortifications.

WAR ON RAILS

Armies were not slow in recognizing the military potential of the railroad. In 1840, the British took a battalion from Manchester to Liverpool by train, and six years later the Russians moved 14,500 men 200 miles (325 km) by rail. The French made great use of the railroad in the 1859 campaign against the Austrians, moving a total of 604,381 men and 129,227 horses.

The railroads were particularly useful to the Prussians. In 1866, in the Austro–Prussian war, nearly 200,000 men were sent to the frontiers by railway, and the numerous lessons learned stood Prussia in good stead in 1870 against France. This, allied to the evidence of the American Civil War, emphasized the railroad's vital role. By 1914, railroads, and the special troops who maintained and managed them, formed an indispensable part of national mobilization plans.

OTHER TECHNOLOGICAL ADVANCES

At the same time as the range and lethality of weapons increased, technology also transformed communications and transport. The development of the railroad was of immense significance, because it speeded up strategic transport and enabled a country with potentially hostile powers on both flanks, such as Germany, to use "interior lines" to her advantage.

Steam was scarcely less crucial at sea. In 1807, Robert Fulton's steamboat made the 150-mile (240-km) journey up the Hudson from New York to Albany in 32 hours. Steam was soon used by naval vessels to power paddle wheels and later to drive underwater propellers. The Battle of Navarino, when a British, French, and Russian force destroyed a Turkish fleet in 1827, was the last general action fought between wooden sailing ships. Natural conservatism, allied to a desire to save coal when the breeze would serve, meant that for much of the century warships remained full rigged. Nevertheless, fleets were at last freed from the tyranny of the wind and were able to maneuver freely.

By the close of the century, the internal combustion engine was beginning to make its presence felt. Between the Boer War of 1899–1902 and the outbreak of World War I in 1914, armies cautiously experimented with automobiles and trucks, although the overwhelming majority of land transport continued to be horse-drawn. It was the application of the internal combustion engine to aircraft that foreshadowed the most dramatic future developments. Armies had already put balloons to military use, but in 1911 the heavier-than-air machine came of age when the Italians flew reconnaissance and bombing missions against Turkish troops in Tripolitania.

Communication and fortification

Not only did technology enable troops and supplies to move faster and more efficiently, it also permitted commanders to communicate with growing ease. The semaphore telegraph had been widely used during the Napoleonic Wars, but its limitations were considerable. In 1829, the electric telegraph came into use, and with the development of Samuel Morse's code in 1850, it became a valuable means of strategic communication. The telephone, patented by Alexander Graham Bell in 1876, was even better, and in 1885 the Germans experimented with linking artillery observers to their guns by field telephone, making indirect fire possible for the first time.

Marconi's work on the wireless was to be of immense long-term importance, but during the period in consideration, wireless was in its infancy, bulky, prone to jamming, and insecure. Indeed, poor security over the wireless was to contribute to the great Russian defeat at Tannenberg in August 1914.

The third area of military affairs affected by the technology of the nineteenth century was fortification. The great engineers of the eighteenth century had established the importance of low, geometrical works, which offered poor targets to an attacker's artillery, and always presented assaulting infantry with ditches, steep walls, and flanking fire. The principles of classical fortification evolved little in the nineteenth century, but technology came to the fortress builder's aid. It enabled him to add concrete (often with a sand "burster layer") to the stonework of yesteryear and, finally, to put the fortress guns in armored turrets. The offensive technology of siege artillery tended to change quicker than the defensive technology of the fortress, as the rapid fall of the Liège forts in 1914 was to demonstrate, but permanent fortifications were to be of considerable importance in World War I. Also, that very simple piece of defensive technology, barbed wire, should not be overlooked. Developed in the United States as a means of cattle control, barbed wire was less dramatic than the steel turret or the concrete casemate but, in its way, it was to have more awesome military consequences than either.

Ironclad ships

It was at sea that defensive technology really came into its own. Adding armor plate to the hulls of wooden warships enabled them to sustain punishment that would have sunk a conventional vessel, and the clash between USS *Monitor* and CSS *Merrimac* in Hampton Roads, Virginia, on March 9, 1862, was the first battle between steam-powered ironclads. Neither ship was really ocean going, but this said more about the circumstances of the American Civil War than about marine engineering.

THE ART OF WAR

The new military technology of the nineteenth century fitted into a world increasingly overshadowed by war. But apart from minor campaigns against insurgents, and the more widespread upheavals of 1848, it was not until 1854 that large-scale hostilities broke out. A dispute over the Holy Places in Jerusalem, and instability resulting from shrinking Turkish power, produced war between Britain, France, and Turkey on the one hand and Russia on the other. The allies sent an expeditionary force to the Black Sea, landed in the Crimea, beat the Russians on the Alma River, and laid siege to the naval base of Sebastopol. Russian attempts to relieve the city led to the battles of Balaklava and Inkerman, and after costly assaults on Sebastopol in the fall of 1855, the Russians at last evacuated it.

⚔ BATTLE OF INKERMAN

DATE November 5, 1854
CAMPAIGN Crimean War
OBJECT A Russian relieving force was to collaborate with a large-scale sortie from Sebastopol and launch a surprise attack on the British and French besiegers.
NUMBERS Russians—19,000 men from the Sebastopol garrison, under General Soimonov; 16,000 men from the field army, under General Paulov; another 22,000 soldiers from the garrison feinted at the allied siege line to prevent the sector under attack from being reinforced. Allies—about 8,000 in the threatened sector.
DESCRIPTION Together, both Russian forces were under the command of General Dannenbeg. The allied armies were under the overall command of Lord Raglan and General Canrobert; Major-General Pennefather, commanding the British 2nd Division, played a leading role in meeting the attack. The Russian attackers were badly coordinated and lost their way in the fog and broken ground. Despite the patchy visibility, artillery played an important part in the battle. The British brought up two long 18-pounder siege guns, and their range and accuracy enabled them to silence the artillery supporting the attack.
CASUALTIES Russians—about 12,000. Allies: French—1,726, British—2,505.
RESULT The allies fought a classic "soldiers' battle" and were able to repulse the Russians, who suffered disproportionately heavy loss.

THE RISE OF THE *DREADNOUGHT*

In the 1840s, ships of the line differed little from those that had fought at Trafalgar. They were full-rigged wooden sailing vessels, their muzzle-loading cannon firing through ports in three gun decks. Just as technology transformed land war, it also revolutionized warship design, and the ships of the 1840s were soon to be obsolete. Developments took place in three areas—propulsion, protection, and firepower. In 1807, the American engineer Robert Fulton proved that steam-powered vessels were commercially viable, but the vulnerability of the paddle wheel limited the application of the steam engine to the warship. In 1843, the first screw-driven warship, the USS *Princeton*, was launched.

Developments in France led to dramatic increases in firepower. Naval guns had traditionally fired solid shot at hostile ships, supplementing this with grape- or case-shot for close-range work against crew or rigging. In 1837, however, the French began to arm their warships with exploding shells. They launched the ironclad battleship *La Gloire* in 1858. The British response, launched in 1861, was HMS *Warrior*, a massive ironclad that rendered all other warships obsolete. Although *La Gloire* and HMS *Warrior* enjoyed armored protection, were powered by screws, and had mounted guns that fired exploding shells, in one important respect they did not progress. Their guns fired broadside, just as Nelson's had. The battle between the USS *Monitor* and the Confederate *Merrimac* (renamed *Virginia*) in March 1862 showed just how helpless sail-powered wooden warships were against ironclads—*Merrimac* destroyed two the day before *Monitor* arrived. It also suggested that a revolving turret, such as that housing *Monitor*'s guns, was a better way to mount main armament than the traditional broadside gun.

The weight of early turrets meant that ships equipped with them tended to ride perilously low in the water and were suitable only for inshore operations. But the Battle of Lissa (1866), in which a technologically inferior Austrian fleet defeated a superior Italian force, encouraged designers to equip warships with armored

The French battleship Jauriquiberry. *Along with her center-line turrets, she carried some heavy guns in barbette turrets, one visible amidships.*

rams, so it became vital for ships to be able to defend themselves fore and aft as well as broadsides. An improved version of the turret was the brainchild of Captain Cowper Coles of the Royal Navy, but his experimental turret ship *Captain* capsized and sank with all hands (including Coles) during a gale in the Bay of Biscay. The instability was caused partly by the need for a full rig. Once the development of more powerful engines and boilers allowed seagoing ships to dispense with sailing rig, from the start of the 1880s, the turret became almost universal in ironclads.

As the century drew to its close the pace of innovation increased. Admiral Fisher, appointed Britain's First Sea Lord in 1904, was encouraged by study of naval developments overseas to set up a committee to design the "all big gun battleship." The result, HMS *Dreadnought*, became the model for the battle fleets of World War I. Although mighty, these ships contained the seeds of their own obsolescence. They were cripplingly expensive, and in face of growing threats from beneath the sea and above it, increasingly vulnerable.

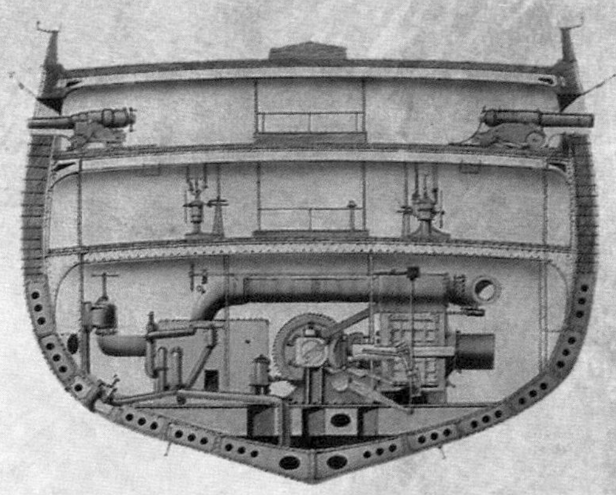

This cross section through HMS Warrior *shows two of her ten 110-pounders. Her main gun deck is protected by 4½-inch (11-cm) wrought-iron plates, backed by 18 inches (36 cm) of teak.* Warrior's *engines could push her along at 14½ knots.*

The 17,900-ton Dreadnought, *launched in 1906, was the fastest battleship in the Royal Navy. Her five turrets housed ten 12-inch (30-cm) guns; smaller quick firers were provided to deal with torpedo boat attacks.* Dreadnought *made all other battleships obsolete, but she was overtaken by new developments and was scrapped in 1920.*

UNIFORM: FROM DRAMATIC TO DRAB

Military uniform had long tended to be flamboyant but impractical, although wartime alterations often modified its more extreme aspects. During the nineteenth century, demands for simpler uniform surfaced, in part as a response to the growing importance of concealment on the battlefield, and in part because of calls for utility and economy.

Armies bowed to the pressure. In the Indian Mutiny of 1857–58, some British units wore khaki (from the Urdu for "dust colored") and the British army replaced scarlet for field service after the First Boer War of 1880–81. The Russo-Japanese war persuaded its belligerents to adopt khaki, too, and the U.S. army took to olive drab in 1902. In 1909, the Austrian army wore "pike gray," while the Germans adopted "field gray" between 1907 and 1910.

The French stood fast against the trend. On the eve of World War I a minister proclaimed "Le pantalon rouge, c'est la France" (the red pants is France,) and French infantry took to the field in 1914 in red pants and long blue coats. This finery did not survive the first clashes, and in 1915 it was replaced by "horizon blue."

The Crimean War was described by Philip Guedalla as "one of the bad jokes of history," and it did, indeed, have an air of black comedy. Yet its consequences were far-reaching. It convinced Russia's new czar, Alexander II, of the need for internal reform, and the abolition of serfdom in 1861 freed more than 40 million peasants. It established France, once again, as a first-rank military power. French soldiers were no longer "the beaten men of Europe," and their achievements drew admiring comments from friend and foe alike. The toughness and resourcefulness displayed by French soldiers in the Crimea was largely a product of long experience of campaigning in Algeria, and it stood out in stark contrast to the privations endured by the British as they wintered on the bare uplands outside Sebastopol. The lamentable performance of Britain's administrative services lent fresh impetus to the demands for military reform. The campaign also drew attention to the shortcomings of military hospitals; and Florence Nightingale, who did so much to organize the hospital at Scutari, emerged as a popular heroine.

French excursions

The French army was in action again just four years later. In 1858, Napoleon III had made a secret agreement with Count Cavour, prime minister of the north Italian state of Piedmont, to come to Piedmont's support if the Austrians, in possession of the neighboring states of Lombardy and Venetia, could be provoked to attack. Napoleon hoped to gain prestige and the French-speaking Piedmontese territories of Nice and Savoy. Cavour, for his part, saw the ejection of the Austrians as a key step toward Italian unification. In 1859, the Austrians were duly duped into attacking and a French army moved into northern Italy, winning scrambling victories at Magenta and Solferino. Then, much to Cavour's fury, Napoleon made peace without ensuring that Venetia was relinquished by Austria, but over the next two years all Italian states, with the exception of Rome and Venetia, came under the sway of Piedmont, which duly became the Kingdom of Italy in early 1861.

Victory in 1859 revealed numerous shortcomings in the French army. While it excelled at "the small change of war," mobilization had been inefficient and the higher conduct of operations clumsy. Magenta and Solferino had been won by the aggressive determination of the French infantry, whose charges swept away the Austrians before they were able to make best use of their excellent Lorenz rifles. Yet the experience did not deter Napoleon from farther

Wilhelm I of Prussia (center) and his staff at the Battle of Königgrätz (1866). Although Moltke had been Chief of the Prussian General Staff since 1857, his was not a household name, even in the Prussian army. At Königgrätz, one general commented that a written order seemed to be all right, "But who is this General von Moltke?" After the battle the question was not asked again.

military adventure. In 1862, he sent an expeditionary force to Mexico, and two years later installed an Austrian archduke, Maximilian, as emperor. But the Mexican escapade turned sour. Maximilian's new subjects were anything but loyal, and Union victory in the American Civil War was followed by vigorous protests about European intervention in the New World, which was seen as contrary to the principles of the Monroe Doctrine of 1823. Prussia's victory over Austria in 1866 was the last straw, and the French withdrew from Mexico to concentrate on the worsening situation in Europe. The unlucky Maximilian was captured and shot, and the episode did much to weaken the prestige of Napoleon's gaslight empire.

THE ASCENDANCY OF PRUSSIA

The waning of French power gave Otto von Bismarck, prime minister of Prussia, the opportunity to proceed toward his aim of German unification. He believed that this first required the defeat of Austria, so that Prussia could become the basis for a united state, which would exclude the German-speaking elements of the Hapsburg empire.

In 1864, he maneuvered the Germanic Confederation into war with Denmark over the duchies of Schleswig and Holstein. The Convention of Gastein (1865) left these under the Prusso-Austrian condominium, which resulted in friction between Prussia and Austria, exactly as Bismarck had expected. He bought off Napoleon, hinting that French neutrality would be rewarded by territorial gains along the Rhine and, with French help, concluded an agreement that would bring Italy into an Austro-Prussian war, forcing the Austrians to fight on two fronts.

The specter of Prussian aggrandizement alarmed many German states, who sided with Austria when war broke out in 1866, after disputes over the federal structure of Germany and the administration of the duchies. Conventional wisdom favored the Austrians and their allies, but this reckoned neither with the needle gun nor with an even more decisive weapon—Helmuth von Moltke, chief of the Prussian general staff. Moltke and the war minister von Roon had carried out far-reaching reform of the Prussian army. Their arrangements for conscription and mobilization were later to become the models for other European armies.

Moltke's conduct of operations was bold but risky. An ambitious "forward concentration" by railroad led to his armies crossing the frontier in widely separated columns, the Elbe army swinging down through Austria's ally Saxony, while the First and Second armies pushed into Bohemia from the north.

MEN OF STEAM AND STEEL

GENERAL ULYSSES S. GRANT

Ulysses Grant (1822–85) passed out of West Point in the bottom half of his class. Although he served with distinction in the Mexican War, boredom with garrison duty led to hard drinking, and he resigned from the army in 1854 to avoid court-martial. He was working in his brothers' Illinois store when Civil War broke out, and he obtained command of the 21st Illinois Volunteers.

On campaign, Ulysses S. Grant rarely looked as well-trimmed as in this portrait. He had few rivals in his grasp of the essentials of war.

Promoted to brigadier general in command of a district based in Cairo, Illinois, Grant found himself playing a crucial role in Union strategy. General Winfield Scott's "Anaconda Plan" demanded seizure of the line of the Mississippi as part of a general attempt to throttle the Confederacy to death. Grant's first thrust down the river failed at Belmont in November 1861, but early the following year he took forts Henry and Donelson. In April, he was surprised at Shiloh on the Tennessee River, but recovered from a disastrous first day's fighting to win a costly victory. His initial attempt to take Vicksburg was thwarted in December 1862, but in a methodical amphibious operation he took the city in July 1863.

Robert E. Lee's style and bearing in this formal portrait are indicative of his origins in the Virginia aristocracy. His father, "Light-Horse Harry" Lee, had commanded cavalry under Washington and served as state governor.

Grant's success at Vicksburg encouraged Lincoln to appoint him commander of all Union forces in the western theater of operations, and he swiftly transformed the situation in Tennessee. In March 1864, Grant was promoted to lieutenant general and appointed general in chief. He accompanied the Army of the Potomac, and set about moving "all parts of the Army together and, somewhat toward a common center." This policy produced a costly slogging match in the wilderness fighting of May–June, followed by the long siege of Petersburg. Sherman, meanwhile, took Atlanta and marched to the sea to bisect the Confederacy. In early April 1865, Lee led his dwindling army out of Petersburg, but was cornered at Appomattox Court House, where he surrendered.

Victory brought Grant immense authority, first as general of the army, and then as Secretary of War in President Johnson's administration. He served two terms as a Republican president, but the malpractices of his colleagues discredited him.

GENERAL ROBERT E. LEE

Robert Lee (1807–70) passed out second of his class at West Point and was commissioned into the engineers. Chief engineer of the central column in the Mexican War, he was badly wounded at the storming of Chapultepec. He was superintendent of West Point in 1855–5 and greatly improved the establishment's efficiency.

Colonel Lee was serving in Texas when the first Confederate states seceded from the Union in March 1861. He felt duty bound to "go with his state" when Virginia seceded, and accepted the command of the state's forces. He prepared the defenses of Richmond, and then opposed Rosecrans in West Virginia, before being summoned back to the eastern theater to take command in the Seven Days' Battles around Richmond in the spring of 1862. Thereafter, at the head of the Army of Northern Virginia, he repeatedly thwarted the Army of the Potomac's advances on the Confederate capital, and twice took the war into the North. His defeat of Hooker at Chancellorsville in May 1863 was a stunning achievement, but at Gettysburg, his last great battle, his management of the battlefield and his faltering subordinates was found wanting.

Reluctance to assert himself with reticent or headstrong subordinates is the only flaw in Lee's military character. He excelled at maneuver, but showed himself no less adept in contending with Grant's bludgeon work in the Wilderness battles of 1863 and in protracting the siege of Petersburg. Appointed commander of all Confederate armies in February 1865, Lee eventually surrendered only when his own Army of Northern Virginia was worn to a thread by casualties and desertion, and its last line of supply was cut.

FIELD MARSHAL HELMUTH VON MOLTKE

Helmuth von Moltke (1800–91) was commissioned into the Danish army, but transferred to the Prussian army in 1822 and almost immediately attended the elite *Kriegsakademie*. In 1835, he was given leave to go to Turkey, and served with the sultan's army at its disastrous defeat at Nisib. He published an account of his travels in 1839.

Foreign service and literary skill helped bring Moltke royal patronage, and in 1857 he was appointed Chief of the Great General Staff. He served as chief of staff to the Austro-Prussian force in the Schleswig-Holstein war of 1864, and in 1866 Prussian victory over Austria-Hungary at Königgrätz made him a figure of European importance. In 1870, his was the directing brain behind the German defeat of France, an achievement that brought him his field marshal's baton, the title of count, and marked him out as a great general.

Count Helmuth von Moltke was proverbially stony faced. It was said that he smiled just twice in his life: once on seeing some obsolete Swedish fortifications, and again when his mother-in-law died.

BATTLE OF KÖNIGGRÄTZ (SADOWA)

DATE July 3, 1866
CAMPAIGN Austro-Prussian War
OBJECT Prussia was challenging Austria for the leadership of the German Confederation—a carefully planned stage in the unification of Germany under Prussia's Hohenzollern dynasty.
NUMBERS Prussians—about 200,000; Austrians and Saxons—about 200,000.
DESCRIPTION The Austrians and Saxons held a strong position northwest of the fortress of Königgrätz. The Prussian First and Elbe armies attacked from the west. Fierce fighting was already in progress when the Prussian Second Army, which had pursued a separate line of advance, appeared on the Austrian right flank. This turning movement proved decisive and the Austrians were heavily defeated, although courageous action by cavalry and gunners allowed Austrian troops to be extracted.
CASUALTIES Prussians—9,000; Austrians and Saxons—44,000, including 22,000 captured.
RESULT The surviving Austrian army fell back rapidly on Vienna, where it met the Archduke Albrecht's army of the South, which had moved up from Italy after defeating the Italians at Custozza. Since a continuation of hostilities could only result in another Austrian defeat, peace preliminaries were signed on July 26. The battle was no less decisive in political terms. Prussia had asserted her right to the leadership of Germany, from which Austria was excluded. Königgrätz was the single most important step on the road to German unification, a path that was to lead directly to war with France in 1870 and thereafter to World War I.

The Austrians had split their forces to face the Italian threat, and although they were victorious in Italy, all the determination of their robust infantry, resolute gunners, and flamboyant cavalry was to no avail against Moltke's huge concentric attack and the savage firepower of the needle gun. On July 3, the Austrians were defeated at Königgrätz in a single battle that decided the war. The peace excluded Austria from active participation in the new German world. The old Germanic Confederation was disbanded, and the states north of the Main River formed the North German Confederation under Prussian leadership.

Although the treaty was generous to Austria, defeat in 1859 and 1866 left her weakened, and in 1867 the empire was reorganized to form the Dual Monarchy, with separate Austrian and Hungarian governments, united in the person of the reigning Hapsburg, who was both Emperor of Austria and King of Hungary.

Franco-Prussian war

France was defeated, indirectly, at Königgrätz. Napoleon failed to obtain any compensation for his neutrality, and found himself facing an increasingly nationalistic Germany whose army had given recent proof of its prowess. His own attempts at military reform were marred by his weakening grip on political power, for it was difficult to sustain both the new "Liberal Empire" and the thoroughgoing reform that the French army urgently demanded. The new military service law, the *Loi Niel* of 1868, went part of the way, and the introduction of the "Chassepot" and *Mitrailleuse* put powerful new weapons in the hands of French soldiers. However, the underlying flaws remained. Mobilization arrangements were archaic and the command structure relied upon a single controlling will, which Napoleon, already painfully ill, was never able to provide.

In the summer of 1870 France stumbled into a war that more astute diplomacy might have averted. A German prince was offered the throne of Spain. Although he eventually withdrew his candidacy, Bismarck phrased reports of the King of Prussia's refusal to guarantee that similar candidacy would not be repeated in such a way that the exasperated French declared war. The first phase of the war was reminiscent of 1866. The French, spread out along the frontier, were defeated on August 6 at Froeschwiller in Alsace and Spicheren in Lorraine. The forces in Alsace withdrew to Chalons under Marshal MacMahon, while those in Lorraine

POLITICAL GENERALS

Both American Civil War armies, faced with the task of raising troops in a nation with little military experience, granted commissions liberally. Men whose political connections would strengthen the government and aid recruitment were especially favored.

Prominent Union political generals included Benjamin F. Butler, a Massachusetts state senator, and the New York Democratic politician Daniel E. Sickles, who lost a leg as a corps commander at Gettysburg. Franz Sigel, a former Baden artillery officer, enjoyed immense influence with the Germans of the North. The Confederate political generals included some of real military ability. John C. Breckinridge, a Kentucky lawyer, rose to the rank of major general before becoming secretary of war. South Carolina planter Wade Hampton raised "Hampton's Legion" at his own expense, and ended the war as a lieutenant general.

Not all politicians who joined the army aspired to high rank. Colonel Frank Wolford of the 1st Kentucky Cavalry was a small-town lawyer and politician. He was known as "Old Meat Axe" to his men, and his phraseology owed little to the drill book, but it was hard to mistake his cries of "huddle up," "scatter out," or "get up and git."

came under the command of Marshal Bazaine. Bazaine tried to withdraw from Metz to Verdun, was defeated at Rezonville on August 16, and fell back into Metz after the inconclusive battle of Gravelotte–St. Privat on August 18. MacMahon, marching to relieve him, was trapped at Sedan on September 1 and compelled to capitulate. Bazaine surrendered Metz in late October.

The second phase of the war tried Moltke's talents more severely, as the French government of National Defense, which replaced the fallen Second Empire, raised troops in the provinces and vigorously defended Paris, the besieged capital. French efforts prolonged the war but could not win it. An armistice was concluded on February 28, 1871, and France made peace on humiliating terms. These included the loss of Alsace and Lorraine, a painful blow that increased the likelihood of another Franco-German conflict. The war not only confirmed German unity under Prussian leadership, but also helped accelerate the militarization of German society, another dangerous portent for the future.

THE AMERICAN CIVIL WAR

By the time of the Franco-Prussian War in Europe, a conflict in North America had foreshadowed many of its developments. The American Civil War, which broke out in 1861, pitted the largely agricultural, agrarian South against the industrial North. The weight of resources was to tell heavily in the North's favor. In 1860, it had 110,274 industrial establishments to the South's 18,026, and $949,335,000 of capital investment against the South's derisory $100,665,000. It is easy to argue that the North's industrial muscle must eventually have proved decisive. However, it took time for the North to

BATTLE OF GETTYSBURG

DATE July 1–3, 1863
CAMPAIGN American Civil War, Lee's invasion of the North, June–July 1863
OBJECT After defeating Federal forces at Chancellorsville, Virginia, in May, General Robert E. Lee decided to invade the North in hopes of farther discouraging the enemy and possibly inducing European countries to recognize the Confederacy.
NUMBERS Union—Major General George G. Meade's Army of the Potomac, 88,000 men. Confederate—General Robert E. Lee's Army of Northern Virginia, with J. E. B. Stuart's cavalry detached, 70,000 men.
DESCRIPTION Lee opened the campaign by taking the war out of Virginia, into Union territory. Stuart's cavalry, the eyes of the army, were out of contact with Lee's main body, and Lee thus encountered Meade's army by accident. A leading Confederate divisional commander had heard that there were large quantities of shoes in Gettysburg and asked permission to obtain them. This brought him into contact with Union cavalry and provoked a general engagement. Once battle was joined, Lee sought first to outflank the Union army from his right, and, when this failed in fierce fighting around Little Round Top (July 2), he launched a frontal assault—known as Pickett's Charge—against the Union center on July 3. After coming very close to success in the Round Top fighting on July 2, the Confederates were bloodily repulsed from the Union center on the next day. The defeat did savage damage to the Army of Northern Virginia and Lee rapidly fell back to Virginia.
CASUALTIES Confederate—between 20,000 and 28,000 men; Union—23,000.
RESULT Gettysburg was inconclusive. However, on July 4, as Lee's beaten army recoiled, Ulysses S. Grant took the Confederate stronghold of Vicksburg on the Mississippi after a long siege. Between them, Gettysburg and Vicksburg marked the climax of the Civil War. Although the North could still lose the war through incompetence or war weariness, the South no longer had the power to force a decision in its own favor. Pickett's Charge was a graphic illustration of the effects of defensive firepower: the remarkable fighting qualities of Confederate infantry were no answer to the fire that Union troops poured down the slopes of Cemetery Ridge.

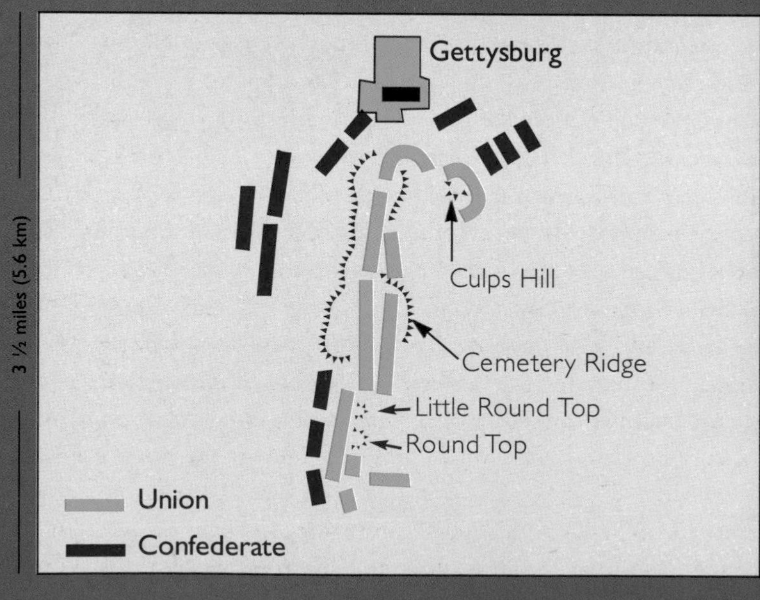

US Navy sailors manning an 11-in (28-cm) Dahlgren gun during the American Civil War. The Dahlgren was cast so as to produce a very hard inner surface to the bore in order to resist wear.

gear its strength to a single cohesive plan; it was not until Ulysses S. Grant remorselessly applied the Union's bludgeon to the Confederacy's rapier that Union victory was assured.

If the South lacked human and industrial resources, it nevertheless possessed some commanders of outstanding ability, Robert E. Lee and Thomas "Stonewall" Jackson among them. Thus the early years of the war were marked by Union defeats, some of which seemed to leave the Confederacy on the very brink of victory. However, all Lee's brilliance could not save the Confederacy from being ground down in a battle of resources. The North's blockade of southern harbors made it increasingly difficult for the South to import arms, and her own factories and battlefield captures were never sufficient to keep the Confederacy's armies fully equipped.

In 1864–65 the combination of Grant's relentless pressure in Northern Virginia and William T. Sherman's destructive march from Atlanta, which he had taken through the heart of the Confederacy to the sea at Savannah, sounded the South's death knell. Sherman continued through the Carolinas, leaving a trail of burned mills and ravaged railroads. The war showed that industrial and economic resources, if properly applied, were decisive.

THE RUSSO-JAPANESE WAR

The American Civil War, with its widespread use of railroads and startling demonstrations of the effectiveness of infantry firepower and field defenses, pointed the way ahead to both 1866 and 1870–71. The Russo-Japanese conflict of 1904–5 did much the same for World War I. The Japanese attacked the Russian fortress and naval base of Port Arthur, at the tip of the Liaotung peninsula in Manchuria, without warning in February 1904, and for the next year besieged Port Arthur and fought the Russian field army in Manchuria. The fighting was inconclusive but gave graphic proof of the effectiveness of magazine rifles and machine guns. The siege of Port Arthur was every bit as significant. Determined Japanese infantry suffered frightful

A Japanese print shows infantry cutting the railroad line at San-Tai-Tzu, north of the Manchurian city of Mukden, during the Russo-Japanese War of 1904–5. There was heavy fighting around Mukden, which was eventually taken by the Japanese. Defeat in Manchuria, loss of Port Arthur, and disaster in the naval battle of Tsushima compelled Russia to make peace, weakening the autocracy's hold at home and its prestige abroad.

casualties in their attacks on Russian forts and field defenses, but the plunging fire of Japanese heavy howitzers proved murderously destructive, not only to the forts themselves but also to Russian ships at anchor in the harbor.

An attempt by the Russian fleet sent from the Baltic to break the siege failed miserably. Admiral Zinovy Rozhestvensky arrived on May 27, 1905. Over that day and the next, in the largest sea battle since Trafalgar and the first fought with steam-powered turreted warships, Admiral Togo utterly defeated the Russian fleet in the straits of Tsushima. Port Arthur had already fallen by the time Rozhestvensky appeared and the demolition of his fleet led the Russians to make peace. Russian defeat had profound consequences, revealing the limitations of the Czarist autocracy and encouraging internal opposition. It also highlighted Russian military weakness, and at the same time picked out the rising power of Japan, a point that was not missed by colonial populations, for whom the defeat of a Western power was especially portentous.

Colonial wars had been in almost constant progress throughout the nineteenth century. The picture was usually a consistent one. Western powers—the British in India and Southern Africa, the Russians in Central Asia, the French in North Africa and Indo-China—

were usually able to defeat indigenous populations by the application of superior technology.

There were times when technology was not enough and most colonial powers incurred at least one serious reverse. In 1879, the British suffered a bloody defeat at the hands of the Zulus at Isandalwana, and in 1896 Baratieri's Italian army was routed by the Abyssinians at Adowa. Moreover, as Western technology spread into Africa and Asia, contests became somewhat less unequal. A small British force was defeated by the Afghans at Maiwand in 1880, in part because the Afghans' Krupp guns outperformed British artillery. The most serious colonial confrontation was the Anglo-Boer War in 1899–1902, when it required the sustained military might of the British empire to defeat the largely irregular forces of the Boer republics and then to cope with a long and exhausting guerrilla war. From the British point of view, however, the war was not without its uses, because it inspired a serious reorganization of the army, as a result of which the armed forces emerged much better prepared to face the challenge of 1914.

THE ROAD TO ARMAGEDDON

The seeds of disaster had begun to sprout while the new century was still in its infancy. An ominous confrontation between France and Germany was an enduring legacy of the Franco-Prussian War. Anglo-German naval and economic rivalry helped push Britain toward an unofficial understanding with France, and the need to counterbalance a powerful Germany encouraged France, for her part, to look toward Russia. Austria-Hungary, riven by the problem of nationalities, was wary of developments in the Balkans, where the decline of Turkish power and the Balkan wars of 1912–13 had aroused new and destabilizing national passions.

The military developments of the late nineteenth century ensured that these political concerns inspired fine-tuned preparations for war. All major European powers recognized the potentially decisive contribution to be made by conscription and mobilization plans, the railroad, and the general staff. The techniques of mass production enabled the huge armies swept together by conscription to be armed and fed. And the new armies had abundant firepower at their disposal. Their infantry and artillery looked so unlike the men who had fought at Waterloo as to be unrecognizable.

The cavalry, striving to confer mobility to a battlefield soon to be locked solid by firepower, still resembled the dashing horsemen of yesteryear. However, despite the beliefs of generals, such as Britain's Douglas Haig, who stated that bullets "had no real stopping power against the horse," the war begun in 1914 was to show that cavalry had lost its place on the modern battlefield.

A mixture of the intellectual currents of the nineteenth century, nationalism high among them, and the industrialization of war had made possible a new kind of conflict, fought between powers with prodigious human and industrial resources at their disposal. It is no small wonder that men looked at the prospect of future war with utter disbelief, arguing that it would prove so destructive as to be impossible. Others, including Britain's Lord Kitchener, prophesied that once the battle of the giants had been joined, it could end only in the exhaustion of the weakest.

QUICK-FIRING ARTILLERY

The development of quick-firing (QF) artillery was in response to the need for better defense against torpedo boats. As these boats became stronger, small machine-gun bullets could no longer do sufficient damage, so heavier-caliber weapons were required. These could not be made to operate in the same manner as machine guns, because of the extra weight of the mechanism and ammunition, but some of the technical features were adapted to facilitate a high rate of fire.

As often happens, the same idea simultaneously arose from two sources. Hotchkiss of France and Nordenfelt of Sweden had both been trying to design a heavy-caliber machine gun for some time. Then, in the late 1880s, both produced 47-mm and 57-mm guns, and these were widely adopted by the world's navies. The guns used rounds of ammunition that consisted of a brass cartridge case containing the propellant charge and a percussion primer for ignition, to which was attached the projectile, a powder-filled pointed shell carrying a simple base fuze. This ammunition, which was virtually a scaled-up rifle or machine-gun cartridge, allowed the gun to be loaded in one simple movement, using a breech mechanism that consisted of a block of steel sliding up and down behind the chamber. The breech

CARTRIDGE QUICK FIRING 6-PR STEEL SHELL CORDITE
SIZE 5 MARK III C
WITH STEEL SHELL FUZED

A typical QF round for a British 6-pounder (2 ¼-inch caliber) coast defense and naval gun. The shell is pointed for piercing ships' hulls.

A German 15-cm (6 inch) field howitzer of 1902, manufactured by Krupp. Once the quick-firing (QF) system had been mastered, it was rapidly extended to larger calibers, although this 150-mm weapon, weighing just over 2 tons was probably as big a QF weapon as could be comfortably managed in the field. Note the cradle beneath the barrel containing the hydro-spring recoil mechanism.

A French 75-mm quick-firing gun of 1897. This formed the pattern for future quick-firing field guns. It was widely adopted, and used until the 1950s in some countries.

mechanism merely had to retain the cartridge in position during firing. The breech was sealed by the expansion of the brass cartridge case, which then contracted and was ejected automatically as the breech block was opened. The French and Swedish guns were identical except for size. At first, they were mounted rigidly on a steel pedestal, which suffered the recoil blow. Later, the gun was carried in a "cradle" and permitted to slide back under the recoil force, its movement arrested by a hydraulic brake. A spring returned the gun to the firing position.

The 47-mm gun, in the hands of a skilled crew, could deliver about 30 shots per minute, the 57-mm about 25. This was adequate to defend warships against torpedo boats, and the same guns were adapted for land use to defend harbors against a similar threat. Their success prompted armies to ask gunmakers for a field artillery gun with a comparable performance.

The difficulty lay with the recoil force. Field guns were more powerful than the 47-mm and 57-mm naval weapons and were not anchored to a massive ship structure to absorb recoil. Unless recoil could be controlled, the gunners would be unable to load the gun fast enough to develop the desired rate of fire.

THE "FRENCH 75"

The problem was eventually solved by the French artillery arsenal at Puteaux, where a Captain Deport developed the 75-mm gun Mle 1897, the famous "French 75." This fired a fixed round of ammunition, had a quick-acting breech mechanism, and controlled the recoil of the gun by means of a complex and highly secret hydropneumatic braking system. This was so effective that a coin balanced on the gun's wheel would remain in place while a shot was fired. Because the gun carriage now remained still, it was provided with a shield so that the gunners were partially protected from small-arms fire.

These four features—the fixed ammunition, shield, quick-acting breech, and an on-carriage recoil system—became the hallmark of the quick-firing gun, and all the major armies rushed to produce their own versions. These guns differed in matters of detail but they all included the four essential features of the French gun, which could throw a 12-pound high-explosive or 16-pound shrapnel shell up to 10,000 yd (9,145 m). However, French offensive doctrine meant that the 75 was not ideally suited to trench warfare, and the shells it fired were too light to pose a threat to a heavily defended position.

10 WORLD WAR I

It is important to emphasize that World War I began in August 1914 much as soldiers had expected, with a fluid war of movement. In the west, the German strategic design for the rapid defeat of France prior to a transfer of strength to the Eastern Front to confront Imperial Russia was highly old-fashioned in the way that it unfolded in August and September 1914. Indeed, the German chief of staff who had originally masterminded it, Alfred von Schlieffen, had been much taken by the classic encircling movement executed by Hannibal at the Battle of Cannae.

THE SCHLIEFFEN PLAN

Although modified by von Schlieffen's successor, the younger Helmuth von Moltke, the plan still resembled a great revolving door in which the arc of the German advance would sweep through Belgium and carry the right wing around Paris and back toward the Rhine. But the Schlieffen Plan took little account of any military realities. The arc of advance would always be within reach of the French strategic rail network, and Schlieffen had hardly considered possible enemy reaction in demanding rigid adherence to a schedule that would commit the German First Army on the extreme right to a 300-mile (485-km) march at a constant 15 miles (24 km) a day for three weeks.

Schlieffen had assumed that use would be made of the Belgian and French railroads but the former were extensively damaged during the German advance and, in the case of von Kluck's First Army, the critical distance between the marching columns and the railheads stretched to an average of 70 to 80 miles (110 to 130 km). The small British Expeditionary Force (BEF) of 75,000 men had the comparatively lavish total of 1,485 motor vehicles of all kinds, while the five northern German armies operating between Luxemburg and Brussels had but 500 motor trucks between them. As they marched deeper into France, the intense summer heat took its toll of the German infantry. German High Command (OHL), initially located at Koblenz, steadily lost contact with its forward elements, 206 miles (331.5 km) away. Von Kluck had two wireless transmitters, but OHL had one receiving set. Codes were slow to decipher and the French were using the Eiffel Tower transmitter to jam German transmissions. OHL had to communicate with commanders by despatching staff officers in motor cars.

Poor communications and lack of coordination between the German First and Second armies led von Kluck to abandon the original plan and pass east instead of west of Paris, thus exposing his right flank and enabling the allies to counterattack in what became known as the First Battle of the Marne. This coincided with German loss of confidence and, on September 9, 1914, the Germans began to retreat.

British soldiers of the 2nd Battalion, Royal Warwickshire Regiment being transported in requisitioned London Transport "Old Bill" buses from Dickebusche to Ypres during the First Battle of Ypres between October 15 and November 22, 1914. The battle marked the climax of the "Race to the Sea." The BEF was brought back from Aisne to Flanders in order to maintain better communications with its bases at Calais, Boulogne, and Le Havre.

BATTLE OF MONS

DATE August 23, 1914
OBJECT British rearguard action in the face of the advancing German army.
NUMBERS British Expeditionary Force—75,000 men, 300 guns; German First Army—160,000 men, 600 guns.
DESCRIPTION Advancing from its concentration area at Mauberge in support of a limited French move toward the Sambre and Meuse rivers, the one cavalry and four infantry divisions of Field Marshal Sir John French's BEF unknowingly came into the path of General Alexander von Kluck's First Army on the extreme right of the German invasion of Belgium and France. After making contact with German patrols on August 21 and 22, the BEF was dug in along the Mons–Condé canal where it was attacked on August 23 by von Kluck's army. In nine hours of fighting, the brunt of the German assault fell on the British II Corps, which suffered most of the British casualties. Unable to advance in face of heavy British fire, the Germans lost heavily. However, with von Kluck having hardly committed his army and with news that the French were already retreating, the BEF also retired that evening.
CASUALTIES British—1,638; German—heavy, although the precise figure is unknown.
RESULT The retreat continued until September 4, which meant that the Mons battle together with the BEF's subsequent delaying actions imposed crucial delays on the Schlieffen Plan.

BATTLE OF TANNENBERG

DATE August 26–30, 1914
OBJECT German counteroffensive to defend East Prussia against the Russians.
NUMBERS Roughly 150,000 men and 700 guns each.
DESCRIPTION Faced with the invasion of East Prussia by the Russian First and Second armies (commanded by Generals Rennenkampf and Samsonov) on August 17, 1914, General Max von Prittwitz ordered the German Eighth Army to retreat. Prittwitz was subsequently convinced by his staff that they could exploit their superior communications to defeat Samsonov, but OHL was not made aware of the change of plan and dismissed Prittwitz. His successor, General Paul von Hindenburg, arrived August 23 with Major General Erich Ludendorff as chief of staff, and approved the existing plan to transfer the Eighth Army to the southern frontier of East Prussia, leaving a cavalry division to cover Rennenkampf. Deploying about an equal number of men against Samsonov's forces, the Germans commenced a double envelopment of the Russian Second Army on August 26. This was completed in four days; Russian losses were high, including 300 guns. Samsonov committed suicide.
CASUALTIES Germans—10,000 to 15,000; Russians—70,000 and 55,000 to 75,000 captured.
RESULT The reinforced Eighth Army turned north to defeat Rennenkampf around the Masurian Lakes in September 1914, a double victory that established the reputations of Hindenburg and Ludendorff.

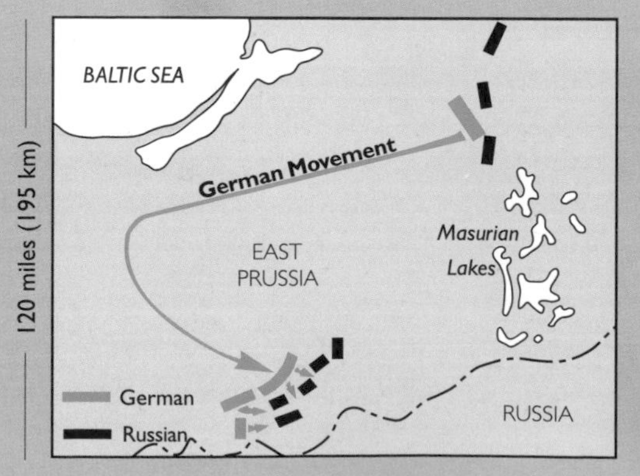

Improvised field fortifications had appeared at an early stage. The BEF had dug in along the Mons–Condé canal on August 23 in its first major engagement. On September 13, however, the French Fifth Army encountered something new in an organized trench system before Reims. In a matter of days, the other Allied armies had similarly come up against a more systematic entrenchment on the part of the Germans. Von Moltke had not actually intended that these trenches should do more than gain a temporary respite for his armies. In search of renewed mobility, each side began to attempt to outflank the other, leapfrogging to the north in turn. By mid-November, this "race to the sea" had resulted in a continuous front from the Alps to the English Channel.

PEACE BY CHRISTMAS?

On the Eastern Front, where there had also been an initial search for a decisive envelopment, positions had similarly stabilized by the end of 1914, although the distances involved—it was more than 600 miles (965 km) from the Carpathians to the Baltic—ensured that the line was not continuous and the war always more fluid. In the Balkans, Serbia had thrown back three major Austro-Hungarian offensives. Clearly, the widespread assumption that the war would be over by Christmas was mistaken and there were already indications of a new kind of warfare. Losses had greatly exceeded expectations, the Germans suffering 750,000 casualties in the first five months in the west and the French some 900,000. Moreover, the sheer expenditure of ammunition was so far above prewar estimates that most belligerents were to suffer "shell shortages" in 1915.

The increased demands for artillery shells significantly changed prewar logistic patterns. Most systems were geared to carrying food and fodder and still dependent upon horsed transport—more ammunition required more horses and more fodder. Thus, between 1914 and 1918, the 5.9 million tons of fodder sent to France for the BEF's animal transport exceeded the 5.2 million tons of ammunition also despatched.

The "bloody paralyser," a Handley Page 0/100 of No.3 Wing Royal Naval Air Service (R.N.A.S.) in France in 1917. The 0/100 was Britain's first designated bomber, the ancestor of World War II's Avro Lancaster. It had a crew of two and was powered by two 260 hp Rolls Royce Eagle engines.

Inevitably, the war necessitated an increase in the ratio of support unit personnel to fighting men, a ratio that has continued to increase through the twentieth century. At least the soldiers of World War I did not yet need vast amounts of gasoline and gasoline-related products but the BEF was still supported by no less than 447,000 motor vehicles by 1918.

AIR POWER

The first campaigns produced revelations about logistics and the importance of greater defensive power, and also encouraged a number of innovations, not least the rapid development of airpower. During the Allied retreat from the Belgian and French frontiers in August and September 1914, British and French aircraft provided a vital reconnaissance function, and had detected the German turn east of Paris. In fulfilling the reconnaissance role, airmen had also begun experimenting with improvised weapons to down their opponents. Three Royal Flying Corps (RFC) machines became the first aircraft to force down an opponent on August 25, 1914. Although no wireless communication was as yet available for aircraft, the RFC undertook its first aerial spotting for artillery on September 13, above the Aisne battlefield.

Air power also made its debut at sea. The Royal Naval Air Service (RNAS) had been the first successfully to launch a torpedo from the air just prior to the outbreak of war but, on December 25, 1914, German Zeppelins made the first actual aerial attack on ships. Ironically, they engaged a British naval force that was launching the first seaborne air attack on the Zeppelin sheds at Cuxhaven. Earlier, on October 8, RNAS aircraft had carried out the first strategic bombing mission in attacking Zeppelin sheds at Düsseldorf and Cologne.

Submarines were making a similar impact, the German U-21 becoming the first submarine to sink a ship in action at sea when attacking HMS *Pathfinder* in the Firth of Forth in Scotland on September 3, 1914. The first merchantman to fall victim was the *Glitra* to U-17 on October 20, while HMS *Birmingham* became the first vessel to sink a submarine by ramming U-15 in the North Sea on August 9, 1914.

LIFE IN THE TRENCHES

Even after the Allies and the Germans settled into static winter positions after the conclusion of the "race to the sea" on the Western Front, it was some months before the trenches became continuous or systematically organized in all sectors over the 475-mile (765-km) front from Switzerland to the coast. Perceptible differences emerged between the armies.

Initially, for example, the Germans concentrated troops in their front line with little immediate support beyond some machine-gun bunkers. By contrast, the British began almost at once to adopt a three-line system of front, support, and reserve trench linked by zigzag communications trenches. The French constructed strong points enfilading less well-defended stretches of line, backed by a support line. Artillery tended to be placed as ranges dictated behind the front line, although the French had a tendency to site their guns farther forward than the British or Germans.

Nonetheless, the pattern of trench warfare became much the same for all the soldiers on the Western Front, despite the fact that the terrain varied greatly from the wooded heights of the Vosges and the flooded coastal plain of the Yser to the dry chalklands of the Somme and Champagne, which alone were suitable for large-scale operations. In fact, such operations were comparatively rare and often tacit truces existed between the opposing front lines in some "quiet" sectors.

The danger presented by artillery, sniper, and mortar fire contributed to a constant stream of casualties, and there was also the ever-present threat of disease resulting from cold, damp, and vermin. Regular rotations between front, support, and reserve positions were essential. Ready access to letters and packages from home and, in the British army at least, an extensive program of recreational activities substantially assisted the maintenance of morale and, to a degree, promoted a "community" of shared experience.

Parapet
Sandbags
Ammunition Hole
Shuttering
Fire Step
Duckboard Flooring
Drainage Sump

(Left) An idealized trench of some 10 to 12 feet (3 to 3.6 m) in depth with sandbag protection and wooden fire step, shuttering, and floor.

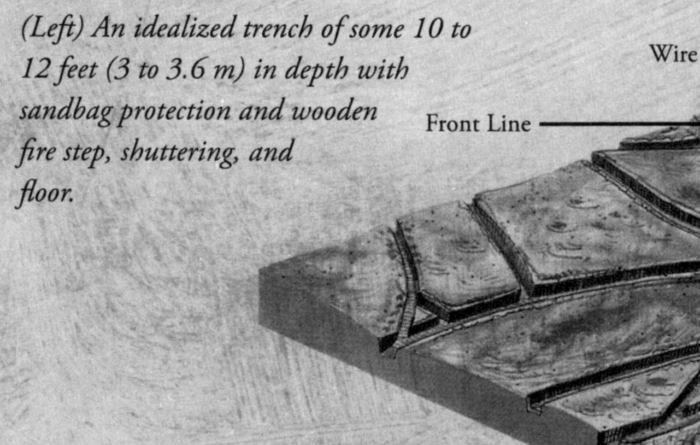

Supply station in a front line trench at La Harazee near Verdun, which saw savage fighting in 1916. The British thought their allies were slovenly trench builders.

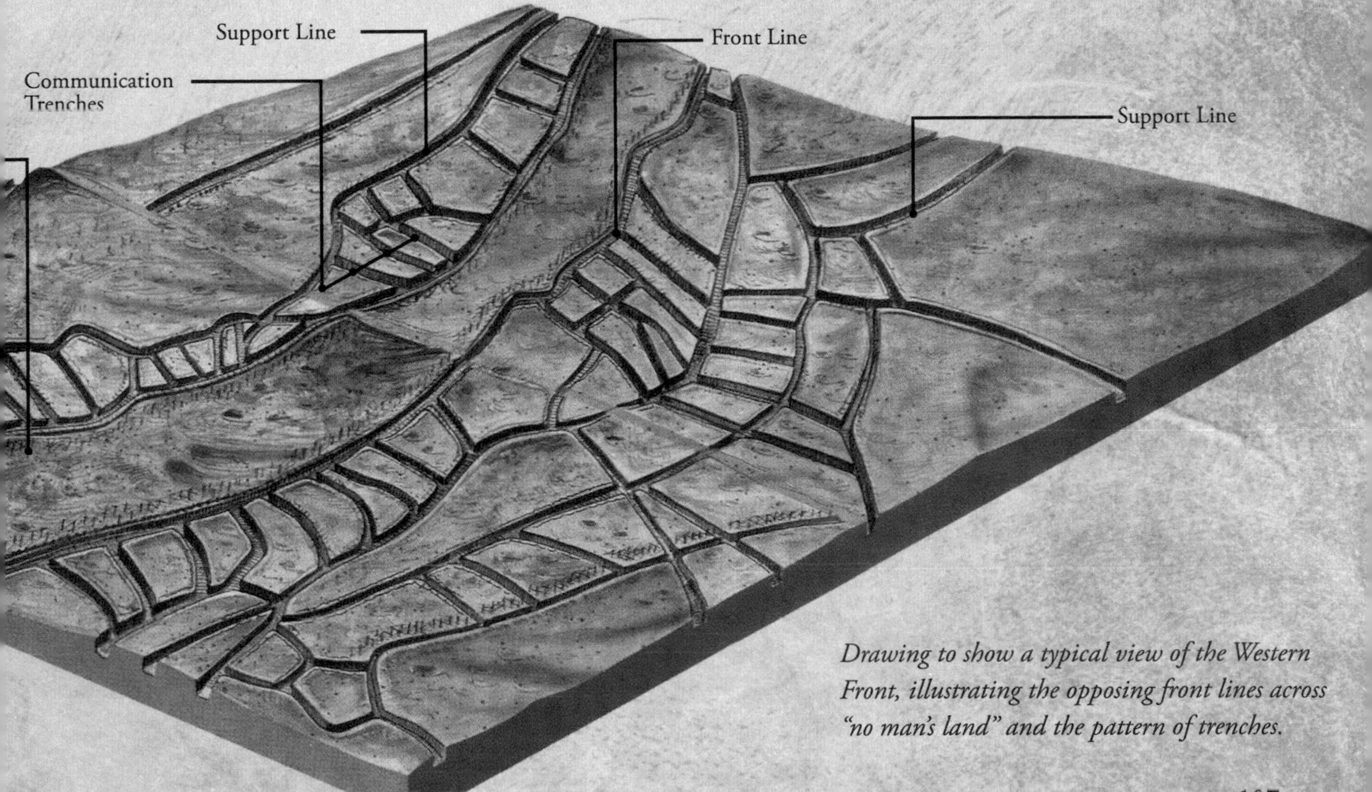

Support Line

Front Line

Communication Trenches

Support Line

Drawing to show a typical view of the Western Front, illustrating the opposing front lines across "no man's land" and the pattern of trenches.

THE SIDE SHOWS

World War I was a global conflict. While the Central Powers eventually embraced Germany, Austria-Hungary, Turkey, and Bulgaria, no less than 22 states eventually comprised the Allies, including Japan and the United States. It was thus inevitable that the war would not be confined to the main Western and Eastern fronts. Even within Europe, war was joined between Italy and Austria-Hungary after the former joined the Allies in May 1915, while the Allied landing at Salonika in October 1915 opened a separate Balkan front against Bulgaria. It could also be argued that the fall of Serbia and Romania to the Central Powers in December 1915 and December 1916 respectively were campaigns separate from the main German and Austro-Hungarian struggle against Russia.

The Allied war against Turkey included the Dardanelles campaign in 1915, the Russian campaign in the Caucasus, and the British campaigns in Egypt, Palestine, and Mesopotamia. Campaigns were also mounted against German colonies, such as the Cameroons, Togoland, and German East and Southwest Africa; and the Japanese participated in the conquest of German possessions in China and the Pacific.

BREAKING THE IMPASSE

The air and sea conflict, however, would not yet make any decisive impact on the war as a whole and, as 1915 opened, the armies of Europe still faced the same problem as in 1914—how to cross the zone of fire. The task was made doubly difficult by the appearance of trenches. Primarily, the creation of static entrenchments robbed the attacker of the element of surprise since it required a lengthy buildup of supplies and manpower in preparation for any attempt to break through an opposing trench line. The place of assault could frequently be determined by the intended victim and arrangements made accordingly. Moreover, the ability of the attacker to protect his infantry as the men crossed what soon became known as "no man's land" was limited to the range of the artillery available. Artillery could not readily be brought forward from its fixed positions behind the lines in order to extend any breakthrough made by the infantry and the attacker generally lacked the mobility required fully to exploit any success.

Of course, artillery could reach the opposing infantry in their trenches if they had no overhead cover, such as bunkers or tunnels, but the artillery available was still not powerful enough to destroy a defensive system totally. Indeed, even when heavier artillery was deployed, sufficient numbers usually survived to break up an infantry attack, particularly by the use of machine guns sweeping the oncoming ranks. Increasingly, the Germans protected their machine guns in bunkers or deep dug-outs and, at the end of any Allied bombardment, a race developed between the German machine gunners and the Allied infantry to determine who reached the German parapet first. Invariably, it was the German machine gunners, with results that are unmistakably associated with the image of the Western Front.

German defense

To a very large extent, overcoming defenses was more a problem for the Allies than for the Central Powers. On the Western Front in particular, the Germans had successfully occupied much of Belgium in the opening campaign, and a good deal of the most industrially productive regions of northern France. It was, thus, a strategic necessity for the Allies to win back such lost ground, while the Germans could afford to indulge in positional attrition in the West while pursuing territorial ambitions in the East. The Allied difficulty was that the Germans had also occupied commanding geographical positions in 1914, which gave them both strategic and tactical control of the Western Front.

The first real British offensive aimed at breaking through the German front line came at Neuve Chapelle on March 10, 1915. It was a highly innovative attack in terms of such techniques as aerial reconnaissance of German defenses, the issue of objective maps to the infantry, and the coordination of artillery fire by schedule to fit the projected lines of advance. A narrow front was selected where the German line formed a salient and where the German trenches lacked real depth or much barbed wire, itself becoming a major obstacle in such positional warfare. The British enjoyed a numerical superiority of something like 5:1 and had assembled the unprecedented number of 340 artillery pieces for a short preliminary bombardment.

However, despite the laying of an experimental network of field telephones, communications broke down almost as soon as the infantry had left the British trenches, mist conspiring to obscure much of what was happening beyond the British front line. A breakthrough was achieved, which in itself was not usual on the Western Front—other comparable breakthroughs by the British were confined to the first day of the battle of Loos on September 24, 1915, the first day at Vimy (by the Canadians) on April 9, 1917, and the first day at Cambrai on November 20, 1917. However, this rare success could not be reinforced rapidly enough and the attack was broken off on March 12, the cost being 12,000 casualties for the gain of just 4,000 square yards (3,345 sq. m).

BATTLE OF ANZAC COVE

DATE April 25, 1915
CAMPAIGN Gallipoli Peninsula
OBJECT The Australian and New Zealand Army Corps (ANZAC) were to support the main landing at Cape Helles by coming ashore a mile north of Gabe Tepe and moving inland to seize the commanding Sari Bari Heights.
NUMBERS British and ANZAC—75,000; Turkish—84,000.
DESCRIPTION Following the failure of the British and French fleets to force the Dardanelles in March 1915, there was little alternative but to attempt an amphibious landing on the Gallipoli peninsula, although only 75,000 men of the British 29th and Royal Naval Divisions and the Anzacs were available to General Sir Ian Hamilton. The German general, Liman von Sanders, had some 84,000 troops in defense, but only about 700 men from the Turkish 19th Division were in the area of the proposed Anzac landing. The first Anzac troops landed at 4:30 a.m. on April 25, but 2 miles (3 km) north of the intended destination in what became known as Anzac Cove, an inlet surrounded by steep cliffs. Despite administrative confusion, they had captured the immediate beachhead by 6 a.m. and came within just 3½ miles (5.6 km) of the Straits before being pushed back by counterattacks organized by the future president of the Turkish republic, Mustapha Kemal.
CASUALTIES By nightfall, the Australians had suffered 2,000 casualties and were fighting simply to retain a foothold on the beach.
RESULT The Australians were pinned down for almost eight months, as were the British at Cape Helles. A farther landing at Suvla Bay also failed. Both Anzac Cove and Suvla Bay were evacuated on December 20; Allied troops left Cape Helles in January 1916.

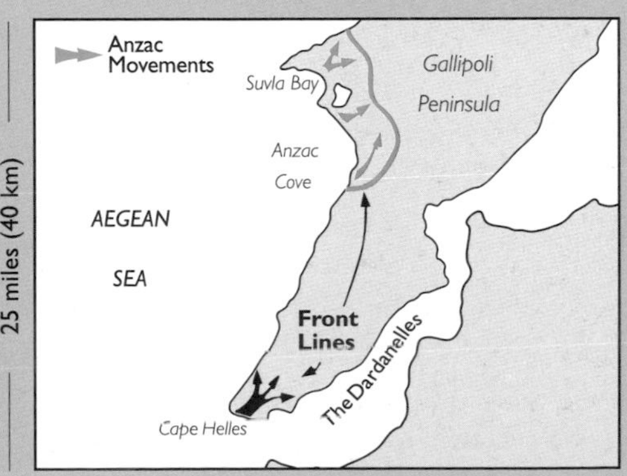

WORLD WAR I AMMUNITION

Enormous changes in ammunition technology occurred during World War I. New types of ammunition were necessary to address new tactical problems, and production techniques had to be radically improved to cope with increased demand. Production on the scale required had to be contracted to civilian engineering firms with no previous experience in this field. In 1914, the standard field artillery projectile was the shrapnel shell, a murderous weapon used against troops out in the open. But once the infantry had dug in, troops came into the open only when attacking. So the demand was for high-explosive shells to blow open the earthworks. In Britain, new factories were built and Lloyd George was appointed Minister of Munitions. In Germany, alternative shell fillings were developed, and so was the use of gas.

In the small-arms field, the use of steel shields in trench loopholes resulted in the development of the armor-piercing bullet. Equally, the need for aviators to be able to see the trajectory of their machine-gun fire led to tracer bullets, which, hollowed out and packed with a pyrotechnic powder, left a trail of smoke and red sparks, from which the firer could adjust his aim. Incendiary bullets were a response to the Zeppelin threat, as were incendiary shells for antiaircraft guns, although the standard shrapnel or high-explosive shell could do sufficient damage to most types of aircraft.

The proliferation of barbed wire on the Western Front created the need for artillery to destroy it or, at least, to cut gaps in it to allow the infantry through. The standard impact fuzes of the day were not sensitive enough for this task, especially in the soft ground of Flanders. More sensitive fuzes, which detonated as soon as they struck the mud, were needed. Despite these, wire clearing by artillery fire was never very effective because barbed wire was flexible enough to resist the blast. The smoke shell was also developed to screen troops advancing over open ground. This was filled with white phosphorus, which ignited when it came into contact with air.

Raids at night were countered, at first, with "star" shells. These had been made before the war and consisted of bright candles that were released from a shell and fell to the ground, giving local illumination. During the war, parachute-suspended magnesium flares were developed. These could be packed into a shell and, by the action of a time fuze, they ignited and lit up the battlefield.

One of the few ways to attack entrenched troops was to burst high-explosive shells in the air over them,

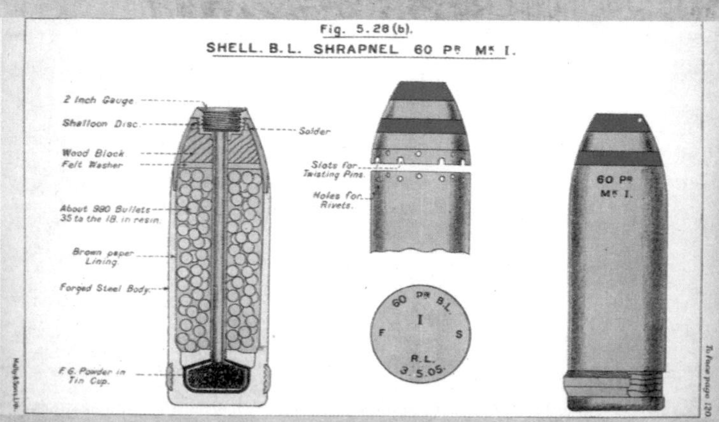

A shrapnel shell for the 60-pounder heavy field gun. The head is retained by pins and rivets; the body contains lead balls packed in resin, resting on a "pusher plate." A central tube passes from the fuze well to a charge of gunpowder below the pusher plate. When the fuze reaches the set time, it sends a flash down the tube to explode the gunpowder.

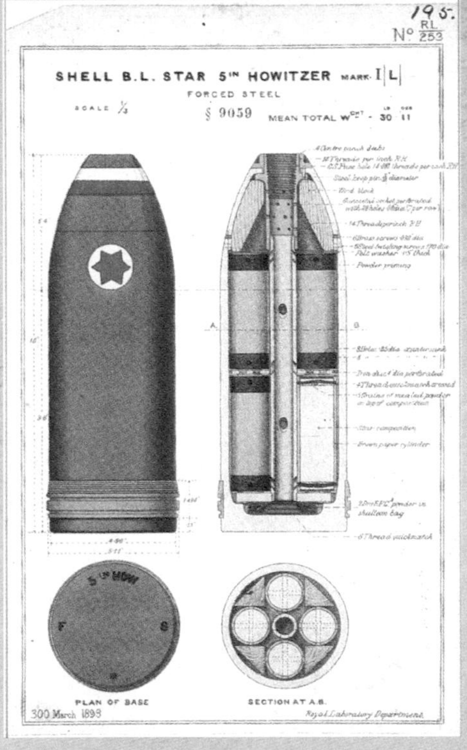

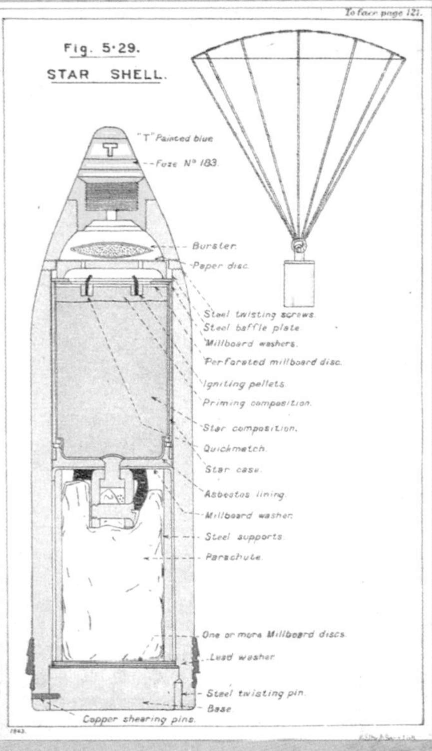

(Far left) This early star shell for the 5-inch (12-cm) howitzer worked in a similar manner to shrapnel, using a gunpowder charge and a pusher plate to eject eight cylindrical stars, which fell to the ground and continued to burn, illuminating the immediate area. They were of more use for signaling than for providing light.
(Left) The parachute star was a later design of star shell, in which a single star unit was attached to a parachute.

but this demanded accurate time fuzes. By 1916, the Germans had developed a clockwork fuze with a prewound spring that was released by the shock of firing. It could be set accurately and permitted precise shooting to the longest ranges. The British and French soon set about devising their own versions.

To enable infantry to break through wire the "pipe charge" or "Bangalore Torpedo" was introduced. This was a 5-foot (1.5-m) length of pipe of 1-inch (2.5-cm) diameter that was packed with explosives. One length of pipe was screwed onto a second length, and then pushed across "no man's land" beneath the enemy wire. Once it was in position, the pushers took cover in their trench and fired the charge, ripping a pathway through the wire. The inventor of this crude but clever device is not known, but it was in the hands of every combatant by 1916. When the tank appeared in 1916, it was soon followed by the land mine, a simple pressure-operated charge of explosive that could be buried in likely places and would break the track of any tank that ran across it.

In naval munitions, pressure-sensitive and magnetic sensors were in development by the time the war ended.

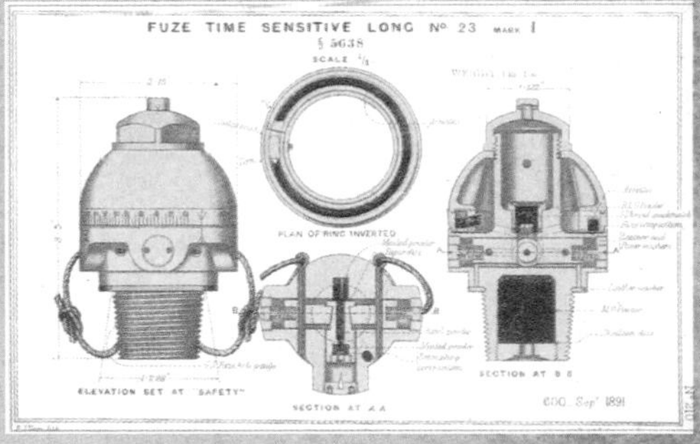

An early time fuze, used with the 5-inch (12.7-cm) star shell. Spin, causing centrifugal force, made the igniting pellet strike the pin and fire the time ring.

Two soldiers search the muddy battlefields of Ypres for lost or abandoned war materials or other valuables. In the first Battle of Ypres, October 1914, German forces failed to reach the English Channel ports but the Allied counter-attack failed. Poison gas was used for the first time on the Western Front in April 1915 by the Germans at the second battle of Ypres. Shelling of all kinds destroyed Flanders's fragile drainage system and left soldiers stranded in mud. At the third battle of Ypres, Passchendaele (1917), many drowned in it.

Unfortunately, the lesson drawn from Neuve Chapelle was not the psychological value of the brief preliminary bombardment but that an even longer bombardment was required both to cut the German wire and to neutralize the opposing defenders. It was assumed that greater firepower would do a more comprehensive job, and it was also believed that future attacks would be better made on a far wider frontage. Thus, opening bombardments, such as those fired by the British before the start of the Battle of the Somme on July 1, 1916, or the opening of the Passchendaele offensive on July 31, 1917, became heavier in the expectation that this would achieve the task.

Creeping barrage

One refinement of artillery support introduced as a result of the initial experience on the Somme was the creeping barrage to take infantry right up to the opposing front line and beyond under a curtain of protecting fire. However, this, in turn, presented difficulties, because it encouraged linear formations and the infantry could not keep up with a moving barrage, which could not be recalled due to the lack of communications. Telephone wires and cables were dug ever deeper but were still cut by artillery fire and, of course, they could be extended forward of the front line into no man's land only as the infantry advanced.

BATTLE OF THE SOMME

DATE July–November 1916
OBJECT The Allies wanted a decisive breakthrough of German lines.
NUMBERS Allies (initially)—24 divisions; Germans (initially)—11 divisions.
DESCRIPTION It was agreed in December 1915 that the Allies would mount a series of offensives in 1916. The main British effort was to take place along the line of the Somme River marking the junction of the British and French armies. In the event, the opening of the German Verdun offensive in February forced the British to take pressure off the French, with the result that Lieutenant General Sir Henry Rawlinson's Fourth Army lacked real strategic purpose in its attack opposite General Fritz von Below's German Second Army. The situation was not improved by disagreements over the objective of the offensive between Rawlinson and his commander in chief, Sir Douglas Haig. After an eight-day preliminary bombardment in which 1.7 million shells were hurled at the German positions, the British attacked on July 1, 1916, the battle being the first real blooding of the "New Armies" of volunteers who had responded to Lord Kitchener's appeal in 1914.
CASUALTIES Almost 500,000 on each side.
RESULT On the first day alone the Allied Fourth Army suffered more than 57,000 casualties, including over 19,000 dead, making it the bloodiest day in the history of the British Army. By the time the battle officially ended on November 19, an area of roughly 25 miles (40 km) long by 6 miles (9.6 km) wide had been won. The Germans suffered as many losses as the Allies and what began, at least as far as Haig was concerned, as a battle for a decisive breakthrough, rapidly became transformed into a battle of sheer attrition.

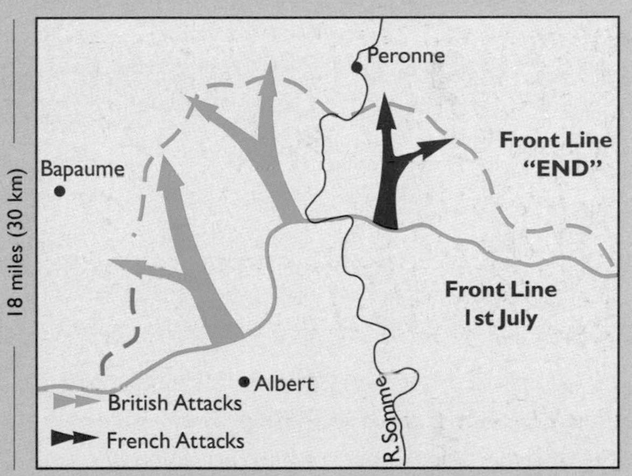

THE ARTILLERY WAR

As early as 1914, it was apparent that artillery was becoming the decisive weapon of land warfare. In the Russo-Japanese War, only 10 percent of the total casualties had been caused by artillery fire, but between 1914 and 1918, this increased to an estimated 70 percent of total casualties. Nevertheless, sufficient numbers of defenders usually survived a bombardment to break up an infantry attack. Thus, the British fired 1.7 million shells in eight days prior to the opening of the Somme offensive in July 1916 and 4.2 million shells in 14 days prior to the Passchendaele offensive a year later without suppressing the defense. Subsequently, advances in instrument location of enemy batteries rendered long bombardments unnecessary.

EASTERNERS, WESTERNERS

Throughout Europe in 1914, politicians of the belligerent countries either willingly surrendered responsibility for the strategic conduct of the war to the professional soldiers or found it effectively wrested from their grasp. The latter was true, for example, of Imperial Germany, where the tradition of von Schlieffen inherited by the younger von Moltke assumed that politicians had no role once war had begun. In Britain, by contrast, the office of Secretary of State for War was given to Earl Kitchener of Khartoum who, having served most of his army career overseas, had virtually no knowledge of pre-war arrangements for expanding the home army and, on one occasion, memorably expressed his distaste for discussing strategic options with gentlemen with whom he was unacquainted, by which he meant the remainder of the Cabinet.

Field Marshal Sir William Robertson, a committed "Westerner" who served as Chief of the Imperial General Staff from 1916–18. Robertson was the only British soldier to rise from the rank of Private to that of Field Marshal.

New plans

Inevitably, when the deadlock and sheer cost of war on the Western Front became apparent in the late fall of 1914, politicians in Britain and France were motivated to seek not so much a new weapon to break the deadlock as an alternative strategy. At that point, however, they had cause to regret the easy transference of their control over strategy to the soldiers, for most professionals regarded any attempt to divert manpower from the Western Front to other theaters as "sideshows," irrelevant to the main effort to defeat Germany's strongest army in the west. Thus, in Britain and France, leading soldiers such as Sir William Robertson, who

Sir Douglas Haig, commander of the BEF from December 1915, with the French Commander in Chief Joffre (1914–16) and David Lloyd George, then Minister of Munitions. Like Robertson, Haig was a convinced "Westerner." Lloyd George was an "Easterner."

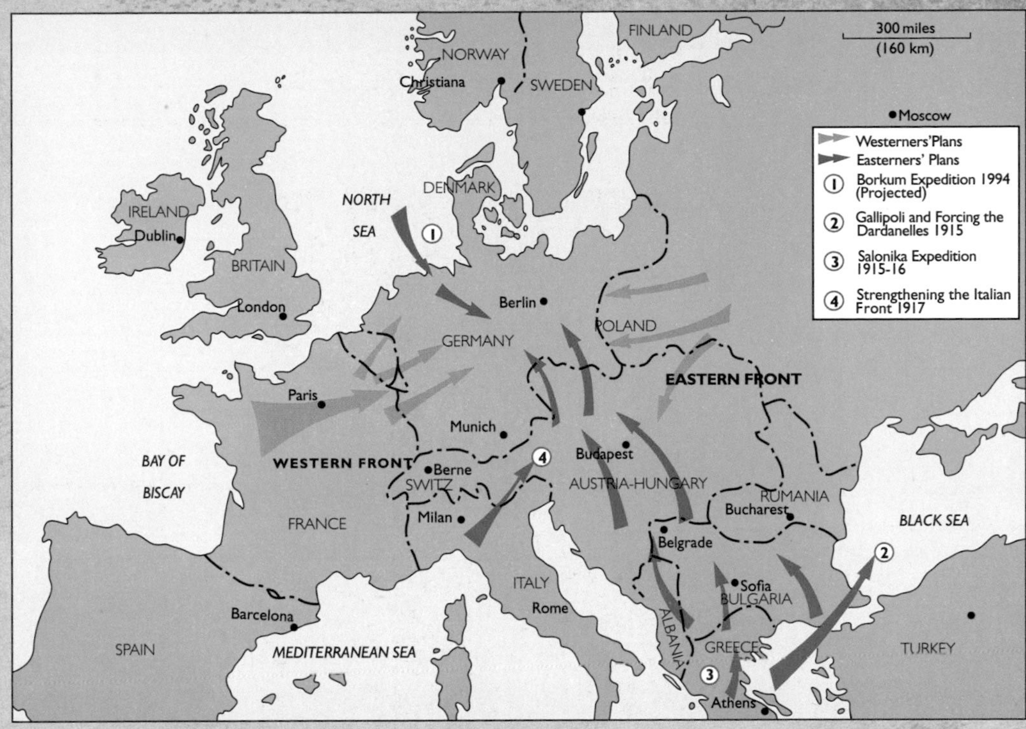

Strategic options considered by British "easterners" in the winter of 1914 included a descent on the island of Borkum as well as expeditions to the Dardanelles and Salonika. Borkum was rejected, but the others were mounted in an attempt to undermine Germany by knocking out her allies and advancing through their territory. When these expeditions failed, Italy became the favored alternative front.

became Chief of the Imperial General Staff in December 1915, and Sir Douglas Haig, who took command of the British Expeditionary Force (BEF) the same month, were "westerners" seeking a decisive victory in the west. Politicians, such as Winston Churchill and David Lloyd George, who became prime minister in December 1916, were "easterners," who were convinced of the desirability of finding an "indirect approach" via Germany's allies.

Different approaches

In one sense the division between the two camps was artificial because both "westerners" and "easterners" were committed to defeating Germany by raising and deploying a large British army, whereas some British politicians, such as Reginald McKenna and Walter Runcimann, believed only in a war of "limited liability." Nonetheless, if the aim was the same, ideas about the means to achieve it differed radically.

Unfortunately for the "easterners," the indirect campaigns they managed to initiate, such as the Dardanelles campaign against Turkey between February 1915 and January 1916, and the Salonika campaign against Bulgaria between October 1915 and September 1918, failed to undermine Germany through her allies. This failure enabled the "westerners" to prevail and, even as prime minister, Lloyd George was reduced to contriving to deny troops to Haig in France by attempting to divert manpower elsewhere.

The division in strategy was paralleled in Germany, where von Moltke's successor as Chief of the General Staff, von Falkenhayn, was committed to a decision in the west while Hindenburg and Ludendorff sought it on the Eastern Front.

British cavalry on the Western Front, ever ready but seldom used. Mud and machine guns swiftly reduced the cavalry to an anachronism. Ironically the tonnage of fodder required to maintain the BEF's cavalry and transport animals exceeded that for ammunition. Between 1914 and 1918 horses and mules ate their way through 5.9 million tons, compared with 5.2 million tons of shells and bullets that crossed the Channel.

Unforeseen obstacles

In attempting to destroy the barrier of the wire, heavier bombardments created a new obstacle by breaking up the ground. In those areas most suited to offensive operations, such as the Flemish plain where the water table was high and the drainage systems were close to the surface, this had disastrous results, leaving the army floundering in mud. In such conditions, even if a breakthrough occurred, it was all but impossible to move reinforcements forward quickly enough to exploit it. The only arm of exploitation available was the cavalry, but on the Western Front horsemen were an anachronism. On July 14, 1916, for example, when the 20th Deccan Horse and 7th Dragoon guards were brought into the attack at High Wood on the Somme, machine guns destroyed them. Similarly, at Arras on April 11, 1917, British cavalry was swiftly brought to a halt. On the Eastern Front, however, there was still a role for cavalry, as well as in peripheral campaigns, such as in Palestine. Indeed, over 4,000 cavalry charges took place on the Eastern Front during the war, including the shattering of the Austro-Hungarian Seventh Army by Russian cavalry at Gorodenko on April 27–28, 1915.

The maintenance of cavalry divisions in the British and other armies epitomized the transition through which the high commands were passing in a painfully gradual learning process. They were isolated from the front line by the new managerial problems that had emerged with the formation of mass armies. Due to the extent of the battlefields and the primitive means of communication available, the war was the first and last fought without traditional voice control by the commander. "Château generalship" by army commanders marked the real tensions that existed in the transition to a new professionalism.

It would be wrong to assume that all generals and all armies failed to appreciate what was happening on the Western Front. Small-units tactics—the attempt by infantry to advance in small groups using their own firepower—had suggested itself to some British officers during the Somme campaign as a means of avoiding the carnage of the first day. However, these ideas were not fully implemented until late 1917; Passchendaele was characterized by the same linear tactics as on the Somme but with longer intervals between lines and individuals.

It is not easy to change doctrine in the middle of a major war, but Germany managed the transition. Having suffered heavily from the opening British bombardment on the Somme, a new concept of "elastic defense in depth," partly based on captured French documents, was implemented during the winter of 1916–17 by Colonel Fritz von Lossberg, Captain Hermann Geyer, and others in the German high command. The front line was thinned in terms of manpower but considerably deepened from front to rear. This enabled a more mobile defense and the possibility of surrendering ground tactically. The defense zone covered between 6,000 and 8,000 yards (5,485 and 7,315 m) in new *Stellung* (positions) constructed behind the existing front. The most formidable was the *Siegfriedstellung* between Cambrai and St. Quentin but the whole system was collectively known to the BEF as the "Hindenburg Line," extending from Arras to Soissons. The new concept also involved special counterattack divisions being placed behind the lines, to which the Germans retired in February and March 1917. The main Hindenburg Line was not effectively broken until August and September 1918, although it was breached by the British at Cambrai in November 1917.

BATTLE OF VERDUN

DATE February–December 1916
OBJECT German chief of staff, Erich von Falkenhayn, appears to have sought a battle of attrition in the Verdun salient. The French defended it desperately as a key fortified frontier zone.
NUMBERS More than 500,000 in total.
DESCRIPTION After a nine-hour bombardment, the German Fifth Army attacked along an 8-mile (13-km) front on February 21. Lack of armament in the surrounding forts and the loss of the largest—Fort Douaumont—on February 25 almost proved fatal to the French defense. The Germans reached the east bank of the Meuse and, on February 29, moved to seize the west bank. German offensives toward the Mort Homme feature were halted on March 6 and April 9 but the French faced repeated assaults during June. The fall of Fort Vaux on June 7 made the situation difficult, but the Russian Brusilov and the British Somme offensives sucked away German reserves; the French recaptured Douaumont on October 24 and Vaux on November 2.
CASUALTIES French—270,000; German—240,000.
RESULT By December, the French had regained almost all the positions lost in February. Heavy casualties were sustained by both sides in what has become a lasting symbol of an attritional battle taken to the extremes of suffering.

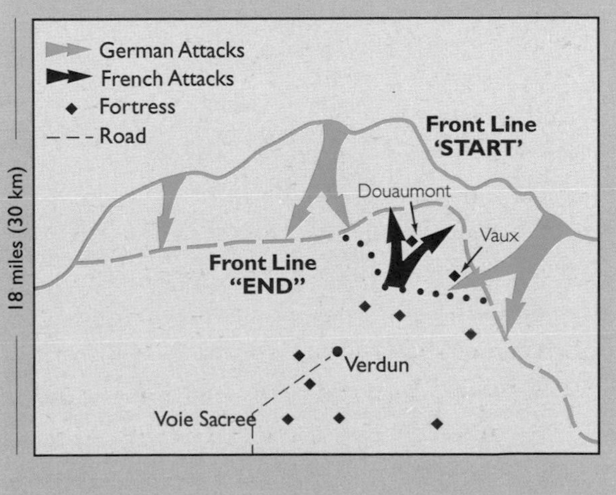

GAS WARFARE 1914–18

Germany, in 1914, was not prepared for a long war, and did not have inexhaustible stocks of munitions. By the end of that year, the German authorities began casting around to find means of rapidly producing artillery shells. The possibility of using nonexplosives was examined and a proposal made to use noxious chemicals. An irritant chemical in shrapnel shells was used against British troops at Neuve Chapelle on October 27, 1914, and xylyl bromide, a tear-provoking gas, in cast-iron shells against the Russians at Bolimov on January 31, 1915. Neither idea worked in practice. The Russians collected some of the shells and, realizing what was being tried, began devising methods of protection against tear gas. The same type of shells were used against the British at Nieuport in March 1915, but were also ineffective. At this stage, neither the British nor the Russians made any public announcement about the use of gas. As a result, the popularly held belief is that gas was first used at Ypres on April 22, 1915, when the Germans deployed 5,730 cylinders filled with 168 tons of chlorine gas along a 4-mile (6.4-km) front. The huge cloud of gas, released at 5:30 p.m. when the wind conditions were right, cut a 5-mile (8-km) gap in the Allied lines. However, as in so many battles of World War I, the attackers were not prepared for their success. No reserves were ready to be thrown in, and the Allies managed to rally and hold their front.

Following the Ypres attack, all the combatants moved swiftly and more than 3,000 substances were tested for their offensive potential during the war, of which some 38 were selected as being capable of use, and of those about a dozen were used in quantity.

This British gas mask was issued in April 1916 as a result of the German use of poison gas. In the bag is a box with layers of charcoal, soda lime, and potassium permanganate. A corrugated tube leads to the rubber cloth facemask. Inside, a mouthpiece and nose clip ensure that only filtered air can be breathed. This was the standard mask for British and U.S. troops until the war ended.

Australian troops in September 1917. The mere threat of gas forced men to don masks and impermeable clothing, ensuring they soon became fatigued, even without strenuous action. A mask restricts the amount of air a man receives and so tends to restrict his physical capabilities.

The Livens Projector, introduced in 1916, was a mortar-like weapon sunk into the ground by the hundreds and fired electrically to launch a salvo of gas canisters into the target area. A canister was fitted with a 30-second time fuze, and the range adjusted by varying the amount of propelling charge; maximum range was 1,300 yards (1.19 km). As well as projecting gas, the Livens was used to fire incendiary canisters against inflammable structures and high explosive against field strongpoints. It remained in the British Army's arsenal until the beginning of World War II.

Gases used in warfare are classified into five groups: lachrimators (tear gases), asphyxiators (lung injurants, such as chlorine), toxic agents (such as phosgene), sternutators (respiratory irritants), and vesicants (blister gases, such as mustard gas). For tactical purposes, they are also divided into nonpersistent gases, which disperse within 10 minutes, and persistent gases, which remain active for hours, days, or even months.

Chlorine and phosgene were dispensed from pressurized cylinders; gases from the first three classes were all used in artillery shells and mortar bombs. The tactic was to swamp an area with a high concentration of gas so as to disable all enemy combatants. To achieve this, the British devised the Livens Projector, first used in quantity at Arras on April 9, 1917, when 3,827 projectiles released 51 tons of phosgene into the German trenches in one colossal salvo. More than 100 men died instantly; another 500 were hospitalized. The Germans developed a similar device after capturing specimens of the Livens Projector.

Germany, which had a larger and more advanced chemical industry than any other combatant nation, pioneered the use of sternutators and vesicants. Mustard gas was first used on July 12, 1917, in the Ypres sector. It caused many casualties because it was an unknown substance to the British and had little smell or immediate effect. Some 12 hours later, men who had been in contact with the gas developed severe blistering of the skin and blindness as well as lung damage.

Sternutators were introduced at about the same time. They were actually smokes containing tiny solid particles that could penetrate the gas masks worn by the British. Because they were not immediately fatal, sternutators were usually used in combination with a toxic gas. The sternutator forced the victim to remove his mask in order to sneeze or vomit, whereupon he inhaled the toxic agent and died.

Although gas was used frequently from 1915 to the end of the war, fewer than one-third of one percent of battle deaths were attributable to it. British records show that 94 percent of men gassed were out of hospital and graded fit within nine weeks. Of the postwar disability pensioners, only two percent were disabled by gas. Where these primitive gases succeeded was in swamping hospitals and evacuation services with casualties, which placed a strain upon the whole supply system. Gas was a casualty producer rather than a killer.

BATTLE OF CAMBRAI

DATE November 20–December 7, 1917
OBJECT Large-scale British tank raid transformed into an attempt to break through the German Hindenburg Line.
NUMBERS Allies—24 divisions; Germans—6 divisions.
DESCRIPTION On November 20, ten days after the end of the Passchendaele offensive, at 6:20 a.m., General Byng's British Third Army, spearheaded by the Tank Corps, attacked the German line at Cambrai. Launched without a preliminary bombardment and utilizing some 378 tanks closely supported by infantry, the attack achieved complete surprise. However, the original concept of a large-scale tank raid had been transformed into another attempt at a decisive breakthrough, without sufficient reserves being available to exploit any breach in the formidable Hindenburg Line. Tanks were still unreliable and just 92 remained serviceable by November 23; the only effective arm of exploitation was cavalry. Thus, although the defense of General von der Marwitz's German Second Army was penetrated to a depth of 3 miles (5 km) along a 6-mile (9.6-km) front, little more could be achieved and a fierce struggle developed around the German positions in Bourlon Wood. On November 30, the Germans counterattacked, and by December 7, the net British gain on the first day had been all but wiped out.
CASUALTIES Some 45,000 casualties on both sides.
RESULT Although it ended in stalemate, the Battle of Cambrai provided a portent of the tactics that would finally end the deadlock on the Western Front.

TECHNICAL INNOVATIONS

In many respects, the innovations that led to the initial success at Cambrai marked the culmination of the BEF's learning process on the Western Front; but it was not the first attempt to use new tactical methods or weapons in order to break the opposing trench lines. Some weapons were revolutionary in concept but others, such as the flamethrower and chemicals, actually looked back to medieval siege warfare. It is perhaps appropriate in any case to liken the war on the Western Front to a protracted siege operation. Developed by a Berlin engineer, Richard Fiedler, in 1900, the modern flamethrower used gas pressure to shoot out inflammable oil for a distance of some 65 feet (20 m). Some attempt appears to have been made to use the weapon against the French in October 1914 and again in February 1915, but its effective debut came at Hooge, near Ypres, on July 29, 1915, when six *Flammenwerferapparate* were used to dislodge men of the British 41st Infantry Brigade from Hooge crater as part of a wider attack. It was extremely successful, but the proximity of the opposing lines—a mere 15 yards (14 m)—was an important factor and it would not have such a decisive impact again. By contrast, the use of gas was to have much more lasting effect.

Even older siege weapons reappeared in a new form with the development of tunneling as a means of breaking through the trench lines. Not all areas were suitable for mining but, where possible, tunneling companies pursued their own specialized and terrifying conflict. The most spectacular success was undoubtedly the explosion of 19 British mines under German positions on the Messines Ridge, southeast of Ypres, on June 7, 1917, which resulted in a swift advance and the capture of 7,000 stunned Germans. The attack was a prelude to the Battle of Passchendaele.

New devices

Trench warfare led to the development of the trench mortar, a deadly weapon. The British eventually deployed 11 different types. The Germans developed steel-cored bullets to pierce sandbags, while the grenade and tin helmet became features of trench life.

The new weapon with the greatest strategic and tactical potential was the tank. The British commander in chief Sir Douglas Haig was a keen advocate of early use of the new weapon, and 49 tanks were involved in a renewed attempt to break through on the Somme on September 15, 1916. Of the 32 machines that reached the start line, however, five had to be ditched, nine broke down, and nine

BATTLE OF PASSCHENDAELE

DATE July–November 1917
OBJECT The British commander in chief, Field Marshal Douglas Haig, wanted to reach the Belgian coast.
DESCRIPTION Officially known as the Third Battle of Ypres, the Passchendaele campaign took the form of eight separate efforts to push the British forward in the Ypres salient between July 31 and November 10, 1917. The offensive was partly justified by the threat allegedly posed to Britain by German submarines operating out of the Flanders ports of Ostend and Zeebrugge, and partly by the fact that only the British remained capable of applying direct pressure on the Germans after the collapse of Russia and of French military morale in the spring of 1917. The offensive also appeared to Haig to offer the opportunity of a real strategic objective in the ports for which the Germans would need to fight. A highly ambitious plan was advanced by which General Sir Hubert Gough's Fifth Army, supported by the Second Army, would be able to advance 15 miles (24 km) in just eight days and on to the coast and the Dutch frontier although, subsequently, some confusion ensued as to the precise objective. After a 10-day preliminary bombardment, the offensive opened against the German Fourth and Sixth armies on July 31 but broke down against the German defense in depth with 31,000 casualties. By the time the battle ended on November 10, it had become even more grisly than the Somme. Indeed, the "battle of the mud" would remain the very evocation of the seeming futility of the war on the Western Front.
CASUALTIES British—ca. 238,000, Germans—ca. 220,000
RESULT Both sides were weakened by attrition but, in the long term, the Germans were less able to afford such losses.

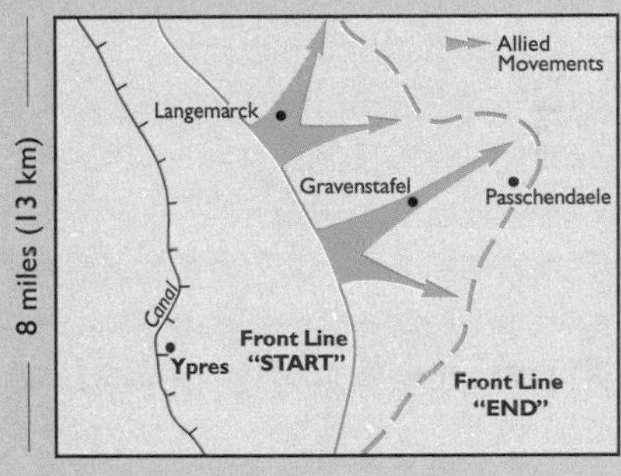

failed to keep up with the infantry. Thus, only nine spearheaded the actual advance on Flers-Courcelette. A breakthrough was partially achieved, but it was an uncertain beginning, and the tank continued to be subject to severe technical limitations. Tanks were vulnerable to artillery and far too slow to exploit any breakthrough they might achieve. In fact, the Germans distrusted tanks and made no significant attempt to use them until the action at Villers Bretonneux on April 24, 1918 when they used 13 of them. That action marked the first duel between tanks, when three British Mark IVs engaged three German A7Vs.

In fact, the tank was not the war-winning weapon sometimes supposed, but the Allied offensive at Cambrai did show that it had potential when used in conjunction with small groups of infantry. Cambrai also heralded the future in other ways because the British had learned the virtue of reverting to a short, or no, preliminary bombardment. Steady advances in instrument location of enemy batteries, including sound-ranging and aerial photography after the introduction of the Thornton-Pickard camera in 1915, immeasurably improved artillery accuracy. Aerial wireless had first been used by the RFC to assist the direction of artillery fire at the Battle of Aubers Ridge on May 9, 1915. By 1917 the Germans had come to fear British counterbattery fire, which was especially effective both at Arras in April and at Cambrai in November. Such accuracy now rendered long preliminary bombardment and preregistration of batteries unnecessary.

Communications had improved with a combination of telephones and spark wireless. Indeed, a wireless deception plan was used for the first time by the Canadians in August 1918. British infantry firepower had also improved through wider distribution of the Lewis light machine gun down to platoon level by 1917.

THE BIRTH OF THE TANK

Most elements of the tank were developed prior to World War I. Indeed, the concept of a caterpillar track originated in the late eighteenth century, although, of course, the internal combustion engine was not invented until 1885. Steam tractors were common before the war and, in fact, the British army had utilized a number for transport purposes during the South African war. Armored cars had made their appearance in warfare during the Italo-Turkish conflict in Libya in 1911 and some civilians, including an Australian named de Mole in 1912, had actually suggested putting tracks on armored vehicles.

However, during the war itself, the idea of utilizing the prewar Holt agricultural steam tractor as a means of overcoming barbed wire and broken ground first occurred to the official British war correspondent, Colonel Ernest Swinton, who submitted his ideas both to General Headquarters (GHQ) and the Committee of Imperial Defense (CID) on October 20, 1914. GHQ rejected Swinton's proposals, but the secretary to the CID, Colonel Maurice Hankey, submitted a paper of his own and the concept was taken up by the First Lord of the Admiralty, Winston Churchill. The Royal Naval Air Service (RNAS) had enjoyed some success with armored cars operating out of Dunkirk in the opening months of the 1914 campaign. The Germans had attempted to obstruct the RNAS cars by digging trenches across the roads, and Churchill had encouraged Admiral Bacon to find a solution to the problem. The work of Swinton and Hankey, thus, happily coincided with this initiative and an Admiralty Landships Committee was established in February 1915.

After some setbacks, a prototype, known as "Little Willie," was built by agricultural engineer William Tritton and Lieutenant W. G. Wilson at the Foster Works in Lincolnshire, of which Tritton was managing director. The next prototype, "Big Willie," was tested at Hatfield Park in January and February 1916 and, as a result of the trials, 40 and then 100 were ordered by GHQ. The first six reached France in August 1916.

(Left) British soldiers of the Tank Corp with some of their vehicles at Bovington Army Training Camp. The Tank Corp was at the forefront of the new technology and had been formed in 1917 from units of the Machine Gun Corps.

(Right) Tactical plan for the use of tanks at Cambrai. The first wave crushes gaps in the wire and fans out to fire down enemy trenches while the second wave drops fascines and advances toward the enemy support trenches; then the tanks gather to advance toward the rear. Infantry grouped in platoons would follow in files to clear the trenches and prepare the way for a general advance.

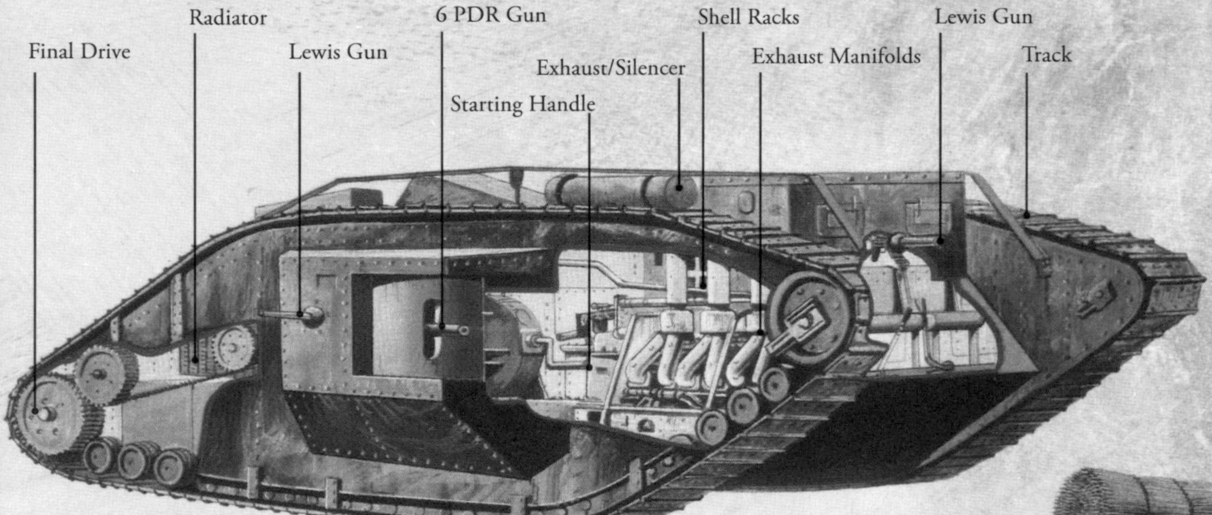

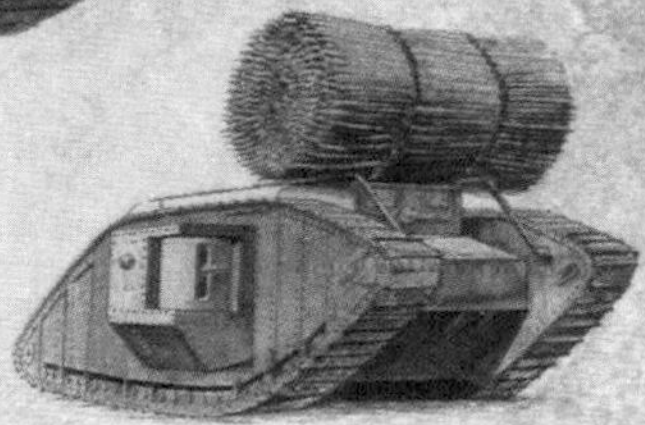

Radiator
6 PDR Gun
Shell Racks
Lewis Gun
Final Drive
Lewis Gun
Exhaust/Silencer
Exhaust Manifolds
Track
Starting Handle

(Above) Section through a Mark IV tank. Prone to mechanical failure of engines, gears, or rollers, it was a cramped, hot, noisy, and fume-ridden environment for its eight-man crew.

(Right) A Mark IV adapted to lay fascines—large rolls of wooden staves tied together—over trenches to enable tanks to cross.

Communication Trench
Fire Trench
Fascines
Fighting Tanks
Outpost
Wire
Support Trench
Wire Crushing Tanks

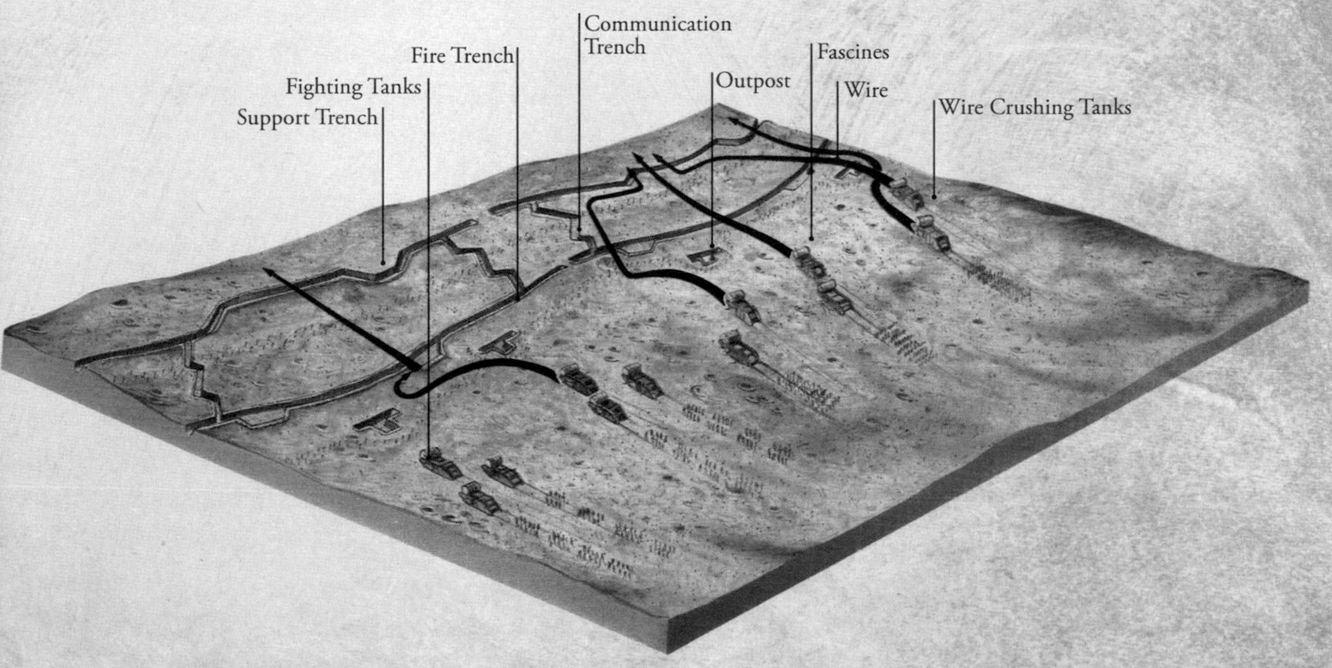

The RFC had undertaken some training in ground attack, and the coordination of artillery, infantry, aircraft, and tanks in attack proved a potent combination at Cambrai, even if the BEF essentially remained an infantry force supported by other arms. But the model was there and the techniques employed at Cambrai would bear fruit in 1918. In fact, British artillery techniques as refined during 1917 did not change again until 1942.

At Cambrai, on November 30, Germany also tried a new technique, this time in counterattack. It was the product of a second remarkable transformation in doctrine, inspired by Lossberg and Geyer and based upon French manuals captured during 1916—a pamphlet by Captain André Laffargue, dating from May 1915, advocated a sudden attack by specially trained troops using automatic rifles or light machine guns. Other French experience also appeared relevant because the French had rediscovered the merit of short bombardment in limited operations at the end of the Verdun battle in 1916.

Similarly, there had been limited artillery bombardment when General Alexei Brusilov had launched Russia's Southwestern armies into an offensive on June 4, 1916. Lacking large reserves of ammunition, Brusilov had relied on surprise, little or no preliminary bombardment, and a combination of separate attacks over a wide front to disguise his objective and disrupt enemy defensive plans. His four armies had attacked on a frontage of not more than 20 miles (30 km), each between the Pripet Marshes and the Dniestr river and had shattered two Austro-Hungarian armies. By June 12, some 192,000 enemy troops were prisoners, but Brusilov had been forced to disperse his own reserves to disguise his plans and the breakthrough could not be sufficiently exploited.

TACTICAL DEVELOPMENTS

Drawing on such examples, the Germans struck back at Cambrai with great success. Specially trained *Sturmtruppen* (storm troopers) led the attack supported by rapid and accurate artillery fire in a short hurricane bombardment.

GERMAN SPRING OFFENSIVE

DATE March 21–April 5, 1918

OBJECT Operation Michael was the first of five offensives, the objective of which was German victory in the West.

NUMBERS Germany—65 divisions; Allies—27 divisions.

DESCRIPTION Variously known as the Ludendorff Offensive or the *Kaiserschlacht* ("Emperor's Battle"), the series of five separate German offensives over five months was a last gamble to achieve victory in the West. The first and largest was Operation Michael, which in 16 continuous days of fighting finally broke the deadlock in France and Flanders. Planned by Ludendorff, Michael hurled 65 divisions from the German Second, Seventeenth, and Eighteenth armies against a maximum of 27 divisions of the British Third and Fifth armies, the latter commanded by General Sir Hubert Gough, starting at 4:40 am. on March 21. Under cover of mist and assisted by an unprecedented concentration of artillery along a 43-mile (69-km) front, German storm troopers took 98 square miles (255 sq. km)—(and 21,000 prisoners)—in a single day, or about the same amount of ground taken by the Allies over 140 days on the Somme in 1916. While German losses were comparatively light at 39,000, they were still more than could be afforded among elite troops, and the Germans met increasingly dogged resistance as the Allies finally created a supreme command to handle the crisis. Once Ludendorff switched objectives on March 27, momentum was lost and Michael ground to a halt on April 5 without achieving a decisive breakthrough.

CASUALTIES German—250,000; Allied—254,000.

RESULT The Allies could afford their losses, Germany fatally squandered its strategic reserve.

U.S. troops in the front line during the Meuse-Argonne offensive, September–November 1918. It was planned by junior officer, Douglas MacArthur.

They bypassed strong points and left these for the ordinary infantry following. Thus, deep penetration was achieved by the tactics of infiltration, with the storm troops maintaining mobility by means of machine guns drawn on sleds, horse-drawn light artillery, and truck-borne observation balloons to spot for the artillery as a whole, and an elaborate series of light signals to mark the advance. The *Sturmtruppen* were also equipped with the new Bergmann light machine gun, which had been introduced in 1917.

Elements of these tactics had been introduced by the Germans before November 1917. Assault troops, for example, had been used as early as August 1914. Similarly, the short but heavy preliminary bombardment, intended not to destroy the enemy but to disrupt his command structure, had also been evolved prior to Cambrai. It owed much to Colonel Georg Bruchmüller, who had tried it first on July 19, 1916, at Tarnopol on the Eastern Front and at Riga on September 1, 1917. It was again used when the Germans broke the Italian army at Caporetto in October 1917 as well as at Cambrai. Thus, when the German spring offensive began on the Western Front in March 1918, some 6,473 guns were used in a five-hour opening bombardment of enormous intensity, lasting just five hours. Ultimately, however, the Germans still faced problems in trying to exploit an initial breakthrough, and their defeat then opened the way for more mobile warfare. At last, the Allies were content to attempt a progressive loosening of the front by a series of limited operations instead of seeking the grand strategic breakthroughs of the past. The final Allied offensive broke the German army, but at a cost, the British losing as many casualties between August and November 1918 as in the previous two years.

Probably only on the Western Front was it possible to impose a defeat comprehensive enough to force a German surrender, given that Germany maintained her strongest army there. However, the sheer cost of warfare on the Western Front prompted some politicians and soldiers to seek alternative fronts, but what were regarded by most Allied soldiers as "sideshows" did not produce the key to breaking deadlock on the Western Front.

Commander C. R. Samson, holding a Webley Mk 1 automatic pistol, standing next to his Nieuport fighter prior to one of his missions, flying from the Aegean island of Tenedos during the Gallipoli campaign of 1915. The aircraft has a Vickers machine gun mounted on the upper wing center section. One of the most effective demonstrations of air power in the World War I was the destruction of a Turkish column on September 21, 1918.

On the other hand, developments in the air and at sea did appear to offer a more viable alternative by allowing the belligerents to bypass an opponent's army and to strike at the heart of a state and its people. An early taste of what was to come was the brief German naval bombardment of England at Great Yarmouth on November 3, 1914 and the more sustained attacks on West Hartlepool, Scarborough, and Whitby on December 16, 1914, which resulted in 133 civilian deaths. A similar attempt to break civilian morale was the German long-range artillery bombardment of Paris between March and August 1918, which compelled 500,000 people to flee.

Sea power

Morale was the prime target of the strategic use of artillery bombardment, but another way to strike at the will of a society to continue the war was provided by the development of sea power. While the Allies blockaded Germany by means of patrols and mines, the Imperial German Navy increasingly retaliated with submarine warfare against merchant ships. But Submarines also posed a challenge to naval vessels and, together with mines, ensured that World War I was the last conflict in which the battleship would be regarded as the main instrument of sea power.

A single line of mines was sufficient to wreck the attempt by the Allies to force a way through the Dardanelles on March 18, 1915, three capital ships being sunk and a fourth damaged by mines or shore battery fire. Another challenge to the capital ship was aircraft—a German guardship became the first vessel to be sunk from the air when it was attacked by Japanese aircraft at Tsingtao in October 1914. Mines were laid by air in the Baltic during the war and an aerial torpedo attack was attempted at the Dardanelles in March 1915. During the same campaign, HMS *Triumph* became the first ship to fire at an opposing vessel it could not see when aircraft spotted it over the Sea of Marmara on April 25, 1915. The first capital ship to be sunk by aircraft was an old Russian pre-*Dreadnought* in April 1916.

At Jutland in May 1916, both the Royal Navy's Grand Fleet and the German High Seas Fleet sailed in line ahead, firing broadsides and seeking the weather gauge (to get the wind to clear the smoke of the guns) as if in the middle of a battle in the age of sail. However, large-scale naval engagements were few and far between. The future lay with naval air power and the submarine.

In terms of the former, a conventional aircraft was successfully flown off HMS *Vindex* in August 1916, while the first conventional aircraft successfully to land on a ship was flown onto HMS *Furious* by Flight Commander E. H. Dunning on August 2, 1917. However, Dunning was killed trying to repeat the feat and the question of the number of obstacles on a ship's deck that could obstruct landing was not finally resolved until the commissioning of the first true aircraft carrier—HMS *Argus*—in October 1918, too late to be used in the war.

AIR SUPERIORITY

From early in the war, the use of aircraft as support for ground operations had increased steadily, once the vulnerability of troops on the ground was fully realized. However, early attempts at ground attack were confused. The French, for example, dropped sheaves of arrowlike steel flechettes onto marching troops. But the fitting of machine guns to aircraft soon led to widespread and effective "ground strafing" (from the German *strafen*, "to punish") against troops and transport. This, in turn, led to more fighters being deployed to protect the troops, and gradually the concept of "air superiority" emerged—the deployment of a large enough number of aircraft to deter the enemy from entering your "air space."

Air power

An even greater opportunity to attack civilians was provided by air power, Great Yarmouth scoring another hapless first as the target of German Zeppelins in January 1915. The main lesson drawn from the bombing of England by dirigibles, and later by heavy bombers, was that most air battles would take place only by mutual consent and that aircraft could hide in the vast space of the skies. Indeed, it appeared exceptionally difficult to win command of the air without seeking constant battles that an opponent could choose to avoid.

For much of the war, the RFC's policy was one of "strategic offensive," although this would now be regarded as a tactical use of air power in which British aircraft sought to win command of the air over the German lines. Inevitably, this resulted in casualties both from direct losses and from the failure of machines to make their way back to Allied lines if in technical difficulties against the prevailing westerly winds. Continuous standing patrols were thus maintained regardless of the situation on the ground, while the Germans chose to concentrate their aircraft to gain local superiority as required. By 1917, therefore, British air losses were four times those of the German airforce.

The difficulties were compounded by an over-reliance on the products of the Royal Aircraft Factory, which trailed behind German production machines in efficiency, and by the refusal to consider parachutes on the grounds that they were unreliable, too bulky, and might lead airmen to abandon their aircraft too readily. Despite the poor quality of many British machines, new lighter aircraft with better speeds and higher rates of climb constantly evolved and presented new challenges to each side. In fact, the personalized air-to-air duel was relatively short-lived as formation flying became the norm in 1916 and 1917. Ground attack had also evolved by 1918, the potential of aircraft in this regard perhaps being best illustrated by the destruction of a Turkish column by seven British squadrons at Wadi el Far'a in Palestine on September 21, 1918. The actual casualties sustained by the Turks were surprisingly few, but vehicles and guns were abandoned and morale shattered.

AERIAL WARFARE 1914–18

On the outbreak of war in 1914, the British Royal Naval Air Service (RNAS) sent a squadron to Dunkirk, and offensive operations against Zeppelin bases began. The German air service retaliated with raids against Paris and other French towns within reach of their airfields, prompting the French to mount attacks against German targets. Bombers were vulnerable and had to be escorted by fighters, so fighter squadrons were withdrawn from the front-line area to defend "the homeland." Artillery was used against aircraft for the first time.

Air fighting emerged as a means of protecting one's own aircraft. In February 1915, two Frenchmen, Roland Garros and Raymond Saulnier, experimented with firing a machine gun forward from the cockpit. They attached steel plates to the propeller to deflect the 7 percent of bullets fired that they expected to hit it. In April, Dutch-born Anthony Fokker invented an interrupter gear based on prewar Swiss designs. His Fokker aircraft was the first true fighter and ushered in the era of the air-to-air duel, which did not last as long as popularly supposed as formation flying and big air battles became the norm.

Long-range bombing was, at first, a German affair, because only they had airships capable of making long flights. However, airships were large and expensive machines and were used principally against major targets. The German navy also operated airships for reconnaissance over the North Sea. The first Zeppelin raid against England took place on January 19, 1915. Of the three machines that set out, two reached England and dropped a scattering of bombs in East Anglia before returning safely to base. This attack was followed, on May 31, 1915, by the first raid on London, when Zeppelin LZ38 dropped 30 high-explosive and 90 incendiary bombs in the eastern suburbs. More raids by German navy Zeppelins and army Schutte-Lanze airships followed. The defenses of London were strengthened, but because the airships flew high, and the fighters took time to reach them, they were invariably able to escape undamaged.

The first Zeppelin to be destroyed was shot down over Ostend in July 1915. Sublieutenant Warneford of the RNAS, flying a Moraine aircraft, managed to get above L-37 and drop a bomb on it, which ignited the hydrogen in the gas-bags. The defenders of London had no success until September 1916, when Lieutenant Leefe Robinson,

Two German Albatross two-seaters (black cross on wings) defending themselves against three British Martinsyde Scouts (red, white, and blue targets on wings). Although eclipsed by the more famous names of Sopwith and Bristol, the Martinsyde company made a number of excellent small fighters, which were well respected by the Royal Flying Corps. Similarly, the Albatross two-seater was usually forgotten in favor of the Fokker and the single-seat Albatross, but it did as much damage to the Allied airforces as they did.

This German Navy Zeppelin L-11 is representative of the airships that bombed England and France. The machine consisted of an aluminum framework covered in fabric, and gasbags filled with hydrogen inside the framework. Four, later six, engines were fitted, giving a speed of 60–80 mph (95–130 km/h). The principal tactical advantage was that the Zeppelin could fly at heights not easily attained by airplanes. It was not until late 1916 that aircraft capable of rapid climb became common, after which the Zeppelin's day was over.

using the newly invented Buckingham incendiary bullets, shot down the Schutte-Lanze SL-11 over Hertfordshire. Within a week, two more had been shot down and the bombing role passed to heavier-than-air machines. Thus, on May 25, 1917, a flight of 26 Gotha bombers—large two-engine biplanes, each capable of carrying 880 pounds (400 kg) of bombs—attacked Kent. Then on June 13, a flight of 14 Gothas flew up the Thames and delivered a severe attack on various areas of London, killing 162 people and injuring 432 others. This was the beginning of a series of attacks that continued until May 1918, when attrition, improved defenses, and the general run-down of the German war effort caused the bombing of England to be abandoned. Five Zeppelins of the German Naval Airship Division launched a last abortive raid on August 5, 1918.

By this time, the Allies had decided to enter the long-range bombing war. The Italian Air Force had become expert at long-distance strategic bombing. In February 1916, trimotored Caproni bombers flew from Italy to bomb Ljubljana, then in the Austro-Hungarian empire, and they later made several raids into Austria. The Italians also bombed the naval base of Pola and the Fiume torpedo factory, both on the Adriatic Sea, using more than 200 bombers on one raid.

By early 1918, plenty of British aircraft were available for front-line duty; surplus aircraft were used in attacks on Germany. These developments strengthened the case for an airforce that was not under army or navy control but existed as a separate branch of the armed forces.

A long-range bombing unit had existed since October 1917, when a wing of the RFC was set up to raid German cities. This was reinforced by three squadrons of Italian Caproni bombers and a French *Groupe de Bombardement*. A U.S. element was planned but never materialized. This force. made a number of raids into Germany, dropping 635 tons of bombs with minimal effect, but it pointed the way for the future development of air power.

The vulnerability of the Zeppelin in the face of agile fighter aircraft led to its withdrawal from bombing in 1917 by the German Army and its replacement by G.IV and G.V airplanes.

René Fonck

Manfred von Richthofen, the "Red Baron" (R)

Albert Ball, VC

Jean Navarre

THE AIR ACES

The emergence of fighter aircraft on the Western Front introduced a relatively short period when air fighting became a romanticized contest between individuals. Removed as it was from the all-too-obvious carnage on the ground, the aerial war caught the public imagination to such an extent that the often tragically short-lived pilots became overnight legends.

For Germany, the earliest ace was Oswald Boelcke, who was killed in October 1916. Boelcke's fame was surpassed both by his former pupil, Max Immelmann, who was killed even before Boelcke, and, of course, by the "Red Baron," Manfred von Richthofen. The latter had shot down a record 80 aircraft by the time of his death in April 1918.

French air aces included René Fonck, Georges Guynemer, and the flamboyant Jean Navarre, who was actually the first to paint his aircraft a distinctive red.

British airmen to achieve similar status included Albert Ball VC, James McCudden, and Edward "Mick" Mannock, whose 73 "kills" placed him second only to Richthofen. None were to survive.

Commander E. H. Dunning's Sopwith Pup just before it goes over the side of HMS Furious *on August 4, 1917. Dunning was drowned in the accident, two days after he had become the first man to land an aircraft successfully on a ship. American Eugene Ely had been the first to take off from a ship successfully in November 1910, but the vessel had not been under power, and the first flight from a moving vessel had been off HMS* Vindex *in August 1916. Landing was somewhat more hazardous.*

WAR OF TRANSITION

The emergence of the *Argus* is an illustration of the nature of World War I. This was a new kind of conflict. Compared with the wars of the previous century, which had been localized and limited in many ways, World War I was a total conflict fought on a global stage. In order to survive the challenge of war, states were required to transform their societies, economies, and even their political structures. This war required mobilization of a state's resources on an unprecedented scale, necessitating increased intervention in all aspects of its citizens' lives, from relatively minor changes, such as the introduction of licensing laws and summer time in Britain—both designed to increase war production—to direction of labor and conscription. The war provided new opportunities at a variety of levels and resulted in radical social changes, particularly for women.

It also created global disruption and brought enormous loss of life and property, although medical advances were such that this was the first war in which deaths from battle wounds exceeded those from disease. It is estimated that the war may have resulted in 10 million dead, excluding 1.5 million Armenian victims of Turkish genocide and a possible 27 million victims of the influenza pandemic of 1918. It also resulted in 20 million being maimed or seriously wounded, 9 million orphans, 5 million widows, and 10 million homeless. The Russians lost some 3 million service personnel, dead before fall of 1917. British empire casualties were 3.2 million, of whom nearly a million were dead or missing. The French had casualties of 5 million, of whom 1.4 million were dead or missing. The Italians, fighting on a narrow front, lost 460,000 dead. The United States sustained some 326,000 casualties, 116,000 of them dead. The Austro-Hungarian empire lost some 1.2 million dead and 3.6 million wounded. The Turks sustained 2.3 million casualties, and the Germans lost some 1.9 million dead and 4.3 million wounded.

Yet, for all the ways in which science and technology had been harnessed, there was much that was traditional in the way the war was fought, from the line of battle at Jutland to the great cavalry battles on the Eastern Front. The tank, manned aircraft, and the aircraft carrier had all emerged on the military stage for the first time, but their potential would only be realized in the future. In that sense, therefore, World War I was essentially a transitional conflict at the dawn of a new age of warfare.

11 WORLD WAR II

The legacy of the Great War in terms of strategy was an important one. The Western Front during 1914–18 had demonstrated the superiority of defense over attack. No one wanted to repeat the costly experience of trench warfare, but during the last part of the war, the tank and the German storm troops had pointed the way to an antidote. Two other weapons also displayed potential for winning wars more quickly in the future. At sea, the U-boat had, during 1917, almost throttled Britain's maritime lifeline, while in the air the German air attacks on London had an effect on civilian morale out of all proportion to the size of the raids.

The significance of these weapons was recognized by the Allies when they drew up the Treaty of Versailles, which formally ended the war with Germany. As well as reducing the German navy to 15,000 men and army to 100,000, the treaty forbade Germany from maintaining an airforce. Tanks, U-boats, and capital ships were also proscribed. As for the Allies themselves, they speedily dismantled their vast wartime armed forces. The United States resumed her prewar isolationism, and France and Britain, especially the latter, turned their attention once more to their empires. The belief that the Great War was the "war to end all wars" encouraged widespread pacificism, and this was reflected in a desire for general disarmament. The first positive indication of this was the 1922 Washington Naval Treaties, by which the major naval powers agreed to suspend capital ship building for 10 years, as well as agreeing to maintain their fleets in the existing strength proportions to one another. During 1927–33, farther disarmament conferences took place in Geneva, but they achieved little apart from banning the use of poison gas.

Interwar theory

Undeterred by the disarmament environment, a number of theorists were considering the shape of war in the future, recognizing the revolutionary effect that the tank and the aircraft could have. In Britain, General J. F. C. Fuller, who had been on the Tank Corps staff in France during the Great War, and Captain Basil Liddell Hart wrote copiously on how the gasoline engine could revolutionize the battlefield, enabling the attacker to defeat the enemy through sheer pace. Although the British and U.S. armies did experiment on a small scale with mechanized forces, lack of money and the international climate at the time inhibited the formation of these forces to any significant degree.

More note was taken of these writings, especially those of Fuller, by the two outcasts of Europe, Germany and Russia. Through secret clauses in the 1922 Treaty of Rapallo,

SPANISH CIVIL WAR

DATE 1936–39

This began in July 1936 when army garrisons in Spanish Morocco, led by General Franco, revolted against the left-wing government in Spain. Within a few months ,Germany and Italy had sent air and ground forces to help Franco, while the Russians did the same for the Republicans. This enabled all three countries to test their latest weapons in combat and the war became a technical laboratory. Amid the inevitable atrocities that civil war brings, the German bombing of the Basque town of Guernica on April 25, 1937, was the most prominent, and confirmed people's worst fears of what a major European war would be like. Although the Republicans, aided by foreign volunteers (the International Brigades) managed to hold Madrid throughout most of the war, Franco's Nationalists gradually brought the whole country under their control. Britain and France adopted a non-interventionist policy and attempted to enlist German and Italian help in mounting a naval blockade to prevent arms and men from being shipped to both sides. Hitler and Mussolini, however, ignored this, and it was their ability to supply Franco at a much greater rate than the Russians that became decisive.

A U.S. Lexington class battlecruiser , a classic example of this type of capital ship. The construction of capital ships was outlawed for 10 years by the Washington Naval Limitations Treaty of 1922.

A Maginot Line casemate in winter 1939–40. Named after the French war minister of the time, the Line, begun in 1928, was the embodiment in steel and concrete of the trench systems of World War I. Much of it was underground, and in many places all that could be seen from the east was a series of small steel cupolas. Its weakness was that it could be outflanked through neutral Belgium.

the Russians allowed the Germans covert armored and air-training facilities in Russia in return for technical guidance. By the early 1930s, the Russians, largely under the guidance of chief of staff Mikhail Tuchachevsky, had developed large armored forces. Once Hitler came to power, the Germans would do the same.

The air prophets took a more extreme stance. Led by the Italian General Giulio Douhet ,they argued that future wars could be won by air-power alone. Aircraft would be able to do what armies and navies could not—strike directly at seats of government, industry, and the civilian population. In the United States, General Billy Mitchell declared that aircraft could destroy capital ships and, hence, make navies vulnerable to air-power. In Britain, Air Marshal Hugh Trenchard used the air-power argument to preserve the Royal Air Force's newly won independence from the other two services. As for the general public, their view was summed up by Stanley Baldwin, soon to be British prime minister, in his often quoted comment of 1932: "The bomber will always get through."

Once Hitler came to power in Germany in 1933, he quickly threw off the remaining shackles of Versailles, putting in place a wide-ranging rearmament program: The German navy was given legitimacy through the 1935 Anglo-German Naval Agreement. While this limited Germany's surface fleet to a third of that of the Royal Navy, she was, significantly, allowed parity in submarines on the basis that convoying, ASDIC (Sonar), and agreements on restricting submarine warfare (1936 London Protocol) had much reduced the threat of this weapon. The German army underwent a massive expansion, while the Luftwaffe grew from nothing to one of Europe's largest airforces in just a few years.

By the mid-1930s, growing tension in Europe, largely created by Hitler, forced Britain and France into a degree of rearmament. France pinned her faith on fixed defenses on her border with Germany, the Maginot Line, believing that this would be sufficient to deter potential aggression. Britain, on the other hand, put priority on maintaining her naval supremacy and in strengthening the RAF in order to match Hitler's Luftwaffe. The army was a poor third, with the main effort going into antiaircraft guns, but much progress was made in replacing the horse by the gasoline engine. Yet, while Germany mechanized from the front, Britain motorized from the rear.

As for the Soviet Union, the impressive progress that the Red Army had made in developing concepts of armored warfare came to nothing. During the great purges of the late 1930s, Stalin removed all the best brains in the armed forces and the tank formations were largely broken up.

THE *BLITZKRIEG* YEARS

The years 1939–41 were marked by a series of spectacular German victories. The secret of their success lay in a new doctrine—*Blitzkrieg*, or lightning war. The concept behind this lay in a move away from the philosophy of defeating the enemy by engaging his armies frontally and destroying them by weight of fire. Instead, the object was dislocation of the command and control system. This was achieved by fast-moving armored formations slicing through the enemy's defenses and penetrating deep into his rear. Having achieved this, they would then trap the withdrawing enemy armies in pockets, which would be reduced by the bulk of the German army, the infantry, who still relied on their feet. In order to help the Panzer divisions get through the defenses, techniques were evolved by which they could call on Luftwaffe support, normally in the shape of the Junkers Ju87 Stuka dive bomber, which was used as aerial artillery. One other aspect was the importance of radio communications, much stressed by *Blitzkrieg*'s prime practitioner, General Heinz Guderian. These gave armored commanders the ability to react quickly to any given situation.

A Ju87B Stuka during the Polish Blitzkrieg.

THE STUKA

The *Blitzkrieg*'s "aerial artillery" had its origins in the Curtiss Hawk, which had been developed as a dive bomber for the U.S. Navy. This had been seen by Ernst Udet, a Great War German fighter ace who was soon to head the Luftwaffe's Technical Office. He persuaded Hermann Göring, then head of Germany's Government Aviation Inspectorate, to back development of a dive bomber for use against pinpoint targets, and the Junkers Ju87 Stuka, first blooded in Spain in 1937, was the result. Its top speed was only some 250 mph (400 km/h) and, armed with 1,100 pound (500 kg) and 110 pound (50 kg) bombs, it attacked its target in a near-vertical dive, its siren wailing, pulling up at the very last moment. However, it was vulnerable to fighter attack, particularly when pulling out of its dive. Later in the war, it became a highly effective "tank buster" on the Eastern Front.

SPECIAL FORCES

One of the significant features of World War II was the use of special forces for intelligence gathering and offensive operations.

The Germans led the way with their Construction Battalion 800. This was raised by the Abwehr, German intelligence, just before the outbreak of war and consisted of plain clothes men whose role was to seize or demolish key points. They were used in Poland and Scandinavia and were later known as the Brandenburgers. The Germans also carried out the first airborne operations of the war when paratroops dropped into Holland and glider-borne engineers knocked out the Belgian fortress of Eben Emael on May 10, 1940.

Immediately after Dunkirk, Winston Churchill instigated the creation of British special forces. The Commandos were formed as a means of striking back at the Germans in occupied Europe, but later, together with their U.S. counterparts the Rangers, they were used as an amphibious spearhead for the major Allied landing operations. The landings also spawned a number of other special units, ranging from beach reconnaissance to the U.S. Navy Construction battalions, the Seabees, whose task was to clear obstacles from beaches, harbors, and airfields. The Middle East was perhaps the most fertile theater for special forces. A wide range of "private armies" was raised, each with a different special role, including the Special Air Service (SAS), whose original purpose in World War II was to destroy enemy aircraft on airfields.

The Special Operations Executive (SOE) and U.S. Office of Strategic Services (OSS) represented another form of special forces. Their role was to support the resistance movements created in every country in occupied Europe. The Resistance itself provided valuable intelligence, as well as carrying out sabotage and other offensive missions in support of conventional Allied operations. In eastern Europe, bands of partisans operating from the densely forested, marshy and impenetrable hinterland—ideal guerrilla countryfulfilled a similar function, diverting German military resources to guard railroads and conduct large-scale anti-gurrilla sweeps.

British Commandos training with fighting knives, which became their symbol.

Otto Skorzeny

The German Otto Skorzeny was a colorful special forces leader, although he did not become involved in the field until 1943. In April that year he was given charge of a special commando, and gained fame for the spectacular glider operation mounted to rescue Mussolini from captivity in the Abruzzi Mountains on September12, 1943. In truth, Skorzeny took part in the operation, but did not command it.

In October 1944, in another spectacular coup, he kidnapped the Hungarian Regent, Admiral Horthy, who was about to negotiate an armistice with the Russians. During the Ardennes counteroffensive of December 1944, Skorzeny commanded 150 Panzer Brigade. His task was to infiltrate men in Allied uniforms through the lines in order to cause chaos. They succeeded in making Eisenhower a virtual prisoner in his own headquarters for a few days, but most were quickly rounded up.

On release from postwar captivity—he was tried and acquitted at Nuremberg–Skorzeny settled in Spain, there helping former SS men to escape from Germany.

Liberation of Benito Mussolini after the successful Gran Sasso operation in 1943. Captain Otto Skorzeny and Mussolini with German paratroopers.

The end for a resistance fighter.

A column of Russian prisoners are marched off to the rear. In June 1941, the Russian troops were caught unprepared by the German invasion. This was largely thanks to Stalin, who did not want to do anything that might antagonize Hitler, despite many warnings of what the Germans intended. By 1942, once the initial shock had passed, the Russian soldier proved to be an equal match for his German counterpart.

The first victim of *Blitzkrieg* was Poland, which was overrun in a campaign lasting just five weeks. While the Poles fought with great bravery, they were under grave disadvantages from the outset. Poland's long frontiers with Germany, including those with the geographically isolated East Prussia, had been lengthened still farther by Hitler's annexation of Czechoslovakia in March 1939, and she was forced to deploy the bulk of her armies on them. Another factor to compel this was that the main industrial region was in Polish Silesia. This resulted in insufficient reserves being available to counter the German thrusts. The Polish army had few tanks and was short of artillery, while the air force was small and its aircraft obsolete. Given these factors, the result was inevitable and any hope that the Poles might have had of prolonging resistance and encouraging a positive response from her allies, Britain and France, was dashed when the Russians invaded eastern Poland on September 17. As it was, except for a very limited advance into the Saarland, the French refused to be drawn away from the Maginot defenses.

The Western Allies were, on paper at least, a much more formidable opponent, and Hitler's generals needed more time to prepare than Hitler was initially prepared to give them. The bad weather of winter 1939–40 came to their aid. While the Allies could match the Germans in tank strength, they did not concentrate their armor, but distributed it along the whole front. The long period of inactivity also did little for the morale of the French army, and the Allied plan for an advance into Belgium to meet and hold the Germans on the line of the Dyle River on the assumption that Hitler would repeat the 1914 Schlieffen Plan, played into the hands of the eventual German plan. This called for the main thrust to be made in the center, creating operational surprise by passing the bulk of the tanks through the wooded and hilly Ardennes, believed by the Allies to be impenetrable by large quantities of armor. When the blow fell on May 10, 1940, the Allies were caught wrong-footed from the outset and never recovered from this. The sheer pace of the German operations was too much for the creaking Allied command structure to react to in time. This was especially true when it came to mounting counterstrokes into the ever-lengthening flanks of the German armored rapier. The German high command itself constantly worried about flank vulnerability and the need for the follow-up infantry to catch up, and this resulted in a number of temporary halts, culminating in that before Dunkirk. Even so, it took just a week longer to overcome France and the Low Countries than to subjugate Poland.

The overrunning of Yugoslavia and Greece in April 1941, although spectacular, were *Blitzkrieg* campaigns on a much smaller scale. What they did do, however, was to force a postponement of the attack on Russia. This was to be fatal, because the German plan relied on the ultimate objectives being gained before the onset of winter. Initially, the Germans were helped by Stalin's refusal to take practical precautions against invasion for fear of provoking Hitler, and the major reorganization of the Red Army as a result of its poor showing against Finland during the winter of 1939–40. Consequently, during the first weeks of the invasion, there were dazzling successes in the form of enormous pockets being created. This was helped by Stalin's refusal to accept large-scale withdrawals. Hitler, however, increasingly meddled in operations, changing his mind over where the ultimate priority lay, the flanks or the seizing of Moscow. This, the effect of poor road/rail communications and ever-lengthening supply lines caused progress to fall behind schedule. The fall rains and subsequent snows caused farther aggravation.

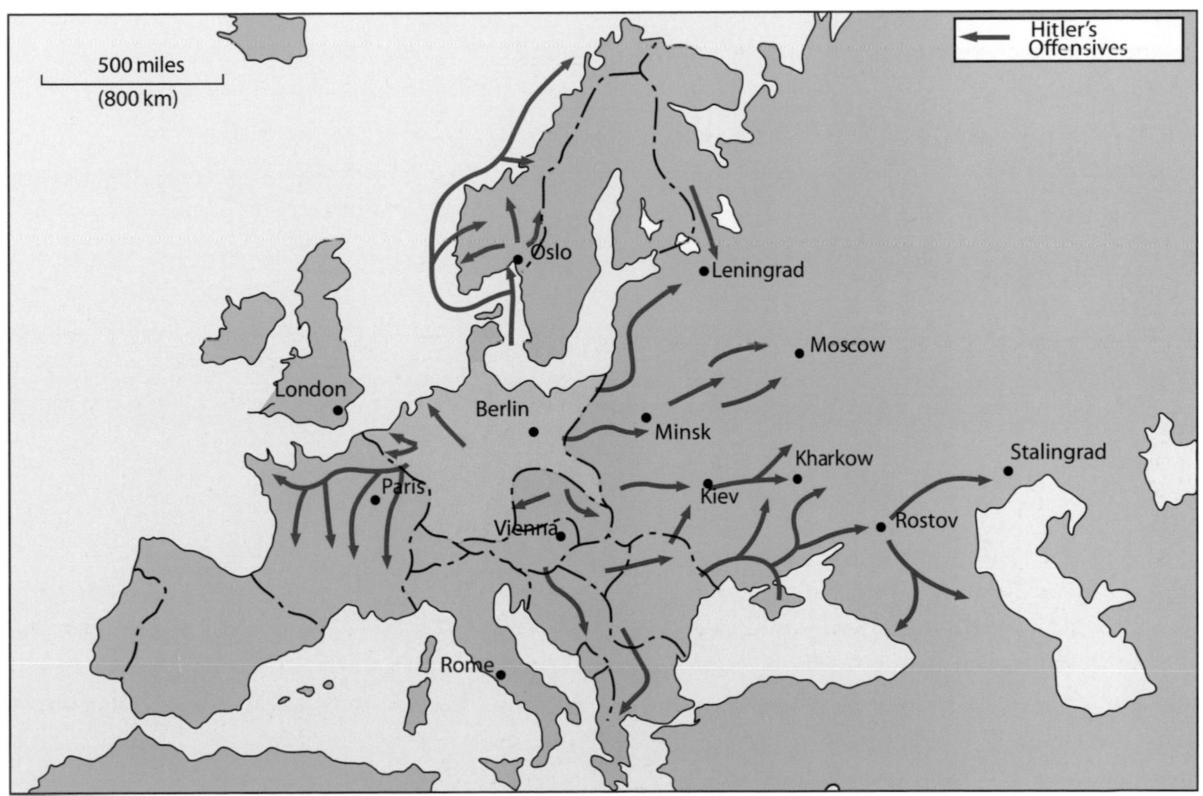

Hitler's offensive campaigns in Europe. Comparing Hitler's invasions of northern, western, and southeastern Europe to his invasion of the Soviet Union makes clear the vastness of this undertaking. From June 1941 until the end of the war in Europe, never less than 70 percent of the German army's combat power was committed to the Eastern Front. In large measure the Russians, with their almost inexhaustible reserves of power, can claim to have vitally contributed to Allied victory.

WORLD WAR II TANKS

As World War II progressed, tanks were fitted with thicker and better armor. They also became more agile and carried larger, more powerful guns. The first major surprise was the Soviet T-34 medium tank, considered by many experts to be the best all-round tank produced during the war. The Soviets ceased production of virtually all other designs aside from their new heavy tanks, the KV series. From 1940, they turned out 18,000 KVs and more than 40,000 T-34s from 42 factories. The T-34 weighed 26 tons, had a 76-mm gun, cunningly angled 45-mm armor, and a road speed of 31 mph (48 km/h). It gave the Soviet tank crews superiority over the Germans once production reached full swing.

The Americans, noting that the side mounting of the 75-mm gun in their tank M3 (the "Lee" to the British) was a drawback, developed the M4 Sherman to replace it. Armed with the same gun as the M3 but in a conventional turret, the M4 had 55 mm of armor and a road speed of 26 mph (40 km/h). Like the Soviets, the Americans saw the industrial and military logic of settling on one design and mass-producing it—they made more than 58,000 M4s before the war ended. However, they failed to back up the Sherman with a good heavy tank, and were slow to take account of faults shown up on the battlefield. By the end of the war, the Sherman was thoroughly outclassed—but there were plenty of them.

The British did not build a reliable tank until the Cromwell in 1944. Armed with a 75-mm gun and protected by 76 mm of armor, it had a speed of 40 mph (64 km/h) and was the most effective British tank by far at the time of the D-Day invasion. However, not enough of them were available and so the bulk of the British armored force used the Sherman. By this time, the artificial distinction between infantry and cruiser tanks had been abandoned. The Churchill was the last infantry tank and its success in special roles, such as breaching defenses and flame throwing, concentrated minds on a "general purpose" design. This led to the Centurion, but not in time for the war.

In late 1942, the Pzkw V Panther appeared, Germany's response to the T-34. It had 80-mm well-sloped armor, a 75-mm gun, and a speed of 28 mph (45 km/h), but suffered constant production hitches. The Pzkw VI Tiger went into production in August 1942. The heaviest tank in the world at that time, it weighed 56 tons, had armor up to 100 mm thick, and was armed with an 88-mm long-barrel gun. The final German design was the King Tiger, which appeared in November 1944, weighing 70 tons with 150 mm of armor, and carrying an even more powerful 88-mm gun. Both Tiger designs were dogged by problems of unreliability.

The Soviet T-34 was better protected, better armed, and faster than any German tank. It led to a crash design program that produced the Panther and Tiger tanks, and to the provision of heavier antitank guns. The Soviets stayed ahead by increasing the gun caliber from 76 mm to 85 mm.

(Top) M4 Sherman tank "Battling Annie". The infantry clustered behind the turret show a somewhat idealized view of how infantry might accompany tanks, but although this tactic was widely adopted by the Russians, it was rarely seen in British or American formations. (Above) The Tiger 1 heavy tank with an 88-mm high-velocity gun and 100-mm thick frontal armor. It often took up to six Shermans to corner and knock out a Tiger.

Design wars

A good tank design strikes a balance between armor, mobility, and gun power. British and U.S. tanks were satisfactory in the first two respects, but were consistently outgunned by German machines. Among the Allies, only the Soviets, with the T-34, had the right balance before 1945, and even they decided to beef up the T-34's main armaments from 76-mm to 85-mm in 1944.

British tanks started by carrying a 40-mm weapon, firing solid armor-piercing (AP) shot. Their German adversaries had 50-mm weapons, firing either AP shot or high-explosive shell, which was useful against soft-skin vehicles and as infantry support. German tanks had also been designed to accept a larger gun in the future, whereas British tanks had not; any increase in armament had to wait for a new tank to be designed. Even this increased gun caliber was only 57-mm, by which time the Americans and Germans were arming with 75-mm. However, the US 75-mm gun was a low-velocity exfield gun, whereas the German one was a high-velocity weapon purposely designed as a tank and antitank gun. Gradually, the U.S. 75-mm was improved and crammed into some British tanks.

The Americans moved to a 76-mm high-velocity gun and the British built their own 76-mm, 17-pounder tank gun. Engineers found a way of fitting the 17-pounder gun into the Sherman turret, creating the Firefly. This was the only tank in northwest Europe in 1944–45 that had any chance at all against the 88-mm of the Panthers and Tigers. The eventual U.S. response was a new heavy tank, the M26 Pershing, which carried a 90-mm gun. However, it came too late in the war to have any measurable effect, and only a handful of them reached Europe.

SECOND EL ALAMEIN

DATE October 23—November 4, 1942
CAMPAIGN North Africa
OBJECT To destroy the Axis forces in Egypt.
NUMBERS British—195,000 men, 1,100 tanks, 900 guns. Axis—100,000 men, 500 tanks, 500 guns.
DESCRIPTION Rommel had been occupying strong defensive positions since the beginning of July. Numerous minefields were in place. Montgomery's plan was to punch through the defenses and then pass his armor through to trap the Axis forces.

After a short but massive bombardment the British attacked in two places, clearing lanes through the minefields as they went. The fighting was bitter and after five days the British had still not broken through. Montgomery therefore changed his plan, aiming to tie down the bulk of the Axis forces in the coastal sector while he punched through to the south. This was put into effect on November 2. Rommel, now short of fuel and ammunition, began to withdraw, in spite of orders from Hitler to continue to stand and fight. On the 4th, the British armor passed through, but failed to cut Rommel off and was then farther delayed by rain. Rommel continued to withdraw through Libya, fighting skillful rearguard actions until crossing the border into Tunisia on January 23.
CASUALTIES British—13,500 men and 500 tanks. Axis—22,000 men and 400 tanks.
RESULT This marked the beginning of the end of the campaign in North Africa, accelerated by the Allied landings in French North Africa on November 8. El Alamein was also the last victory gained by British and Dominion forces alone.

Consequently, the Germans, ill equipped for winter, were not only halted in front of Moscow, but thrown back in a series of counterattacks. *Blitzkrieg* had met its match.

NORTH AFRICAN SEESAW

For three years after the fall of France, the only area in which Western Allied ground forces were actively engaged against the Axis was in North Africa. The fighting in the Egyptian–Libyan desert was characterized by each side making long rapid advances, only to be halted by overstretched supply lines, and then, in turn, being driven back. The desert made the tank seemingly the dominant weapon, but the generally better success enjoyed by the Axis armor was not so much to do with technical superiority, but Rommel's better handling of it. Too often, British armored commanders tended to emulate their horsed-cavalry forebears in unsubtle charges at the enemy, or failed to take timely advantage of windows of opportunity. Rommel's sixth sense, something he shared with the other Panzer commanders, for being at the critical point at the right time, and his tactic of drawing the British armor onto his formidable 88 mm antitank guns time and again, won the day for him. The German ability quickly to form ad hoc all-arms battle groups was also significant. In the end, it was the virtual throttling of the Axis supply lines across the Mediterranean and quantitative superiority in material, aggravated by the fact that in German eyes North Africa was always a very minor campaign, that eventually brought Allied victory in May 1943.

THE RECONQUEST OF EUROPE

The lessons of *blitzkrieg* initially caused the Western Allies drastically to increase their numbers of armored divisions, although their programs were later cut back with the realization that the generally close terrain of northwest Europe needed a high proportion of infantry. Much effort was also made to perfect systems for employing close air support on the battlefield, which came to fruition during 1944 campaigns, where, through the "cab rank" system, ground-attack aircraft circled overhead waiting to be called down to attack targets of opportunity.

In spite of the increasing quantitive Allied superiority in all departments, the Germans showed themselves to be as tenacious in defense as they had been adventurous in attack, particularly in Normandy in 1944 and during the winter 1944–45 campaign in northwest Europe. The tank, too, proved as effective in defense as in attack, especially the German Tiger, which outgunned all Allied tanks. The German principle of training all ranks to be able to assume the responsibilities of two levels higher was also a factor, especially since operational orders allowed subordinate commanders greater freedom of action within the constraints of a mission than on the Allied side. The Allies' greatest problem was, as was so often the case in warfare driven by the gasoline engine, logistics. Hitler had decreed that all the English Channel and Atlantic ports were to be held to the last man. So, when the Allies finally broke out of the Normandy beachhead in August, they were still reliant on all supplies coming through there. Thus, their spectacular dash across France on the broad front on which Supreme Commander Dwight Eisenhower insisted, for political reasons as much as anything, could not be sustained. Only when the port of Antwerp was opened up at the end of November 1944 did the situation improve, but by then winter and a coagulating German defense put an end final victory before the end of 1944.

On the Eastern Front, the German offensive in the south in the summer of 1942 tried to complete what had been left unfinished in December 1941. The plan failed partly because the Russians, learning from their 1941 mistakes, traded space for time, and the destruction of their forces in large pockets did not occur.

General Bernard L. Montgomery watches his tanks move up. North Africa, November 1942. While on the surface this theater was ideal for the tank, being very open and with few natural obstacles, cleverly deployed antitank guns could often neutralize their effect. Both sides mounted them on vehicles, "porteeing," as it was called by the British, to increase their flexibility.

U.S. Marines in the jungle of New Britain in the Bismarck Archipelago, January 1944. This gives a good idea of the problems the jungle undergrowth presented for stealthy movement. On the other hand, it provided the perfect medium for laying ambushes. Often the only way to ensure resupply was by air.

JUNGLE FIGHTING

War in the jungle was as much a battle against the jungle itself as against the enemy. Soldiers who were unfamiliar with their surroundings had to overcome feelings of isolation, especially when enemy infiltration was all too easy, and learn the practicalities. Jungle navigation was an art in an environment where smoke, even from cigarettes, could be detected at a distance and, by night, jungle noises could mask the approach of an enemy. The discomfort of the monsoon and the threat of disease also had to be coped with. Casualties from malaria during the early part of the campaigns in Burma and the Far East far exceeded those from fighting.

Also Hitler, instead of concentrating on overrunning the Caucasus, became increasingly mesmerized by Stalingrad, and his attacking forces found themselves thrusting in divergent directions. The Soviet counteroffensive in front of Stalingrad in November 1942, which cut off Paulus' German army and brought about its eventual surrender three months later, marked the debut of the reborn Red Army. Reequipped both through weapons sent by Britain and the United States ("lend lease") from the West and the Russian armaments industry safe behind the Urals, it relied on success by initially achieving overwhelming superiority, especially in artillery, at the point of attack. Once the door of the defenses had been forced slightly ajar, mechanized formations, known as mobile groups, would be passed through to penetrate deep into the rear, seizing key terrain to aid the advance of the follow-up forces, disrupt command, and control and encourage precipitate enemy withdrawals. Echelonment of forces helped sustain the exploitation of the breakthrough, but when one thrust began to lose momentum the Russians would launch a fresh offensive in another area, thus preventing the Germans from reinforcing a threatened sector from elsewhere along the front. The German counter was to increase the depth of their defenses. Once the Russians did break through, the German forward forces were to accept being bypassed and cut off and to rely on relief by armored forces striking the Russians in the flank. This worked to a degree, but growing Russian superiority in resources, especially manpower, proved too much. At Kursk in July 1943, the largest tank battle of the war, German armor losses were insupportable and they were strictly on the defensive from then on.

THE JAPANESE WAY OF WAGING WAR

The successes enjoyed by the Japanese army in the months immediately following the strike at Pearl Harbor in December 1941 were as dramatic as those of the German army in the West and the Soviet Union in 1940–41. Much of the Allied failure can be attributed to the low regard in which the Japanese fighting man and his equipment was held. This was to forget that the Japanese army entered World War II hardened and combat-experienced from its war against China and brushes with the Red Army on the Russo-Manchurian border. The Japanese army also held an advantage over Western armies in that its soldiers were hardier and used to subsisting on a mere fraction of the logistic support required by their counterparts. The ability to advance unencumbered by an elaborate supply system played no small part in their speedy overrunning of Malaya, Singapore, Burma, and the Philippines. Their military code, which laid down that death for the emperor in battle was the highest reward and that surrender was dishonorable, also meant that they pursued attacks more relentlessly and defended more bitterly.

Another key to the early Japanese successes on land was their ability quickly to feel their way around the enemy's flanks. This was especially noticeable during the advance down the Malayan peninsula (January 1941–February 1942). The British assumed that the Japanese would keep as much as possible to the roads and laid out their defenses accordingly. Also, they had an aversion to operating in the jungle. The Japanese coming up against these defenses would melt into the jungle and then reappear deep in the rear of the defenders.

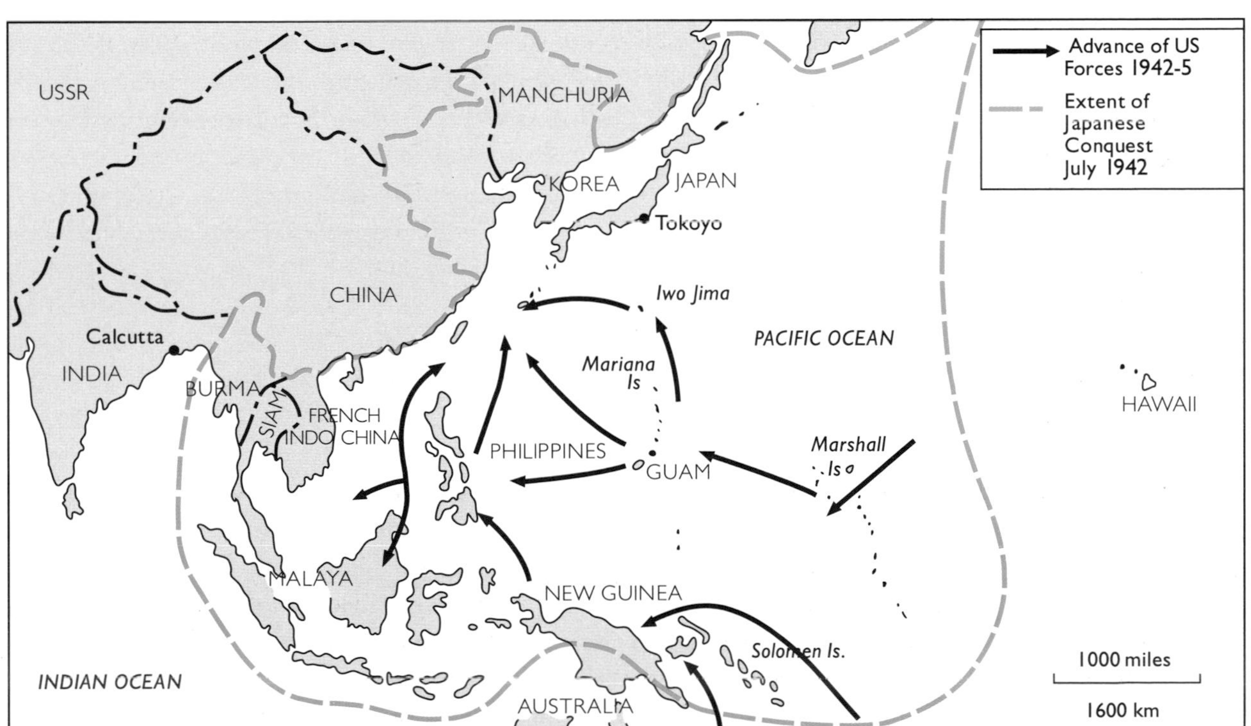

The limits of the Japanese Greater East Asia Coprosperity Sphere. This gave Japan the vital raw materials that she needed, but with American naval victories in the Coral Sea and at Midway in spring 1942, and the landings on Guadalcanal in August, the tide begin to turn in favor of the Allies.

An Atlantic convoy. There were two types of convoy: slow (7.5 to 9 knots) and fast (9 to 15 knots). Ships steaming at 15 knots or above relied on their speed to outwit the U-boats. The convoy itself was commanded by a commodore, usually a retired senior naval officer, who sailed in one of the merchant vessels. The escort commander was, however, responsible for the safety of the convoyed ships and overrode the commodore in this respect. During the first part of the war, too few escorts for the convoys was a major reason for U-boat successes.

Consequently, try as they might, the British were unable to anchor their defenses and hasty withdrawals became more frequent and longer. The Japanese could use the same tactic in defense and demonstrated this during the disastrous British Arakan offensive in Burma at the end of 1942.

Japanese victories created a belief among Allied soldiers that the Japanese were superior in the jungle, and before they could be overcome on the battlefield, this perception, and fact, had to be overcome. Jungle warfare schools were set up, which taught soldiers not only how to fight effectively but also how to live confidently in the jungle. A key to defensive warfare in the jungle was not to withdraw when attacked. The Americans at the Guadalcanal beachhead and the British during the 1943 and early 1944 Japanese offensives in Burma stood and fought, even though surrounded.What, however, proved essential for this strategy was having air superiority so that resupply by air could be undertaken.

While many of the battles on the Pacific islands allowed little scope for generalship, being reduced to little more than concentrating all available firepower to blast the Japanese from each strongpoint, the final campaign in Burma in 1945 did incorporate deception and fast-moving advances, in which armor played a not insignificant part in providing close support for the infantry.

Most dramatic was the brief Soviet offensive against the Japanese armies in Manchuria in August 1945. This reflected the synthesis of the Red Army's four years' fighting on the Eastern Front and was marked by a high degree of deception (*maskirovka*) and surprise—two factors that the Russians now regarded as inseparable from one another—and impressive penetrations by mobile groups, as well as vast numerical superiority.

In sum, the main lessons to come out of the war on land during 1939–45 were not so much new as confirmation of the old. The degree of success of operations was dependent on the ability of the logistic system to sustain them, no one arm was paramount and victory went to the commander who best conducted the all-arms orchestra. Gasoline-driven warfare and radio placed even more emphasis on the need to act quicker than one's opponent, and what had been realized by the end of 1918, that air superiority over the battlefield could be decisive, became of prime importance.

THE WAR AT SEA

The navies of World War II pursued traditional objectives, of which the two foremost were maritime supremacy and destruction of trade. In both cases what differed from previous wars was the role played by naval air power, although, by 1918, its potential had been recognized. This was reflected in the building of aircraft carriers, of which the first were in service before the end of World War II. The size of the navies themselves generally reflected the proportions agreed by the 1922 Washington Treaties: the U.S. and Royal navies were the largest, followed by those of France, Italy, and Japan. The Japanese navy was supposed to be equal to the French and Italian navies but, resentful of not being allowed parity with the U.S. navy, Japan had embarked on an ambitious ship-building program in the 1920s, and by 1939 it was the third largest in the world. The German navy was much smaller, but modern. In 1937, Hitler had laid down Plan Z, which was drawn up on the assumption that war with Britain was inevitable. This plan, however, would not come to fruition until 1943–48, and, hence, the outbreak of war came long before the navy was ready for it.

MARITIME SUPREMACY

Given the small size of her navy, there was no question in September 1939 of Germany risking, as she had before, a major confrontation with the British fleet. Instead, her major surface vessels would concentrate on attacking British trade. Indeed, the only significant surface actions took place during the opening days of the Norwegian campaign, and these largely involved destroyers.

Once Italy entered the war in June 1940, the situation changed. Mussolini termed the Mediterranean *Mare Nostrum* (Our Sea), but the British had traditionally regarded themselves as the dominant naval power here, maintained through the powerful Mediterranean Fleet and the naval bases at Gibraltar and Malta.

BATTLE OF MIDWAY

DATE June 3–6, 1942
OBJECT Japan wished to capture the Midway Islands.
NUMBERS Four Japanese and three U.S. aircraft carriers.
DESCRIPTION Midway was perhaps the most significant turning point in the war in the Pacific, and a prime example of carrier warfare. The Japanese target was the U.S. base on Midway in the central Pacific Ocean, which they described as "Pearl Harbor's sentry." To deceive the Americans, they also intended simultaneously to capture the Aleutians in the northern Pacific. U.S. code breakers got wind of the plan and the U.S. Pacific Fleet, still lacking battleships after the December 7, 1941, strike on Pearl Harbor, sent two task forces, built around its three aircraft carriers, to Midway. The Japanese strike forces set sail on May 27. On June 3, the two U.S. task forces met near Midway. Next day, Japanese carrier aircraft attacked Midway, but failed to neutralize U.S. land-based aircraft. The Japanese immediately rearmed with torpedoes to attack the U.S. task forces, but were then ordered to rearm with bombs in order to attack Midway again. After one abortive attempt, U.S. carrier aircraft found the Japanese Midway strike force and damaged three of its four carriers while their aircraft were still being rearmed. The three sank during June 5. On that afternoon, after air reconnaissance had spotted the Japanese force once more, a farther U.S. aircraft strike sank the remaining carrier, forcing a Japanese withdrawal. Japan's only successes came on June 7, when their forces landed in the Aleutians and a submarine sank the U.S. carrier *Yorktown*.
CASUALTIES Japanese—four carriers, one heavy cruiser, 322 aircraft; U.S.—one carrier, one destroyer, 150 aircraft.
RESULT The Battle of Midway forced the Japanese onto the defensive. Never again could they risk a major fleet-versus-fleet action.

KEY COMMANDERS

Those who led the air, sea, and land forces of each nation between 1939 and 1945 represented many different command styles. At the very top were the supreme warlords, the national leaders. Of the dictators, Hitler and Stalin displayed many similarities. Both immersed themselves in the minutiae of operations, taking personal control. Hitler relied on his commanders' observance of the traditional Prussian code of duty, honor, and loyalty; Stalin controlled his generals, as he did the whole of the Soviet Union, through fear. Mussolini merely postured. In Japan, the emperor was treated as a god, but the power lay with the generals, especially war minister Hideki Tojo, nicknamed "The Razor."

Winston Churchill undoubtedly inspired not only the British but others as well with his famous speeches, but he, too, could not resist meddling at times in operational matters. The bond forged between Churchill and Franklin D. Roosevelt became crucial in coordinating Anglo-U.S. strategy, but Roosevelt inspired his fellow Americans not through great oratory but with his more homely "fireside chats." Both men were lucky to have able chiefs of staff, Marshall and Alanbrooke, to guide them. Hitler merely had the subservient Wilhelm Keitel.

For the Western Allies, it was essential that the senior commanders were diplomats as well as soldiers. Dwight Eisenhower was the personification of this and it needed all his skills to damp down the friction that arose between his U.S. and British subordinates. This was especially true between Montgomery and Patton, both of whom were fighting soldiers and prima donnas, but who instilled enormous confidence in their troops.

There were, too, the Bomber Barons—Spaatz, Eaker, and Harris—who believed that their strategic air forces could win the war single-handed. Other supreme Allied commanders who proved to be good diplomats were Alexander in the Mediterranean and Mountbatten in South east Asia. In contrast, Douglas MacArthur, who

(Top) Rommel (left) in North Africa. Known as the "Desert Fox," he outwitted the British for almost two years.
(Above) Guderian was nicknamed "Schnell Heinz" (Fast Heinz), a name he more than lived up to.

commanded for so long in the southwest Pacific, was equally successful but drove his troops instead of led them. The Pacific was primarily a maritime war and U.S. admirals "Bull" Halsey and Chester Nimitz commanded their fleets with dash and verve, as did the British admiral Cunningham in the Mediterranean.

The British and Americans considered Gerd von Rundstedt, known as the Last Prussian, to be the ablest German commander, but he grew old, and his peer was Erich von Manstein, who fought largely on the Eastern Front. The Panzer generals, especially Heinz Guderian and Erwin Rommel, believed in leading from the front and gained the most spectacular successes. They had their Russian counterparts, particularly Georgi Zhukov and Ivan Koniev. Japan's Tomoyuki Yamashita, conqueror of Malaya and Singapore, was another of this breed, while Admiral Isoroku Yamamoto, who masterminded the Pearl Harbor strike, was the foremost strategist of the war. He later made the Americans fight hard for Guadalcanal.

(Above) From left to right: Bradley, Ramsay, Tedder, Eisenhower, Montgomery, Leigh-Mallory, Bedell-Smith. This team planned and executed the Normandy landings.

Hermann Göring (second in on the left) was head of the Luftwaffe and, for much of the war, Deputy Führer. He increasingly and unfairly blamed his pilots for the air force's failures.

A U.S. naval task force under Japanese air attack during the Battle of Santa Cruz, October 24–26, 1942. This was one of the many naval actions surrounding the battle for Guadalcanal. Two Japanese carriers were damaged and the U.S. carrier Hornet *was sunk.*

However, the British had enough respect for the Italian navy and for the fact that Italian air coverage from the mainland, Sicily, and islands in the eastern Mediterranean extended over much of the sea. Accordingly, all but the most urgent convoys to the Middle East were rerouted around South Africa, the Cape route, and the main fleet anchorage at Malta was moved to Alexandria, Egypt.

Nevertheless, Malta was to remain crucial to the British strategy, for if the Axis powers could seize it, Alexandria would be isolated from Gibraltar and the Axis supply routes to North Africa would be impossible to interdict. Thus, much effort was made to keep the island resupplied in the face of Axis air attacks, which were unceasing until fall 1942. During 1940–41, there were several brushes between the British and Italian fleets, of which the largest was that off Cape Matapan in March 1941. More significant, however, was the strike made by carrier-based aircraft on the port of Taranto on the night of November 11–12,1940, which severely damaged three of Italy's six battleships. Yet, while the British had the best of these engagements, they did not have things all their own way, especially once German air units had been sent to Sicily in early 1941. During that year, the British lost one aircraft carrier to a U-boat and another was badly damaged by Sicily-based aircraft. Heavy losses were also suffered during the German airborne invasion of Crete in May, and in December Italian frogmen crippled two battleships in Alexandria Harbor. Yet, while the British carriers played a part, especially in reinforcing Malta with aircraft, given that the Mediterranean is virtually an enclosed sea, it was land-based aircraft that were dominant. Until the Axis forces had been driven out of Libya at the beginning of 1943, they enjoyed the advantage in their ability to operate almost at will over the Mediterranean.

War in the Pacific

In the Pacific, where land bases were few and far between, the situation was different, although again air power quickly proved to be the dominant factor. The rationale behind the Japanese attack on the U.S. Pacific Fleet base at Pearl Harbor on December 7, 1941, was the need for Japan at least to neutralize U.S. maritime power in the Pacific while they secured their Pacific and southeast Asia empire, which would provide them with oil and other vital natural resources that they lacked at home. The inspiration behind the plan was the British success against the Italian fleet at Taranto. On the surface, the attack was brilliantly successful. No less than six battleships were destroyed as well as most of the aircraft based in Hawaii. Yet, two vital targets had been missed—the oil storage tanks and the Pacific Fleet's two aircraft carriers, which were both at sea at the time. These omissions, especially the latter, were to prove fatal.

During the next few months, the Japanese overran almost all their objectives, and among their successes was the sinking of the British ships *Prince of Wales* and *Repulse* off the Malayan coast on December 10, 1941, another demonstration of the vulnerability of capital ships to aircraft. Their Pacific onrush was finally halted by two naval actions, which marked the first carrier versus carrier battles. In the Coral Sea (May 7–8), a U.S. task force, which included two carriers, engaged a similar Japanese force. One U.S. carrier was sunk, as was one Japanese carrier, and the other Japanese carrier was disabled. Although it was the U.S. task force that withdrew, the Americans had frustrated a Japanese landing attempt at Port Moresby, Papua New Guinea. The following month came the more decisive Battle of Midway, which forced the Japanese fleet onto the defensive.

U.S. troops landing on Leyte in the Philippines, October 1944. The leading waves were now well inland, but it would take two months of hard fighting to clear the island of Japanese.

There now began the long haul to recapture the territories seized by the Japanese and eventually to invade the Japanese mainland itself. This took the form of a series of amphibious landings, beginning with that on Guadalcanal in the Solomon Isalnds in August 1942. For these to be successful, it was essential that the landing forces had sufficient air and naval support, especially since the Japanese fiercely resisted every new thrust not just on land, but also on the sea and in the air. This inevitably meant more major naval actions, again dominated by carriers, beginning with the Battle of the Eastern Solomons just after the Guadalcanal landings. This forced the Japanese to continue to reinforce Guadalcanal by only night, in what became known as the Tokyo Express. There were numerous clashes in "The Slot," between Guadalcanal and Florida Island to its north, and often the Japanese performed better because of superior night-fighting techniques.

The last major fleet action in the Pacific was Leyte Gulf (October 1944), when the Japanese tried to destroy the U.S. naval forces supporting the landings in the Philippines. The result was the loss of their remaining carriers and the death knell of the Japanese navy. The battle also marked the debut of the kamikaze suicide aircraft, just about the last weapon left in the Japanese naval armory and one that would cause the Allied fleets some discomfort, but no more.

What the Pacific demonstrated, more so than any other naval campaign, was that the carrier, with a strike range limited only by that of its aircraft, had now taken over from the battleship as the main surface unit. Furthermore, a prerequisite to achieving maritime supremacy was gaining maritime air superiority.

THE WAR AGAINST TRADE

Beside the Allies' battle to throttle the Axis maritime communications across the Mediterranean to North Africa, two other campaigns were waged against sea communications. The first was the German effort to sever Britain's maritime lifelines, described as the Battle of the Atlantic, the longest campaign of the whole war. There was also the primarily U.S. campaign to suffocate Japan by preventing her from importing the necessary raw materials needed to sustain the war effort. Both illustrate the dependence of island nations on the sea for survival, something that has not changed over the ages.

At the outbreak of war, Germany had 57 U-boats, of which 17 were at sea, and the first shot of the Battle of the Atlantic was fired on September 3, the day Britain declared war, when the liner SS *Athenia*

ULTRA/MAGIC

ULTRA and MAGIC were blanket codewords for the Allies' ability to decipher respectively the top-secret German and Japanese ciphers. In the case of ULTRA, the Poles did the groundwork. They had acquired Enigma cipher machines, which were available commercially before the war, and brought them west after the defeat of Poland. Teleprinter signals were picked up by radio eavesdroppers and then passed to the British decrypting center at Bletchley Park. Modifications to the Enigma machine, and the fact that the teleprinter was not the only means of communication, meant that a complete picture of German plans and intentions could not usually be obtained. Often, too, the ideal counter might alert the Germans, or was not possible to execute in time. Nevertheless, vital intelligence was obtained from this source. The same applied to MAGIC, an operation based in Washington DC, which was obtaining important intelligence even before Pearl Harbor. Neither the Germans nor the Japanese ever realized that their codes had been broken, a tribute to the tight security that surrounded both operations, and they made significant contributions to Allied victory.

was torpedoed and sunk. Britain immediately instituted convoying and declared a naval blockade of Germany. For the first nine months of the war, however, the U-boat would not be the main threat. Beside the small number operational, convoying kept them at bay, and their torpedoes proved unreliable. Even so, the British were conscious of their lack of suitable means to combat them and regretted their prewar complacency, especially after U-47 penetrated the Home Fleet's anchorage at Scapa Flow in the Orkneys, Scotland, in October 1939, sinking the elderly battleship *Royal Oak*. The lack of suitable escorts, aggravated by the necessity to secure the cross-Channel supply lines, which were essential to support the army in France, meant that convoys were protected for most of the transatlantic passage by little more than a single armed merchant cruiser. Little thought had been given to hunting down U-boats. Indeed, during the first weeks, task forces built around a carrier were used, but these were quickly abandoned after one carrier suffered a near miss from a torpedo and another was sunk.

General Heinz Guderian, armored warfare expert, in his command vehicle. Note the Enigma cipher machine in the foreground. The operator keyed in the message, which was then automatically encoded by the machine through preset rotors. Allied mathematical and technical ingenuity enabled the codes to be broken. The decrypts, codenamed Ultra, were among the great Allied triumphs, and secrets, of the war.

Atlantic forays

It was the surface threat that made the deepest impression on the British during the Phoney War (September 1939 to April 1940). Two pocket battleships, *Deutschland* and *Graf Spee*, had set sail for the Atlantic in August 1939, but they were not let loose on the sea lanes until the end of September. While the *Deutschland* was forced to return to port early because of mechanical problems, *Graf Spee* soon began to leave a trail of havoc in the South Atlantic and Indian Ocean. No less than seven naval task forces were organized to hunt her down, and it was eventually the southernmost, based on the Falkland Islands, that cornered her off the Plate River, Argentina, in December.

In the meantime, two more capital ships had made brief forays into the Atlantic, triggering a sally by the Home Fleet, which failed to intercept them. Another early threat was the magnetic mine, laid by aircraft and submarine off British estuaries and ports. These caused a number of sinkings before the technical antidote, degaussing (producing an opposing magnetic field), was found.

THE ATLANTIC BLACK GAP

It became apparent during the Battle of the Atlantic that use of aircraft was the one means by which a truly aggressive defense against the U-boat could be conducted. To provide total coverage across the North Atlantic meant having sufficient very long-range (VLR) aircraft. Until 1943, the Allied maritime air forces had to compete for funds and production time with the strategic bombing forces, who argued that they were taking direct offensive action against Germany while the Battle of the Atlantic was merely defensive. The bombing forces enjoyed priority in four-engine aircraft and airborne radar. Hence, part of the Atlantic could not be covered because aircraft were not available—the Black Gap. It was only after the need to win the Battle of the Atlantic was affirmed at the January 1943 Casablanca Conference that the situation changed, and the gap was closed.

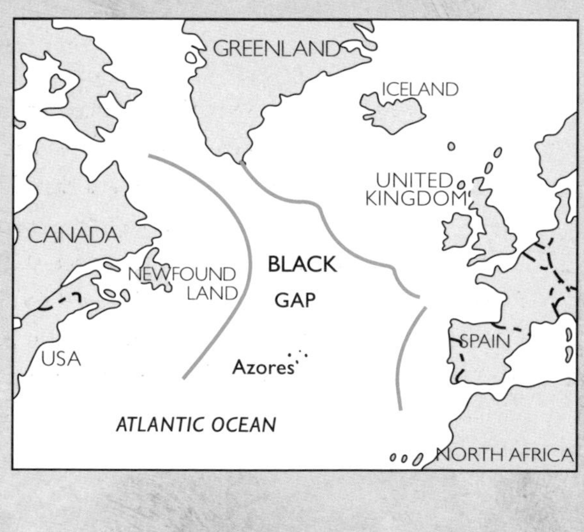

The fall of France dramatically altered the situation. By now, the Germans had overcome their torpedo difficulties and they were more reliable. More important was that they could make use of the French Atlantic ports. This radically cut down the sailing time to the Atlantic and meant that more U-boats could now be on patrol. The result was the first so-called "Happy Time" for the U-boats. From July 1940, shipping losses rose steeply, with the U-boat claiming the lion's share. The Luftwaffe joined in. Long-range Fockewulf Condors located convoys and guided the U-boats onto them, as well as sinking ships themselves. While winter gales reduced U-boat activities, there was a resurgence of the surface threat. This culminated in May 1941, when the battleship *Bismarck* sank the pride of the Royal Navy, the *Hood*, only to be slowed herself by carrier-based air attack and then sunk by the Home Fleet. This effectively marked the end of the surface raider in the Atlantic, although the threat remained.

Air support versus U-boats

In the meantime, the British managed to increase the number of escorts, initially thanks to 50 elderly U.S. destroyers exchanged for Caribbean bases, and at the end of May the first transatlantic convoy sailed with continuous escort, ending the first "Happy Time." The basing of aircraft on Iceland increased air coverage and decryption of the U-boat Enigma cipher meant that convoys could sometimes be steered around U-boat concentrations. Increasing U.S. involvement also helped, but once the United States entered the war, there was a second "Happy Time" for the U-boats. During the first half of 1942, they concentrated on the vulnerable U.S. Eastern Seaboard, which lacked the necessary anti-submarine defenses until the late summer.

By now, it was becoming increasingly vital for the Allies to win the Battle of the Atlantic, in the context of reentering the continent of Europe in order to defeat Germany, an agreed priority over Japan. Better escort drills, more escorts, including carriers, and improved

DESTRUCTION OF CONVOY PQ 17

DATE June 27–July 5, 1942
CAMPAIGN Russian convoys
OBJECT To deliver war materials to Russia.
NUMBERS Britain—33 merchant vessels and one tanker escorted by six destroyers, two antiaircraft ships, four corvettes, three minesweepers, four trawlers, two submarines; supported by two battleships, one carrier, six cruisers, 17 destroyers. Germans—202 aircraft and a naval squadron built around a pocket battleship, *Tirpitz*, and two heavy cruisers.
DESCRIPTION The British had been sending war supplies to the Russian ports of Murmansk and Archangel since September 1941. At the beginning of 1942, the Germans deployed *Tirpitz* and other naval units to northern Norway and also began to attack the convoys with U-boats and Norwegian-based aircraft. With the coming of the Arctic summer and perpetual daylight, shipping losses increased. PQ 17 left Iceland on June 27 and was located by U-boats four days later. On July 4, it came within aircraft range and lost two vessels. At the same time, the British learned that *Tirpitz*, *Sheer*, and *Hipper* intended to intercepted the convoy. The supporting ships would not reach PQ 17 in time to prevent this, so the convoy was ordered to scatter. During the next three days, the Luftwaffe attacked and just 10 merchant vessels eventually reached port. *Tirpitz* and her consorts did sally out, but returned to port after a Russian submarine nearly torpedoed the battleship.
CASUALTIES 23 merchant vessels lost.
RESULT The heavy losses caused a halt to Russian convoys until September. PQ 18 got through with a much strengthened escort, for the loss of one destroyer and 13 merchantmen. There was then a farther lull before a proper resumption was made in December.

technical aids for detecting and destroying U-boats helped, but the other side of the coin was that, in spite of efforts to slow the U-boat-building industry by bombing, U-boat production was on the increase. However, new tactics employing "wolf packs," which swept convoy routes line abreast and, once a convoy was located, concentrated in attack, were also proving effective. Allied aircraft were playing an increasingly significant role, but the battle could not be won until the Black Gap in mid-Atlantic had been closed.

Farther north, German Norway-based aircraft and ships, including the battleship *Tirpitz*, were creating grave problems for the Arctic convoys supplying Russia through her northern ports.

The climax came in spring 1943. After the "wolf packs" had worsted two convoys, the pendulum suddenly swung the other way. In May, 41 U-boats were sunk, forcing the Germans to withdraw those remaining from the Atlantic. The merchant ship-building rate began to overtake that of losses. The U-boats soon returned to the Atlantic, but were not the force that they had been, in spite of improved torpedoes and the Schnorkel, which enabled the U-boat to spend a longer time submerged and hence reduce the air threat. Not until 1945 did submerged long-range, high-speed boats come into service, and then only a handful. Introduced earlier, they might have had an effect, but by then, it was too late. The Allies had won the technological and operational battle.

Flawed Japanese strategy

The Allied campaign against Japan's maritime trade was successful, too. The Japanese submarine fleet concentrated on U.S. warships, with no great success. The Japanese sunk just 149 U.S. ships of all types, while the United States placed priority on merchant shipping, knowing that without it Japan would be starved of vital war-supporting raw materials. By 1944, U.S. submarines

THE U-BOAT

Throughout the war, there were two basic types of U-boat—coastal (mainly Type VIIs) and ocean-going (Type IX.) Both were primarily powered by diesel engines. The coastal U-boats had a surface range of some 5,000 nautical miles and the Type IX 11,000 miles.

Underwater propulsion was achieved through auxiliary electric engines, but speeds were no more than 4 knots, slower than any merchant vessel, and underwater range was limited to 80 nautical miles, because of the need to surface in order to recharge the batteries. This meant that U-boats in the Atlantic had to spend most of their time on the surface and, as Allied detection methods and antisubmarine weapons improved, U-boats became more vulnerable. This was especially so with regard to the threat from the air—aircraft accounted for half of U-boat losses during the war. The Germans, therefore, worked hard to improve underwater endurance and speed.

The first solution was the *Schnorkel* tube, an idea examined by the Dutch navy prior to the war, which enabled the main diesel engine to be operated underwater. When the submarine was on the surface, the tube was clipped to the deck and then raised and attached to the conning tower before the U-boat dived. The *Schnorkel* tube was not completely satisfactory. Underwater speeds of no more than 8 knots were achieved, navigation was very difficult, and in heavy seas, water would slop down into the control room. Nevertheless, from 1943 onward, a number of existing U-boats were converted.

Two other solutions were developed during the latter half of the war. The first of these was the electro-boat—Type XXI (ocean-going) and Type XXIII (coastal). A combination of very powerful batteries and streamlined hull increased the submerged speed to 17 knots and submerged ranges to 200–300 nautical miles. The other concept, the Walter boat, used a revolutionary new turbine engine driven by steam and hydrogen peroxide, both created by breaking down sea water. Walter boats could steam at 20 knots underwater for short periods, but their submerged range was somewhat less than the electroboats. These new types appeared too late to affect the course of the war significantly.

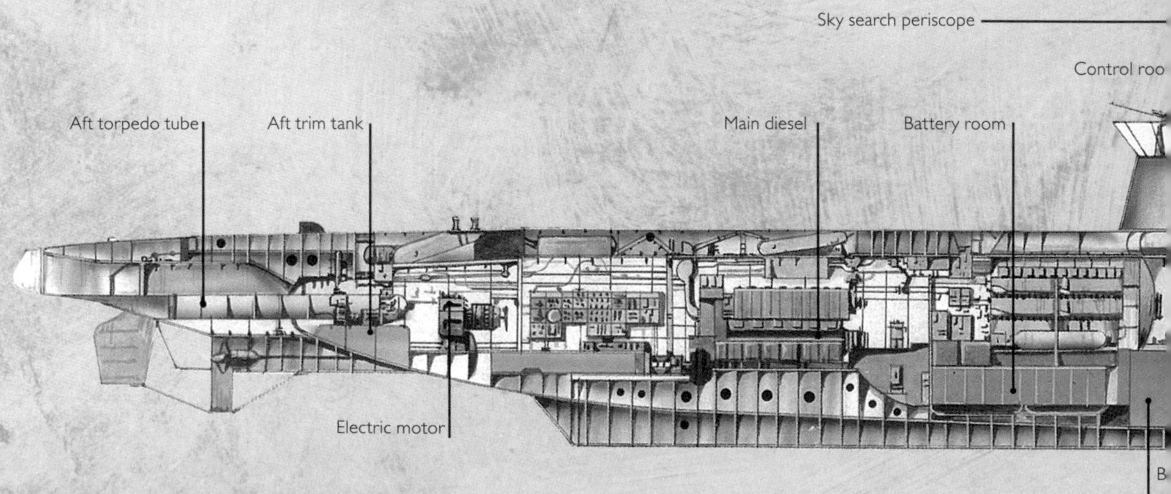

A Type IX U-boat under air attack. Allied aircraft normally used depth charges, bombs, and machine guns. From March 1943, a very effective air-dropped passive acoustic homing torpedo, Fido, was introduced. Airborne radar also proved useful.

A Type VIIC/42. She had a crew of 45 and had four bow and one stern torpedo tubes, with capacity for 16 torpedoes. The top surface speed was 18 knots and she had a surface range of 10,000 miles (16,093 km) at 12 knots.

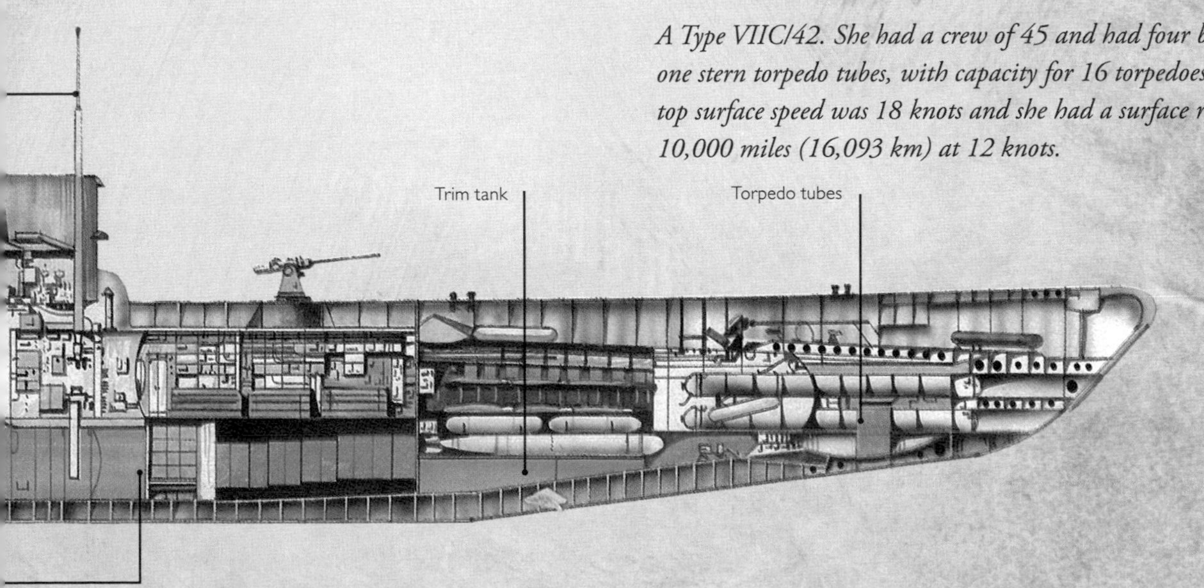

were sinking 50 Japanese merchantmen a month; the success rate fell away simply because of the lack of targets. Japan's failure to implement a proper convoy system and to develop effective antisubmarine weapons and detection aids were the reasons. By spring 1945, Japan's maritime communications had been virtually throttled, more than 1,000 ships had been sunk, and war production declined rapidly. The fatal flaw in the Japanese strategy had been to concentrate too much on destroying enemy surface sea power at the expense of protecting her ultimate lifeline.

THE WAR IN THE AIR

Air power played an essential part in supporting the other two major dimensions of war. Indeed, one of its two major roles was achieving either total (supremacy) or partial (superiority) command of the air space over land and maritime combat zones. Having achieved this, it was possible for air forces to give both land and naval forces intimate or close air support within the battle area itself and also to attack the area immediately behind, through which the enemy had to pass the supplies and reinforcements needed to sustain his effort in the battle area. This was, and still is, termed "interdiction."

Supremacy and interdiction

During the *Blitzkrieg* campaigns, which relied on achieving shock and surprise from the outset, the aim of the German airforce was to destroy its opponent on the ground, which meant attacking airfields on the opening day. The Poles, in September 1939, prevented this by moving their aircraft to satellite airfields, but this made little difference given their small numbers and obsolescence. It worked to a degree in May 1940 and was very effective against the ill-prepared Russians in June 1941. The Japanese, too, used the same technique during their initial offensives.

The one failure that the Germans had during the early years of the war was during late summer 1940. Air supremacy was an essential prerequisite for a successful invasion of Britain. In the Battle of Britain, once early

BATTLE OF BRITAIN

DATE July 10–October 31, 1940
CAMPAIGN Western Europe
OBJECT To achieve air supremacy over southern England as a prerequisite to a cross-Channel invasion.
NUMBERS At the beginning of the battle, Germans—2,600 aircraft of all types; RAF—644 fighters.
DESCRIPTION The battle consisted of five distinct phases. The first, which lasted until August 7, was known as the "contact" phase. The Luftwaffe, by attacks on Channel convoys, tried to tempt the RAF into battles close to the French shore. RAF policy at this stage was conservation and they largely refused to be drawn. During the period of August 8–23, the Germans switched their attention to fighter airfields and the RAF's vital early warning radar system, Chain Home (see also page 254). The Luftwaffe nearly crippled RAF Fighter Command's infrastructure, but the Luftwaffe's commander, Hermann Göring, convinced that attacks against the radar stations were ineffective, began, from August 24, to be drawn toward London, concentrating on airfields and aircraft factories. The more inland the target, however, the less able were the German fighters, because of their limited range, to protect the bombers. Then, from September 7, came the offensive on London, primarily by day. Finally, during October, the bombing effort switched to nighttime and the Blitz got properly under way. Daytime nuisance raids, taking advantage of poorer weather, targeted airfields.
CASUALTIES 1,700 German and 600 British aircraft lost.
RESULT Failure to gain air superiority quickly made Hitler lose enthusiasm for invasion. Instead, he tried to bomb Britain into submission, but his plans to invade Russia brought this to an end in May 1941.

strategies failed, the Luftwaffe turned to attacks on radar stations, airfields, and industry in an attempt to destroy the infrastructure of RAF Fighter Command. German fighters were now operating at extreme range, having only 20 minutes' flying time over England, which put the RAF fighters at an advantage. Also, they failed to concentrate sufficiently on each target. Thus, while they put some radar stations and airfields out of action for a time, they also allowed them breathing space for repairs. Finally, the switch to attacks on London at the beginning of September was an admission that they had failed to subdue the RAF.

By the time the Allies had begun to take the offensive on all fronts, toward the end of 1942, they had adopted a more methodical approach. For example, during the preparatory period before the Normandy landings in June 1944, attacks by Allied air forces on airfields and radars in northern France were very much more systematic than the Luftwaffe's 1940 effort. Targets were attacked time and again until it was certain that they were destroyed. The result was that when the landings took place, hardly a single German aircraft could be mustered over the invasion front.

It was realized from the outset that the best way to achieve this was to concentrate on communications and thus block the routes that the enemy was using to bring supplies and reserves. The abortive Allied efforts to destroy the Meuse bridges in May 1940 were an indicator of this. Having achieved early air supremacy, the Luftwaffe also concentrated on these types of targets. During the latter part of the war, the Allies made interdiction a priority during the preparatory phase. Classic examples of this are the aptly named Operation *Strangle*, which was carried out prior to the successful May 1944 attacks on the Gustav Line in Italy and the sealing off of Normandy prior to D-Day through the destruction of road and rail bridges leading into the region.

AVRO LANCASTER

The Avro Lancaster was the outstanding heavy bomber of the war and became the backbone of the RAF strategic bombing offensive against Germany. It was derived from the Avro Manchester, which made its operational debut in February 1941, but soon proved unpopular because of the unreliability of its two engines. The four-engine Lancaster entered service at the beginning of 1942; its first operation was to drop mines off Brest on the night of March 3–4,1942. By 1945, no fewer than 7,377 had been built. Highly maneuverable and able to withstand heavy punishment, the Lancaster could carry 14,000 pounds (6,350 kg) of bombs 1,660 miles (2,670 km), a performance exceeded only by the U.S. B-29. It could also carry the heaviest bomb of the war, the 22,000-pound (9,979-kg) Grand Slam, which destroyed the Bielefeld viaduct in Germany in March 1945.

U.S. B-17 Flying Fortresses, with the contrails of their escort fighters above them, en route for a target in Germany. Heavily armed, but carrying only half the bombload of the RAF Lancaster, they flew in a boxlike formation. This was not enough to keep the Luftwaffe at bay without fighters escorting them all the way to the target.

STRATEGIC BOMBING

The one mission that air forces could undertake totally independently of the other armed services was strategic bombing, the means by which prewar theorists believed that wars could be won single-handedly. Given the technological state of the art at the time, there was some justice in Stanley Baldwin's comment on the invincibility of the bomber. Ground detection devices, which were based on sound and visual means, had a very limited range and the relatively poor climb performance of the wooden biplane fighter meant that they could not intercept the bombers in time. The only alternative was standing patrols of fighters, a prohibitively expensive use of assets. The situation had changed dramatically by the late 1930s, however, thanks to the introduction of the all-metal monoplane fighter and of radar. The effect of these was well illustrated by the Battle of Britain.

Yet, in September 1939 the rival air forces did not undertake the "knockout" blow that fearful civilian populations expected. Governments bound themselves by the 1923 Hague Draft Rules of Air Warfare, which, although never ratified, outlawed indiscriminate bombing and forbade attacks on other than strictly military targets. The bombing of Warsaw in September 1939 and Rotterdam in May 1940 were the first cracks in these ground rules. However, Warsaw had become a military target by virtue of its refusal to surrender, although Rotterdam was a more marginal case. But, in spite of these, a small degree of indiscriminate bombing was being carried out, albeit unintentionally.

The problem was that the bomber of 1939 could not bomb accurately. Navigation was reliant on dead reckoning and astro fixes, both of which were prone to error. Indeed, that is why most bombing during the early months of the war was undertaken by day. By early 1940, due to significant aircraft losses, the British were forced to switch to bombing by night, which increased navigational inaccuracy. Even if the target was correctly identified, the bombsights of the time, which had not been significantly improved since 1918, were not very accurate. The Germans were the first to improve navigation with their *Knickebein* (Crooked Leg) system, which was based on radio signals intersecting over the target, but this could be countered by jamming or transmitting "spoof" signals.

The "area bombing" or "city busting" that was to dominate the strategic-bombing offensives against England, Germany, and Japan began by accident when a German bomber dropped bombs on London in error in late August 1940. The British retaliated by attacking Berlin, which was followed by the long drawn-out Blitz on London and other British cities during the winter of 1940–41. The Blitz showed, however, that the prewar belief that civilians would quickly cave in under bombing attacks was mistaken. If anything, it strengthened the citizens' resolve to resist and hit back.

The Blitz also revealed a serious shortfall in the Luftwaffe's order of battle: the lack of a true strategic bomber, with long range and large bombload. The reason was that the Luftwaffe was seen by Hitler when he created it as a *Risikoflotte* (Risk Fleet) designed to impress Germany's neighbors by its size rather than its quality. The production rate for two-engine aircraft was much greater than that for four-engine and the Luftwaffe needed to grow quickly. The RAF fell into the same trap in the mid-1930s when it tried to match the Luftwaffe in numbers, although, by 1937, specifications had been drawn up for heavy bombers, which began to come into service at the beginning of 1941. The Luftwaffe's lack of a strategic bomber was exposed during the war against Russia. Not only was it unable to mount a sustained air offensive against Moscow, but it also lacked the range to attack the Russian war industry behind the Urals.

Campaign against Germany

It was not until 1942 that the British bombing offensive against Germany really got under way. Before then, bomber numbers had been too few to make much of an impression. New technical aids, increasing numbers of heavy bombers, and a dynamic new commander, Arthur Harris, began to make the bombing bite. But no technical aid was invulnerable to countermeasures and while bombing accuracy improved to an extent, it was still not precise enough, although there were exceptions, such as the Dams Raid in May 1943.

THE DAMS RAID

DATE May 16–17, 1943
OBJECT To disrupt German war production.
NUMBERS 19 Lancaster bombers.
DESCRIPTION The idea of destroying the Ruhr dams in order to seriously affect German war production in the region had been postulated before the outbreak of war in 1939. However, it was not until designer Dr. Barnes Wallis had developed a revolutionary bomb that it became more than an idea. By skipping across the water, the bomb, which became known as the "bouncing bomb," could attack the dams horizontally. To induce the bomb to skip, meant flying at a very precise and very low height, and a special RAF squadron (617), using modified Lancaster bombers, was formed in March 1943. The nighttime operation was mounted two months later. The primary targets were the Möhne, Sorpe, and Eder dams; three others, the Ennepe, Lister, and Diemel, were secondary targets. The Möhne and Eder dams were successfully breached, causing widespread flooding and disruption of communications; the Sorpe was slightly damaged.
CASUALTIES Eight aircraft failed to return.
RESULT The effect on the Ruhr industries was not serious. Even so, the technical ingenuity involved and the cold-blooded courage of the crews provided a very welcome fillip to morale, not just for RAF Bomber Command, but also for the Western Allies as a whole.

RAF Bomber Command was drawn increasingly to area bombing because it lacked the means to do anything else. The self-justification for it was that it was effective in both lowering civilian morale and keeping munitions workers from their beds and hence reducing production. Spurred by the Pointblank Directive of January 1943, which identified the dislocation of the German military, economic, and industrial systems and the fatal undermining of morale as the main aims of the strategic bombing offensive, RAF Bomber Command waged three consecutive campaigns, against the Ruhr, Hamburg, and Berlin, during 1943–44. The campaign against the Ruhr was made more difficult by the industrial haze that covered the region, but did help to drive German industry into the countryside, where, during 1944, its production would peak. Hamburg was the closest that Harris got to undermining morale, when in July 1943 the heart of the city was torn out by fire storms, but Berlin proved too tough to overcome. Bomber casualties mounted in the face of an ever more technically sophisticated air-defense system and it was as well that the decision to switch the strategic-bombing forces to support of the Normandy landing preparations halted the Battle of Berlin at the end of March 1944.

Round the clock bombing

The U.S. strategic bombing "barons" thought differently. While they agreed that bombing could be decisive, they argued that daylight attacks gave better accuracy and so were more effective. By giving their bombers the maximum defensive armament, they believed that they could ward off enemy fighters. It was not until spring 1943 that they were able to take a full part in the offensive and began to concentrate on industrial targets by day, while the RAF attacked cities by night, a strategy that was known as "round the clock bombing." Belief in the invincibility of the B-17 Flying Fortress and other bombers was cruelly shattered during operations in the late summer and fall of 1943, when the loss rate in bombers was as high as 30 percent. The bomber could not get through modern air defenses on its own by day, and the U.S. Air Force seriously thought of switching to night attacks. Salvation came in the shape of the long-range escort fighter, the P-51 Mustang, and confidence was restored during the last year of the war in Europe.

The temporary placing of the strategic air forces under Eisenhower's command during the spring and summer of 1944 did not please the bomber commanders, who believed that this would give Germany valuable breathing space. Yet they played a significant part in the interdiction operations and were also used in direct support of the ground forces, although their "carpet-bombing" techniques more than once caused casualties to their own side and created added mobility problems. When they returned to concentrating their attacks on Germany in mid-September 1944, the German transportation system was quickly brought to a virtual halt. When the Allies eventually overran Germany in spring 1945, it was a totally devastated country.

There is no doubt that strategic bombing contributed to victory against Germany; and it was, for so long, the only means of striking directly at the German heartland. However, it was not in itself decisive, and the belief that Germany could be reduced to such a state that Allied land forces would be left with a mere police action on their hands was incorrect. Too much faith was placed on morale attacks, which continued until the end of the war. The attack on Dresden in February 1945 was the most controversial. As the Blitz did not break British morale, so the Germans stood up against a much longer and heavier campaign. The Allied policy of unconditional surrender probably contributed to this because German propaganda was able to instill a belief that there was nothing to be gained by early surrender, but even so the prewar theorists had been disproved.

Campaign against Japan

The strategic bombing offensive against Japan took very much longer to be mounted for the simple reason that the Japanese mainland remained out of reach of the bombers for so long. Indeed, the only U.S. air attack on Japan before 1944 took place in April 1942, when carrier-launched B-25s dropped a few bombs on Japanese cities and then crash-landed in China, but this was as much to boost Allied morale at an especially dark time as to achieve any larger purpose.

It was not until the B-29 Superfortress came into service that the U.S. Air Force took possession of an aircraft capable of reaching Japan from land bases while carrying a useful payload. They began by operating from bases in South China in June 1944, but the results were disappointing, and a Japanese offensive then forced them to evacuate.

SCHWEINFURT–REGENSBURG RAIDS

DATE August 17, 1943
OBJECT To disrupt German war production.
NUMBERS 376 B-17s, 276 P-47s, 180 Spitfires; 540 Fw190, Me109, Me110 sorties flown.
DESCRIPTION This was a twin daylight operation carried out by the U.S. Eighth Air Force against the ball-bearing industry at Schweinfurt and Luftwaffe fighter plants at Regensburg deep in southern Germany. On August 17, 376 bombers took off, escorted by P-47 Thunderbolts and Spitfires. The Schweinfurt group was to return to its East Anglian bases after the attack, while the airplanes attacking Regensburg were to fly on to North Africa. Shortage of fuel forced the escort fighters to turn back just short of the German border, but even before they did so, German fighters were beginning to hack down bombers. The attacks grew in intensity the deeper into Germany the U.S. airplanes penetrated. Even so, the Regensburg attack was remarkably accurate and caused some extensive damage. This group, by turning south over the Alps, was able to surprise the air defenses in the area and quickly shook off its attackers. The bombing of Schweinfurt, in contrast, was scattered and the bombers had to endure the same punishment during the homeward trip as they had gone through on the outward journey.
CASUALTIES The combined attack cost 60 U.S. bombers compared with 27 German fighters shot down.
RESULT This operation forced the Eighth Air Force to concentrate on short-range targets for a time. A second raid on Schweinfurt on October 14, accompanied part of the way by longer-range P-38 Lightning escorts, suffered even greater casualties and finally convinced the Americans that deep-penetration daylight operations were too costly without a fighter that could escort the bombers all the way to the target.

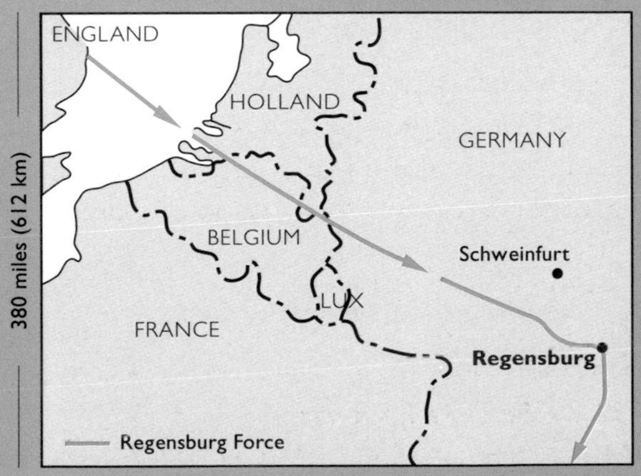

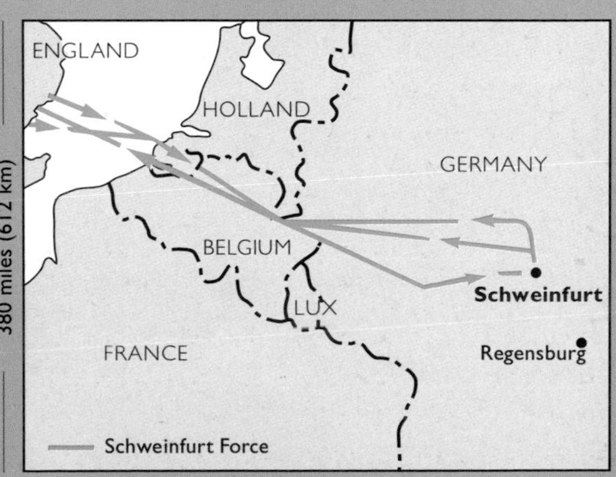

RADAR

The idea of using radio waves to measure distance occurred to the scientists of several nations at more or less the same time. In the 1920s, weather researchers had discovered that they could "bounce" a radio signal off the upper atmosphere and detect its return to earth. From this discovery, scientists began thinking that perhaps signals could be bounced off other things. In 1934, Dr. Kuhnhold of the German navy's Radio Research Establishment began experiments, which by 1936, were sufficiently advanced to be able to persuade the German navy to place a contract for a range-finding radar for use with naval guns.

U.S. navy scientists had noticed by 1930 that a radio signal showed distortion when an aircraft passed between transmitter and receiver. In 1933, the U.S. army's Signal Corps joined in the investigation, and by 1936, both services had produced prototype equipment. The French were also experimenting, aiming to develop an iceberg-finding device for transatlantic liners.

In Britain, the radar principle was fully explored and developed. In January 1935, the Committee for the Scientific Study of Air Defence asked Dr. Robert Watson-Watt, a radiophysicist, to investigate whether a "death ray" capable of stopping aircraft engines, as discussed in newspapers at the time, was a feasible proposition. He replied that it was not, but there might be other aspects of radio that could be useful. Within a month he submitted a report in which he laid out, in considerable detail, a potential system for detecting aircraft by means of radio waves. The report went farther, proposing a defensive system to cover the identification of friendly aircraft, the possibility of countermeasures, and much more. The idea was adopted, and by June 1935, aircraft had been detected at a range of 17 miles (27 km).

Three years later, Britain had a complete chain of radar stations along the east and south coasts. These were used during the Munich crisis of 1938 and have been operating continuously ever since. However, warning of

Although radar began as a detection system, it was quickly expanded to provide other vital information. The H2S system was adopted in British bombers in January 1943. Tests of night-fighter radars in 1940 had shown that centimetric radar could distinguish between built-up areas and featureless countryside. Because bombing targets were usually in built-up areas, this led to development of a downward-pointing radar that could, effectively, "draw a map" of the ground, with enough detail for the navigator to correlate the picture with the map and so pinpoint his position.

RADAR IN BRITAIN 1940

The radar screen around Britain in 1940 consisted of two "chains" of stations. Chain Home was the first, providing cover at high altitude and long range. Chain Home Low came later, giving low-altitude cover against raiders flying over the sea. As technology improved, so the boundaries of radar coverage were extended.

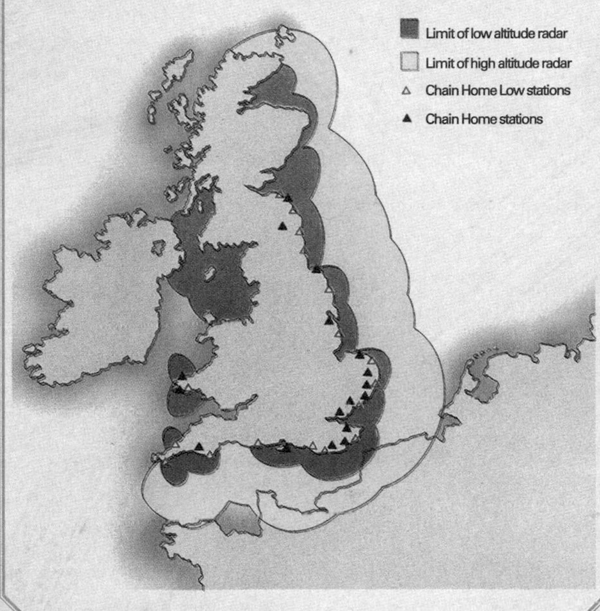

the approach of enemy aircraft by itself is not enough. Working from Watson-Watt's proposals, a complete communication system between radars and defensive aircraft was set up and integrated with Air Marshal Hugh Dowding's fighter control system. Incoming raiders were detected, positions were plotted on the control room table, and fighters were "talked" into a suitable position for intercepting the enemy. Without this command and control system, the Battle of Britain might have taken a very different course.

Germany developed a similar system, beginning in 1940 with a handful of "Freya" early warning radar sets borrowed from the Germany navy. The Luftwaffe's own design, "Wurzburg," followed, and by the middle of 1941 a comprehensive warning system was operating.

The United States had a handful of sets operating by 1941. One set covering Pearl Harbor actually detected the incoming Japanese bombers, but its operators assumed they were a flight of U.S. bombers expected from the West Coast.

Shorter-wave radar

Low-powered early sets operated at a wavelength of about 3 feet (1 m). It was known that if the wavelength were shorter, more power could be generated, giving wider range and better precision, but it was practically impossible to generate such waves using conventional glass valves or tubes. Eventually, two young English physicists devised the "cavity magnetron," which was capable of producing powerful 3.9-inch (10-cm) waves. Since the wavelength governed the size of the transmitting and receiving antenna, the shorter wavelength made it possible to install effective radar sets inside an aircraft.

This allowed night fighters to detect bombers once they had been directed to the general area by the ground radar and controllers. Submarines, risen to the surface at night or in fog, could be detected at long range. Radar allowed a bomber navigator to scan the ground beneath for landmarks and to correct his navigation, and also allowed him to detect approaching enemy fighters.

Watson-Watt had also proposed measures to counter an opponent's radar. Metallic paper strips, cut to half the wavelength of the radar and scattered in the air, could swamp the enemy radar with spurious echoes. This tactic was code named "Window." The dilemma over the use of Window was whether the enemy could make better use of it than the Allies. Britain eventually took the plunge in July 1943 to cover the first of the great raids on Hamburg. Window remained effective throughout the war and it was soon joined by other, more sophisticated electronic devices to confuse radar reception.

Probably the earliest successful jamming operation was performed in February 1942, when the German navy blinded British south-coast radars to conceal the escape of three battleships from Brest Harbor. The British returned the compliment in 1944 with a massive radar decoy that kept the Germans guessing about where the Allies would land on D-Day.

THE NORMANDY LANDINGS

DATE June 6, 1944
OBJECT Invasion of France by Allied forces.
NUMBERS 8 Allied divisions—2 U.S., 1 British airborne plus 5 landing divisions (2 U.S., 2 British, 1 Canadian) tasked with landing on 5 beaches: Utah, Omaha, Gold, Juno, Sword. Germans—1 Panzer, 4 infantry divisions.
DESCRIPTION The planning of Operation "Overlord" began in April 1943. The Germans expected a landing and the most likely place was the Pas de Calais, where the English Channel is at its narrowest, so somewhere else had to be found, not too far from the English south coast. Much detailed topographical intelligence was acquired before the decision to opt for Normandy was taken, and elaborate plans to keep the Germans from finding out were drawn up under the code name "Bodyguard." The necessary landing craft for such a huge undertaking had to be gathered, and specialized equipment developed from scratch to ensure its success. The invasion fleet had to be secured against air, surface, and subsurface threats. Because no port lay within the landing area, artificial "Mulberry" harbors and PLUTO (Pipeline under the Ocean) were created so that the forces in the beachhead could be supplied and reinforced. The tides had to be right and the weather fair, the cause of a 24-hour postponement. All elements taking part had to be thoroughly rehearsed over British beaches similar to those in Normandy. Air and French Resistance operations during the preparatory phase had to be closely coordinated. The Allied supreme commander for "Overlord" was General Dwight D. Eisenhower; the British general Bernard Montgomery was placed in command of the Allied land forces.
CASUALTIES Allies—approximately 15,000; Germans—approximately 10,000.
RESULT Consolidation of the beachhead marked the beginning of the end for German forces in the West; once the Allies broke out of Normandy, it was only a matter of time before they reached the German border.

The securing of Saipan and Tinian in the Marianas by the beginning of August 1944 gave the Americans a Pacific base close enough to Japan for the B-29s. They began operations in November, with high-altitude bombing by day, but haze interfered with accuracy and results were again disappointing. Accordingly, the decision was made to employ lower-level attacks by night using a high proportion of incendiary bombs. The new offensive opened in March and brought devastating results to the largely wooden structures of Japanese cities. In just a week, four cities, including Tokyo, suffered heavy destruction, but then there was a pause for restocking of the incendiaries. By early April, farther U.S. conquests had brought P-51 escort fighters within range of Japan and the B-29s were able to resume attacks by day. This, combined with U.S. submarine operations, proved calamitous for Japanese war production but, as in Germany, there was no thought of surrender. Indeed, as the fighting on Iwo Jima and Okinawa showed, Japanese resistance was as fierce as ever and the prospect of invading the islands of mainland Japan was daunting. Again, conventional strategic bombing had made a significant but not decisive contribution to final victory.

AMPHIBIOUS WARFARE

Between the two world wars no nation paid much attention to amphibious warfare. The British experience in the Dardanelles in 1915 had convinced most people that major landings on hostile shores were too risky to be a viable operation of war. Yet nine months after the outbreak of the war, the Germans were confronted with the possible necessity of having to carry out this very operation.

Operation *Sealion*, the invasion of Britain, was not a contingency that they had thought of before the end of the campaign in France, let alone earlier. Even though they tried to convince themselves that it would be no more than a large-scale river crossing, and Poland and the recent campaign in the west had given them plenty of opportunity to perfect these, they were completely unequipped to cross the English Channel. Indeed, Hitler himself recognized this to the extent of refusing to order more than preparations for it. He recognized that an essential prerequisite was air supremacy over both the Channel and landing area and was not prepared to execute the operation until this had been achieved. While Göring set out to achieve this, the German naval commander in chief, Erich Raeder, increasingly expressed his doubts over his ability to protect the invasion armada from the ravages of the Royal Navy.

Field Marshal von Rundstedt, who was to command the landing forces, showed no interest in the concept, never believing that it would happen. As it was, the task of gathering together suitable craft from the waterways of Europe was immense, especially given the time available, and the fact that few were really suitable. The invasion's indefinite postponement, after the Luftwaffe had failed to overwhelm the RAF, was, therefore, generally greeted with relief and the Germans never would carry out a major amphibious operation.

The Japanese, on the other hand, planned for amphibious landings during the 1941–42 offensive. While they did not possess the special equipment on which the Western Allies came to rely, they were successful during the early months of the war in the Pacific because they were able to surprise their opponents, and assert naval and air supremacy.

Royal Marine Commandos coming ashore on Sword Beach, Normandy, June 6, 1944. On the beach itself can be seen various types of specialized armored vehicle. Known affectionately as "funnies," they included swimming tanks, bridging vehicles, vehicles equipped with devices for clearing lanes through minefields, and for destroying concrete strongpoints.

European landings

In December 1941, at the first of their major wartime conferences, the Western Allies formally recognized that total victory in Europe and the Far East could not be achieved without landing forces from the sea. Indeed, the British had already been doing this, albeit on a very small scale, with their Commando raids, and had set up the Directorate of Combined Operations, the title reflecting the triservice nature of this operation of war. With regard to Europe, the Americans wanted to carry out cross-Channel landings in France as soon as possible, but the British preferred to secure the Mediterranean periphery first, in spite of Stalin's demands for the instant creation of the Second Front. The disastrous Dieppe Raid of August 1942 showed that the Allies were not ready to launch a successful invasion of France, but the lessons learned from it proved invaluable. Farther experience was gained from the successful *Torch* landings in French North Africa (November 1942) and the Sicilian (July 1943) and Italian (September 1943) landings. The culmination in Europe came with the Normandy landings in 1944.

V-1 MISSILES AND V-2 ROCKETS

The Germans began experimenting with rockets as a substitute for artillery from the late 1920s. Their work using solid-fuel rockets led to the Nebelwerfer, and using liquid fuel, to the A-4 rocket, more commonly called the V-2. This was short for Vergeltungswaffen 2 ("Vengeance Weapon 2"), a title bestowed by Hitler.

In 1931, General Walter Dornberger and Werner von Braun, based near Berlin, designed the A-1, which never flew; the A-2 flew successfully over the Baltic in December 1934 and the German army was sufficiently impressed to finance a missile development station at Peenemunde, on the Baltic coast. Subsequent rockets were developed there. The A-3, fired in 1938, tested technology later used in the A-4. The A-4 weighed about 13 tons at launch; the motor burned for about 70 seconds, during which period the rocket was turned onto a ballistic trajectory. Once correctly aligned, a radar signal cut off the motor and the A-4 coasted to its target. The rocket went into production in 1944; about 10,000 were built, of which 1,115 were fired against Britain, 1,341 against Antwerp, and 194 against other targets.

Once the final design of the A-4 was settled, the Peenemunde scientists proceeded to work on even bigger weapons, such as the A-10, a two-stage rocket intended to bombard the United States, but the war ended before these ideas could be translated into hardware.

Several private companies also set about designing guided missiles. Among them was Messerschmitt, who designed Enzian, a radio-guided air-defense rocket with an infrared homing head. Various prototype models were built between 1943 and 1945, of which 38 were fired experimentally. The Rheinmettal company developed Rheintochter, another radio-controlled air-defense missile, and other designers worked on X-5, an air-to-air missile; Wasserfall, an air-defense missile; Rheinbote, a surface-to-surface weapon; Moewe, another air-defense

(Left) V-1 missiles crossing the Kent coast in 1944. Beneath are the guns of the "Diver Belt," the concentration of air-defense artillery that stretched along the southeast coast of England.

(Right) An A-4 rocket after being launched from Test Stand VII at Peenemunde Army Experimental Station in the summer of 1943. The flight went to a range of 160 miles (257.5 km) and landed within 2 ½ miles (4 km) of its target. A film of this flight was instrumental in converting Hitler to the use of rockets.

missile, and many more. Of all these projects, only Rheinbote achieved success, and some 200 or more were fired at Antwerp in 1945. The war ended before any of the others could be brought into service.

The "Flying Bomb"

In 1942, the Luftwaffe began developing the FZG-76, better known as the V-1 "Flying Bomb." The first test launch was in December. The V-1 resembled a small aircraft, with fuselage, wings, and tail. A ramjet motor was mounted above the rear of the fuselage. Launched by catapult, to ensure sufficient airflow through the motor to make it function, it carried 1,870 pounds (850 kg) of explosives, flew at about 370 mph (595.5 km/h) and had a range of more than 120 miles (193 km). Production began in March 1944 and about 35,000 were made; 9,251 were fired against Britain, of which 4,261 were destroyed, and 6,551 against Antwerp, of which 2,455 were destroyed.

The V-1 could also be slung beneath an aircraft and launched in the air. Flying at speed, the pilot could start the rocket's motor by remote control and release the bomb. Provided it was pointed in the right direction, gyroscopic stabilization ensured that it would fly straight, and its range was governed by the amount of fuel it carried. Once it ran out of fuel it stalled, dived to the ground, and detonated.

Initially, defense against the V-1 was difficult. Although it flew straight and level (ideal for the anti-aircraft gunner), it was a hard target because it flew high and fast and could not be easily tracked by the larger guns. With the introduction of the U.S. SCR-504 autotracking radar and electronic predictor, targeting became very much easier, and the widespread use of proximity fuzes greatly improved the kill rate. RAF fighter aircraft played their part, but most V-1s were destroyed by gunfire.

The A-4 rocket was a different matter. It flew faster than the speed of sound, so there was no audible warning of its approach, and it was so fast that even if it was picked up by radar, there was not enough time to target it. The only hope was to place a screen of bursting shells in its path on the chance that a fragment might detonate the warhead while it was still well up in its trajectory. Some degree of early warning was achieved by using long-range radar to watch likely launch areas, but because the launching apparatus was mobile, it was pure luck if the radar happened to be looking at the right place at the right time.

The Luftwaffe also used the Hs-293, a gliding bomb. This air-to-ground missile, rocket-propelled and radio-guided, was released from an aircraft and steered to its target. It carried a 550-pound (250-kg) warhead. Introduced in 1942, it was used against shipping in the Bay of Biscay and around the Dodecanese Islands in the Aegean Sea, and also at Anzio in Italy in 1944, but Allied radio countermeasures were soon developed to jam the control link, and its use was discontinued.

U.S. Marines during the bloody fighting on Tarawa in the Gilbert Islands, November 1943. This and the landing on its sister island of Makin marked the first of a series of operations in the central Pacific, which culminated in the landings on Okinawa in April 1945. The Tarawa garrison of 5,000 men fought to the last, inflicting 3,500 American casualties.

Pacific landings

The first major U.S. landing in the Pacific, on Guadalcanal in August 1942, was planned in a hurry and with few resources. Indeed, it was called "Operation Shoestring." Consequently, although the troops successfully got ashore, it was weeks before the initial beachhead could be expanded; it took six months to secure the island. The main lesson learned was that the launching base must not be too distant if the buildup of force and sustainability necessary to exploit the landings inland was to be achieved. This, and the desirability of land-based aircraft able to cover the landings, influenced what became known as the "island-hopping" strategy practiced by MacArthur in the southwest Pacific and, with more difficulty, Nimitz in the central Pacific.

So great a role did amphibious operations come to play in Allied strategy, that the rate of production of the specialized equipment needed for them could not keep up with demand and, inevitably, some feasible plans, which might have shortened campaigns, had to be rejected. As U.S. chief of staff George C. Marshall is reputed to have said: "Prior to the present war I never heard of any landing craft except a rubber boat. Now I think about little else."

LEGACY OF WORLD WAR II

World War II did not produce any startlingly new principles of war. Rather, it served to reaffirm the tried and trusted principles that have been observed throughout the history of warfare. Likewise, the age-old problems of coalition warfare, especially that of trying to reconcile national interests with the good of the alliance as a whole, did not change. Where it did differ from its predecessors was in its totality and complexity.

Technological advances both during the prewar years, and accelerated during the war itself, especially in the fields of communications and propulsion, generally meant that it was conducted at a much faster pace than hitherto. Commanders, therefore, had to think and react much more quickly. At the same time, the increase in information sources and the factors that they had to consider, largely brought about by the much wider range of resources available with which to conduct war, made decision making a much more difficult business. While total victory was still represented by the man with his rifle and bayonet standing in the enemy's seat of government, the means to get him there had grown more complex. At the highest strategic level, the problem was compounded by the fact that it was very much more of a global war than its predecessor, with many more parts of the world being actively fought over. Indeed, it became almost two separate wars, one against the Axis powers in Europe, the other the conflict with Japan. The increased technological character of war also meant that the "tail to teeth" ratio, the numbers supporting each individual directly engaged with the enemy, had dramatically increased, at least in Western armies.

While 1939–45 was by no means the first total war—there are numerous instances of these throughout history—it directly affected people in many more parts of the world than ever before. National resources and populations were, to use Giulio Douhet's expression, "sucked into the maw of war" to a greatly increased extent. Conscription of the civil population for war work was widespread. Strategic bombing placed the civilian increasingly in the firing line. Women became more directly involved, whether in the Resistance movements of Axis-occupied Europe, tracking enemy aircraft by radar, or, in the Russian case, actually fighting. Increased totality brought increased ruthlessness in the way in which the war was waged. The Holocaust and the Japanese treatment of prisoners of war are but two examples.

The development of increasingly destructive weapons added to this totality, and none was more destructive than the atomic bomb. While it finally brought World War II to an end, it opened the door to an ever more awesome concept of future war. Although Hiroshima and Nagasaki might have finally proved the prewar air prophets right, they would have taken little comfort from it.

OKINAWA

DATE April 1–June 22, 1945
OBJECT To establish a forward base for land, air, and naval formations assembled for the invasion of the Japanese home islands.
NUMBERS U.S.—50,000 troops on the first-day landings, rising to nearly 250,000 by June; Japanese—120,000.
DESCRIPTION The Japanese allowed the Americans to land unopposed and then drew them on to formidable defense lines within the island, simultaneously throwing massed kamikaze attacks against the invasion fleet lying offshore. The kamikaze attacks began on April 6 while the 78,000-ton battleship *Yamato* sailed from Japan on a kamikaze mission against the U.S. amphibious force, but on April 7 was sunk, along with five of her escorts, by aircraft of the U.S. Task Force 58. It was the Japanese navy's last sortie of the war. Ashore, fanatical resistance, successive ridges, and heavy rain hampered the U.S. advance. Resistance continued through June. All the garrison's senior officers, including their commander General Ushuru Ushijima, committed ritual suicide before the Japanese surrender
CASUALTIES U.S.—48,193 service personnel killed, wounded, or missing, plus 763 aircraft and 34 ships; 25 more were damaged beyond repair. Japan—110,000 dead and some 10,000 taken prisoner, plus 16 ships and 7,800 aircraft. Additionally, up to 160,000 of Okinawa's civilian population died during the course of the fighting.
RESULT The ferocious kamikaze onslaught proved unavailing. By the end of the Okinawa campaign, the Americans had adopted new tactics and deployments to deal with the threat. Okinawa was also the first occasion on which Japanese troops surrendered in any appreciable numbers.

NUCLEAR WEAPONS

The column of smoke and radioactive dust above Nagasaki after the detonation of "Fat Man." This was the second atomic bomb, also of 20 kt power, dropped on August 9, 1945.

After Albert Einstein's formulation of the equivalence of mass and energy, the prospect of releasing energy contained within the atom fascinated physicists. Until the 1890s, it had been assumed that the atom was indivisible and indestructible. Then, in 1903, Ernest Rutherford and Frederick Soddy were the first to discover a subatomic particle, the electron. More discoveries followed until, in 1939, Lise Meitner and Otto Frisch split the nuclei of uranium atoms to release a disproportionate amount of energy—nuclear fission. Almost immediately, a conference of American physicists was held in Washington, as a result of which a proposal was made to the U.S. President Franklin Roosevelt to develop an atomic bomb using uranium as the explosive. Roosevelt consulted Einstein and then appointed a Uranium Consultative Committee. The first controlled chain reaction, in which a neutron striking a uranium nucleus and releasing energy liberated other neutrons, which, in turn, acted on neighboring atoms, took place in Chicago in 1942.

Similar work had taken place in Britain, where the "Tube Alloys" committee had been formed. Much informal exchange of information took place, but it was not until 1943 that an official accord was firmly established. By that time, Fermi had set the first chain reaction in operation and an enormous constructional effort, code named the "Manhattan Engineer District," was set in motion to manufacture the material for a bomb.

Germany had also realized the potential of the atom and set up a research program. But German scientists mistakenly elected to base their studies on "heavy water." Under British direction, Norwegian resistance forces destroyed successive shipments of heavy water from the only plant—in Norway—capable of making it. This action reinforced the Germans' belief that they were on the right track and also cut off their supplies, so their efforts came to nothing.

At 5:30 a.m. on July 16, 1945, the first detonation of an atomic bomb occurred in the New Mexico desert, with devastating effect. The invasion of Japan was scheduled for November 1, 1945. Faced with the possibility of hundreds of thousands of U.S. casualties, President Harry S. Truman decided to bomb the Japanese into submission instead. Hiroshima was the target on August 6, 1945. The B-29 bomber chosen for the mission was commanded by

Enola Gay, *a B-29 long-range Super Fortress bomber used in the raid on Hiroshima. A similar aircraft was used for the second raid, against Nagasaki, both flying from the American base in Okinawa.*

Colonel Paul W. Tibbets, and called *Enola Gay*, after his mother. A photo of movie star Rita Hayworth had been attached to the "Little Boy" atomic bomb the aircraft carried. Seconds after 8:15 a.m., its bomb-bay doors opened and "Little Boy" began its descent from 31,000 feet (9,500 m). As *Enola Gay* pulled away, the crew saw a vivid flash, then felt a double shock wave. Below them, some 15 miles (24 km) away, a ball of fire seethed skyward as the bomb detonated 2,000 feet (600 m) above the aiming point, with a force equivalent to 29,000 tons of conventional explosive, devastating five square miles (13 sq km) and killing some 75,000 people. The Japanese did not surrender, and on August 9, "Fat Man" was dropped on the city of Nagasaki. Approximately 35,000 people died. Thousands more in both cities died later of the after effects. On August 14, Emperor Hirohito accepted terms for an unconditional surrender. On September 2, the surrender documents were signed by General MacArthur and representatives of the Japanese government aboard the U.S. battleship *Missouri* in Tokyo Bay. With his instinctive sense of theater, MacArthur declared, "These proceedings are now closed." The atomic era had been born.

The United States assumed it would hold a monopoly on the atomic bomb after 1945, but the Soviets, who had begun work on one in early 1943, probably knew as much about nuclear technology as the Western Allies; not only was their own research far developed but they were greatly helped by their spy network, which informed them of Western developments. Due to the USSR's backward industrial base, it took time, but in 1949, the Soviets were able to detonate their own atomic bomb. The United States went ahead again in 1952, when it exploded the first thermonuclear hydrogen bomb, but less than a year later the USSR detonated its own H-bomb. The nuclear arms race was under way.

12 WARFARE TODAY AND TOMORROW

In August 1945, the Allies achieved total victory over Germany and Japan. However, the wartime alliance between the Western powers and the Soviet Union was quickly replaced by the Cold War, a long period of tension and conflict between East and West, the consequences of which are still unfolding in the twenty-first century.

Adolf Hitler's long-held aim was the destruction of Soviet Communism, but in May 1945 the Red Army, far from being defeated, was 100 miles (160 km) from the Rhine River, Germany's main artery, and was in unchallenged possession of the whole of Eastern Europe and much of the Balkans. Although the USSR had suffered huge losses during the war, and the majority of its cities and factories west of the Urals lay in ruins, it was now the strongest military power in Europe.

By the time Churchill, Roosevelt, and Stalin met at Yalta in February 1945, in the closing months of the war, the cracks in the wartime alliance were beginning to open up. Churchill was deeply suspicious about Stalin's ambitions in Europe, while Roosevelt had convinced himself, against much compelling evidence, that he could "do business" with the Soviet leader. Roosevelt was also eager to secure the USSR's entry into the war against Japan, which was occupying Manchuria, part of China. The Soviets took their time about this, invading Manchuria on August 8, 1945, two days after the atom-bomb attack on Hiroshima. Nonetheless, Roosevelt was prepared to make concessions to Stalin over Eastern Europe, a theater about which the Americans and the British could do little or nothing.

For his part, Stalin was unconcerned. His immediate postwar aim was to ensure that Poland—the age-old invasion route into Russia—would remain under Soviet control. Beyond the boundaries of an enlarged Soviet Union, he would rely on a protective buffer of satellite Eastern European nations that the Red Army had either liberated (Poland, Czechoslovakia, and the Baltic states) or invaded (Hungary, Romania, and Bulgaria.) Stalin had a simple, brutal attitude to their fate, declaring, "Everyone imposes his own system as far as his army can reach. It cannot be otherwise." Churchill's riposte came in a speech delivered at Fulton, Missouri, in March 1946: "From Stettin in the Baltic to Trieste in the Adriatic, an iron curtain has descended across the continent [of Europe]. Behind the line lie the capitals of the ancient states of Central and Eastern Europe."

NATO AND THE WARSAW PACT

The new East–West confrontation was felt most keenly in Berlin, lying deep in the heart of Soviet-controlled East Germany but itself divided into Soviet, U.S., British, and French occupation zones. Berlin was the one chink in Churchill's "iron

Supplies for West Berlin are loaded aboard a U.S. Air Force C-54 transport plane at Wiesbaden Air Base, West Germany, in March 1949. The Soviet Union's imposition of a land blockade of the part of the city administered by France, Britain, and the United States crystallized the postwar hostility between the superpowers and stimulated the formation of NATO.

curtain." In Soviet-controlled East Berlin, it was possible to buy a subway ticket to Allied-controlled West Berlin and travel on to the Western-occupied zones of West Germany. Many East Berliners made the journey and never returned.

Top of the agenda of the newly formed Western European Union (Britain, France, Belgium, the Netherlands, and Luxembourg) was the establishment of a democratic West German government. This prompted a Soviet withdrawal from the Allied Control Council, which oversaw the administration of occupied Germany. When the United States, France, and Britain merged their zones of occupation into a single unit and boosted the German economy by introducing the Deutschmark, the Soviets responded with a blockade of West Berlin, starting in June 1948. Road and rail links to the city were severed and electricity was cut off. There was enough food to last a month and fuel for 10 days. The Western powers beat the blockade with a massive airlift. The U.S. Air Force and the RAF flew thousands of missions to Berlin. On May 12, 1949, the Soviets admitted defeat and lifted the blockade, but the airlift continued until September, by which time more than 2.3 million tons of supplies had been flown into Berlin.

The Berlin airlift solidified the battle lines of the Cold War. In April 1949, the United States, Canada, and 10 Western European nations formed a defensive alliance, the North Atlantic Treaty Organization (NATO), aimed at deterring a Soviet attack on Western Europe. West Germany (which came into being in September 1949) joined NATO in 1954. The Soviet response was the Warsaw Pact, formed in May 1955 and comprising the Soviet Union, Albania, Bulgaria, Czechoslovakia, East Germany, Hungary, Poland, and Romania. The Warsaw Pact, dominated by the Soviet Union, did not survive the collapse of the Soviet empire and was disbanded in 1991.

In contrast, NATO continued to expand in the 1990s. A reunited Germany joined in October 1990, with the proviso that foreign troops and nuclear weapons would not be stationed in the former East Germany. Thereafter, former Soviet satellites formed a waiting line. In 1999 the Czech Republic, Hungary, and Poland joined, followed in 2004 by Bulgaria, Estonia, Latvia, Lithuania, Slovakia, and Romania. In 2009, Croatia and Albania joined but a year later, after coming under pressure from Russia, Ukraine abandoned its application. In 1966, France had withdrawn from NATO's integrated military structure, but in 2009 rejoined, keeping its own nuclear deterrent.

Soviet tanks deployed on the streets of Budapest in November 1956 to suppress the Hungarian uprising underlined the Soviet Union's determination to maintain its authority over the East European states that had joined the Warsaw Pact in the previous year. Such scenes were repeated in Prague in August 1968.

THE PEOPLE'S REPUBLIC OF CHINA

The third claimant to superpower status during the Cold War was China. The Chinese civil war ended in 1949, with the proclamation by the victorious communist leader Mao Tse-tung of the People's Republic of China. Originally aligned with the USSR, China broke off relations in 1959. Five years later China exploded its first atomic bomb.

In the last 20 years, China has been transformed both economically and technologically, although its military capacity still lags behind that of the United States. Its huge army of some 2.5 million men and women remains poorly equipped by comparison with the U.S. Army, although China's advanced weaponry includes the Russian Sukhoi-30 variable-geometry multirole fighter. In December 2004, China launched a new class of submarine capable of firing nuclear warheads to strike targets across the Pacific. In August 2011, the first Chinese aircraft carrier, purchased as a shell from the Ukraine in 1998, underwent sea trials. Satellite images showed that the carrier lacked the arrestor system to catch landing aircraft before they slid into the sea. Nevertheless, China's rapid military expansion was watched nervously by Washington, Tokyo, and its neighbors in the South China Sea, and has already prompted a significant response from the United States (see page 292).

THE COLD WAR

In 1949, the division of Germany was recognized when the Western-backed Federal Republic of Germany (West Germany) and its counterpart in the East, the Soviet-sustained German Democratic Republic, came into existence. Continuing tension between East and West ensured that Germany remained the epicenter of the Cold War in Europe, a conflict made concrete by the erection of the Berlin Wall by the East German government in 1961 in an attempt to staunch the flow of refugees from East to West. Nevertheless, the fact that Germany was now divided removed the problem that in the twentieth century had led to two world wars—a powerful, populous, and united Germany at the heart of central Europe. Not everyone rejoiced when the Berlin Wall came down in 1989.

From 1945, for the next few years, the United States was the world's only superpower, a status confirmed by its sole possession of nuclear weapons. The Soviet Union exploded its first atomic bomb in 1949. By 1950, the American nuclear program was producing more than 100 warheads a year. A stark measure of the power of nuclear weapons is the terminology used to describe their yield, or explosive force. This is measured in kilotons and megatons, or the approximate equivalent in thousands or millions of tons of conventional TNT.

New delivery systems and new forms of atomic weapons were also investigated. In 1952, the U.S. army deployed a 280 mm gun with nuclear shells. By 1955, it had added the Corporal and Honest John surface-to-surface missiles as well as nuclear landmines. Meanwhile, the Soviet Union had tested its first plutonium bomb in 1949, and by 1953, both the United States and the USSR had developed hydrogen bombs. So-called H-bombs use fusion instead of fission to release atomic energy, and they can have yields measured in tens of megatons rather than the few tens of kilotons to which the early bombs were limited.

Farther advances were achieved with the development of intercontinental ballistic missiles (ICBMs) and submarine-launched ballistic missiles (SLBMs), some of which, in turn, were equipped with multiple warheads. Later, the warheads themselves were made independently targetable, and accuracy was increased to the point where half the warheads launched would be expected to land within a few hundred yards of a designated target at ranges of anything up to 5,000 miles (8,050 km). Even more accurate were air-launched cruise missiles.

DETERRENT STRATEGY

Initially, the United States aimed for superiority in nuclear forces. By the mid-1950s, the goal had been reduced to sufficiency, but the strategy was still one of massive retaliation in the event of an attack. In the early 1960s, the strategy of flexible response was developed, in which both conventional and nuclear weapons would be used.

The American sector of Berlin, the city which became the epicenter of the Cold War, notoriously divided by the Berlin Wall. The Wall was erected in 1961 by the East German government to staunch the flow of its citizens to the West. By June 1962 it stretched for some 87 miles (140 km).

DISMANTLING COLD WAR ARSENALS

The dramatic collapse of Soviet hegemony in eastern Europe in 1989 was prefigured by Soviet moves to reduce the numbers of troops deployed in non-Soviet Warsaw Pact countries. Even before the conclusion of the 1989–90 Vienna negotiations on conventional forces in Europe (CFE), unilateral force reductions on both sides of the NATO-Warsaw Pact divide had made it clear that the peak of the postwar arms buildup had been passed.

The aim of the CFE talks was to agree ceilings on the numbers of weapon systems in various categories deployed in NATO and Warsaw Pact European countries. Accurate totals for the numbers of systems actually deployed were needed first, although to some extent, differences in each side's estimates of the other's holdings were academic. But they were important as negotiating points and to enable each side to verify the other's reductions.

The U.S. Multiple Launch Rocket System (MLRS) was one of the principal weapons developed to help NATO forces deal with the threat of a potentially overwhelming Soviet armored offensive in central Europe.

The figures that emerged show the scale of the arsenals that were created during 45 years of Cold War between East and West. Even after the substantial reductions called for by a CFE treaty, each side was allowed to retain 20,000 tanks. Yet, in 1940, the German army embarked on a campaign that was to defeat most of western Europe with barely one-eighth that number, deploying 2,574 tanks against the 3,609 mustered by France and Britain between them.

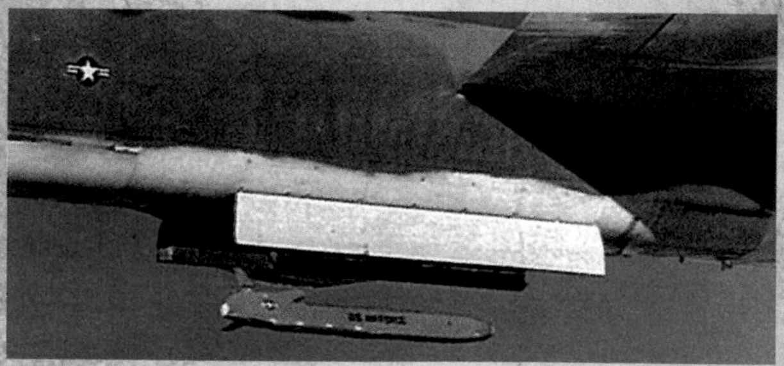

Air-launched cruise missiles, first deployed aboard U.S. Air Force B-52 strategic bombers in the mid-1980s, added flexibility to the U.S. strategic deterrent force by enabling manned bombers to launch attacks from stand-off ranges.

The revelation of the scale of chemical weapon stockpiles in Europe, and the difficulties involved in disposing of them, was one of the most disturbing aspects of the arms reduction process. NATO transported 100,000 artillery shells containing some 7,000 tons of nerve agent to Johnston Atoll in the Pacific, where they were burned in special incinerators.

The agreements on chemical and conventional weapons were preceded by the December 1987 treaty committing the United States and the USSR to eliminate all nuclear missiles with ranges of between 311 miles (500 km) and 3,417 miles (5,500 km). It was revealed that the U.S. had deployed 309 Tomahawk ground-launched cruise and 120 Pershing II ballistic missiles. At the same time, Soviet short-range 311–621-miles (500–1,000-km) missile deployments amounted to 220 SS-12 and 167 SS-23; in addition, 405 SS-20 and 65 SS-4 long-range missiles were deployed at operational sites.

Italian Army Tank Destroyer on patrol in Sarajevo, Bosnia-Herzegovina, 1996, during Operation Joint Endeavor, a peacekeeping effort by a multinational Implementation Force (IFOR), comprised of NATO and non-NATO military forces, deployed to Bosnia in support of the Dayton Peace Accords.

Nuclear stockpiles

More than 20 years after the end of the Cold War, the world's combined stockpile of nuclear warheads remains at a dangerously high level. By 2012, there were five nuclear weapon states (NWS)—China, France, Russia, the United Kingdom, and the United States—officially recognized as possessing nuclear weapons by the nuclear Non-Proliferation Treaty (NPT) of 1968. The secrecy that surrounded the accumulation and maintenance of these weapons makes it impossible to present anything other than an estimate of each of these states' holdings of both strategic and lower-yield tactical warheads.

China currently deploys some 240 warheads in total, France approximately 300, and the United Kingdom fewer than 160 from a stockpile of up to 225. In May 2010, the United States Department of Defense released for the first time the total number of active and inactive warheads in its stockpile. In 2012, this amounted to 5,113 plus some 3,500 retired warheads and those awaiting dismantlement. The active and inactive nuclear warheads included 1,737 deployed strategic warheads, approximately 500 operational tactical weapons, and some 2,645 inactive warheads. At the same time, Russia deployed some 1,492 operational strategic warheads and some 2,000 operational tactical warheads, and was stockpiling another 7,000 or so strategic and tactical warheads.

Three states—India, Pakistan, and Israel—did not sign the NPT and are known to possess nuclear weapons. By 2012, India deployed some 100 nuclear warheads and Pakistan a similar number. Israel has neither confirmed nor denied that it possesses nuclear weapons but it is estimated that its stockpile contains anything between 75 and 200 warheads. In addition, North Korea deploys an unknown but small number of nuclear weapons while Iran is pursuing a uranium-enrichment program, which could provide it with bomb-grade fissile material for nuclear weapons. In September 2007, Israel launched an air strike against an alleged nuclear reactor in Syria, which had been built in collaboration with North Korea.

Following the 1991 collapse of the Soviet Union, Belarus, Kazakhstan, and Ukraine have returned the nuclear weapons on their territory to Russia and have joined the NPT as nonnuclear weapons states. South Africa, which dismantled its small number of nuclear weapons after the fall of the apartheid state, joined the NPT in 1991. Iraq's ambition to develop weapons of mass destruction (WMD), including nuclear, under Saddam Hussein was brought to an end by the U.S.-led invasion in March 2003. In 2004, Libya's nuclear program was abandoned by the Libyan dictator Muammar Gaddafi in an attempt to improve his relations with the West. Additionally, Argentina, Brazil, South Korea, and Taiwan have shelved their nuclear programs.

President Gerald Ford and Soviet leader Leonid Brezhnev sign the Strategic Arms Limitation Treaty (SALT I) in Vladivostok, November 24 1974. The subsequent SALT II was not ratified by the United States because of the 1978 Soviet invasion of Afghanistan. In 1986 the United States withdrew from SALT II.

The goal was the "assured destruction" of enemy armed forces, not civilian populations. There was also a move to develop antiballistic missiles to limit the damage that an enemy attack could inflict on the United States itself.

By the end of the 1980s, the purpose of U.S. nuclear forces was defined as being to deter aggression, particularly nuclear attacks, against the United States and its allies. To do so, they had to be effective, flexible, survivable, and enduring. Effectiveness was achieved by accuracy both of weapons and target information, so large numbers of strategic reconnaissance systems—satellites, aircraft, and electronic systems—were deployed. Flexibility came from manned bombers, notably the Rockwell International B-1B (which entered service with the USAF in 1985) and the Northrop Grumman B-2 (which made its operational debut in 1999). ICBMs in hardened silos and missile-armed submarines in distant oceans contributed to survivability. By the end of the 1980s, the Soviet Union had a similar range of weapons, but more ICBMs, some of them mobile, and a more effective air-defense system against bombers.

LIMITING THE ARMS RACE

One purpose of the strategy of mutually assured destruction was to make instability so dangerous to both sides that it would inhibit the development of new capabilities that could disturb the strategic balance. Accordingly, the deployment of nuclear forces was accompanied by efforts to agree limits on their size and capabilities.

One development that threatened to upset the strategic balance was the deployment of missiles designed to intercept and destroy ballistic-missile warheads. Both the United States and the USSR deployed such systems in the early 1970s. The American Safeguard system involved Sprint and Spartan interceptors being based in North Dakota to protect ICBM silos, while the Soviet Galosh missiles were installed around Moscow. After detailed negotiations, the 1972 Anti-Ballistic Missile Treaty limited each side to just 100 ABMs, at a maximum of two sites; the U.S. system was dismantled, although the Soviet system was maintained and upgraded.

Along with the ABM Treaty, Stage I of the Strategic Arms Limitation Talks (SALT) resulted in an agreement to freeze the number of ICBMs and SLBMs on each side at their existing levels for five years. In 1979, SALT II concluded with an agreement to limit the total number of delivery systems on each side to 2,400 initially and 2,250 by the end of 1981, with sublimits on the numbers of ballistic missiles carrying multiple independently targetable warheads. The two Strategic Arms Reduction Treaties (START I and START II) both sought to reduce the number of warheads and delivery systems available to the United States and Russia. START I was originally signed in July 1991, but after the breakup of the USSR, former Soviet states Belarus, Kazakhstan, and Ukraine also became signatories. By 2001, the strategic arsenals of the United States and Russia had been reduced by 30–40 percent, and Belarus, Kazakhstan, and Ukraine had returned the nuclear weapons left over from the former Soviet Union to Russia. Building on this, START II aimed to eliminate heavy ICBMs and all other multiple warhead (MIRVed) ICBMs, and to reduce the total number of nuclear weapons deployed by both nations by two-thirds below pre-START levels.

In May 2002, the United States and Russia signed the Strategic Offensive Reductions Treaty (SORT) under which they agreed to reduce their strategic arsenals to 1,700–2,200 warheads each. The treaty came into force in 2003, but was replaced by the legally binding New START, signed in 2010 by the United States and Russia. This envisages a farther reduction in warheads and delivery vehicles, limiting each side's deployed strategic nuclear warheads to 1,550, and strategic delivery systems (ICBMs, submarine-launched, and heavy bombers) to 800 deployed and 800 nondeployed (such as on submarines undergoing overhaul) with a sublimit of 700 deployed. New START came into force in 2011 and will expire in 2021.

CONVENTIONAL WARS AND LOW-INTENSITY CONFLICT

In some countries, World War II never really stopped. In many others, the new order of the postwar world represented an opportunity to pursue dreams of liberation. The result was an astonishing variety of wars in the Cold War period, with superpower involvement ranging from full-scale military intervention to behind-the-scenes support for one side or the other.

Many of the conflicts during the Cold War were the result of straightforward territorial or economic disputes, but other factors were also at work. One was the enlistment of Third World nations in the geopolitical strategies of the two superpowers. Another was the sheer quantity of surplus military equipment that had been produced during World War II. A third was the often arbitrary new national boundaries that the tides of conflict had left in their wake. Yet another was the example set by the movement that was soon to win control of the most populous nation on earth.

The Chinese revolution, along with independence for India, resulted in the emergence of new regional superpowers in Asia. In the Middle East, the creation of the state of Israel provided a focus for hostilities going back thousands of years. In Africa, the end of colonialism was by no means always a peaceful affair. And Central America became a battleground for rival ideologies in an area where the cocaine trade introduced new economic distortions.

THE CHINESE REVOLUTION

The success of the communist revolution in China was an inspiration to would-be revolutionaries around the world and a practical model for the organization and execution of their uprisings. By the end of World War II it had already passed through what have become recognized as the first and second phases of classic revolutionary warfare; the way was clear for the final phase.

The Japanese surrender in 1945 left the U.S.-backed Kuomintang forces under Chiang Kai-shek as the only opposition to the Red Army of the Communist Party of China. The Red Army expanded and reorganized, drawing on the support built up over decades of political and military activity, and prepared for the transition from guerilla warfare to full-scale civil war. In July 1946,

MAO'S PRINCIPLES OF WARFARE

Mao Zedong defined his principles of revolutionary warfare in a theory of "people's war." In the first phase of Mao's revolution, he established base areas among the peasants. The second phase was what is now recognized as classic guerrilla warfare. Opportunistic attacks were mounted against government forces, but with no attempt to engage them in battle. Afterward, the guerrillas would melt into the countryside. Only when the guerrillas were strong enough would they form conventional armies and begin open warfare.

The main advantage of the insurgent is the ability to avoid combat with superior forces. As the North Vietnamese showed in the 1968 Tet offensive, a premature escalation of guerrilla into conventional warfare is likely to be counterproductive; on the other hand, as the Tamil Tigers in Sri Lanka demonstrated in a war lasting from 1983 to 2009, conventional forces using conventional tactics in an asymmetric war against guerrilla opponents often struggle against an elusive enemy.

Mao announced the formation of the People's Liberation Army (PLA), and although Chiang controlled the major towns and cities at this stage, the PLA occupied the countryside between them.

By the summer of 1947 the PLA had expanded to the point where it was gaining the upper hand. During 1948, the Fourth Field Army picked off the cities of Manchuria one by one; by October, the Kuomintang was faced by a total of five PLA field armies; and within the next 12 months Chiang's forces were routed.

At the Battle of Xuzhou (Suchow) in November 1948, the best-equipped Kuomintang formations were defeated by combined PLA forces. The remaining pocket of resistance in the north, centered on Beijing (Peking) and Tianjin (Tientsin), was eradicated in January 1949. In April, the PLA crossed the Chang Jiang (Yangtze) River in the course of its southward advance. Nanjing (Nanking) and Shanghai were taken. Finally, Chiang and the remnants of his forces fled to Taiwan, leaving Mao to proclaim the People's Republic of China on October 1, 1949.

WAR IN KOREA

Victory in the civil war did not leave the PLA idle. Attempts to pursue Chiang to Taiwan were soon abandoned, but in 1950 seven PLA divisions occupied Tibet, and soon afterward a force of 300,000 volunteers crossed the Yalu River into Korea.

Previously occupied by Japan, Korea had been divided along the 38th parallel at the end of the war, with Soviet troops occupying the north and U.S. forces in the south. The North Korean president Kim Il Sung claimed the whole of the country, but elections in the south produced a government that was friendly to the United States, and by 1949, both Soviet and U.S. troops had been withdrawn.

In June 1950, however, the North Korean People's Army (KPA) invaded the south. Within weeks the KPA had occupied all of South Korea except for a small area around Pusan in the southeast, where the United States had assembled a predominantly American multinational force under the banner of the United Nations (UN). However, on September 25, the UN commander in chief, General Douglas MacArthur, mounted an amphibious landing at Inchon, high up the west coast of South Korea, which combined with a successful breakout from Pusan to drive the KPA back into the North and bring the UN forces within striking distance of the Yalu. Then, on November 26, the Chinese mounted a counterattack, driving the UN troops back across the 38th parallel as quickly as they had advanced into the North.

The PLA intervention was not a success. It suffered heavy losses before being forced back to the prewar border by UN counterattacks in the spring of 1951. MacArthur, too eager to involve China itself, was dismissed by President Truman, and the war settled down into two years of attrition. By mid-1953, with the South Korean army strong enough to defend the country and the North's supporters tired of what had become an unwinnable struggle, the two sides were ready for an armistice, which came into effect on July 27.

INDIA AND PAKISTAN

In 1945, India was still a part of the British empire, but a decades-old independence movement could not be resisted much longer. It achieved its goal on August 15, 1947. However, the problem of a society divided between 250 million Hindus and 90 million Muslims was not wholly resolved by partitioning the subcontinent into Hindu India and Muslim East and West Pakistan, and within weeks of the two countries becoming independent they were at war.

The northern state of Kashmir had a Muslim majority population but a Hindu maharajah who attempted to remain independent of both sides. However, a Muslim uprising in October 1947 forced his hand, and he accepted union with India. The ensuing fighting between the armies of India and Pakistan ended in a UN-negotiated cease-fire on December 31, 1948, with the former in control of the south and Pakistan occupying the northern mountains.

Subsequently, India became involved in skirmishes with China over disputed border areas in the far northern Ladakh district and the Northeast Frontier Agency (now Arunachal Pradesh), where Indian border posts were overrun in October 1962, before the Chinese called a halt to the fighting in November and withdrew. India's reaction was a concerted drive to expand and modernize its armed forces, with results that would be apparent within 10 years.

THE BLUE HELMETS

In June 1948, the United Nations (UN) established a Truce Supervision Organization (UNTSO) to oversee the truce in Palestine. Since then, UNTSO has supervised the 1949 General Armistice and the cease-fire following the 1967 Arab–Israeli War, while the UN has mounted peacekeeping operations around the world.

A UN Emergency Force (UNEF I) was formed in November 1956 to manage the withdrawal of British, French, and Israeli forces from Egypt. UNEF II was set up in October 1973 to oversee the cease-fire after that month's war between Israel and Egypt, and in June 1974 a Disengagement Observer Force (UNDOF) was established to monitor the cease-fire between Israel and Syria.

The Military Observer Group in India and Pakistan (UNMOGIP) was formed in January 1949 to supervise the cease-fire between those two countries in the disputed north Indian states of Jammu and Kashmir. The UN mounted a major operation in the Congo (ONUC), and since March 1964 the Peacekeeping Force in Cyprus (UNFICYP) has tried to keep Greek and Turkish forces on the island apart.

In recent times, UN forces have been deployed to monitor the Gulf War cease-fire and the Soviet pullout from Afghanistan; to supervise Namibia's transition to independence; to keep peace in the former Yugoslavia; and in 2012 to monitor the uprising in Syria.

India has been troubled by other border insurrections, but Pakistan has remained its main opponent. In 1965, there was renewed conflict in Kashmir and in the Rann of Kutch, on the border between India and West Pakistan, with sporadic clashes erupting into undeclared war in September. A new UN cease-fire was imposed after 22 days, but not before the biggest tank battle since World War II had taken place in the area around Sialkot.

Bangladesh

The major war that had been threatening to break out between India and Pakistan ever since independence came finally in 1971, after East Pakistan had declared itself the independent state of Bangladesh. West Pakistan attempted to suppress the independence movement, and the ensuing civil strife cost hundreds of thousands of lives. Up to 10 million Bengalis took refuge in India, where initial support for guerrilla operations soon gave way to preparations for full-scale military intervention with the assistance of the Soviet Union.

On December 3, Pakistan attempted to forestall the impending Indian invasion of Bangladesh by launching a preemptive invasion of Kashmir and the Punjab. The Indian Air Force survived attacks on its airfields, and the next day the Indian invasion in the east began. Within 13 days the Pakistani commander in Bangladesh had surrendered with 85,000 men, while in the west the Indian army halted the Pakistani advance. By December 17 it was all over—Pakistan had lost Bangladesh.

In 1998, the two nations were involved in a tense nuclear stand-off. Following a Pakistani test of a nuclear missile in April, India detonated five nuclear bombs underground in May, near the Pakistani border. Pakistan responded with five underground tests of its own later that same month. In May 2002, the disputed region of Kashmir once again brought India and Pakistan to the brink of nuclear war. The mountainous region remains a potential flash point between the two nations. Many people in Indian-administered Kashmir, particularly in the Muslim-majority Kashmir Valley, do not want the territory to be governed by India, preferring independence or secession to Pakistan. Although there has been a decline in militant violence in recent years, this phenomenon has been accompanied by a growing number of civilian demonstrations against Indian rule. Kashmir remains a potential flashpoint.

AFGHANISTAN

The Soviet invasion of neighboring Afghanistan in the December following the September 1979 coup against Nur Muhammad Taraki's government resulted in Pakistan becoming a reluctant host to refugees from the fighting and a major conduit of arms destined for the *mujaheddin* resistance groups.

Although the *mujaheddin* succeeded in forcing the Soviets to increase their originally modest invasion force and to adopt new tactics to counter the threat of U.S. Stinger surface-to-air missiles, they never managed to unite in their opposition to the new government installed in Kabul and its Soviet backers. At the same time, the Soviet forces could not quell the resistance, and after eight years of war, the Soviet withdrawal was announced in March 1988.

After years of fighting, a group called the Taliban finally took control of the country in 1996, following its capture of the Afghan capital, Kabul. The Taliban, an extremist militant movement based on Pashtun tribesmen wedded to the strict interpretation of Sharia (Islamic) law and the brutal suppression of women, was aided and trained by Pakistan's intelligence agency (ISI) and also received aid and diplomatic recognition from the United Arab Emirates and Saudi Arabia.

Following the al-Qaeda attacks on New York and Washington in September 2001, the Taliban was driven from power by a U.S.-led coalition. The coalition forces, ably led and fielding a fearsome array of high-tech weaponry, drove the Taliban into the lawless tribal areas of northwest Pakistan, where they regrouped to fight what became the coalition occupation of Afghanistan.

The coalition found it easier to win the war in Afghanistan than to rebuild the country and win the peace. There were some grim precedents for their failure.

A mujaheddin *guerrilla poses for cameramen with one of the U.S. Stinger antiaircraft missiles supplied to the resistance following the ultimately unsuccessful Soviet invasion of Afghanistan. Armed by the United States in the 1970s, many of these Afghan Cold War proxies were to clash with their former allies 30 years later during the so-called War on Terror.*

Afghanistan's predominantly mountainous terrain has been crossed and recrossed by invading armies since the time of Alexander the Great in the fourth century BC. In the nineteenth century, the preeminent colonial power, Great Britain, fought a succession of bloody Afghan wars to secure its hold on the Indian subcontinent. Britain's imperial rival, czarist Russia, meddled in the region and more than a hundred years later the Soviet Union invaded Afghanistan and fought a fruitless 10-year war to subdue *mujaheddin* guerrillas.

The coalition's failure in Afghanistan was a major failure of Counter-Insurgency (COIN) operations. Initially, the U.S. military was distracted by the disintegration of Iraq after the conclusion of the second Gulf War (see page 292). It was not until 2009 that U.S. commanders in Afghanistan focused on protection of the civilian population instead of the elimination of the threat posed by the Taliban. However, their task was fatally hindered by the massive corruption of the Afghan government, headed by Hamid Karzai, whose writ hardly ran farther than the capital, Kabul. Karzai also presided over a vicious and venal warlord network that the Afghans loathed even more than the departed and unlamented Taliban.

Farther obstacles were placed in the way of coalition commanders by the mendacity of the Pakistani intelligence service, their nominal ally, which was intent on playing both ends against the middle in Afghanistan, as it had for many years. Nor were they helped by the low quality of many of the civilian advisers brought in to rehabilitate Afghanistan's shattered infrastructure, or the undertow of bickering between the coalition partners. In a tragic footnote to the misconduct of the war, the agricultural base in previously productive areas, such as Helmand in southern Afghanistan, has been replaced by cultivation of the opium poppy. Afghanistan is now the world's leading supplier of opium.

Even after the U.S. surge of troops in 2009, the number of coalition soldiers in the Afghan theater was insufficient to turn the tide against the Taliban before the declared date of withdrawal in 2014. Moreover, the additional troops wasted much of their energies

U.S. ground trooops on patrol in Afghanistan. By November 2012, 3,027 members of the coalition forces had been killed in the theater, many of them by Improvised Explosive Devices (IEDs), crude, cheap but effective weapons and a characteristic element of asymmetric warfare in the early years of the 21st century.

operating in remote hamlets rather than securing important population centers. It is unlikely that the Afghan army will be able to hold the country together after the departure of the coalition. It is more likely that, for the foreseeable future, Afghanistan will remain a chaotic cockpit in a strategically crucial part of the Indian subcontinent. Moreover, the formidable problems associated with the withdrawal by the coalition of some 100,000 troops and their equipment along land lines that have often been blocked by the Pakistani government will be a headache for the NATO nations in the coming two years. Afghanistan is an easy country to get into but not so easy to get out of.

SRI LANKA

India's direct involvement in Sri Lanka began in July 1987, when an Indian Peacekeeping Force (IPKF) was sent to the island in response to a request from President Jayawardene. The army, largely drawn from the Sinhalese Buddhist majority population, had found it impossible to contain the Hindu Tamil separatists' guerrilla campaign for a separate Tamil state in the northeast of the island. Since the former British colony of Ceylon had become independent in 1948, there had been repeated outbreaks of intercommunal violence, and the arrival of Indian troops only precipitated more.

While the Indians tried with as little success as the Sri Lankans themselves to disarm the guerrillas, the government found itself facing a new insurgency in the south, where the left-wing Sinhalese JVP organization began a violent campaign against the Indian presence. In the end, the Indians withdrew their last troops from the island in March 1990, but this failed to halt the violence. In 1991 a Tamil Tiger suicide bomber, Themuli Rajaratnam, blew herself up with the former Indian prime minister Rajiv Ghandi. The Tamil Tigers' war with the authorities continued until 2009, when they were forced to concede defeat. In 2012, a reconciliation commission was established to examine the lessons of the conflict amid accusations from human-rights activists that the Sri Lankan government had flagrantly breached human rights in the concluding phases of the conflict, when some 27,000 Tamil Tigers and 24,000 government troops had died, along with many thousands of civilians. Afterward, it was estimated that more than 770 square miles (2,000 sq. km) of Sri Lanka were seeded with some 1.6 million land mines.

SOUTHEAST ASIA

Most of the prewar British, French, Dutch, and U.S. colonies in southeast Asia had been overrun by the Japanese during World War II, and the defeat of the colonial powers had given new hope to the budding independence movements in the region. In the wake of the Japanese surrender, Vietnam, Laos, Cambodia, and Indonesia were declared independent by nationalist leaders. By 1949, the Dutch had been forced by guerrilla resistance, and U.S. and United Nations pressure, to accept the inevitability of independence for Indonesia, which duly became a federal republic in the following year. Its subsequent history has included local uprisings and a confrontation with the British over northern Borneo in the early 1960s, while its annexation of West Irian (now Irian Jaya) in 1963 and of the former Portuguese colony of East Timor in 1976 have provided farther opportunities for conflict with separatist insurgents.

In Vietnam, the communist Viet Minh, under political leader Ho Chi Minh and military commander Vo Nguyen Giap, were ready to resist the return of the French. The reoccupation of Hanoi by the French in 1946 was to prove a misleading prologue to an eight-year war in which a classic guerrilla campaign was waged under Giap's leadership. The Viet Minh consolidated their hold on rural areas and then, with the support of the newly victorious Chinese communists, prepared to go on the offensive. Giap's first forays, in 1951, ended with three major defeats, but in 1953 the French established a base in the northern highlands at Dien Bien Phu, to which Giap laid siege. In May 1954, after five months, 10,000 French troops surrendered and France agreed to leave Vietnam, Cambodia, and Laos. Vietnam itself was to be divided, with the Republic of Vietnam in the south run by a noncommunist government.

THE VIETNAM WAR

Ho Chi Minh and the North Vietnamese did not rest on their laurels after ousting the French, and their infiltration of the South, along with continuing communist insurgency in Laos and Cambodia, meant that U.S. support for South Vietnam's new president, Ngo Dinh Diem, grew steadily more military in nature. In the late 1950s, it progressed from training the new republic's army to deploying military advisers in the country, and by 1962, the arrangement had been formalized with the establishment of the Military Assistance Command. Within three years, the number of U.S. advisers had grown to 27,000, and in March 1965, President Johnson's decision to commit combat troops to the war was symbolized by the landing of U.S. Marines on the beaches at Da Nang.

Two decades of war

During the ensuing 10 years of war, the U.S. forces' frustration grew in line with their size. Operating largely

The door gunner of a U.S. army helicopter fires his M60 machine gun at an unseen target on the ground in Vietnam. The search-and-destroy tactics developed by the Americans in Vietnam, with troops landed by helicopter at remote locations for sweeps through the countryside in search of their elusive opponents, proved ineffective despite the massive scale of the U.S. military involvement in the country. U.S. combat operations had ended by January 1973, and South Vietnam finally fell in April 1975.

by helicopter from fortified bases, but also mounting massive bombing raids involving a whole panoply of new aircraft and weapons, the Americans rarely found targets to match their massive firepower. An exception was provided by the all-out Tet (New Year) offensive mounted by the North Vietnamese Army in February 1968, but although this proved an expensive failure for the North, its unprecedented scale served to undermine U.S. claims that it was making progress in the war.

By the beginning of 1969, there were more than half a million U.S. military personnel in the country, but public support for the war had begun to erode. President Johnson had declined to stand for reelection, and his successor, Richard Nixon, had committed himself to "Vietnamization" of the war and "peace with honor" for the United States. In effect, this meant a steady reduction in the number of U.S. personnel in South Vietnam, the transfer of military hardware to the Army of the Republic of Vietnam (ARVN), and an increased reliance on bombing, first to extend the war into Cambodia and

Laos, and later to repel a new North Vietnamese offensive in the spring of 1972.

The 1972 U.S. bombing campaigns, Linebacker I and II, were ended in December, and in January 1973 peace talks in Paris finally produced a cease-fire agreement. By this stage, the U.S. army had ceased combat operations in the country and, during the next two years, the North Vietnamese army increased the number of troops deployed in the South in support of the Viet Cong guerrillas. In March 1975, the North Vietnamese began a new full-scale offensive, and on April 30 Saigon fell, finally ending a war that had lasted 20 years.

APOCALYPSE AND AFTER: VIETNAM AND CAMBODIA

The communist victory in Vietnam was paralleled by the Khmer Rouge takeover in Cambodia in April and the accession to power of the Pathet Lao in Laos later in the year. In Cambodia, Pol Pot's regime renamed the country Kampuchea, emptied the capital of its inhabitants, and set up a "reeducation" program that involved wholesale slaughter of the population.

The resulting flood of refugees into Vietnam, coupled with Khmer incursions across the border, provoked Vietnam to invade Kampuchea in 1978, driving Pol Pot back into the jungle and installing a new government in Phnom Penh.

Under the administration of the UN in 1993, Cambodia held elections, which led to the establishment of a new constitution and the reinstatement of Norodon Sihanouk as king. The Khmer Rouge refused to take part in the elections and rejected peace talks, and were finally outlawed by the Cambodian government in 1994. Following Pol Pot's death in 1998, the UN pulled out of trials of other top-level Khmer Rouge leaders because of doubts that the tribunals were independent. Today, Cambodia is ruled by Hun Sen's Cambodian People's Party.

In 2009, Kang Kek Iew was the first Khmer Rouge commander to be found guilty of war crimes and crimes against humanity in his role as commandant of the S21 extermination camp. In a UN-backed Cambodian court, he was sentenced to 40 years' imprisonment, a term that, in 2012, was increased to life. However, the presence of former Khmer Rouge at the highest levels in the current Cambodian government, notably Hun Sen, himself a Khmer Rouge before he broke with Pol Pot, has militated against wholesale prosecutions.

ISRAEL AND ITS NEIGHBORS

Wars in the Middle East between Israel and its neighbors have not matched events farther east in terms of the size and numbers of countries involved, the numbers of casualties, or the sheer scale of conflict. However, the Israeli armed forces have established a reputation as one of the most effective military organizations ever seen with their repeated victories over the armies of much bigger Arab states across the country's borders.

FATAH AND HAMAS

Fatah was founded in the 1950s with the goal of creating a Palestinian state, principally by waging a terrorist war against Israel. One of its founders was Yasser Arafat. In 1995, Fatah spawned an offshoot, Tanzim (Organization), dedicated to high-profile attacks on Israeli targets. Hamas came into being in 1987 at the time of the Palestinian uprising (Intifada) in Gaza and the West Bank. Although Hamas shares Fatah's belief in the destruction of the state of Israel, it has often been both politically and militarily at odds with its Palestinian rival. Tensions were exacerbated after the death, in 2005, of the Palestinian Liberation Organization's leader Yasser Arafat, and relations farther declined after Hamas's victory in the 2006 elections in Palestine. Fighting between the two factions in 2006–7 left Hamas in control of Gaza while Fatah presided over the Palestinian National Authority on the Weat Bank. Attempts in Doha and Cairo to effect a reconciliation were unsuccessful.

A knocked-out Egyptian Sherman tank in the Sinai desert, 1956. Israel's swift and tactically brilliant conquest of Egyptian territory east of the Suez Canal, masterminded by the Israeli Defence Force's astute and dashing Chief of Staff, Moshe Dayan, paved the way for the abortive joint invasion of the Suez Canal Zone by Britain and France.

Israel's Declaration of Independence in 1948 effectively constituted a declaration of war, and the new state's armed forces were confronted immediately by the armies of Transjordan, Syria, Lebanon, Iraq, and Egypt. United Nations intervention helped secure a series of temporary truces, which reinforced Israeli military success, and by July 1949, all five Arab countries had conceded defeat, swelling the exodus of hundreds of thousands of Palestinians from the new state.

However, none had conceded Israel's right to exist, and the region has been subject to a series of subsequent wars. In 1956, Israel joined Britain and France in invading Egypt, demolishing Egyptian resistance in the Sinai before withdrawing from the conquered territory. In June 1967, the Israeli armed forces defeated those of Egypt, Syria, and Jordan in the space of six days, and in 1973 they took barely three times as long to repel attacks by Egypt and Syria. Subsequently, Israel became involved in the Lebanon, where Palestinian guerrillas had begun operations after being expelled from Jordan in 1970 and where conflict between the Christian and Muslim populations erupted into civil war in 1975.

Israel invaded southern Lebanon in 1978 and mounted a full-scale invasion in 1982, forcing the Palestinian Liberation Organization (PLO) to quit the country but finding itself entangled as a result. Israel finally withdrew its forces in 1985, although it has continued occasional military intervention, and since December 1987 it has had to cope with civil insurrection in the territories on the West Bank of the Jordan and the Gaza Strip. It withdrew from the last in September 2005.

The so-called "road map," setting out a two-state solution to the Palestine problem, has stalled while Israel built a security fence on the West Bank along its pre-1967 border, which looped into Palestinian areas, and focused its attention on strengthening and expanding the biggest Jewish settlements on the West Bank.

Iranian soldiers on a Soviet tank during the Iran–Iraq War (1980-88), the longest conventional war of the 20th century after the Sino-Japanese War (1937- 1945). The cost of the war, some half a million soldiers and civilians killed and many more wounded, evoked the slaughter of the Great War, as did the crude "human wave" infantry tactics employed by both sides and the use of chemical weapons, including mustard gas.

Nevertheless, Israel's northern and southern borders remained under constant threat. In 2006, an artillery assault launched from Lebanon by the Shiite Muslim organization Hezbollah (Party of God) on Israel's northern border communities, the cross-border killing of two Israeli soldiers, and the abduction of another soldier prompted a short Israeli incursion into Lebanon.

At the end of 2008, the Israelis, stung by some 3,300 rockets fired into their territory over a 12-month period by the military wing of the Palestinian organization Hamas (Islamic Resistance Movement), launched a three-week assault on the Gaza Strip. Air strikes were followed by ground incursions in which 1,300 Palestinians were killed and 13 Israeli soldiers died. This provoked a storm of international criticism. While the Gaza Strip has one of the highest population densities in the world, Israel has the highest ratio of defense spending to gross domestic product (GDP) of all developed nations.

IRAN–IRAQ WAR

In contrast to the short-lived Arab–Israeli wars, the war that began in September 1980, when President Saddam Hussein of Iraq began an invasion of the new Islamic republic of Iran, was to drag on for nearly eight years. By the time it ended in July 1988, it had cost a million lives and an estimated thousand billion dollars.

Militarily inconclusive, the war involved some worrying new developments. It fostered a growth in new sources of modern weapons, as the arms industries of developing countries helped to fulfill the appetite for guns, artillery rockets, and ammunition that the traditional suppliers of munitions officially declined to meet. Chemical weapons were used, and both countries started to manufacture ballistic missiles, as each sought means to strike at the other's cities, highlighting the spread of such missiles to large areas of the Third World. In addition, attacks on third-party oil tankers drew Western naval forces into the Persian Gulf, and the Iranian threat led Saudi Arabia to acquire intermediate-range ballistic missiles from China.

END OF EMPIRE IN AFRICA

In 1945, much of Africa was administered by the old colonial powers of Europe. During the ensuing decades their administrations have been replaced by independent national governments, frequently after wars of independence and seldom without subsequent conflicts.

Probably the biggest conflict on the continent in recent years is the war fought in the Democratic Republic of Congo, which raged between 1998 and 2002. Dubbed by some as "Africa's World War," the conflict involved the armies of six nations, split the vast country into rebel- and government-held regions, and killed an estimated two-and-a-half-million people, largely through disease and starvation. Rwanda and Uganda joined Congolese rebels in their fight against Congo's leader, Laurent Kabila, because they accused him of backing groups, particularly the Hutu militia, that threatened their security. In response to this, the surrounding countries of Zimbabwe, Namibia, and Angola joined forces with Kabila. A peace treaty was signed in 2002, following a pledge by Congo to disarm and arrest Rwandan Hutu militia in return for the withdrawal of Rwandan troops. The following year, agreement was reached between the warring factions within Congo to end hostilities. Under the agreement, Joseph Kabila (Laurent's son) remained president until 2006, after which he retained the post in democratic elections.

However, in spite of its massive reserves of strategic metals and minerals—including half the world's cobalt and nearly two-thirds of the global supply of coltan, a vital element of cell phones—the Democratic Republic of Congo, which is two-thirds the size of Europe, languished at the bottom of the UN's index of human development. In 2008, fighting flared in the eastern half of the country and in 2009 Rwandan troops were invited in by the government to mount a joint operation against rebel Rwandan Hutu militias. The fighting was ended with a peace agreement signed on March 23, 2009.

In the summer of 2012, a resurgence of fighting in Congo sparked by self-styled M23 rebel forces, named after the March 2009 agreement and led by Bosco Ntaganda, brought the rebels to within 30 miles (50 km) of Goma, the capital of the province of North Kivu and the headquarters of the UN mission in Congo.

The town fell at the end of November. The M23 rebels had taken the most important city in eastern Congo, which had become the world's largest peacekeeping operation, although the UN troops tasked with this role offered no resistance. The attitude of the war-weary civilian population of Goma was extremely circumspect, as M23 had gained an unenviable reputation for human rights abuses during its brief life. Its leader, Bosco Ntaganda, and four of his colleagues have been identified by Navi Pillay, the UN commissioner for human rights, as "among the worst perpetrators of human rights violations in the Democratic Republic of Congo, or in the world". In the autumn of 2012 there was little doubt that that Ntaganda's intention was to control Congo's abundant mineral wealth but the precise details of his agenda were difficult to disentangle from the ambitions of Rwanda, which in all probability, was supplying Ntaganda with direct military support, including night-vision goggles and 120 mm (4¾ in) mortars. What remained abundantly clear was that Joseph Kabila's government in Kinshasa, fatally compromised by the deal struck with Rwanda in 2009, had lost control over the territory in eastern Congo.

Rwandan genocide

Related to the war in the Democratic Republic of Congo, the 1994 slaughter in Rwanda of around 800,000 people of the Tutsi tribe will go down as one of the bloodiest episodes in African history. Carried out by soldiers, policemen, and ordinary members of the public, the Hutu population's 100-day genocide was sparked by the death of Hutu President Juvenal Habyarimama, whose plane was shot down over Kigali airport on April 6, 1994, but had its roots in 80 years of resentment and inequality between the two tribes. Until 2012, Rwanda employed traditional "gacaca" community courts to try those suspected of taking part in the 1994 genocide. Key individuals suspected of orchestrating the massacre were tried before an International Criminal Tribunal in Tanzania. However, Congo and its smaller eastern neighbor Rwanda remain locked in a deadly embrace, a running sore exacerbated by Rwandan designs on the huge mineral wealth in eastern Congo.

With the exception of the December 1989 invasion of Panama, the United States has largely avoided direct military involvement in Latin America, but various forms of military assistance are used to help combat insurgency and, more recently, the drugs trade. Here, soldiers from the U.S. and Ecuadorean armed forces take part in a combined exercise.

CONFLICT IN LATIN AMERICA

The Central American states of Guatemala, Honduras, El Salvador, Nicaragua, Costa Rica, and Panama appear to exist in a perpetual condition of actual or incipeint insurgency. The endemic lack of stability in the region was highlighted by the 1969 war that erupted between Honduras and El Salvador, ostensibly over the riots that accompanied a World Cup soccer match between the two countries in San Salvador but actually reflecting Hondurans' resentment at the numbers of Salvadorean immigrants in their country.

In the 1980s and early 1990s, general economic inequality, frequently sustained by military rule and the widespread use of terror as an instrument of government, ensured no shortage of recruits to the various guerrilla movements, and counterinsurgency campaigns against them had little effect.

Farther south, at the start of the 1990s, the trade in cocaine grown in Bolivia and Peru and processed in Colombia for shipment to the United States and Europe was coming to be seen as a potential military problem. Sendero Luminoso (Shining Light) guerrillas were active throughout Peru and particularly in the coca-growing area of the Upper Huallaga Valley. Their protection of the coca growers and shippers raised concern both locally and in Washington. Alliances between the enormously wealthy cocaine cartels and guerrillas with long experience of jungle warfare added a new dimension to the insurgents' activities.

Falkland Islands

The military coups that have been a feature of South America's modern history have usually involved more violence against their own inhabitants than external aggression, although the military government that came to power in Argentina in 1976 managed to become involved in a war with Britain over the sovereignty of the Falkland Islands (or Malvinas) in the South Atlantic. Ultimately, the task force despatched by Britain was able to recapture the islands from the Argentine forces that had occupied them in April 1982. Democracy was restored in Argentina in 1983 but tensions over the Falklands rumbled on. In 2012, the Argentine president Christina Fernandez de Kirchner restated Argentine claims to the islands.

In the autumn of 2012, the Falklands were defended by a garrison of some 1,200 troops, comprising infantry, engineers and logistics and signal units. Rapier missile batteries and four Typhoon Eurofighter jets provided air defence. Maritime patrolling was performed by a C-130 Hercules. The United Kingdom's Joint Rapid Reaction Force, containing elements of all three services, could be deployed to the Falklands if the UK government received intelligence of a specific threat posed to the Falklands' integrity.

However, doubts persist about the United Kingdom's ability to defend the Falklands against Argentine aggression. In 1982 Britain was able to despatch two aircraft carriers, Invincible and Hermes, to the South Atlantic. In 2012 the Royal Navy was unable to project air power by sea as the two new Queen Elizabeth class carriers, similar in size to the US Navy's Nimitz class carriers and flying Lockheed Martin F-25 Lightnings, will not enter operational service until 2018. Until that time the air defence of the Falklands, wholly dependent on the island's airstrips at Mount Pleasant and Port Stanley, will remain problematic if their runways are disabled by the Argentine air force. It remains highly unlikely that our NATO ally France would agree to provide air cover for a future British task force in the South Atlantic.

INTERNATIONAL JUSTICE

In 1993, the UN Security Council created the International Criminal Tribunal for the Former Yugoslavia, the first international war crimes tribunal since the Nuremberg process opened in November 1945. In 1993, impunity for wartime atrocities remained the norm. However, by 2012, international justice is a regular feature of conflict resolution, and amnesties are no longer readily traded for peace. Of the 161 individuals indicted by the Yugoslavian tribunal, none remain at large.

The International Criminal Court (ICC) came into being in July 2002 and can prosecute individuals for genocide, crimes against humanity, and war crimes, but only those committed after the court's creation. From 2017, it will be able to prosecute those who commit crimes of aggression. The ICC is based in the Hague, in the Netherlands, but its proceedings can take place anywhere.

In the summer of 2012, states that accepted the jurisdiction of the ICC included all those in South America, the majority of the European states and approximately half those in Africa. Some 50 countries, including Russia, have signed but not ratified the Rome statute, which established the court. Some 40 other states, including China and India, have neither signed nor ratified the statute.

By 2008, the ICC was staffed by some 600 staff drawn from 83 states. By fall of 2012, the court had launched investigations into seven specifically African cases, in the Democratic Republic of Congo, Uganda, the Central African Republic, Darfur, Sudan, Kenya, Libya and Ivory Coast. There has been criticism of the African bias of the ICC, but it should be noted that since 1993 the United Nations has also established more than 50 international fact-finding or investigative commissions to examine incidents ranging from the 2007 assassination of Benazir Bhutto to the 2009 suppression of demonstrations in Guinea.

HIGH-TECH BATTLEFIELD

In the immediate postwar years, atomic weapons were the main area of military research and development, but other advances increased the range, power, and effectiveness of conventional weapons. In the course of subsequent decades, tanks, warships, submarines, and aircraft have used new methods of propulsion, new classes of weapons, and new types of sensors plus the computers needed to control them.

The result is that aircraft now routinely achieve supersonic speeds, submarines remain submerged for weeks on end, many surface warships have been relieved of the need for frequent refueling, and tanks have achieved new levels of speed and agility. Missiles have affected every area of warfare. Satellites, radar, infrared, and laser technology have provided new levels of accuracy in the detection and tracking of targets and the aiming and guidance of the weapons used to engage them.

JETS AND ROCKETS

The first jet aircraft were in service before the end of World War II. They were already faster than their piston-engined counterparts, but the full potential of jet propulsion is even now a long way from realization.

The U.S. F-86 Sabres and Soviet MiG-15s that fought the first jet combats over Korea were powered by heavy, thirsty engines that were capable of speeds of more than 600 mph (965 km/h). By the end of the 1950s, the addition of afterburners, which mix fuel with the jet exhaust and reignite it to boost the thrust, had enabled fighter aircraft to exceed twice the speed of sound, if only for brief periods because of the sheer amount of fuel consumed.

Since then, engines have become steadily lighter, more powerful, and more fuel efficient. Vectored thrust has enabled aircraft to take off in a matter of a few tens of yards and land vertically. And techniques for deflecting the exhaust of a standard fighter have added new levels of maneuverability.

Of course, it was rocket propulsion that took the first manned aircraft through the sound barrier, but the main application of rocket technology has been in missiles. These are now deployed in all sizes from lightweight shoulder-launched antiaircraft and antitank weapons to multistage ballistic missiles.

The missile threat

There have been several times during the last 50 years when the lethality of missiles has seemed to be about to make whole classes of weapons redundant. Instead, the result has been the development of new forms of anti-missile defense and, in turn, new methods of increasing missiles' effectiveness.

In 1967, the Israeli destroyer *Eilat* was sunk by a Soviet Styx missile fired by an Egyptian gunboat. The initial conclusion drawn from this encounter was that warships of any size had suddenly become hopelessly vulnerable to any attacks by the smallest missile-armed vessel. However, just as the analogous threat of the torpedo at the end of the nineteenth century was contained by appropriate defensive measures, so new warships were equipped with rapid-fire guns and antimissile missiles capable of reducing the threat to acceptable levels. The sinking of HMS *Sheffield* by an air-launched Exocet missile in the South Atlantic in 1982, during the Falklands War, and the damage done to USS *Stark*, also by an Exocet, in the Persian Gulf in 1987, happened because the sensors that should have detected the approach of the missiles were not functioning.

Similarly, in the early stages of the 1973 Arab–Israeli war many Israeli tanks and aircraft were destroyed by the Egyptians' shoulder-launched Soviet missiles. Once again, some analysts were quick to conclude that the missile threat had made armor and air power too vulnerable to survive on the battlefield. But yet again, countermeasures in the shape of new forms of tank armor and air-launched infrared decoys sent the missile designers back to the drawing board to work on multiple or top-attack warheads for antitank missiles, and more discriminating surface-to-air missile-seekers, able to distinguish real jet exhausts from decoys.

PRECISION GUIDANCE

The most dramatic advance in military technology of the last half century has been the application of precision-guidance techniques to virtually every class of weapon. The earliest form of missile guidance to be used operationally—in the shape of the German Fritz X and Hs 293 air-to-surface missiles of 1943—was command guidance. This method uses a wire or radio link to transmit the operator's steering commands to the missile.

Early manual command-guided missiles were steered by the operator using a joy stick, but the process is automated in modern semiautomatic systems, such as the U.S. Tube-launched, Optically tracked, Wire-guided (TOW) antitank missile and Patriot long-range Surface-to-Air Missile (SAM). In both cases, the system must track both target and missile—visually in the case of TOW or by means of radar in the case of Patriot's aircraft and missile targets—in order to generate the appropriate steering commands. Many missiles dispense with this complication by providing the missile itself with a means of tracking and homing on the target.

Homing guidance relies on the ability of a seeker carried by the missile to detect radiation emitted by or reflected from its target. It is classified as active, semiactive, or passive, according to whether the missile generates the radiation itself, detects the reflections of a signal from another source, or homes on the target's own emissions.

To guide the missile effectively, the seeker needs to be able to distinguish the target

Threat warning and target information are vital if guided weapons are to be used effectively. The E-3 airborne warning and command system (AWACS) aircraft operated by the U.S. Air Force and several of its allies can monitor a large volume of sky and transmit target coordinates to friendly forces.

The U.S. Army's Apache uses a sophisticated nose-mounted sensor system to detect and track targets for the Hellfire laser-guided anti-tank missiles mounted on its wings.

The U.S. Copperhead guided projectile is fired from a conventional 155-mm howitzer. Like the Paveway laser-guided bomb, the Copperhead is unpowered but can be steered in the terminal stages of its flight, using its laser seeker and control system, to hit a designated target.

from background radiation, so aircraft against the neutral background of the sky are a principal target for radar-homing missiles. Active radar guidance is used by the U.S. Phoenix long-range air-to-air missile (AAM) and advanced medium-range air-to-air missile (AMRAAM), both of which carry their own radar transmitters to illuminate the target. Other medium-range AAMs, such as the U.S. Sparrow and its British Skyflash and Italian Aspide derivatives, rely on the launch aircraft's radar to provide the target illumination.

Some Soviet missiles were reported to have seekers capable of homing on hostile aircraft radar emissions, but the main Western application of passive radar homing is in weapons, such as the U.S. Harm and British Alarm, which are designed to locate and attack hostile ground-based radar transmitters.

Aircraft are also good targets for passive infra-red homing missiles, which seek out the heat radiated by engine exhausts or hot areas of the airframe. Both short-range AAMs, such as Sidewinder, and low-level SAMs, such as Stinger, use infrared seekers to guide them to their targets. Laser homing, using the coherent light beams emitted by lasers, is used to illuminate targets for many types of guided weapon, from the Copperhead artillery round to the Hellfire antitank missile that is carried by the U.S. Army's AH-64 Apache helicopter.

Long-range weapons, such as cruise and intercontinental ballistic missiles, are guided by navigational instead of homing systems. The most common is inertial navigation, which uses accelerometers and gyros to measure the rate and direction of the vehicle's acceleration and calculate its range and bearing from the launch point.

In the 60 years since the end of World War II, whole new classes of weapons have appeared. The Tomahawk sea-launched cruise missile, shown here being launched from a U.S. warship, has a range of 1,500 miles (2,415 km) against land targets or 300 miles (485 km) against ships, and can carry nuclear as well as conventional warheads.

air combat. The first missiles designed to be launched by aircraft against other aircraft were unguided, so they were fired in salvoes to increase the probability of a hit. More promising was the addition of infrared homing warheads designed to locate and home in on hot jet exhausts. The first such heat-seeking missile was the U.S. Sidewinder, advanced versions of which are still in service along with similar weapons produced in many other countries.

Infrared homing missiles are limited to relatively short ranges. Radar seekers, such as those used on the U.S. Sparrow and the more recent advanced medium-range air-to-air missiles (AMRAAM, or Am-ram), promised to be able to engage hostile aircraft at much longer ranges. However, there are problems in distinguishing friendly aircraft from hostile ones at ranges beyond the visual, and Sparrow has achieved only limited success in combat. A new complication is the appearance of anti-radar missiles designed to home in on the radar signals of either the fighter or the missile itself, a development that some analysts have suggested could make current radar-guided air-to-air missiles obsolete at a stroke.

LAND COMBAT

The perceived threat to the tank in the early 1970s was very serious because the tank was, and remains, the principal battlefield weapon. Its combination of mobility and firepower makes it the most powerful and versatile weapon in the modern army, and consequently the linchpin of both offensive and defensive tactical operations.

The armies with the most sophisticated arsenals are Russia and members of NATO, particularly the United States. Designed to fight and win a conventional war in central Europe, tanks were developed in accordance with contrasting strategies and operational concepts, although their weapons show many similarities in function and capabilities. Soviet determination to avoid a repetition of the enormous casualties suffered during World War II gave rise to a strategy of offensive operations involving massive firepower and rapid maneuver, using heavy concentrations of self-propelled artillery to soften up defenses before tanks and mechanized infantry formations would move quickly to exploit any openings created, to seize strategic objectives, such as cities, so that tactical nuclear weapons used against

The British Aerospace Harrier Vertical/ Short Take off and Landing (V/STOL) fighter, close-support and reconnaissance aircraft. Developed in the 1960s, the Harrier has seen combat in the Falklands, Bosnia, Kosovo, Iraq and Afghanistan. The RAF controversially scrapped its fleet of Harriers in 2010 but the multi-role aircraft has been flown in upgraded form since 1983 by the US Marine Corps as the Harrier II.

them would end up destroying the very things they were supposed to protect.

In January 2006, the Polish government published more than 1,000 declassified documents. Among them was the Soviet 1979 battle plan "Seven Days to the Rhine," which envisaged a blitzkrieg-style attack on Western Europe, and the use of nuclear weapons in response to a NATO nuclear first strike. This remained Warsaw Pact battle doctrine until the late 1980s and explains why, toward the end of the Cold War, up to 250 tactical-range nuclear-armed rockets were based in Poland.

NATO's ability to withdraw and counterattack in the face of an offensive was constrained by the need to protect the territory it was designed to defend from becoming a battlefield. It tried to counter Soviet numerical superiority by the application of advanced technology. In the days when a Soviet offensive was a possibility, NATO's defenses involved the use of everything from long-range artillery to short-range missiles and rockets, with tanks, supported by infantry and tactical air assets, concentrating on their opposing counterparts.

Air support

Air power has become an integral part of land warfare. The rapid deployment of troops and equipment is effected by helicopters, while armed gunships have been developed to engage armored targets. The U.S. Army's AH-64 Apache, which entered service in 1984, has proved a superb tank-killer. With a range of 300 miles (483 km) the Apache is built to endure high-intensity battle conditions, operate in bad weather and uses advanced avionics to function by day or night. It is armed with an M230 chain gun and carries Hellfire anti-tank missiles and Hydra 2¾ in (70 mm) unguided rockets. Its FLIR (forward-looking infrared) system, housed in its nose sight, gives the Apache a deep strike capability hundreds of miles ahead of a front line.

Tactical fighter-bombers carrying out close air-support and battlefield-interdiction missions are part of any commander's ideal tactical repertoire. Airborne sensors provide much of the information on which decisions must be based. Air-combat fighters are essential to provide battlefield air superiority.

STEALTH AIRCRAFT

Stealth, or low-observable (LO) technology, is a quality and design goal affecting the configuration of many large items of military kit. Although it is a pressing preoccupation of today's weapons designers and engineers, stealth technology, which is in effect a combination of technologies, has a history stretching back to the development by the British in the 1930s of radio direction finding (RDF) or, as the Americans later called it, radar. Bomber aircraft and surface ships could be easily detected by radar, and submarines by its sound equivalent, sonar—the sending and receiving of sound impulses through water. Stealth technology aims to reduce or eliminate this vulnerability.

In World War II, the Luftwaffe experimented with primitive stealth technology. The Horten HO 229, a jet configured like a "flying wing," first flew in January 1945 but never became operational. The HO 229 had a lower radar reflection than conventional aircraft with their tailplanes and round fuselages. Its innovative design was later reflected in the postwar eight-engined Northrop YB-49, the so-called "Flying Wing," a project that was canceled by the U.S. Air Force in 1949.

In the 1950s, military designers on both sides of the Iron Curtain developed ways of reducing radar cross section (RCS). One of the most striking examples was the introduction in 1964 of the SR-71, designed at Lockheed's "Skunk Works" to operate at heights and speeds beyond radar detection. In the 1970s, the US Airforce used the latest computers to develop the first generation of true stealth warplanes. By using carefully selected synthetic materials with low radar reflectivity, and a shape that reduced the area of reflecting surfaces, an aircraft could be designed with a very low "radar signature," enabling it to remain invisible to radar at ranges at which other aircraft would be detected.

The first true stealth aircraft was the single-seat Lockheed F-117 Nighthawk, a fighter-bomber that entered service in 1983 and usually carried a 5,000 pound payload. The Nighthawk's stealthily faceted airframe required a huge amount of maintenance and it was retired in 2008. Its successor was the two-man Northrop Grumman B-2 Spirit. A stealth heavy bomber designed to penetrate deep antiaircraft defenses, the B-2's primary Cold War mission was eliminated by the collapse of the Soviet Union in the early 1990s and production was cut back. At today's prices, the cost of each B-2 represents an outlay of just over a billion dollars.

The B-2 made its operational debut in 1999 in the NATO action over Kosovo. It was later used in Operation Enduring Freedom against targets in Afghanistan and in Operation Odyssey Dawn, the UN-mandated enforcement of the no-fly zone over Libya. The B-2 has an operational range of some 6,900 miles (11,000 km) and a maximum speed at 40,000 feet (12,000 m) of 630 mph (1000 km/h). It can bomb up to 16 targets in a single pass when armed with 1,000 pound or 2,000 pound bombs, and up to 80 when armed with 500 lb bombs.

A B-2 Stealth bomber from the 509th Bomb Wing at Whiteman Air Force Base, Mo., flies over the St. Louis Arch on Aug. 10 2006.

NAVAL WARFARE

In common with other examples of modern military technology, warships have become vastly more capable since 1945. Only the U.S. Navy has managed to sustain the enormous expense of nuclear-powered aircraft carriers, from which a comprehensive range of fighters, bombers, and antisubmarine aircraft operate. But the Harrier, Sea Harrier, and Harrier II STOVL (short take-off, vertical landing) aircraft have enabled several smaller navies to operate compact but effective carriers, and both the Soviet and French navies developed new large aircraft carriers in the 1980s.

IRAQ WARS

The six-week war that ended Iraq's occupation of Kuwait in January/February 1991 demonstrated the effectiveness of the latest generation of Western military technology, as Iraq's ostensibly powerful armed forces were overwhelmed by a sustained campaign of aerial bombardment and a crushing armored ground offensive. The Iraqi dictator, Saddam Hussein, was allowed to remain in power at the war's conclusion.

However, he was captured, tried, and executed at the conclusion of the second Iraq war of 2003, which was justified largely on the basis of the erroneous claim that Iraq possessed weapons of mass destruction (WMDs) and Saddam's supposed links to terrorist organizations. The war was declared all but over by US President George W. Bush 34 days after the start of hostilities. Thereafter, the victorious coalition's lack of plans for post-war Iraq were starkly exposed.

The occupation of Iraq became a potent global recruiting pretext for extreme Islamist fighters, compounded the huge refugee problem created by the war, and allowed Iran to exert regional influence through terror networks operating inside Iraq and active intervention in Iraqi territory by its Revolutionary National Guard. The last US combat brigade left Iraq in August 2010. The cost of the war and occupation to the USA was some $3 trillion.

A new player on the naval strategic board, China deployed its first aircraft carrier in 2011 in the South China Sea and in so doing compelled the United States to reassess the thrust of its global-power projection, which is massively dependent on 10 carrier task forces that operate worldwide. Much thought has been given to the possibility that, in a future crisis, the Chinese might be tempted to attack and sink a target such as a U.S. aircraft carrier, however well it may be defended. The loss of even a single carrier would reduce the U.S.'s naval air power by some 10 percent and has the potential to cause thousands of U.S. casualties.

At the same time, even small frigates are capable of operating antisubmarine helicopters while mounting a medium-caliber gun along with varying mixes of antiship, anti-aircraft, and antisubmarine missiles and the means of detecting and tracking targets for them. Electronic countermeasures, ranging from jammers able to interfere with the seekers of hostile missiles to launchers for radar decoys, are a vital part of their armory. And lightweight sonar systems provide the means for guarding against the ever-present menace of the submarine.

In fact, underwater warfare is an area where there is little scope for relaxation. Ballistic-missile-armed submarines are the last line of nuclear deterrence, and ceaseless activity is aimed at identifying their characteristics so that they can be tracked and attacked if necessary.

Conventional submarines also threaten the surface ships on which international trade depends, and the navies that are the principal means of projecting national power overseas in defense of national interests. Accordingly, maritime patrol aircraft, surface ships and their helicopters, and hunter-killer submarines constantly practice the techniques of detecting, tracking, and attacking hostile submarines against the day when they may need to do it for real.

In the context of the global projection of naval power, NATO has extended its reach from 2000 in the international effort to control the scourge of piracy on the high seas. This rapidly spreading phenomenon is reflected in the hijacking, and subsequent ransoming, of high-value merchant vessels and individual sailors by gangs of pirates. In recent years, the epicenter of this criminal enterprise has spread from the Straits of Malacca in the Far East to the waters off Nigeria, in West Africa, and the seas off the Horn of Africa, on Africa's eastern seaboard, where chaotic failed states provide havens for pirate gangs. In 2009, NATO launched Operation Ocean Shield, an antipiracy mission, the backbone of which was provided by the U.S. Navy. Its operations were subsequently extended into the Indian Ocean and the South China Sea.

THE COMPUTER REVOLUTION

The ability of modern military hardware to carry out its designated tasks rests to a large extent on computer technology. Everything from radios designed for counterjamming by rapid changes in frequencies, to aircraft in terrain-following flight, depends on the ability of computers to sort and analyze data fast, and then to come up with the appropriate response. The eventual aim is to use computers to analyze the whole tactical picture and suggest appropriate courses of action to the commander.

TERRORISM

To many, the world seemed a safer place after the collapse of the USSR in the early 1990s. However, the fragmentation of the USSR ensured that the certainties of the Cold War were replaced by the myriad strategic uncertainties of the early twenty-first century. For example, the successor Russian federation's determination to retain the Caucasus—the pathway to Caspian Sea oil and the Middle East—has led to two brutal wars in Chechnya and the destabilization of the region. The Russians presented the Chechnya campaigns as part of the West's War on Terror, which echoes Soviet cynicism of the Stalin era. Another echo of Stalin's time is Russia's continuing heavy investment in espionage as a method of penetrating Western institutions, stealing their secrets, particularly those relating to advanced technology, and distorting decision making. In this murky arena, little has changed since the days of the Cold War. Nevertheless, it is as well to remember that in 2012 Russia was a nation with a shrinking population and a shriveling industrial and technological base. But in spite of its problematic future, Russia's 2011 arms exports amounted to some $7.9 billion, compared with a U.S. figure of $9.9 billion. This indicates that both nations retain a stake in fighting Cold War-type proxy battles on foreign soil. In this context, rugged, relatively simple Soviet-era weaponry—notably the AK-47 assault rifle—has proved effective against the overengineered and more expensive armories deployed by the Americans and their surrogates.

In contrast, in 2011 the United States spent an overall $689 billion on arms compared with Russia's spend of $64.1 billion. However, that huge discrepancy has to be seen in the light of the United States' huge commitments in Iraq and Afghanistan.

U.S. dominance

The United States remains the preeminent global military power, although it has taken a battering in recent asymmetrical wars—conflicts fought by technologically advanced First World countries against far weaker but tactically agile Third World opponents. The seeds of doubt planted during the Vietnam War have germinated into a morale-sapping harvest in the second decade of the twenty-first century. The United States courted farther controversy with its War on Terror strategy by introducing the policy of "special rendition"—in effect, the abduction of terrorist suspects to countries where, in all probability, torture might be used to extract information of use to U.S. intelligence agencies, which were themselves closely involved in the business of rendition. In September 2006, President George W. Bush confirmed the reality of rendition while denying the use of torture, to which he ascribed a very narrow definition.

Linked with the policy of rendition was the part played in the War on Terror by the Guantanamo detention camp, established on a U.S. naval base in Cuba. The facility was opened in January 2002 and eventually housed some 779 terrorist suspects. Bush's successor,

UNMANNED AERIAL COMBAT

The Central Intelligence Agency (CIA) began experimenting with remotely piloted reconnaissance drones in the 1980s, and in 1995 the US Air Force deployed the General Atomics Predator in the Balkans for operations in the former Yugoslavia. By 2001, when the US Air Force began operations in Afghanistan, it had acquired 60 Predators, which had been modified to undertake a strike role, firing Hellfire missiles. In the process, Predator had been transformed from an unmanned aerial vehicle (UAV) into an unmanned combat aerial vehicle (UCAV). By 2000, improvements in communications systems made it possible to fly Predator remotely from distances as far away from bases in Pakistan as air force facilities in Nevada.

Predator's successor was the General Atomics Reaper, which is faster than Predator, has greater endurance, and is more heavily armed with Hellfire missiles, laser-guided bombs, and Joint Direct Attack Munitions (JDAMs). JDAMs' guidance kit turns "dumb" bombs into all-weather "smart" munitions. The AGM-Hellfire is an ASM (air-to-surface missile) initially designed for use against armor, although it now has a multimission, multitarget, precision-strike capability and can be launched from air, sea, and ground platforms. Its name derives from its original specification as a HELicopter-Launched FIRE-and-forget weapon. Hellfire II, developed in the 1990s, has spawned a number of semiactive laser variants that home in on a reflected laser beam aimed at the target from the launching platform.

The General Atomics MQ-1 Predator, the primary unmanned aircraft employed by the USAF and the CIA for reconnaissance and offensive operations. In 2001, Predator was modified to carry Hellfire missiles and became operational in this role in October of the same year.

The General MQ-9 Atomics Reaper. The Reaper is not a variant of Predator but is a separate and much larger aircraft. It carries a variety of weapons, including Hellfire missiles, 500 lb (225 kg) laser-guided bombs and Joint Direct Attack Munitions (JDAMs) whose guidance kit turns "dumb" unguided bombs into all-weather "smart" weapons.

A Lockheed Martin AGM-114 Hellfire missile is manhandled into position on one of the four weapons stations on a Sikorsky MH-60 Sea Hawk helicopter for use against surface targets.

Hellfire II, weighing 106 pounds (48 kg) with a 20-pound (9-kg) warhead, has a range of 3 miles (4.8 km) and is currently carried by Reaper.

Reaper has a range of nearly 3,700 miles (6,000 km), can fly at 50,000 feet (15,200 m), and is well suited for "loitering operations" in reconnaissance and in support of ground troops. Loaded with sensors and thermal cameras, Reaper can read a license plate at a range of 2 miles (3 km). An operator's command takes a fraction over one second to reach it via a satellite link. Reaper achieved its first kill in Afghanistan in October 2007.

By March 2011, the USAF was training more pilots for advanced unmanned aerial vehicles than for any other single weapon system. In 2011, there was an average of one Predator strike every four days. Some critics claimed that the use of Predator was often a form of licensed assassination of terrorist targets outside theaters of war in which the United States was directly engaged. It also caused considerable collateral damages and civilian casualties.

Reaper throws into sharp focus the many moral and political questions attendant on the prosecution of what is now termed "asymmetrical warfare"—the waging of war by the governments of technologically advanced and expensively armed First World countries against agile but poorly armed nongovernmental opponents in the Third World. There is little doubt, however, that UCAVs such as Reaper represent the warplanes of the future.

AL-QAEDA

The Islamist terror grouping al-Qaeda (which means "base") was formed in 1988 by the Saudi-born Osama Bin Laden and a number of like-minded militants. In 1996, in his first public statement, Bin Laden declared war ("jihad") on the Americans and announced that he was fighting U.S. foreign policy in the Middle East, particularly U.S. support for the house of Saud and the state of Israel.

Bin Laden was to be the overall inspirer, but not the operational commander, of such subsequent terror attacks as those in 1998 on the U.S. embassies in Kenya and Tanzania. The U.S. government, preoccupied with state-based threats and ballistic-missile defenses, did not at this time regard al-Qaeda as the most serious threat facing the country. However, by 2001, Bin Laden had access to the financial resources to project al-Qaeda's power internationally and with enormous effect. After the attacks on New York and Washington in September 2001, al-Qaeda essentially became the brand name for worldwide Islamic terrorism in Europe, North Africa, former Soviet Central Asia, and the Middle and Far East.

Although the United States destroyed al-Qaeda's power base in Afghanistan, it is clear that military action alone will not be sufficient to halt the terrorist group's activities. Bin Laden evaded U.S. special forces at the end of the war in Afghanistan, but in 2010 U.S. intelligence, tracking one of his couriers, identified a possible refuge in a compound in Abbottabad, Pakistan. In May 2011, the decade-long, trillion-dollar pursuit concluded with the dispatch of Bin Laden by U.S. special forces. Nevertheless, al-Qaeda still has a powerful base in Yemen and a string of ferocious affiliates in West Africa.

President Barack Obama, originally undertook to close the camp, but it remained operational throughout his presidency. In July 2012, it still held 168 detainees amid a swirl of argument and counterargument over the legality of the Guantanamo inmates' detention and the conditions under which they were kept.

The third element in this geopolitical equation is the emergence in the last 20 years of an industrially powerful and militarily stronger China. Although China is unlikely to challenge U.S. military dominance in the coming years, it has already forced the Americans to tilt their global strategy away from Europe toward a new theater of potential conflict in the South China Sea.

African turmoil

One theater in which China has been flexing its economic muscle in recent years is the continent of Africa. In 2012, an upbeat social and economic narrative on Africa was gaining hold, but the continent still harbors large areas of systemic conflict, not least in the Democratic Republic of Congo. At a lower but no less depressing level, ethnic or Muslim–Christian conflict also disfigures Mali, Somalia, and Nigeria, where Boko Haram has come to the fore in recent years. This violent anti-Western Islamic movement, based in the northeast of Nigeria, seeks to establish sharia law, is aggressively anti-Christian, and is, in all probability, linked to AQIM (al-Qaeda in Islamic Magreb). Boko Haram expressly forbids all interaction with the Western world.

Unholy trinity

Nevertheless, most Western analysts believe that the greatest threat facing the modern world is the coming together of terrorist organizations, certain "rogue states," and weapons of mass destruction (WMD). The terrorist threat is particularly difficult to combat, because, unlike a nation, a terrorist organization is not bounded by national borders or territory. As a result of this, Western strategy consists of a combination of intelligence gathering, military force against states suspected of fostering and supporting terrorism (as in the case of Afghanistan and Iraq), and diplomacy aimed at bringing certain "rogue states" in from the cold (as in the case of Libya). It is hoped that this three-pronged approach will stop WMDs from falling into terrorist hands.

Demonstrators in Istanbul mount a protest in March 2012 against the Syrian government's shelling of the city of Homs, dubbed the "center of the revolution" and home to 1.6 million people.

THE ARAB SPRING

In December 2010, the Arab world was rocked by a series of convulsions that sent shock waves around the Mediterranean littoral, eastward into Iranian Khuzestan, and southward into Mali. By the summer of 2012, dictatorial rulers had been forced from power in Tunisia, Egypt, Libya, and Yemen, and a civil uprising in Syria had descended into an all-out sectarian civil war.

In Egypt, the newly elected president Mohamed Morsi of the Muslim Brotherhood, was initially sidelined by the Egyptian army, reluctant to surrender the power it had long exercised over Egypt's economic and political life. However, the rise of the Muslim Brotherhood, which had not taken an active role in the major protest that preceded the ousting of Morsi's predecessor, Hosni Mubarak, indicated a potential shift in the *modus vivendi* Egypt had reached with Israel after the 1973 war.

The situation in Syria, where President Bashar-al-Assad clung to power with the help of his army and loyal Alawite militias, also presented a threat to Israeli security, as the rebel Free Syrian Army was reinforced by *jihadi* fighters from across the Arab world. The fighting had repercussions in neighboring Turkey, which received a flood of Syrian refugees, and posed problems for Russia since the Syrian port of Tartus provided the Russian navy with its only base outside the former Soviet Union.

In Libya, the rising against Colonel Muammar Gaddafi was given decisive momentum by the intervention on March 19, 2011, of the United States, Britain, and France with a bombing campaign against pro-Gaddafi forces. The intervention was eventually joined by 27 states from Europe and the Middle East. In August, anti-Gaddafi forces captured Tripoli, forcing the dictator to regroup in Sirte, where he was captured and killed on October 20. Democratic elections followed in July 2012 but the Libyan militias that had removed Gaddafi remained reluctant to come under the umbrella of a new national army. The entire Middle East remains in a dangerous state of flux.

CYBER WAR

In the twenty-first century, warfare has been transformed by the computer revolution, a phenomenon that has reached into every aspect of contemporary life. In similar fashion, during the nineteenth-century Industrial Revolution, the torrent of technological innovation was harnessed to destructive effect by the world's most advanced military machines.

The survival of today's advanced societies—and their industrial power, financial, and transport hubs, and communications, health, and security infrastructures—is now heavily dependent on information technology, which is itself immensely vulnerable to blitzkrieg attack from external enemies and hostile agencies. Cyberspace—characterized as the fifth domain of warfare after land, sea, air, and space—is an arena in which nation states remain the major but by no means the exclusive players. Indeed, in China, which devotes huge resources to cyberspace, the state operates hand-in-glove with criminal surrogates.

By 2011, approximately one in three of the world's population was an Internet user, a platform on which it is sometimes difficult to distinguish friend from foe. Moreover, the Internet remains a potentially fragile instrument. More than 90 percent of digital traffic travels through undersea fiber-optic cables, which are crammed into a number of vulnerable choke points. Among them are the waters off New York, the Red Sea, and the Luzon Strait in the Philippines.

The origins of the cyberspace battlefield can be traced back to June 1982, when the U.S. Central Intelligence Agency (CIA) sabotaged computer-control software used to regulate gas pipelines, which was stolen by Soviet spies from a Canadian firm. In this early demonstration of a so-called "logic bomb," pump and valve settings went haywire, causing a huge blast in Siberia, which was monitored by U.S. early warning satellites.

The first so-called cyber war is often cited as the aftermath of an April 2001 incident in which a U.S. EP-3 Aries II spy plane collided with a Chinese jet over the South China Sea. In the following weeks, thousands of Web sites in China and the U.S. were the subject of defacement and hacker attacks.

The stakes are higher when government agencies, or their surrogates, step in. Cyber war played a significant

In September 2010, the Lipman Report listed terrorism, cyber warfare, industrial espionage, and weapons of mass destruction as threats to the U.S. economy along with that of other nations. Cyber attack posed a threat to public and private facilities, banking and finance, transportation, manufacturing, medical institutions, education, and government, all of which are now dependent on computers without which they could not operate.

April 13, 2001: U.S. Secretary of Defense Donald H. Rumsfeld briefs reporters in the Pentagon in Washington, D.C. on the facts associated with the recent collision between the EP-3 Aries II reconnaissance aircraft and a Chinese F-8 fighter aircraft. Rumsfeld told reporters that the U.S. spyplane was flying in a level position when the Chinese jet became aggressive and hit the U.S. plane from below.

part in Israel's 2006 incursion into Lebanon to deal with Hezbollah, the militant Shia Muslim faction. Using black propaganda tactics, the intelligence arm of the Israeli Defence Force (IDF) compromised Hezbollah-backed television and radio stations and launched denial-of-service attacks on Hezbollah Websites. In September 2007, in Operation Orchard, Israeli warplanes carried out an air strike on a Syrian nuclear facility, using the IDF's version of Suter, a military computer program that attacks enemy computer networks and communications systems.

In April 2007, Estonia came under cyber attack from Russia after the relocation of a controversial war memorial, the Bronze Soldier of Tallinn, erected by the Soviet Union in 1947. Estonian ministries, banks, and the national media were the principal targets. In August 2008, during the brief South Ossetian War, cyber attacks were launched by the Russian military to coincide with air strikes and troop movements against the former Soviet republic of Georgia.

Regional rivalries on the Indian subcontinent have also led to an outbreak of cyber warfare. In November 2010, a group calling itself the Indian Cyber Army hacked Web sites controlled by the Pakistani army and a number of Pakistani ministries. The attack was launched as a response to the involvement of Pakistani terrorists in the 2008 Mumbai massacre. A month later, the so-called Pakistani Cyber Army hit back by hacking into the web site of India's leading investigative agency, the Central Bureau of Investigation (CBI).

The United States is not immune from attack. In April 2009 reports surfaced that China and Russia had penetrated the U.S. electrical grid, leaving behind software programs with the potential to disrupt the system. President Barack Obama declared that the U.S.'s digital infrastructure was a "strategic national asset," and in May 2010 the Pentagon established the Cyber Command (Cybercom) under General Keith Alexander, director of the National Security Agency (NSA). His brief was to establish "full spectrum" operations to defend U.S. military networks and to attack the systems of other nations, although precisely how remains secret. The UK has its own cyber-security apparatus, based at GCHQ, the British equivalent of the NSA. After the 2007 Bronze Soldier incident, the North Atlantic Treaty Organization (NATO) set up a Cooperative Cyber Defense Center of Excellence in Tallinn, the capital of Estonia.

China aims to attain cyber supremacy by the end of the twenty-first century, although it vehemently denies involvement in cyberspying. Nevertheless, few doubt that in 2009 the Chinese successfully hacked into the USAF's $300 billion Joint Strike Fighter Project. In the

U.S. Army General Keith Alexander, Commander of Cyber Command, addresses the audience during the activation ceremony of Cybercom on Fort Meade, Md., May 21, 2010.

breakneck Chinese drive for growth, it is clear that their intelligence services have more to gain from penetrating U.S. military and industrial establishments than the Americans have in penetrating theirs. Even so, there are sound geopolitical reasons for American intelligence to keep a close eye on its Chinese counterparts.

For military commanders, modern technology is both a blessing and a curse. Cruise missiles and smart bombs are guided by Global Positioning System (GPS) satellites; drones are piloted remotely against the Taliban in Afghanistan from bases in Nevada; warplanes and warships are huge data-processing centers; even the "poor bloody infantry" are being wired up. Yet exponentially increasing connectivity over an insecure Internet multiplies the avenues for e-attack.

At present, cyber war is seen as a vital adjunct to the ongoing business of espionage rather than a critical component in the waging of all-out war. The technology of espionage never stands still, although the principal aims of the spy master—the acquisition of military and industrial secrets—have changed little since the days of John Buchan and *The 39 Steps*. The blurring of the lines between criminality and war is a sinister phenomenon but hardly a new one. Inevitably, experts are divided on the threat posed by cyber war. Some predict the galloping collapse of modern societies under sustained e-attack, a scenario that recalls governments' apprehension in the 1930s of the devastating effect of strategic bombing raids on European capital cities. Then it was affirmed that "the bomber will always get through." Today, the hacker, often with little more than a laptop, poses a similar threat. Nevertheless, it is equally likely that cyber attack will not be a decisive weapon but a means of disrupting and delaying the enemy's response to achieve a limited objective. One scenario frequently advanced in this context is the Chinese seizure of Taiwan without having to engage the U.S. in a shooting war.

STUXNET

Malware, an abbreviation of "malicious software," is a form of programming designed to disrupt or destroy target computer systems, or infiltrate them to harvest information. The Stuxnet worm is an example of complex malware, which is programmed to spy on and subvert specific industrial systems, operating like a sniper rifle rather than a blunderbuss. Its targets are the Windows operating system and industrial software applications developed by German firm Siemens.

In 2009–2010, Stuxnet's chief targets were the Iranian uranium enrichment facilities at Natanz, ostensibly part of a civilian energy program but suspected of being the preliminary to the development of nuclear weapons. Stuxnet, probably introduced via infected memory sticks, altered the speed of Natanz's centrifuges, of which approximately 1,000 were eventually dismantled and removed. The effect was been to push back the Iranian nuclear program by two or three years.

It is widely thought that Israeli intelligence was behind the Stuxnet attack. The Israelis possessed the ability, with American help, to develop a cyber tool such as Stuxnet. The Iranians use P-1 centrifuges and it is likely that the Israelis acquired one on the international black market before testing Stuxnet at their own nuclear facility at Dimona. Alternatively, the United States, which received P-1s from Libya's disbanded nuclear program, may have supplied the equipment. Continuing debate over the precise origins of the Stuxnet attack suggests that Israel may well have preferred to employ it against Iran instead of mount a conventional military attack on Natanz.

Iranian President Mahmoud Ahmadinejad visits the Natanz hardened fuel enrichment plant, which covers some 100,000 square metres and was the target of a Stuxnet attack by the Americans and the Israelis in 2009–2010.

TIMELINE TO 1945

Wars and battles, whether prolonged or lightning strikes, big or small, have helped to shape the world since time immemorial. No list of them can be totally comprehensive but nevertheless can be a useful reference and helpful in putting the main conflicts in context.

ca. 2154 BC	Sacking of Kish and fall of Sargon and the Akkad empire
ca. 1481 BC	Egyptian campaign against Syria and Palestine; Battle of Megiddo
ca. 1296 BC	Egyptians and Hittites fight over Syria; Battle of Qadesh
701 BC	Assyrian campaign in Palestine
546–539 BC	Persian Wars
499–401 BC	Graeco–Persian Wars
490 BC	Marathon
480 BC	Thermopylae
480 BC	Artemisium
480 BC	Salamis
460–404 BC	Peloponnesian Wars
433 BC	Sybota
418 BC	Mantinea
406 BC	Arginusae
371 BC	Leuctra, Thebes overcome Sparta
338 BC	Chaeronea, Philip of Macedon in central Greece
338–322 BC	Macedonian advance under Alexander the Great
331 BC	Gaugamela
264–241 BC	First Punic War
256 BC	Ecnomus
219–202 BC	Second Punic War
216 BC	Cannae
198 BC	Cynoscephalae, Second Macedonian War
168 BC	Pydna, Third Macedonian War
149–146 BC	Third Punic War
86 BC	Chaeronea, First Mithridatic War
58–52 BC	Gallic Wars
52 BC	Alesia
42 BC	Philippi, Roman Triumvirs defeat Brutus and Cassius
27 BC–AD 476	Wars of the Roman empire
AD 69	Second Cremona, Roman civil war
69–178	Danubian Wars

72	Siege of Masada, Roman–Jewish War
114–97	Parthian Wars
193–95	Siege of Byzantium by Romans
208–11	Romans, under Emperor Septimius Severus, in Britain
241–44 and 250s	Persian invasion of Roman empire
278	Siege of Cremna by Romans
312	Milvian Bridge, Constantine's invasion of Italy
357	Strasbourg, Roman response to Alamanni invasion
359	Amida, Persian invasion of eastern Roman Empire
363	Roman invasion of Persia
378	Adrianople, Romans versus Goths
395–1453	Byzantine Empire Wars
410	Sack of Rome by Goths
535–554	Byzantine conquest of Italy
768–812	Campaigns of Charlemagne
865–79	Viking Great Army in England
991	Maldon, Vikings versus English
1053	Civitate, war between Pope Leo IX and Norman lords
1061	Norman invasion of Sicily
1066	Hastings, Norman conquest of England
1096–99	First Crusade
1097–98	Siege of Antioch
1145–49	Second Crusade
1189–92	Third Crusade
1189–91	Siege of Acre
1191	Arsuf
1202–4	Fourth Crusade
1203–4	Château Gaillard, King John of England and Philip II of France fight for Normandy
1213–21	Fifth Crusade
1260	Ayn Jalut, invasion of Syria by Mongols
1314	Bannockburn, England versus Scotland
1337–1453	Hundred Years War between England and France
1346	Crécy, defeat of the French by Edward III of England
1402	Ankara, defeat of Ottomans by Tamerlane, Mongol ruler
1410	Tannenberg, defeat of Teutonic Knights by coalition of states
1415	Agincourt, invasion of France by Henry V of England
1416–1573	Venetian–Turkish Wars
1418–19	Siege of Rouen, conquest of Normandy by Henry V of England
1422	Siege of Meaux, death of Henry V in France
1428–29	Siege of Orléans, English repulsed by French led by Joan of Arc
1453	Siege of Constantinople by Turks

1455–87	Wars of the Roses, between House of Lancaster and House of York
1461	Towton
1471	Tewkesbury
1474–75	Siege of Neuss by Burgundians
1477	Nancy, death of Charles the Bold of Burgundy; rise of Swiss soldiers
1480	Siege of Rhodes by Ottomans
1481–92	Spanish–Muslim Wars
1485	Bosworth, Wars of the Roses, death of Richard III
1519–21	Spanish conquest of Mexico
1525	Pavia, war between France and the Hapsburg empire
1526	Mogul–Afghan War
1531–33	Spanish conquest of Peru
1571	Lepanto, Ottomans defeated by the Holy League coalition
1588	Spanish Armada, attempted Spanish invasion of England
1618–48	Thirty Years War in Europe
1631	Breitenfeld, Thirty Years War
1642–51	English Civil War
1643	Rocroi, Thirty Years War
1645	Naseby, English Civil War
1689–45	Jacobite rebellions, Scottish uprising against England
1700–21	Great Northern War, Russian challenge to Swedish empire
1701–14	War of Spanish Succession
1704	Blenheim, War of Spanish Succession
June 28, 1709	Poltava, Great Northern War
1740–48	War of Austrian Succession
1745	Fontenoy
1756–63	Seven Years War, first global conflict
1757	Plassey, Anglo-French war in India
November 5, 1757	Rossbach, Seven Years War
December 6, 1757	Leuthen, Seven Years War
September 13, 1759	Quebec, Seven Years War
1775–82	American War of Independence
1775	Bunker Hill
1781	Yorktown
1792–1802	French Revolutionary Wars
1794	Fleurus
1798	Aboukir Bay (Battle of the Nile)
1800	Marengo
1803–15	Naploeonic Wars
1805	Ulm
1805	Trafalgar
1805	Austerlitz
1808–14	Peninsular War

1811–87	North American Indian Wars
1812–15	War of 1812, United States versus British empire
1812	Borodino, Naploeonic Wars
1813	Leipzig, Naploeonic Wars
1815	Waterloo, the Hundred Days of Napoleon's restoration
1815	New Orleans, War of 1812, United States defeat the British
1836	Texan War of Independence
1839–42	First Afghan–British War
1846–47	U.S.–Mexican War
1853–56	Crimean War
1854–55	Siege of Sebastopol
1854	Inkerman
1859	Solferino, French campaign in Italy
1861–65	American Civil War
1863	Chancellorsville
1863	Gettysburg
1864–65	The March to the Sea
1866	The Seven Weeks War between Austria and Prussia
1866	Koniggratz (Sadowa), Seven Weeks War
1870–71	Franco–Prussian War
1870	Rezonville–Mars-la-Tour
1870	Gravelotte–Saint Privet
1870	Sedan
1878–80	Second Afghan–British War
1879	Zulu–British War
1880–81	First Anglo–Boer War
1898	Spanish–American War
1899–1902	Second Anglo–Boer War
1900	Paardeberg
1904–5	Russo–Japanese War
1905	Tsushima
1914–18	World War I
1914	Mons
1914	Tannenberg
1915	Anzac Cove (Gallipoli)
1916	Verdun
1916	Jutland
1916	The Somme
1917	Passchendaele
1917	Caporetto
1917	Cambrai
1917–1922	Russian Civil War
1918	German Spring Offensive

1918	Megiddo
1919	Third Afghan–British War
1919–23	Turkish War of Independence
1935–36	Second Italo-Abyssinian War
1936–39	Spanish Civil War
1937–45	Sino-Japanese War
1939–40	Russo-Finnish War
1939–45	World War II
1939	Invasion of Poland
1940	Fall of France
1940–41	The Blitz
1940	Battle of Britain
1941	Cape Matapan
1941	Invasion of Yugoslavia
1941	Invasion of Greece
1941	Invasion of Crete
1941	Invasion of the Soviet Union
1941–44	Siege of Leningrad
1941	Crusader, relief of Tobruk
1941	Pearl Harbor
1942	Fall of Malaya and Singapore
1942	Coral Sea, Midway
1942	Destruction of Convoy PQ 17
1942–45	U.S. Pacific "island-hopping" campaign
1942–43	Guadalcanal
1942	Second El Alamein
1943	Landings in Sicily
1943	Italian campaign
1943	Dams raid
1943	Hamburg raid
1943	Kursk
1943	Schweinfurt–Regensburg bombing raids
1944	Normandy landings
1944–45	V-weapons Offensive
1944	Operation Bagraton
1944	Arnhem
1944–45	Ardennes counteroffensive
1944–45	Invasion of the Philippines
1945	Ruhr campaign
1945	Iwo Jima
1945	Okinawa
1945	Hiroshima
1945	Nagasaki

CHRONOLOGY OF POSTWAR CONFLICT

Major wars and disruptions are given here, but, of course, since humankind has yet to learn to live together in peace and harmony, the list is ongoing. Skirmishes, rebellion, and tribal conflict continue to be pursued with varying degrees of vigor all around the globe. Any number of acts of aggression will be taking place at any given time that, if not full-scale war between nations, are certainly bloody and have the potential to turn into something much bigger and more involving.

1945 Chinese civil war between Mao Zedong's Red Army and Nationalists under Chiang Kai-shek resumed after Japanese surrender at end of World War II; Nationalist resistance ended December 1949.

1945–49 Indonesian war of independence in which Indonesian People's Army resisted restoration of Dutch colonial rule; independence achieved December 1949.

1946–49 Greek civil war Communist guerrillas of the Democratic Army of Greece opposed to restoration of monarchy were defeated in October 1949 by U.S.-backed Greek government forces.

1946–54 Indo-China war Return of French colonial rule to Indo-China resisted by Viet Minh; French withdrew and North and South Vietnam created; independence of Laos and Combodia recognized July 1954.

1946–48 Israeli war of independence Jewish guerrilla campaign against British forces administering Palestine under 1920 League of Nations mandate; state of Israel proclaimed March 1948.

1946–44 Philippines HUK rebellion Revolt by People's Anti-Japanese Army following independence in July 1946.

1947–49 India–Pakistan war Kashmir acceded to India in October 1947 after Muslim rebellion; Indian and Paskistani troops involved in fighting until January 1949 cease fire mediated by UN.

1948– Burmese civil war Struggle for autonomy by Karen National Liberation Army plus (until April 1989) insurgency by Communist Party of Burma following independence from UK in January 1948.

1948 Costa Rica civil war Rebel army formed March 1948 to enforce results of general elelction after attempt by incumbent government to annul it; regular army defeated and abolished.

1948 Colombia civil war Insurgency by Revolutionary Armed Forces of Colombia plus, subsequently, guerrilla movements.

1948–49 Arab–Israeli war Egypt, Iraq, Jordan, Lebanon, and Syria invaded Israel when British mandate ended in May 1948; final armistice recognized Israeli victory.

1948–60 Malayan emergency Declared by Britain June 1948; Malayan Communist Party insurrection contained by Malaysian independence August 1957; emergency lifted July 1960.

1950–53 Korean war Initial success of June 1950 invasion of South Korea by North Korea followed by successful UN counteroffensive in September; UN forces pushed back by Chinese involvement from October; then prolonged war of attrition before cease fire and new border with demilitarized zone along existing front line agreed July 1953.

1950 Chinese invasion of Tibet Started October 1950; Lhasa occupied September 1951.

1952–60 Kenyan emergency Declared by Britain in response to Mau Mau terrorism; revolt contained by 1956; emergency lifted 1960.

1954–75 Laos civil war Pathet Lao resistance movement supported by North Vietnam defeated U.S.-backed Royal Laotian army in civil war following July 1954 independence from French colonial rule.

1954 Guatemala coup and guerrilla war Overthrow of Guatemalan government by U.S.-backed exiles in June 1954 followed by continuing counterinsurgent war against Guerrilla Army of the Poor (EGP), Revolutionary Armed Forces (FAR), and Revolutionary Army of People in Arms (ORPA) guerrilla groups.

1954–62 Algerian war of independence Algerian National Liberation Front started terrorist attacks November 1954; revolution largely suppressed 1957–58; independence granted 1962 after violent opposition by French colonists.

1955–59 Cyprus emergency Declared by Britain November 1955 in response to National Organization of Cypriot Fighters (EOKA) bombings; emergency ended December 1959; independence granted August 1960.

1955–72 Sudan civil war Conflict between northern Arab Muslim government forces and Anya Nya guerrilla army of southern black minority population following January 1956 independence.

1956 Hungarian uprising Soviet troops withdrew in response to October uprising, but returned and crushed opposition November 3–14 after Hungary abrogated the Warsaw Pact and declared neutrality.

1956 Suez invasion British and French paratroops landed in Suez Canal Zone November 5 after October invasion by Israel; cease-fire announced November 7 followed by Israeli withdrawal, concluded March 1957.

1956–59 Cuban revolution Guerrilla movement started by Fidel Castro November 1956; overthrew government of Fulgencio Batista, January 1, 1959.

1958 Lebanese civil war Fighting between Syrian-backed Muslim and Maronite Christian militias from May ended in September after U.S. intervention in July.

1958 Nicaraguan civil war Sandinista guerrilla movement founded in 1958 finally succeeded in overthrowing government of Anastasio Somoza in July 1979; Sandinista government subsequently opposed by U.S.-backed contra rebels until defeated by opposition parties in 1990 election.

1960–65 Congo civil war Civil unrest, army mutiny, and attempted secession by Katanga from former Belgian Congo (now Zaire) following independence in June 1960 and involving Belgian forces plus foreign mercenaries and the biggest ever UN peacekeeping operation; situation stabilized November 1965 after second coup by army commander Joseph Mobutu.

1961–75 Vietnam war U.S. involvement in South Vietnam expanded from small-scale aid to full-scale campaign involving more than 500,000 troops by 1969. U.S. withdrawal in 1973 followed by North Vietnamese victory in April 1975.

1961–93 Eritrea war Ethiopian annexation of Eritrea in 1961 opposed by Eritrean (later Eritrean People's) Liberation Front and Tigrean People's Liberation Front; peace talks held in 1991, followed by Eritrean independence in 1993.

1962 Sino-Indian conflict Chinese offensives across Himalayan borders October 1962 followed by November cease-fire and subsequent partial withdrawal.

1962–66 Borneo confrontation December 1962 rebellion by Kalimantan Liberation Army in Brunei followed by Indonesian incursions into British colonies (Malaysian states from September 1963) of Sarawak, Sabah, and Brunei from Kalimantan on Borneo; opposed by British forces; peace agreed August 1966.

1961–93 Indonesian civil war Continuing insurgency in Java and, since 1963 uprising, in West Irian.

1962–69 North Yemen civil war Fighting between Republican Army and Royalist forces before Yemen established 1970.

1963–64 Cyprus civil war Intercommunal fighting between Greeks and Turks erupted December 1963; deployment of UN peacekeeping force April 1964.

1964–67 South Yemen war of independence Guerrilla war in British colony of Aden and South Arabian Federation develops into civil war between rival groups; British withdrawal November 1967 followed by formation of People's Republic of Yemen.

1964–75 Mozambique war of independence Frelimo guerrilla war against Portuguese colonial authorities; independence 1975.

1964–80 Zimbabwe civil war British colony of Southern Rhodesia declared independent as Rhodesia 1965; Rhodesian security forces opposed by guerrilla armies of Zimbabwe African National Union (ZANU) and African People's Union (ZAPU) until 1980 cease-fire and independence under ZANU leader Robert Mugabe.

1965 Dominica civil war Military coup to restore ousted President Juan Bosch caused civil war; ended by U.S. military intervention May 1965.

1965 India–Pakistan war Renewed fighting in Kashmir and in the Rann of Kutch September 1–23 ended by UN intervention.

1965–75 Dhofar rebellion South Yemen-backed Dhofar Liberation Front opposed by Sultan of Oman's armed forces with British and (after 1970 coup in Oman) Iranian assistance; large-scale Iranian operations from December 1973; war declared over in December 1975.

1966–89 Namibia war of independence People's Liberation Army of Namibia (PLAN) opposed by South African forces from July 1966 until Namibian independence April 1989.

1967–70 Nigerian civil war Attempted secession of Biafra May 1967 defeated by federal government of General Gowon.

1967 Arab–Israeli war In six days from June 3, Israel responded to Arab states' aggression by destroying the Egyptian airforce on the ground, occupying Sinai and Jordanian territory on the west bank of the Jordan River, and defeating Syrian forces in the Golan heights.

1968 Soviet invasion of Czechoslovakia Occupation by Soviet troops on August 21, 1968, to reverse liberalization instituted by Czech President Alexander Dubcek's April "Prague spring" reforms.

1968–88 Chad civil war Government of former French Equatorial Africa opposed by Frolinat guerrillas; subsequent intervention by France and Libya before 1987 cease-fire left Libya with Aouzou Strip and French forces deployed in the south.

1969 Honduras–El Salvador war Invasion of Honduras by El Salvadorean troops on July 14 after riots following a soccer match; ended by withdrawl of forces on July 30.

1969–2005 Northern Ireland troubles British troops deployed in UK province of Northern Ireland to counter Irish Republic Army (IRA) terrorism; IRA cease-fire in 1990s and establishment of power-sharing government; IRA destroyed arms in 2005.

1969 Philippines insurgency Marcos and subsequent governments opposed by communist New People's Army in most provinces, Muslim separatist Moro National Liberation Front on Mindanao.

1970 Jordanian civil war Clashes between Palestinian guerrillas and Jordanian government forces in February and June, followed by large-scale fighting in September; cease-fire September 24.

1971–93 Cambodia civil war North Vietnamese-backed Khmer Rouge victory in 1975 followed by genocide and invasion by Vietnamese forces in 1978; Vietnamese withdrawal (1989) left Cambodian government facing continued guerrilla operations by Khmer Rouge and other factions; peace and elections 1993.

1971 Sri Lanka revolt April 1971 rebellion by People's Liberation Fron (JVP) suppressed by early May.

1971 India–Pakistan war India defeated West Pakistan in Bangladesh (formerly East Pakistan) and on India's western border, December 3–17.

1971 Bangladesh guerrilla war New government's attempt to evict tribal peoples from Chiltagong hills resisted by Buddhist Jana Sanghati Samity and Chakma Shanti Bahini movements.

1973 Arab–Israeli war Egyptian and Syrian attacks launched October 6 succeeded initially but then repelled; by October 24 cease-fire, Israel had occupied additional territory; Sinai ultimately returned to Egypt by April 1982.

1974 Turkish invasion of Cyprus Coup by (Greek) National Guard on July 15 followed by landing of Turkish troops on July 20; August 16 cease-fire left eastern third of island in Turkish hands.

1975–90 Lebanese civil war Renewed fighting in April 1975 between Christian and Muslim factions ended October 1976 by Syrian invasion, but sporadic fighting continued involving Druze and Shi'ite Muslim militias, Christian militias, and Syrian, Lebanese, and Israeli armed forces; March 1978 Israeli invasion of southern Lebanon followed by withdrawal of troops in June after UN interventon.

1975–90 Angolan civil war Since Angola's independence from Portugal in 1975, UNITA, backed by South Africa and the United States, fought the Soviet-backed MPLA government and its Cuban troops in a civil war that started in 1960 as a war of independence; peace deal agreed 1990.

1975–99 East Timor resistance war Opposition to November 1975 Indonesian annexation of former Portuguese colony by Fretilin independence movement guerrillas; UN administration took over in 1999; East Timor fully independent 2002.

1975–91 Morocco–Polisario war February 1976 declaration by Algerian-backed Popular Front for the Liberation of Saguia al-Jamra and Rio del Oro (Polisario) of independent Sahrawi Arab Democratic Republic in Western Sahara opposed by Morocco and Mauritania; Morocco's subsequet attempts to occupy the former Spanish colony, including construction of 1,000-mile (1,609-km) Hassan Wall, frustrated by Polisario forces from Mauritania; cease-fire and peace process agreed 1991.

1977–92 Mozambique civil war Renamo resistance movement formed 1977 by Rhodesian intelligence officer to oppose Frelimo government; backed subsequently by South Africa, Portugal, Morocco, Saudi Arabia, Zaire, and U.S. religious fundamentalists; Renamo's activities included massacring thousands of peasants and making hundreds of thousands of people homeless; peace agreed 1992.

1977–88 Ogaden civil war Guerrilla campaign by Western Somalia Liberation Front (WSLF) against Ethiopian army in Ogaden region of southeastern Ethiopia; open war involving Somali government forces from 1977; negotiated settlement May 1988.

1979 China–Vietnam war Chinese invasion of Vietnam on February 17, 1979 in retaliation for deployment of Vietnamese troops in Cambodia followed by fierce fighting and heavy casualties, and destruction of several Vietnamese cities; Chinese withdrawal completed March 17.

1979–96 Afghanistan war Soviet invasion in December 1979, intended to quell popular Muslim uprising followed by unsuccessful 10-year fight against *mujaheddin* guerrillas; Soviet withdrawal complete February 1989, followed by war between the resistance groups themselves; war ended with victory for the Taliban.

1980–88 Iran–Iraq war Iraqi attack on Iran in September 1980 followed by a war of attrition involving attacks on neutral shipping, ballistic missile bombardments of cities, and the use by Iraq of chemical weapons as well as conventional warfare; cease-fire agreed August 1988.

1980–92 El Salvador civil war Insurgency by Farabundo Marti National Liberation Front (FMLN) guerrillas opposed by armed forces and death squads.

1980 Peruvian insurgency Guerrilla war against government forces by Sendero Luminoso (Shining Light) movement.

1982 Falklands war Occupation of Falkland islands by Argentine forces in April 1982 ended by British invasion and Argentine surrender on June 14.

1982 Israeli invasion of Lebanon Full-scale Israeli invasion in June 1982; Syrian and Palestine Liberation Organization (PLO) forces defeated and PLO made to evacuate Beirut before 1985 withdrawal of Israeli forces to south Lebanon buffer zone.

1983 U.S. invasion of Grenada U.S. forces invade October 25, 1983, after assassination of Grenadan leader Maurice Bishop.

1983–2009 Sri Lanka civil war Rebellion by ethnic separatist Tamil groups against Sinhalese government leads to army reprisals and emergence of Liberation Tigers of Tamil Eelam (Tamil Tigers) as dominant resistance group; July 1987 Indo-Lankan Peace Accord and deployment of Indian forces against Tigers results in Sinhalese leftist JVP rebellion, subsequently suppressed; Indian forces withdrawn in 1990 but fighting resumes; cease-fire started in 2002 but renewed violence in late 2005 leads to the return of civil war ending with defeat of Tamil Tigers in 2009. Reconciliation commission established in 2012.

1983–2005 Sudan civil war Sudan People's Liberation Army (SPLA) formed in southern Sudan 1983 to oppose northern government following imposition of Islamic law; war estimated to have caused over two million deaths, and some four million are displaced.

1987–93 Palestinian intifada Arab "shaking free" campaign involving stone-throwing, strikes, economic boycotts, and other nonmilitary methods of resistance against Israeli occupation of West Bank started December 1987.

1989 U.S. invasion of Panama U.S. forces crush Panamanian resistance in 16 days, following President Noriega's declaration of war; invasion, which was given the name "Operation Just Cause," involved 27,684 U.S. troops and more than 300 aircraft.

1989–2003 Liberia civil war 14 years of fighting ended in 2003 with introduction of power-sharing government.

1990–91 Gulf war Conflict in response to Iraqi invasion of Kuwait in August 1990; invasion met with immediate economic sanctions by UN against Iraq; hostilities commenced in January 1991 with air assaults directed against a range of military, command, communication, and infrastructure targets; such was the ferocity and effectiveness of the air campaign that the ground campaign lasted less than a week; Kuwait declared liberated on February 27, 1991.

1991–2001 Yugoslav wars Series of conflicts in the six former Yugoslav republics; caused by old ethnic and cultural tensions, and also by Serb expansionism and political, cultural, and economic dominance. Three longest-running conflicts were those in Croatia (1991–95), Bosnia (1992–95), and Kosovo (1996–9). The war in Kosovo ended following NATO military action against Serbian forces. Around 300,000 people are estimated to have died in the decade of conflicts, with many more forced to leave their homes, making them the bloodiest in Europe since the end of World War II.

1991–2002 Sierra Leone civil war Revolutionary United Front (RUF) attacked villages in the east of the country near the Liberia border. In the coming years, fighting escalated, with rebel forces capturing much of the country and getting ever closer to the capital, Freetown. UN forces helped to establish peace in 1999, but war not officially ended until 2002.

1994 Rwanda genocide Around 800,000 people, mostly belonging to the Tutsi tribe but also moderate Hutus, were slaughtered in a 100-day campaign of violence following the assassination of Hutu President Juvenal Habyarimana. The first killings were carried out by military personnel, but civilians were encouraged to join in and many thousands did. Tensions between the two tribes became worse during Belgian occupation in the early twentieth century. Belgian colonists treated Tutsis better than Hutus, creating resentment and increasing division.

1994–96 First Chechen War Russia invades the Chechen Republic of Ichkeria, winning the fierce Battle of Grozny, but Russian forces, despite being vastly superior, are thwarted by Chechen guerrillas in their attempt to take control of the mountains. The 1996 cease-fire is followed by the signing of a peace treaty in 1997 under which Chechnya retains its de facto independence.

1996–2012 Congo wars The bloodiest conflict of recent history, the first war began in late 1996 and ended in 1997 when rebel forces, led by Laurent Kabila, overthrew President Mobutu Sésé Seko. The second war began a year later and involved nine African nations and many armed groups. The conflict officially ended in 2002, but many of the armed groups continue to operate, especially in the east, and thousands of people continue to die every month as a result of starvation and preventable diseases. Turmoil in Congo, precipitated by civil war and the military intervention of five neighboring states, continues.

1999–2009 Second Chechen War The Islamic International Peacekeeping Brigade (IIPB) take over Dagestan in Chechnya in 1999, prompting a Russian military response. Russian forces defeat Chechen separatists and establish direct rule in 2000 but resistance continues. Human-rights violations by one side and terrorist atrocities by the other are condemned worldwide. By 2009, most fighting has stopped and Russian control over the territory has been reestablished, although some insurgency continues.

2001–2012 Afghanistan war U.S.-led coalition, including many Afghan tribes, defeats Taliban regime, who provided refuge for al-Qaeda, including Osama bin Laden. Democratic elections have been held since the end of the conflict, but the situation remains far from stable; coalition forces are due to withdraw by 2014.

2003 Iraq war Controversial conflict fought as part of the War on Terror. Saddam Hussein's regime toppled after little more than a month of fighting, but, despite free elections, sectarian violence threatens to derail attempts to establish democracy.

2003–10 War in Darfur Conflict between the Sudanese government and Janjaweed Arab militias and rebels of the Sudan Liberation Army (SLA) and Justice and Equality Movement (JEM), resulting in atrocities perpetrated against civilians and hundreds of thousands of deaths.

2004– Ongoing persecution of Pakistani Hindus and other minorities has been in part ameliorated by the signing of the National Commission for Human Rights Bill in May 2012 by Pakistan President Asif Ali Zardari.

2004– Ongoing Iraqi Shia insurgency is fueled by car and suicide bombs targeting security forces, causing heavy collateral and civilian damage.

2005-10 Chad civil war Sudan's government's attempt to overthrow Chadian President Idrisse Deby using Chadian rebels as middle-men concludes with a peace treaty signed in January 2010.

2006–11 Middle East conflict Clashes between rival Palestinian organisations Fatah and Hamas on the West Bank and Gaza concludes with an uneasy truce.

2006– Ongoing Mexico drug war Ongoing war waged by the Mexican military and drug cartels

2006–09 Ethiopian intervention in the ongoing Somali civil war, flaring since 1991.

2007–12 Mali, Niger civil wars Insurgencies by the nomadic Tuaregs, the latest in a long line of uprisings dating back to the early years of the 20th century.

2008– Ongoing Cambodia–Thai border dispute Border dispute in the area around a Buddhist temple which in 2008 was designated a UNESCO World Heritage Site.

2006–9 Israeli incursions into Gaza Israeli attacks on Gaza, culminating in November 2012 with a week-long naval and air bombardment which included 1,500 air strikes.

2009– Ongoing insurgency in North Caucasus In spite of the official end of the decade-long Second Chechen War, insurgency continues in the North Caucasus republics of Chechnya, Dagestan, Ingushetia and Kabardino-Balkaria.

2009– Ongoing Boko Haram uprising in Nigeria Insurgency by the extreme Muslim adherents of Boko Haram, linked with Al-Qaeda and aimed at the Christian population

2010–11 Ivorian civil war Civil war following disputed elections leading to French intervention and the trial before the International Criminal Court of Laurent Gbagbo, former President of the Ivory Coast.

2011– Ongoing civil war in Syria Civil war between the Ba'athist regime and the rebel Free Syrian Army supported by jihadists from across the Arab world.

2012 State of Palestine receives United Nations recognition United Nations General Assembly votes overwhelmingly to recognize Palestine as a state.

INDEX

Page numbers in **bold** *refer to illustrations.*

ACKNOWLEDGMENTS

Quantum would like to thank the following for the use of their pictures reproduced in this book:

Alamy 144
Amber Books (MARS) 94, 110, 113, 114, 141, 149, 156, 171, 178, 183 (bottom), 188, 193, 218, 226 (both), 228, 239 (all images), 247, 258
Art Archive (ET Archive) 98 (top), 86, 101, 254
Bibliothèque Nationale Paris 56
Boeing Airspace 250, 268 (bottom), 286
Bridgeman (Peter Newark) 99 (bottom), 133, 136 (all images), 139
British Aerospace 289
Corbis 22 (top), 80 (bottom), 174, 266, 267, 281, 301
Dave Longley 55
Duncan Campbell 47
DAVA 283
Getty 82, 163
Ian Hogg 172 (both images) 190 (both images), 200-201 (all images), 219 (both images), 230, 231 (bottom), 286-287
iStock 10 (both images), 17 (both images), 21, 24, 37, 39, 57, 70 (both images), 72, 75, 76, 108 (both images), 212
LTV Corporation 268 (top)
Martin Marionetta 287
Shutterstock 9, 42, 70, 119, 131, 153, 160 (all images), 208, 297

PUBLIC DOMAIN IMAGES:

Bindersarchiv Bild, 225 (183 J16050 / CC-BY-SA), 227 (101I-567 1503A-08 / Toni Schneiders / CC-BY-SA), 238 (101I-785-0287-08 / CC-BY-SA), 238 (101I-139-1112-17 / Knobloch, Ludwig / CC-BY-SA)
Wikimedia: 9, 24, 43, 44, 45, 54, 55, 61, 64 (both images) 69, 80, 83, 93, 99 103, 106, 112, 115, 117, 118, 125, 127, 128, 129, 132, 137, 144, 152, 157, 164, 167, 181, 182, 187, 197, 204 (top), 206, 208, 209, 221, 225, 231, 233, 243, 262
Classical Numismatic Group inc 67
Executive Office of the President of the United States 270
Library of Congress 98, 175, 182 204 (bottom), 214, 223
National Archives Canada 195
NASA 259
U.S. Airforce 263, 265, 290-291, 294, (both images)
U.S. Army 266, 269, 278, 280
U.S. Defense Department 234, 260, 275, 276, 300
U.S. Navy 161, 236, 240, 241, 247, 295

All other photographs, maps, and illustrations are the copyright of Quantum Publishing. While every effort has been made to credit contributors, the publisher would like to apologize should there have been any omissions or errors—and would be pleased to make the appropriate correction for future editions of the book.